TRAVEL AND MEMOIRS OF TIBET

ENCYCLOPAEDIA OF TIBET SERIES — 2

TRAVEL AND MEMOIRS OF TIBET

Edited by

S.K. SHARMA & USHA SHARMA

ANMOL PUBLICATIONS PVT LTD

NEW DELHI-110 002 (INDIA)

ANMOL PUBLICATIONS PVT LTD
4374/4, Ansari Road Daryaganj,
New Delhi-110 002

Travel and Memoirs of Tibet
First Edition 1997

ISBN 81-7488-451-3

PRINTED IN INDIA

Published by J.L. Kumar for Anmol Publications Pvt. Ltd. New Delhi, Typeset by Akshar Graphics, Delhi and Printed at Mehra Offset Press, Delhi.

Dedicated

to

His Holiness Tenzin Gyatso the Fourteenth Dalai Lama

(For his distinguished writings on Buddhist philosophy, for the role he has played in fostering ecumenical relations between the great religions of the world and for his able leadership of the Tibetan people)

Preface

FOR CENTURIES, the unworldly world of Tibet has remained a mystery. Also known as—the Roof of the World, the Hidden Land, the Mystic Land, the Forbidden Land, or the Land of the Lamas—Tibet is situated on a high plateau surrounded by mountain passes. Covering an area in excess of 2.5 million square kilometers, it borders of India, Nepal, Bhutan and Burma to the south, Eastern Turkistan to the north and China on the east. Owing to its unique physical features, Tibet occupies not only the highest but also the most strategic position in Central Asia. In Tibet proper the mountain ranges, run from northwest to southeast with deep or shallow valleys forming innumerable furrows between them. The lofty Himalayan chain sprawls along the entire southern frontier and shuts off the warm monsoon from the Indian Ocean. Rich in minerals and with a variety of flora and fauna, Tibet is also the source of many great rivers — the Tsang-po (Brahmaputra), Senge Khabab (Indus), Drichu (Yangtse), Zachu (Mekong) etc.

Prjevalsky has described Tibet in the following words—"The grandeur of nature in Asia, revealing itself in endless forests and tundras of Siberia, or in the waterless deserts of an overwhelming grandeur in a wide flat upland which forms the southern half of the central part of this continent." Actually, everything that is said about Tibet, is full of significance, whether it be by Plano Carpini or Rubruquis or Marco Polo or Oodoric of Friuli or many other travellers. For them, Tibet has remained as something unusual and exotic.

Tibet is the homeland of a distinct and ancient nation. It is known as the ancient but yet a living home of Mahayana Buddhism. For centuries, Tibet remained a seat of Buddhist practices and learning. The impact of its smooth transmission was felt far and wide.

The Tibetan people have had a chequered history coupled with a unique cultural heritage. They are a distinct race with their own spoken and written language, own socio-cultural traditions, food and dress. Slowly but surely, it grew into a great military power and carved for itself a huge empire in Central Asia, and ultimately renounced the use of arms to practise the teachings of the Buddha. Unfortunately, on 17 March 1959, the Dalai Lama left Lhasa and escaped from pursuing Chinese to seek political asylum in India. He was followed by an unprecedented exodus of Tibetans into exile.

The study of Tibetan history, political developments, socio-cultural and religious traditions etc. is attracting the interaction of an increasing number of scholars all over the world. The present volume *Travel and Memoirs of Tibet* gives a descriptive account of the numerous and significant narrations/reminiscences of famous travellers.

The editors of the present work made it a point to maximise the intellectual benefit of the wealth of literature embedded in the pages of various books, journals, reports etc. Efforts have been taken to economise the precious time of scholars and the alike.

We express our deep gratitude to Dr. P. L. Mehra, Pema Rigzen and many others for their academic support. Finally, we gratefully acknowledge with thanks, the various institutions and a galaxy of authors whose contributions have become part and parcel of our present endeavour.

–Editors

Dedicated
to
His Holiness Tenzin Gyatso the Fourteenth Dalai Lama
(For his distinguished writings on Buddhist philosophy, for the role he has played in fostering ecumenical relations between the great religions of the world and for his able leadership of the Tibetan people)

Preface

FOR CENTURIES, the unworldly world of Tibet has remained a mystery. Also known as—the Roof of the World, the Hidden Land, the Mystic Land, the Forbidden Land, or the Land of the Lamas—Tibet is situated on a high plateau surrounded by mountain passes. Covering an area in excess of 2.5 million square kilometers, it borders of India, Nepal, Bhutan and Burma to the south, Eastern Turkistan to the north and China on the east. Owing to its unique physical features, Tibet occupies not only the highest but also the most strategic position in Central Asia. In Tibet proper the mountain ranges, run from northwest to southeast with deep or shallow valleys forming innumerable furrows between them. The lofty Himalayan chain sprawls along the entire southern frontier and shuts off the warm monsoon from the Indian Ocean. Rich in minerals and with a variety of flora and fauna, Tibet is also the source of many great rivers — the Tsang-po (Brahmaputra), Senge Khabab (Indus), Drichu (Yangtse), Zachu (Mekong) etc.

Prjevalsky has described Tibet in the following words—"The grandeur of nature in Asia, revealing itself in endless forests and tundras of Siberia, or in the waterless deserts of an overwhelming grandeur in a wide flat upland which forms the southern half of the central part of this continent." Actually, everything that is said about Tibet, is full of significance, whether it be by Plano Carpini or Rubruquis or Marco Polo or Oodoric of Friuli or many other travellers. For them, Tibet has remained as something unusual and exotic.

Tibet is the homeland of a distinct and ancient nation. It is known as the ancient but yet a living home of Mahayana Buddhism. For centuries, Tibet remained a seat of Buddhist practices and learning. The impact of its smooth transmission was felt far and wide.

The Tibetan people have had a chequered history coupled with a unique cultural heritage. They are a distinct race with their own spoken and written language, own socio-cultural traditions, food and dress. Slowly but surely, it grew into a great military power and carved for itself a huge empire in Central Asia, and ultimately renounced the use of arms to practise the teachings of the Buddha. Unfortunately, on 17 March 1959, the Dalai Lama left Lhasa and escaped from pursuing Chinese to seek political asylum in India. He was followed by an unprecedented exodus of Tibetans into exile.

The study of Tibetan history, political developments, socio-cultural and religious traditions etc. is attracting the interaction of an increasing number of scholars all over the world. Viewing Tibet and the Tibetan people in a global perspective, the present theme—*Encyclopaedia of Tibet*—has been systematically and carefully conceived, and finally categorized into the following volumes:

1. History and Geography of Tibet
2. Travel and Memoirs of Tibet
3. Society and Culture of Tibet
4. Religious Heritage of Tibet
5. Dalai Lama and Tibet
6. India and Tibet
7. Tibet and the World

The editors of the present work made it a point to maximise the intellectual benefit of the wealth of literature embedded in the pages of various books, journals, newspapers, reports etc. by way of compiling a multi-volume encyclopaedia. Efforts have been taken to economise the precious time of scholars and the alike.

We feel much beholden to His Holiness, the Fourteenth Dalai Lama for many of his speeches/writings which we have incorporated in our humble attempt. We also express our deep gratitude to Dr. P. L. Mehra, Pema Rigzen and many others for their academic support. Finally, we gratefully acknowledge the various institutions and a galaxy of authors whose contributions have become part and parcel of our present endeavour.

—*Editors*

Contents

Contents

1

Narratives of the Mission of Mr. George Bogle to Tibet (1774)

By
CLEMENTS R. MARKHAM

I

LETTER FROM THE TESHU LAMA TO WARREN HASTINGS

(Received March 29, 1774)

THE AFFAIRS of this quarter in every respect flourish. I am night and day employed in prayers for the increase of your happiness and prosperity. Having been informed by travellers from your quarter of your exalted fame and reputation, my heart, like the blossom of spring, abounds with gaiety, gladness, and joy; praise that the star of your fortune is in its ascension; praise that happiness and ease are the surrounding attendants of myself and family. Neither to molest nor persecute in my aim; it is even the characteristic of my sect to deprive ourselves of the necessary refreshment of sleep, should an injury be done to a single individual. But in justice and humanity I am informed you far surpass us. May you ever adorn the seat of justice and power, that mankind may, under the shadow of your bosom, enjoy the blessings of happiness and ease. By your favour, I am the Rajah and Lama of this country, and rule over numbers of subjects, a particular with which you have no doubt been made acquainted by travellers from these parts. I have been repeatedly informed that you have been engaged in hostilities against the Deb Judhur, to which, it is said, the Deb's own criminal conduct, in committing ravages and other outrages on your frontiers, has given rise. As he is of a rude and ignorant race (past times are not destitute of instances of the like misconduct, which his own avarice tempted him to commit), it is not unlikely that he has now renewed those instances; and the ravages and plunder which he may have committed on the skirts of the Bengal and Bihar provinces have given you provocation to send your vindictive army against him. However, his party has been defeated, many of his people have been killed, three forts have been taken from him, and he has met with the punishment he deserved; and it is as evident as the sun your army has been victorious, and that, if you had been desirous of it, you might, in the space of two days, have entirely extirpated him, for he had not power to resist your efforts. But I now take upon me to be his mediator, and to represent to you that, as the said Deb Rajah is dependent upon the Dalai Lama, who rules in this country with unlimited sway (but on account of his being in his minority, the charge of the government and administration for the present is committed to me), should you persist in offering further molestation of the Deb's country, it will irritate both the Lama and all his subjects against you. Therefore, from a regard to our religion and customs, I request you will cease all hostilities against him, and in doing this you will confer the greatest favour and friendship upon me. I have reprimanded the Deb for his past conduct, and I have admonished him to desist from his evil practices in future, and to be submissive to you in all matters. I am persuaded that he will conform to the advice which I have given him, and it will be necessary that you treat him with compassion and clemency. As to my part, I am but a Fakir, and it is the custom of my sect, with the rosary in our hands, to pray for the welfare of mankind, and for the peace and happiness of the inhabitants of this country; and I do now, with my head uncovered, entreat that you may cease all hostilities against the Deb in future. It would be needless to add to the length of this letter, as the bearer of it, who is a Gosain, will represent to you all particulars, and it is hoped that you will comply therewith. In this country worship of the Almighty is the profession of all. We poor creatures are in nothing equal to you. Having a few things in hand, I send them to you by way of remembrance, and hope for your acceptance of them.

II

MINUTE BY WARREN HASTINGS
(May 4, 1774)

The President acquaints the Board that, since he laid before them the letter from the Teshu Lama of Tibet, he has written an answer to it, and, among other things, has proposed a general treaty of amity and commerce between the two states of Bengal and Bhutan. He begs leave to observe that such a treaty has ever been a favourite object with our Honourable Masters, and that they have repeatedly recommended the establishment of an intercourse with that country. The present juncture appeared to him the most favourable which has yet occurred for pursuing these views.

The letter from the Lama invites us to friendship, and the late final arrangement of the disputes on the frontier renders the country accessible without danger either to the persons or effects of travellers. Therefore, no sooner was the treaty for the affairs of Kuch Bahar signed and ratified than he thought seriously of carrying this project into execution; and conceiving it to be most proper that a European, and servant of the Company, should be entrusted with the negotiation in preference to any native, he wrote immediately for the necessary passports for such a person, which he informs the Board he has now obtained. The person he has made choice of for this trust is Mr. George Bogle, a servant of the Company, well-known to this Board for his intelligence, assiduity and exactness in affairs; and the President further expects to draw much advantage in the conduct of the business from the coolness and moderation of temper which he seems to possess in an eminent degree. He proposes that Mr. Bogle should set out without loss of time, and will charge himself with furnishing him proper instructions and despatches. He hopes the Board will approve of his choice, and as Mr. Bogle undertakes this difficult and hazardous commission without any immediate prospect of advantage, and with great uncertaintly as to its success, he would recommend to the Board that he be continued in possession of the appointments which he now holds at the Presidency, and permitted to act by deputy till his return, or till it shall be thought proper to dispose of him another way. The President further acquaints the Board that he has nominated Mr. Alexander Hamilton, assistant-surgeon on the establishment, to accompany Mr. Bogle on this expedition.

The President has only further to observe that he is far from being sanguine in his hopes of success, but the present occasion appears too favourable for the attempt to be neglected. He also can assure the Board that the information which he has been able to procure of the people, the country, and government of Tibet, gives considerable encouragement to it. They are represented as a simple, well-disposed people, numerous and industrious, living under a well-regulated government, having considerable intercourse with other nations, particularly with the Chinese and northern Tatars, and possessing at home the principal means of commerce, gold and silver in great abundance. For the more particular satisfaction of the Board he subjoins to this minute the substance of this information, which, being on record, will also exhibit to our Honourable Masters the grounds of the present undertaking, whatever may be its success, and enable them to judge how far it may be advisable to prosecute it on any future occasion.

He also annexes to his an account of such goods as he has ordered Mr. Bogle to provide for presents to the Lama, or as samples of the commodities which this country is capable of supplying, and he moves that the Board should order the amount to be paid out of the treasury.

III

LETTER FROM WARREN HASTINGS TO THE COURT OF DIRECTORS

The President, having received a letter from Teshu Lama, who is the guardian and minister of the Dalai Lama, the sovereign and high-priest of all Tibet, thinks it a proper opportunity to open intercourse between these countries and Bengal, through Mr. G. Bogle, whose merits and abilities we have frequently noticed to you, and who by his patience, exactitude, and intelligence seemed peculiarly fitted for the duty. Accordingly, Mr. G. Bogle will be sent to the Lama, with a letter and presents and different samples of goods, to see which would sell best there. Mr. Hamilton, assistant-surgeon, is to accompany him, but the great length of the journey and the natural difficulties which Mr. Bogle has to encounter from the severity of the climate and the rudeness of the country will make it a long while before we shall hear from him.

IV

APPOINTMENT OF MR. BOGLE

Fort William, 13th May, 1774

Sir,—Having appointed you my deputy to the Teshu Lama, the sovereign of Bhutan, I desire you will proceed to Lhasa, his capital, and deliver to him the letter and presents which I have given you in charge.

The design of your mission is to open a mutual and equal communication of trade between the inhabitants of Bhutan and Bengal, and you will be guided by your own judgment in using such means of negotiation as may be most likely to effect this purpose.

You will take with you samples for a trial of such articles of commerce as may be sent from this country according to the accompanying list, marking as accurately as possible the charge of transporting them.

You will inquire what other commodities may be successfully employed in that trade. And you will diligently inform yourself of the manufactures, productions, goods, introduced by the intercourse with other countries, which are to be procured in Bhutan, especially such as are of great value and easy transportation, such as gold, silver, precious stones, musk, rhubarb, munjit, etc.

The following will be also proper objects of your inquiry—the nature of the road between the borders of Bengal and Lhasa, and of the countries lying between; the communications between Lhasa and the neighbouring countries, their government, revenue and manners.

Whatever observations you may make on these or any other subjects, whether of useful knowledge or curiosity, I desire you will communicate to me from time to time, reporting the success of your negotiations.

The period of your stay must be left to your discretion. I wish you to remain a sufficient time to fulfil the purposes of your deputation, and obtain a complete knowledge of the country and the points referred to your inquiry. If you shall judge that a residence may be usefully established at Lhasa without putting the Company to any expense, but such as may be repaid by the advantages which may be hereafter derived from it, you will take the earliest opportunity to advise me of it; and if you should find it necessary to come away before you receive my orders upon it, you may leave such persons as you shall think fit to remain as your agents till a proper resident can be appointed, and you will apply to the Lama for his permission and the necessary passports for the persons who may be hereafter deputed in this character.

You will draw on me for your charges and your drafts shall be regularly answered. To these I can fix no limitation, but empower you to act according to your discretion, knowing that I need not recommend to you to observe a strict frugality and economy where the good of the service on which you are commissioned shall not require a deviation from these rules.

I am, Sir,

Your most obedient servant,

Mr. George Bogle. *Warren Hastings.*

P.S.—I have appointed Mr. Alexander Hamilton, assistant surgeon, to attend you on this deputation.

V

PRIVATE COMMISSIONS TO MR. BOGLE

Fort William, 16th May, 1774

1. To send one or more pair of the animals called tu's, which produce the shawl wool. If by a dooley, chairs, or any other contrivance they can be secured from the fatigues and hazards of the way, the expense is to be no objection.

2. To send one or more pair of the cattle which bear what are called cowtails.

3. To send me carefully packed some fresh ripe walnuts for seed, or an entire plant, if it can be transported; and any other curious or valuable seeds or plants, the rhubarb and ginseng especially.

4. Any curiosities, whether natural productions, manufactures, paintings, or what else may be acceptable to persons of taste in England. Animals only that may be useful, unless any that may be remarkably curious.

5. In your inquiries concerning the people, the form of their government, and the mode of collecting their revenue, are points principally meriting your attention.

6. To keep a diary, inserting whatever passes before your observation which shall be characteristic of the people, the country, the climate, or the road, their manners, customs, buildings, cookery, etc., or interesting to the trade of this country, carrying with you a pencil and a pocket-book for the purpose of minuting short notes of every fact or remark as it occurs, and putting them in order at your leisure while they are fresh in your memory.

7. To inquire what countries lie between Lhasa and Siberia, and what communication there is between them. The same with regards to China and Kashmir.

8. To ascertain the value of their trade with Bengal by their gold and silver coins, and to send me samples of both.

9. Every nation excels others in some particular art or science. To find out this excellence of the Bhutanese.

Warren Hastings.

10. To inform yourself of the course and navigation of the Brahmaputra, and of the state of the countries through which it runs.

W.H.

VI

MEMORANDUM OF TIBET, BY WARREN HASTINGS

(Accompanying the Instructions to Mr. Bogle)

Tibet is a cold, high, mountainous country. The inhabitants approach more in figure to the Persians and other inhabitants of Western Asia, than to any of their neighbours, Chinese, Hindus, or Tatars.

It should seem that Tibet consisted of a great variety of tribes more or less addicted to the pastoral life. At times they appear to have united into powerful confederacies, and become formidable to their neighbours. At other times, when divided, they fell a prey to irruptions to Tatars, or to the policy and power of the Chinese. The Caucasus formed a barrier on the south that protected reciprocally both Hindustan and Tibet from any dangerous hostilities in that quarter.

In the fourth century, the Tatar confederacy of the Typa subdued the north and east of Tibet. In the eighth and ninth centuries, when the Tatar confederacy of the Turks became feeble, the power of those nations, which now acknowledge the supremacy of the Dalai Lama, was very great. Sometimes they penetrated into the heart of China, but at other times the Chinese took advantages of their divisions to recover what had been lost.

In 1102, the chief of Great Tibet seems to have resided at Lhasa. He at that period found it necessary to become lama, in order to strengthen his authority over the different tribes that had raised him to be their leader, and for the same reason, it is said, that he submitted to become a vassal of the Chinese empire in 1125.

In the thirteenth century, the Tatar confederacy of the Moghuls under Mangu Khan overran Tibet, and soon after Kublai Khan, who was Emperor of China as well as chief of the Moghuls, divided it into provinces, and gave the title of King to the Lama of Lhasa. The Moghul princes being expelled from China, the Emperor Yonglo, of the dynasty of Ming, which succeeded them, gave the title of King, in 1373, to eight more lamas in Tibet. In 1426, these took the title of Grand Lamas; and then, or sometime afterwards, the Lama of Lhasa took the distinguishing title of Dalai Lama. At least, we find the Chinese Emperor Kang-hi appointing, in 1705, a Dalai Lama, who is said to be the sixth in succession who had borne that title.

It was in the middle of the fifteenth century that the Dalai Lama of Bhutan, or Greater Tibet, first named a Typa Lama for the administration of civil affairs. The late intercourse opened between the Presidency of Bengal and Bhutan shows that the office of Typa remains and actually engrosses the authority of the state. It is not likely that the Dalai Lama retains the power of nominating to this office.

Although the Chinese historians ascribe to their emperors the power of nominating the Dalai Lama, it does not follow that this nomination is more than a bare acknowledgement or confirmation of his appointment by the lamas or Tibetan tribes. It may likewise not be improbable that the Typa Lama is chosen by the priests. It is, at least, generally said that the chiefs of the Tibetan tribes that acknowledge a sort of supremacy in the Dalai Lama are all elected by the priests, or lamas, the nobility at the same time having some influence in the transaction.

A curious enough precaution against hereditary succession in the chiefship is ascribed to these tribes. No sooner, it is said, is a new chief chosen, than his wife and children are for ever separated from him. I have never heard what is one with *them*, nor whether the chief is, after his elevation, debarred the use of women.

If the institution is true, it seems to indicate a very high advance in political establishments. Rude men have no apprehension of losing their independence; people only become jealous of their liberty when they grow doubtful of their resolution to retain it.

The religion and hierarchy established in Tibet is, however, a matter of much greater curiosity. We are told that the Dalai Lama is held to be an incarnation of the legislator prophet, or god Buddha or Fo, who over all Hindustan gives his name (like Thanth or Mercury, the prophet legislator and god of the Egyptians) to the planet Mercury, and to the fourth day of the week. When the Dalai Lama dies, a child is said to be pitched on as possessing certain marks which show that the soul of the deceased has been transmigrated into him; and the divinity and identity of the new manifestation of the god is of course acknowledged.

Among the different Tatar tribes which are of this religion, there are persons called Ku-tchuck-tus, who are likewise esteemed living Fos. It is, however, said that though each tribe pays a particular respect to its own Ku-tchuck-tu, the divinity of those of other tribes is not the less acknowledged and it is even pretended that the Ku-tchuck-tus admit a superiority in the Dalai Lama, so that his excrements are sold as charms at a great price among all the Tatar tribes of this religion. I have already mentioned that no less than eight Lamas in Tibet, besides the Lama of Lhasa, have the title of King, and are called Grand Lamas. But I do not know whether these, too, are esteemed incarnations of the divinity, or what subjection, if any, they pay to the Dalai Lama.

Any information with regard to the antiquity and to the creed of this religion, as well as to the authority, civil and ecclesiastical, of the lamas, could not fail to be extremely interesting.

It would also be desirable to have any facts relative to the state of Tibet with respect to China and Tatary. I have been told that a large river forms a boundary between China and Tibet, which was carefully guarded by the troops of both countries; and that Tibet received European commodities by the valley of Kashmir. But I have learned nothing satisfactory on these subjects, not so much as whether Kashmir and Lesser Tibet are at present dependent on Bhutan or Greater Tibet, or whether the Dalai Lama is still a vassal to China.

It is said that in Tibet it is very common for one lady to have several husbands. I should wish much to know if this practice obtains in all the ranks of society, and whether those husbands who all have intercourse with one woman have not likewise other women that are their wives, with whom likewise they hold an intercourse in common. We have instances in other countries where, though each man in a family had a wife that was properly his own, all the men in the family had likewise an intercourse with all the women in it. Perhaps this may be the case also in Tibet; and if we knew anything of the laws of succession in Tibet, or to whom the children of a wife with several husbands were understood to belong, one might be able to discover how the fact stood, though we had no direct information with regard to it.

The history, government, and religion of Tibet are no doubt more interesting objects of inquiry than its climate or typographical and physical characters; yet these, too, are highly curious. The great rivers of the south and east of Asia appear to issue from its mountains. It is probably, therefore, the highest land in the old continent, and this circumstance, together with the difficulty of access to it, give it a striking analogy to the valley of Quito, in South America, which is the highest land in the new continent, and whose climate and situation M. de la Condamine has exhibited in so interesting a point of view. Though Lhasa is situated in a more southern latitude that

Alexandria, in Egypt, we are told that people sent by Colonel Cumming had to travel to it through snow so late as the month of April. Any observations made in such a country a thermometer would, therefore, be valuable.

I have preferred stating what I know of the subject to putting mere interrogatories. By this means I flatter myself it will be better perceived what information I want, and what information is desirable.

[From *Narratives of the Mission of George Bogle to Tibet, and of the Journey of Thomas Manning to Lhasa*, 1879.]

2

Memorandum on our Relations with Tibet

By
COLMAN MACAULAY

I

1. It is difficult for those who have always been accustomed to look upon Tibet as a closed land for Europeans, to realize that a century and a half ago a Christian Mission was established at Lhasa. Nowadays a solitary English traveller, approaching any of the passes, finds himself confronted by a party of guards who point to an inscribed board planted on the frontier pillar, and proceed to execute a pantomime, of which the unmistakeable purport is that, if he crosses the boundary, their throats will be cut. The number of Europeans who, since the beginning of this century, have set their eyes, much less their feet, upon Tibetan ground,—at any rate in the provinces of U and Tsang, or Tibet Proper,—might almost be counted on the fingers of the two hands. Yet in beginning of the last century, missionaries passed freely backwards and forwards between India and Tibet, and for many years preached the gospel under the very shadow of Potala. Two Jesuits, named Desideri and Freyre, travelled over the Mariam-La pass to Lhassa in 1716, and Desideri remained there till 1721. In his journal, which was discovered at Pistoia in the end of 1875, Father Desideri states that he openly gave out at Lhassa that he was a foreign Lama come to convert the people; that he was received with much toleration; and that the king (i.e., the Nomenkhan or Gesub Rimboochay, the head of the temporal Government of the Tale Lama) was so much struck with a pamphlet of his that he arranged for a religious discussion to take place between him and some great Lamas. A revolution, however, intervened; the "king" was assassinated; and the discussion fell through (Geographical Magazine, 1st September 1876). Again Father Horace della Penna, with 12 Capuchins, reached Lhassa by way of Nepal in 1719. In 1735 he returned to Rome for reinforcements, and in 1740 he again reached Lhassa with nine companions.

He died in Nepal in 1747, but other missionaries remained at Lhassa, till they were expelled about 1760. As Mr. Clements Markham, in the admirable introduction to his edition of the Narratives of Bogle and Manning, says:— "The way in which Horace della Penna passed to and fro between Tibet and India proves that the intercourse was free and unrestrained, and that the traffic was protected by the enlightened policy of the Lamas of Tibet and the Newar Kings of Nepal." It was the supersession of these two authorities,—the extension of Chinese influence in Tibet, and their assumption of the control of the foreign relations of the Lamas on the one hand, and the conquest of the peaceful and enlightened Newars by the turbulent and ignorant Goorkhas on the other,—that led, first to the discouragement, and then to the prohibition, of intercourse. These two causes acted and re-acted upon one another till the present state of affairs was brought about, and while Nepalese and Cashmeerees hold their own in the market places of Shigatse and Lhassa, British subjects, Indian or European, are, as such, unceremoniously turned back almost within sight of the smoke of our locomotives.

2. The event to which Desiderri refers when he speaks of a revolution occurring, was the first of a train of circumstances which led to results more disastrous to European intercourse than his own disappointment at the loss of a triumph over his Lama opponents. The storming of Lhasa and the murder of Gesub by the Zungarians in 1717 was followed by Chinese intervention, and from 1720 two Chinese Ampas were permanently stationed at Lhasa. At first they do not seem to have had very much authority in Tibet. Their presence, in fact, would appear to have called into being a national party, headed by the Gesub, which jealously watched all their attempts to assert the authority of China. At length a catastrophe occurred which, though fatal to the actors in the tragedy itself, led to a great increase in the influence of China. About the middle of the last century the Ampas, Pou and Li, wished to increase the Chinese garrison, on the pretext of a movement among the Nepalese tribes, and interfered more and more in the government of the country. The Gesub and the national party offered an uncompromising opposition to them, and the Ampas had the Gesub assassinated before their eyes. The result was an outburst of popular fury; the Ampas were torn to pieces; and a general massacre of the Chinese in Tibet ensued. The Emperor Kien Lun sent an army to re-establish Chinese authority, and for sometime afterwards the Gesubs, instead of leading a national party of opposition, were completely the creatures of the Ampas. Mr. Clements Markham gives 1749 as the date of this revolution. Huc and Gabet say it occurred in the 35th year of Kien Lun, which would be 1770. It is to be observed, however, that Bogle, who visited Tashi Lunpo in 1774, refers to it as antecedent to the death of the Tale Lama, Lossan Kalsang, which took place in 1758. Mr. Markham's date would therefore appear to be correct. At any rate it is clear that the change in the relations between the Ampas and the Tibetan Government was closely followed by the expulsion of the European missionaries. As long as there was a party to keep the Chinese in check, the missionaries were unmolested. As soon as the Chinese got the power into their hands, they were expelled. It is curious to note the points of resemblance between the position of Huc and Gabet in 1846, and the position of the Capuchins a century earlier. In both cases we find tolerance and kindness from Tibetans, and bigotry and hostility from the Chinese. Huc and Gabet were treated with marked attention and respect by the Regent Pe-Chi, or Shaffe, Shete, who did his utmost to protect them. It was Ki-Chan, the Chinese Plenipotentiary, anxious to regain credit after his disgrace at Canton, who insisted on their expulsion.

3. While Chinese influence was thus gaining a remarkable accession at Lhassa, events were in progress in Nepal, which were destined to culminate in the complete severance of Indian intercourse with Tibet. As long as the chiefs of the Newar dynasty ruled the petty kingdoms of Kathmandoo, Patan and Bhatgaon, a flourishing trade was carried on through Nepal between High Asia and the plains. Mr. Clements Markham notices that as early as 1583 a traveller named Ralph Fitch gave an account of it. Mr. Bogle, writing in 1775, says:—"Every encouragement was given to trade. A very moderate duty was levied on goods; the country, populous and well-cultivated, easily furnished the means of transporting them, and the merchants, free from spoil or exactions, settled in Nepal, and contributed to enrich it at the same time that they improved their own fortunes." Mention has been made above of a movement among the Nepalese which gave the Ampas, Pou and Li, a pretext for increasing the number of the Chi-

nese troops in Tibet. This was no doubt a phase of the dissensions between the Newars, which gave Prithi Narayan, the Chief of the Goorkhas, an opportunity of intervening, and of finally, in 1769, subduing the whole of the Nepal valley. The Goorkha conquest was fatal to trade. A military despotism succeeded to the mild and enlightened sway of the native chiefs. A standing army was maintained to overawe the people, and grinding taxes were imposed to defray the expenses. "The merchants," wrote Mr. Bogle, "subject to heavy and arbitrary fines upon the most frivolous pretences, and obliged to purchase the protection of a tyranical Government by presents scarcely less oppressive, quieted a country where they could no longer enjoy that freedom and security which are the life of commerce. Only two Kashmiri houses remain, and the Rajah, afraid of their also abandoning him, obliges them to give security for the return of such agents as they have occasion to send beyond the boundaries of his dominions." It will be pointed out further on that to this day heavy import and export duties are levied on the frontiers of Nepal.

4. Meanwhile, to the eastward, Deb Judhur of Bhootan had invaded Cooch Behar, and stopped all trade with Tibet through these channels. There remained the road through Demo Jung, now known as Sikkim, and Mr. Bogle says that "the fakirs, when expelled from Nepal, generally frequented this road; but being esteemed unhealthy, it was not adopted by any creditable merchants." It was soon closed altogether by the Goorkha Raja invading the country.

5. The third quarter of the 18th century, therefore, saw Europeans expelled from Tibet by Chinese influence, after residence extending over nearly half a century. It also saw trade paralysed, and the road from India closed by the turbulence of the intervening States.

6. But, though the fair prospect was overcast, it was obscured only by clouds that might pass away. There was to be yet a gleam of sunshine before it disappeared in the darkness of the long night that was to follow. In 1774 the Tashi Lama, or Penchen Rimboochay, sent to Warren Hastings his memorable letter of intercession for Deb Judhur. Lossan Paldan Yese was the 13th of the illustrious line of Avatars which, beginning with Subhuti, the Stavira, one of the favourite disciples of Buddha, has, after intervals of varying length, established the continuous dynasty of the Penchen Rimboochay or Tashi Lamas of Tashilunpo. The first four incarnations took place on this side of the Himalayas, and the Penchens have always been conspicuous for the reverence and affection with which they regard the holy places of the land of Aryavarta. Mr. Mayers, of the Consular Service of China, in a paper read before the Royal Asiatic Society of Great Britain in April 1869, said : "Joint heir with the Dalai (Tale) Lama of the spiritual inheritance derived from Tsungkaba, the Panshen Erdeni is believed by the Tibetans to be worthy of the higher degree of adoration, his office and functions being the less contaminated by worldly influences." The Tashi Lama, or Penchen Rimbochay ordains, or is ordained by, the Tale Lama, or Gyow Rimboochay, according as one or the other is the elder. The immediate predecessor of Lossan Paldan Yese was formally invested by the Emperor Yung Ching with the sovereignty of the whole of Tibet west of the Painam, and he himself was destined to raise oven higher than before the reputation of the dynasty for sanctity, wisdom and strength of character. Warren Hastings seized the opportunity of the Tashi Lama's letter of intercession to endeavour to remove the obstacles to trade. He dealt leniently with the Bhootanese, and sent George Bogle as his ambassador to the Lama. Bogle's narrative shows that his journey was retarded, and the object of his mission thwarted, by the jealousy of the Gesub and the influence of the Chinese. It also brings out very strongly the wonderful power, dignity and liberality of the Lama's

character. Two expressions quoted by Bogle from the Lama's conversation are instructive. "As to me," he said, "I give encouragement to merchants, and in this country they are free and secure." But, speaking of the Gesub as the representative of the policy of Lhassa, he said "his heart is confined, and he does not see things in the same view as I do." He clearly saw that it was essential to remove the objections of the Chinese before anything effectual could be done to establish free intercourse between India and Tibet, and he promised to continue his efforts to this end. He subsequently visited China at the invitation of Kien Lun, and was received with great demonstrations of respect, the Emperor himself advancing to meet him and placing him on a seat beside his own. The Lama lost no time in broaching the subject of communication between India and China, and the Emperor promised, at his instance, to write a letter of friendship to Warren Hastings. All hope of success in this direction, however, was destroyed by the sudden death of the Lama from small-pox. Still something had already been gained. Warren Hastings had won the confidence of the Lama's brother, the Chanzoo Cusho, who became Regent upon his death, and Bogle had succeeded in inducing the Deb Raja to allow native merchants to pass to and from Tibet through Bhootan. As soon as the Regent announced the reappearance of the Penchen, Mr. Hastings deputed Captain Turner to convey his felicitations to Tashi Lunpo. Turner had an interview with the child and confirmed the friendly relations with the Regent. But like Bogle, he was debarred from a visit to Lhassa by the jealous of the Gesub. He wrote in his report: "I have obtained the Regent Chanzoo Cusho's promise of encouragement of all merchants, natives of India, that may be sent to traffic in Tibet on behalf of the Government of Bengal. No impediment, therefore, now remains in the way of merchants, to prevent their carrying their commercial concerns into Tartary. Your authority alone is requisite to secure them the protection of the Regent of Teshoo Loombo, who has promised to grant free admission into Tibet to all such merchants, natives of India, as shall come recommended by you; to yield them every assistance requisite for the transport of their goods from the frontiers of Bhootan; and to assign them a place of residence for receiving their commodities, either within the monastery, or, should it be considered as more eligible, in the town itself." Subsequent reports showed that these measures bore excellent fruit. Purunghir Gossain, the companion of the late Tashi Lama on his visit to China, and the bearer of many letters from Warren Hastings to Tibet, was sent to Tashi Lunpo by the great Governor-General with despatches announcing his approaching departure for Europe. Captain Turner communicated Purunghir's report of his journey to Mr. Macpherson, the Acting Governor-General. "It is with infinite satisfaction," he writes, "I learn from the reports of Purunghir the flourishing state of the lately projected scheme of trade, to promote which, he assures me, not anything has been wanting in facility of intercourse; that the adventures, who had invested their property, had experienced perfect security in conducting their commerce, had carried their articles to an exceeding good market and found the rate of exchange materially in their favour." Not only was Purunghir charged with the verbal communication of the anxious desire of the Regent to continue with the new Governor-General "Those offices of friendship so long supported by his predecessor," but he brought two letters for the Governor-General, one in the name of the young Tashi Lama, and one from the Regent himself. The Tashi Lama's letter runs thus—"We have made no deviation from the union and unanimity, which existed during the time of the first of nobles, Mr. Hastings, and the deceased Lama; and may you also grant friendship to these countries, and always make me happy with the news of your health. which will be the cause of ease to my heart and confirmation to my soul." The

Regent wrote: "Every day make me happy by the news of your health and prosperity, and bestow favours like the first of nobles and make me happy with letters, which are the cause of consolation." No response whatever appears to have been given to these cordial invitations to correspondence, and six years later an event occurred which might have been made an occasion for winning permanently the affections of the Tibetans, but which was allowed to undo all that Warren Hastings had achieved, and to close Tibet against British subjects for a hundred years.

7. The temple of Tashi Lunpo had been enriched for generations by the munificence of its abbots and the piety of the faithful. Rich tapestries and silks, rare pictures and precious stones, vessels and images of solid gold, ornamented its walls and its altars. The gilt roof of the tomb of Chokyi Gyaltshan cost six lakhs of rupees, that of Yese Pal Sanpo cost over seven. With the remains of Paldan Yese (Bogle's Tashi Lama), Kien Lun sent to Tibet a temple of copper and another of solid gold, which were placed inside the mausoleum at Tashi Lunpo, and the Tibetan chronicler, whose account has been translated by Baboo Sarat Chandra Das, says: "All the presents made by the Emperor, together with those obtained from other sources, of the estimated value of 4,15,665 *San* (Rs. 2,49,39,900) were spent in erecting his tomb and decorating and adorning it with precious stones and satin flags." The story of all this wealth tempted the Goorkhas, who, having conquered Nepal and a part of Sikkim, were in want both of money and of occupation. In 1782 they suddenly appeared before Tashi Lunpo: the Regent and the child Tashi Lama escaped across the Sanpo; and the Goorkhas, after stripping the monastery and the palace of their treasures, hurried back to Nepal with their booty. The Regent conveyed the young Lama to Lhassa, and information was despatched to Pekin. An avenging army was soon in motion from China, and within few months of the occurrence of the outrage, the Goorkhas were signally defeated close to Kathmandoo itself, and compelled to disgorge their plunder and to undertake to pay an annual tribute to China and to send an Embassy in token of submission every five years. The Chinese turned these events to bitter account against us. They reported that we were the allies of the marauders, that he had drilled that we were the allies of the marauders, that we had drilled their troops, that British soldiers had been recognized among them. A line of Chinese posts was established along the frontiers of Bhootan and Nepal, and every native of India was expelled from Tibet. An expression in Turner's "Account of the situation of affairs in Tibet from 1785 to 1793" would seem to show that the Tibetans applied to us for assistance, and that we refused it. Mr. Edgar doubts whether aid was really asked for. However, this may be, the circumstances were such as to render intervention a right and almost a duty. Warren Hastings would have required no pretext beyond the fact that an unprovoked act of brigandage had been committed on a helpless child, and that a party of marauders, whom it was in his power to coerce, had driven his young rally a fugitive from the palace where British envoys had recently been received with honour. Mr. Duncan was actually signing a treaty of commerce with Nepal, while the Goorkhas were planning their attack on Tashi Lunpo, and the only notice Lord Cornwallis appears to have taken of the outrage was an offer to mediate between China and Nepal, which was treated with indifference on both sides. "From this period," says Turner, "unhappily is to be dated the interruption which has taken place in the regular intercourse between the Company's possession and the territory of the Lama." "The approach of strangers, even of the natives of Bengal and Hindustan, is utterly prohibited. A most violent prejudice prevails even against the Hindoo Goseins, who are charged with treachery against their generous patrons, by becoming guides

and spies to the enemy, and have in consequence, it is said, been proscribed their accustomed abode at Teshoo Loomboo, where they had been ever patronized in great numbers by the Lama, and enjoyed particular favour and indulgence."

8. Thus the curtain fell upon the Tibetan stage, and from this time up to the present the journey of an Englishman to Lhassa (which is considerably nearer to Darjeeling than Darjeeling is to Calcutta, and which is separated from it by no pass of any difficulty whatever) has been considered something about as visionary as a voyage to Laputa or Atlantis would have appeared to a contemporary of Swift or to a disciple of Plato. Manning indeed made his way to the holy city in 1811—the only Englishman, so far as we certainly know, who ever reached it. He spoke Chinese, he travelled in disguise, and his knowledge of medicine gave him great advantages. But his disguise was penetrated, and he was compelled to return to India. Our next glimpse of Tibet is obtained from the narrative of Fathers Huc and Gabet, who reached Lhassa on 29th January, and were deported from it on 15th March 1846. Both Manning and Huc and Gabet were well treated by the Tibetans, and were expelled by the Chinese. Manning, who wished to go on to China, was forced to return to India: Huc and Gabet, who begged to be allowed to go on to India, were forced to return to China. In the pages of these missionaries we find a most interesting mention of the Penchen Rimboochay, to whom Warren Hastings sent Turner more than 60 years before, and whom Lord Cornwallis saw driven from his home by the Goorkhas. "The celebrity," they write, "of the present Penchen is prodigious; his partisans assert that his spiritual power is as great as that of the Tale Lama, and that the sanctuary of Tashi Lunpo does not yield in sanctity to that of Potala. The present Penchen Rimboochay is sixty years of age; he is, they say, of a fine and majestic frame, and astonishingly vigorous for his advanced age. The Tibetans, the Tartars and the other Buddhists call him by no other name than the Great Saint, and never pronounce his name without clasping their hands and raising their eyes to heaven. The Tartars have so strong a faith in his power that they invoke him continually. In dangers, in affections, in all matters of difficulty, they have in their mouths the magic word bokte (saint)."

9. Our next information comes from the reports of the hardy explorers of the Survey Department despatched between 1865 and 1878, and from the (politically) more important reports of Baboo Sarat Chandra Das. This gentleman, while head-master of the Bhutia School in Darjeeling, devoted himself to the study of Tibetan literature, and conceived the design of penetrating to Tashi Lunpo. This design he carried out with a prudence, a courage and an intelligence which entitle him to high distinction. In 1879 he reached Tashi Lunpo travelling, not by the Sikkim passes, where he would have been liable to detection, but by the Kang La, which leads into a corner of Nepal, and then over the Chotang La and the Chorten Nyema into Tibet. He went in the character of an Indian pundit, desirous of studying Buddhism in the places where it now flourishes. He was most hospitably received by the Minister of the Penchen, Singchen Rimboochay, and by the Penchen Rimboochay himself. This Penchen was born in 1853, and was the immediate successor of the Penchen of Turner and the Huc and Gabet. Sarat Baboo did not see much of the Grand Lama, who was only at Tashi Lunpo during seven weeks of his stay; but he saw enough to convince him of his strong individuality of character. The Minister, throughout his stay, manifested the strongest desire to become acquainted with European science. He was indefatigable in his application to photography and took lessons in English and Hindi, in physical science, and in mathematics. Sarat Baboo left 'T'ashi Lunpo with a warm invitation from the Minister to

return in the succeeding year. The Minister begged of him to fetch a lithographic press, some vaccine matter, a telephone and other things. In 1881 Sir Ashley Eden obtained the sanction of the Supreme Government to Sarat Baboo's deputation with Lama Ugyen Gyatso, the companion of his previous journey, on a visit to Tashi Lunpo and Lhassa. The Baboo again took the Nepal route, but this time crossed the Kanglachen Pass. He was received with open arms by the Minister, and resided with him at Tashi Lunpo and Dongtse for several months. He had better opportunities than on his first visit for prosecuting his acquaintance with the Grand Lama, and gave him lessons in Sanskrit. The Lama showed himself to be a man of broad and liberal views, and strongly inclined to further intercourse with India. He even proposed to take the Baboo in his own suite to Lhassa, when unfortunately he died of small-pox in August 1882. Sarat Baboo's report of his second visit is now in the press. It is sufficient to say here that he visited Lhassa in the train of the wife of one of the Shaffes, or Chief Secretaries, who is related to the Minister, and that he saw the Tale Lama, then a boy of eight. He returned to India in the beginning of 1883. The Minister had asked him if he could take about Rs. 2,500 for him in money to Calcutta for the purchase of European articles. On the Government of India learning this, they desired that the Minister might be informed that they would be glad if he would consider this sum as placed to this credit in Calcutta in recognition of his kindness to the Baboo.

10. We have been awaiting a favourable opportunity for formally communicating this message, and an occasion recently presented itself. There have been various rumours afloat for the last year or so of the stoppage of the trade through Darjeeling by the Tibetan officials. This was at one time said to be owing to the quarrel between Tibet and Bhootan in August 1883, when the Paro Penlow plundered Phari Jong and carried off the Jongpen a prisoner. At another it was attributed to the influence of the Nepalese, who, after the settlement of the dispute arising out of the riot at Lhasa in March 1883, when the Sera, Depung, and Gahdan monks, disregarding the authority of the Tibetan Government, plundered the shops of the Newar traders, are said to have pressed the Tibetans to close the road to Darjeeling for three years. That the trade was stopped at times, and so lately as September last, there can be no doubt. It was considered desirable that enquiries should be made on the subject in Sikkim, and as some questions of importance regarding the Maharaja's allowance and the levy of transit duties were pending, there was a good opportunity for interesting the Sikkim Durbar in the matter. At the same time circumstances had suggested the advisability of opening a direct road between Darjeeling and the province of Tsang, where a large supply of wool is found and where the people have always been well-disposed to us in consequence of the friendly relations subsisting between the Tashi Lamas and the Indian Government a hundred years ago. The Lieutenant-Governor accordingly deputed me to make enquiries from the Maharaja at Tumlong, and to visit the Lachen valley to ascertain if a road, practicable all the year round, could be constructed. It was also hoped that, if I could have a friendly interview with the Tibetan authorities on the frontier at the head of the Lachen valley, an opportunity might be found for communicating the message of the Government of India to the Minister at Tashi Lunpo, the capital of Tsang. A special report deals with the question relating to Sikkim. I may here say that the Maharaja was able to state that, when he left Choombi on 20th October, the trade had been opened again. He attributed the stoppage to the dispute with the Bhootanese which was then being investigated; he said he knew nothing of a Nepalese intrigue. Intimation of my projected visit to the frontier was sent by the Maharaja to Kamba Jong, and on the 8th November I met

one of the Jongpens of Kamba (the other was ill) at Giagong. I may here quote the description given by Baboo Sarat Chandra Das of the functions of a Jongpen:—"The Jongpens are the district officers who, in addition to their revenue and executive duties, are entrusted with powers to try Civil and Criminal cases within the limits of their *jongs* or districts. The chief duty of the Jongpen is the collection of the Government revenues and occasional taxes, levied by the issue of *kargya*, or *purwanas*, from the Court of Kahlons. His power therefore is very great in revenue and executive matters. In every *jonj* two Jongpens with equal powers are appointed from among the most distinguished Doongkhors. The Jongpens of Tibet closely resemble in their duties and powers and district officers under the British Government, with this difference, that the Jongpens have also to do military duty in times of war. In military matters the Jongpen is subordinate to the Daphem (General) and the Ampa (Senior Imperial Resident)."

11. At the beginning of our first interview, the Jongpen was reserved and distant in his manner, and was evidently uneasy, lest I should ask leave to cross the frontier. He also declined to receive a letter or presents for the Minister, on the ground that it was not the custom to hold any communication with the British. As the conversation proceeded, however, and I pointed out that the letter was a mere matter of courtesy, and a sign of respect for the character and position of the Minister, made enquiries about the reappearance of the Penchen and explained the entirely pacific and friendly nature of our policy, and as he saw that I had no intention of crossing the frontier or of giving trouble, he became more communicative, and finally agreed to take charge of the letter and some presents. After this the communications became very cordial, and he displayed much curiosity and interest in the things presented or shown to him, and finally he himself asked me to have a photograph of the group taken. Next morning I had a long confidential interview with him, only Sarat Baboo being present as interpreter. He begged that I would treat what he said as confidential, and I trust, therefore, that this portion of my memorandum may be regarded as such. To my enquiry what was the cause of the suspicion with which we were regarded, he answered that there was no real dislike or suspicion of us among the people, and that on the contrary they were now well-aware that the "Maharani's" subjects are governed with justice and are very rich and happy. This knowledge is spreading every day, and a stronger and stronger desire is growing up for further communication with India. The only party really opposed to us are the monks of the monasteries at Lhassa,—Sera, Depung, Gahdan, Mulu, and the four "Lings" (Kenduling, Chemeling, Checheling and Tankyaling),—who are afraid of losing their influence, and also afraid of losing the profits of the practical monopoly which they now hold of the trade through Darjeeling. The monks have hitherto had their own way, but he and most of the officials, and all the people, would like to see all restrictions on communication with us removed. I asked him what he thought of the proposal of constructing a road through the Lachen valley for the convenience of traders. As an official, he said, he could not say he would like to see it made; as a private individual he would be glad. I asked him if it would lead to increase in trade. He said that it would certainly do so, if traders were allowed to pass. People are now most anxious to trade with India, and are most eager to get English goods, particularly broadcloth, cutlery and piece-goods. "Now-a-days," he said, "whenever a man gets an article of English manufacture, a hundred people come to look at it." He said, however, that there would be no use in making a road while the present policy is upheld, as he would be forced to prevent people from using it in large numbers. I asked him if he levied any duty now on traders, such as I had met in the Lachen valley. He said, he had no orders to

levy duty, but he had strict orders not to let many people pass Kamba Jong, and he had had before this to turn people back for fear of getting into trouble. In the same way at Phari, he believed it was a matter more of prohibition than of taxation. He did not believe in the pretext of the Bhootanese and Nepalese difficulties so far as the question of the trade by the Jeylep (the eastern pass) was concerned. The Sera and Depung monks are keen traders, and they have influence enough to cause difficulties to be thrown in the way of their competitors. I asked him if he and others of the same views had any hope of seeing a change in the policy of exclusion. He said that if we could only get China on our side, the present was an excellent opportunity. The riot of March 1883 occurred during the grand prayer meeting, when the police of Lhasa is every year given over for a month to the charge of the monks under a Provost called Tshog-chhen-shal-no. The quarrel originated in the maltreatment of the Tibetan lady by some Nepalese shopkeepers. The Sera, Gahdan and Depung monks all took part in the disturbance because the Nepalese are rival traders. The Sera and Gahdan monks had the additional incentive of a desire to discredit the Depung monks, who, they complain, monopolise the appointment of Provost. The Gesub, who tried to quell the tumult, had to take refuge in the Tale Lama's palace and afterwards tendered his resignation of the office. The outcome of the matter was that the Lhassa Government had to pay Nepal an indemnity of 10 lakhs of rupees. They have this year asked China to send four Ampas instead of two, in order to support their authority against the monks. This, the Jongpen said, was an excellent opportunity for us. The Lhassa Government, he assured me, are themselves liberal and friendly, and if the Chinese would allow us to approach them and the monks were suppressed, trade, he was confident, would be freed from all restrictions. I had also a long talk with the Jongpen about the Tashi Lamas. He was well-acquainted with the story of Bogle's and Turner's missions, and said that every villager in Tibet knew of the pearl necklace which the Governor of India sent to the Tashi Lama. He also spoke quite seriously of the belief that Her Majesty is the incarnation of the Divine Mother Tara, who is the special protectress of the Penchens. The monks at Lhassa, it may be observed, have tried to spread the belief that she is the incarnation of Mag-jorgyamo, the God of War, but throughout Tsang, and in a great part of U, the other view is held. He was very much surprised and pleased at even my limited stock of information regarding Tibet and its religion, but he was aware that the Indian Government are tolerant towards Buddhists, and that it had even expended money on repairs of Buddhist monuments. He also knew that Warren Hastings gave the Tashi Lama a piece of land on the Hooghly for a Buddhist temple. My interview with the Jongpen was cordial in the extreme, and he repeatedly asked Sarat Baboo to say that he had never hoped to see a Peling (European) with so much sympathy for Tibet and its people. I hope I may be pardoned for going so much into personal detail with regard to this interview. I have done so because it seems to me that no better illustration could be given of the willingness of these people to enter upon friendly relations with us, if they are properly treated, or of the superiority of personal intercourse over formal correspondence, then the change between the Jongpen's manner at the beginning of our interview on the 8th and his manner at the close of our interview on the 9th. We parted, I promising to send him copies of his photograph as soon as possible, and he promising to write to me at times with news of Tibet. I may add that the Jongpen's attendants, 106 in number, were very friendly and respectful.

12. The Jongpen has carried out his commission most faithfully, and the Minister has not failed to respond promptly to my letter. A copy of his letter to me and the letter

for His Excellency, with the significant present accompanying it, have been separately forwarded to the Government of India. We have thus at length succeeded, after much neglect and many failures, in opening friendly communication with Tibet. His Grace the Duke of Argyll wrote in his despatch of 5th May 1870: "I entirely concur with Your Excellency's Government that benefit may reasonably be expected from the proposed measure of abandoning our recent policy of isolation towards Tibet, and resuming the former friendly communications with its rules, which were originally opened by Mr. Warren Hastings, when Governor-General of India, and which have unfortunately been too long in abeyance." The letter now received are the first that have come from the authorities at Tashi Lunpo since December 1785. But they derive a further special interest from their contents; for the letter of the Minister announcing the incarnation of the 16th Penchen Rimboochay in 1884 is a precise parallel to the letter of the Regent announcing the incarnation of the 14th in 1782.

II

13. It is unfortunately, from the special circumstances of the case, impossible to make any approach to an accurate estimate of the expansion of trade that would follow if our native merchants were admitted without restriction to Tibet. We know that a flourishing trade did exist while the road, even through Nepal, was open, and moderate duties only were levied. We know that as soon as our merchants were again admitted through Bhootan, a profitable commerce at once sprang up. And we might assume, if we had no other materials for forming an opinion, that the trade would be valuable to-day, when Calcutta is brought within 15 days' journey of Shigatse and three weeks journey of Lhassa, if it was valuable when the journey even to Shigatse took six weeks, and when Darjeeling, where the whistle of the steam-engine now resounds along the hills, was still hushed in the silence of the primeval forest. The registered import and export trade of Nepal was last year Rs. 1,48,71,315. How much of this,—and of the trade which escapes registration,—goes to and comes from Tibet we have no means of ascertaining with accuracy. Some light, however, is thrown upon the extent of the trading operations of the Nepalese merchants by the fact that the amount which the Tibetan Government had to pay on account of the losses sustained by them in the disturbance at Lhassa on 31st March 1883 was 10 lakhs of rupees. They have establishments at Shigatse, Gyantse and Chethang as well as at Lhassa. We do not know what even our present trade through Darjeeling really amounts to. I have shown in the report for the past year that I ascertained by personal enquiries made through Baboo Sarat Chandra Das that the value of the goods under nine heads alone, known to have been taken to Tibet by individual traders, was Rs. 1,54,805 against Rs. 8,080, the value of the total exports of the year under those heads as shown in the registers. The Commissioner's attention has been drawn to this, and he has been asked to make proposals for a change in the system of registration, which can never be efficient while the mohurirs are supposed to work at Rungeet and Pheydong throughout the year. Several instances of the same nature have come to my notice during the current year. I may observe that there has been a considerable increase in the recorded export of piece-goods, indigo, tobacco and copper and in the recorded import of horses, blankets, musk, and yak-tails, though the figures only represent the trade passing at the times when the registering officers have been present at their stations. I have ample evidence, however, that the most valuable and portable articles frequently escape notice altogether. Musk, for instance, is a very favourite article of import, the pods selling in Calcutta at Rs. 20 to Rs. 25 each. It is known that there was a rush of general trade in the

beginning of the year,—when the passage of goods through Phari was comparatively free,—in consequence of the very large profits said to have been made by those who owned ventures in 1883-84 after the withdrawal of the Nepalese traders from Lhassa. The Pheydong mohurir appears to have attended to his work in June, as his register shows Rs. 64,000 worth of musk imported in that month. In September the register shows Rs. 14,100. The returns for October and November are blank, and the return for December shows Rs. 6,000. Now Sarat Baboo has procured for me a list of nine men who came through Pheydong in November and December with musk worth Rs. 88,500. Some had silks and bullion as well. The imports of musk alone were therefore not less than Rs. 1,66,600 in the four months of June September, November and December. The value registered in 1883-84 was Rs. 2,560, and in 1882-83 was *nil*. I have little doubt that the total value of the trade between Tibet and Darjeeling—apart from the local trade of Sikkim,—is quite ten lakhs of rupees even now.

14. But, as I shall proceed to show, this gives us no indication whatever of the value of the trade that would be carried if our traders were placed on the same footing as the Nepalese occupy in Tibet. The trade of Tibet with India is now carried on by Nepalese, Cashmeerees and Tibetans. We may leave the Cashmeerees out of consideration, as the trade of India through Ladakh can never be large. The Nepalese are compelled to use the routes through Nepal in order that their Government may have the opportunity of handing them over to the tax farmers on the frontiers. The journey from Calcutta to Kathmandoo takes 9 days, and the journey from Kathmandoo to Shigatse takes 28 days. From Shigatse to Lhasa is 8 days' march. The journey from Calcutta to Lhassa by Kathmandoo therefore takes over six weeks without halts. Now Darjeeling can be reached in 26 hours from Calcutta. I came in myself in 1877 from the Jeylep Pass to Darjeeling between Thursday morning and Saturday evening, and, had the railway then existed, I could have reached Calcutta at noon on Monday, having had my food in Tibet at the Jeylep Chorten on Thursday morning. A week would be an ample allowance for a trade with laden coolies or mules from Darjeeling to the Jeylep. From the Jeylep to Gyantse may be counted 7 days, and from Gyantse to Lhassa 6. The journey, therefore, from Calcutta to Lhassa by Darjeeling may be taken at three weeks, or less than half the journey by Kathmandoo. The rates of duty on goods passing north or south across the southern frontier of Nepal vary at the different stations. There is no regular customs establishment, but the vicious system of farming is employed. The effect on trade may be gathered from the remark of the Collector of Mozufferpore: "The farmers make as much as they can during the term of their lease, and their exactions are passed over unnoticed." It is understood that export and import duties are also levied at Kirong on the northern frontier. In Sikkim, on the other hand, there are no duties of any kind. It is impossible that a trade through Nepal could flourish with such difficulties to surmount as a tedious journey of six weeks and a harassing system of import and export duties. Why the trade through Darjeeling is so cramped is clear enough. Our merchants not being allowed to settle in Tibet and carry on a regular commerce with correspondents in the plains, the trade remains in the hands of individual Tibetans who have themselves to take charge of their own small ventures. Even they, as we have seen above, are constantly harassed and stopped. What we require is to have our own native merchants stationed in the principal towns with liberty to carry on unrestricted communications with the plains through Darjeeling. If this could be effected, there can be no doubt that a very large trade would spring up, and English goods would not only have a large market in the valley of the Sanpo,

but displace the Russian goods which now, from the facilities they enjoy, find their way into southern Mongolia and Tibet. I have already referred to the statement of the Jongpen of Kamba regarding the demand that exists for European goods. A glance at the map is sufficient to show that, with our railway to Darjeeling, and good roads to the neighbouring frontier, is only requires commercial organization and freedom from obstruction to ensure a flourishing trade between Calcutta and Lhassa.

The Nepalese are well-aware of the danger with which their monopoly is threatened, even under present circumstances, by the Darjeeling route. The goods imported by Darjeeling can be sold at Lhassa at a very large profit, and still at lower prices than the Nepalese have to charge. They have accordingly again brought great pressure to bear upon the Tibetan Government to close the Sikkim route, and a Lhassa trader informs me that there is a general apprehension that the pressure will be effectual, and that trade between India and Tibet through Darjeeling may soon be wholly prohibited. This man has never before visited Calcutta, though he has travelled from Lhassa to Nepal, and he very graphically described the ease and rapidity of the one journey compared with the other. It will not be forgotten, in this connection, that the Tibetans paid the Nepalese tribute under the Treaty in 1856.

15. The chief articles of export from Tibet would be musk, gold and wool. Of musk I have spoken above. The supply of this article appears to be practically unlimited, as the musk deer abounds throughout the country.

16. The mineral wealth of Tibet has formed the basis alike of Indian fables and of Chinese proverbs. Indian fancy placed the home of the gods far away among the snows, on mountains glittering with gems and gold. The Chinese have a saying that Tibet is both the highest and the richest country in the world. The tradition that the country contains rich mines of gold and silver found expression eleven hundred years ago in a work called Sang-ling ("the secret land") by the great apostle Padma Sambhava, which is now in the Tale Lama's library at Lhassa. There appears to be little doubt that gold is really plentiful. The profusion with which the metal is used in the adornment of the great temples of Tashi Lunpo, Lhassa and Samye shows that it can be obtained without much difficulty. Turner says: "They find it in large quantities and frequently very pure. In the form of gold dust it is found in the beds of rivers, and at their several bindings, generally attached to small pieces of stone, with every appearance of its having been part of a larger mass. They find it sometimes in large masses, lumps and irregular veins; the adhering stone is generally flint or quartz, and I have sometimes seen a half-formed impure sort of precious stone in the mass." Regarding Western and Central Thibet, one of the Bathang missionaries writes: "Must it be supposed that Central Tibet is rich in nothing but rocks and mud when the largest gold-fields actually worked lie to the west, at Thokjalung and Chakchak in the Ngare province, and on the Kuenlum mountains at the very boundary between Tibet and the Gobi desert? The gold dug from the Thibetan mines is shining in the rays of the sun on the gilt pinnacles of the pagodas, on the idols, on the beams and columns of the temples, on the chairs, couches and ornaments of people of high rank." And we have evidence that gold is plentiful in Eastern Tibet also. Huc and Gabet say: "Tibet, so poor in agricultural and manufacturing products, is rich beyond all imagination in metals. Gold and silver are collected there so readily that the common shepherds have become acquainted with the art of purifying these precious metals. You often see them in the ravines or in the hollows of the mountains, seated round a fire of argols amusing themselves with purifying in a rude crucible the gold dust they have found while tending their herds." M. Desgodins, in "La Mission du Tibet," writes thus: "Le sable d'or

se trouve daus toutes les rivieres et meme dans les petits ruisseaux du Thibet oriental. On peut voir autour de la malheureuse petite ville de Bathang, prise comme centre, en bien des endroits, vingt ouvriers chinois ou thibetains leveurs d'or selon l'ex pression, tres occupes a leurtravail e tres circonspects aussi parce que les lois thibetaines defendent, sous des peines severes, tout creusement dans les mines d'or et d'argent." The prohibition here referred to has its origin in the popular superstition—a remnant of the old worship of the forces of nature—that ill luck must attend any attempt to discover the secrets of the earth. This superstition, as Mr. Edgar points out, is also prevalent in Sikkim. In Tibet, however, the prohibition has, for individuals, legal as well as popular sanction. The sacred books declare that Tibet is a land of treasures, and that the spirits appointed to guard them will wreak vengeance on any one who seeks to trepass on the mystic store-house. It is ordained that if any one accidentally discovers a mine of precious metals or of gems, he shall go his way and tell no man, satisfied that he has been accorded a glimpse of the wealth committed to the care of the terrible genii, the Tanma Chuni, but presuming not to look further. The need of gold for the adornment of the temples, and a liking for tea and other commodities has, however, led to some relaxation of these ordinances in favour of the Government, so that the Tale Lama's administration works two gold mines, and the Tashi Lama's one. The progressive party of course ridicule all this. Sarat Baboo has told me a characteristic story of the Minister, who asked him to examine some black stones near his country seat at Dongtse to see if he could find any evidence of coal, adding, however, that he must be careful not to be observed, as the regulations could not be openly defied. These antiquated ideas will soon give way before self-interest, if commerce is developed, and then the vast mineral resources of Thibet will at length have an opening. As regards other minerals, I may again quote turner: "Two days' journey from Tissolumboo there is a lead mine; the ore is much the same as that found in Derbyshire, mineralized by sulphur, and the metal obtained by the very simple operation of fusion alone. Most lead contains a portion of silver, and some in such proportion as to make it an object to work the lead ore for the sake of the silver. I have seen ores and loose stones containing copper, and have not a doubt of its being found in great abundance in the country."

17. The quantity of wool available for export is known to be enormous. Between Kamba and Shigatse, within a march and a half of the Sikkim frontier at the head of the Lachen sheep are killed, not for the sake of their hides of fleeces, which are practically valueless for want of a market, but in order that their carcasses may be dried into jerked meat and sold for eight annas each. At Kamba itself carpets and rugs are manufactured of the finest quality, and of patterns evincing excellent taste and skill; but there is no outlet for these fabrics. Further north on the great Chang Thang (or northern plateau), which begins just beyond the Sanpo, within five marches of the Kongra Lama, are prodigious flocks and herds which roam at will over the endless expanse. "The whole Jangthang," writes Mr. Hennessy in his review of the explorations of A—k in 1879-82, "is coated by a short succulent grass, which from May to August covers the undulations with the softest of green carpets;" and he adds that hundred, and even thousands, of maunds of shawl wool are "necessarily produced every year and *wasted*" on this great prairie.

18. As regards imports, the Jongpen laid stress chiefly on the demand for broadcloth, piece-goods and cutlery. Indigo and tobacco, he said, would also be largely consumed; but the other goods were universally prized. On the subject of tea he was more reserved. All he could say was that the prohibition against the import of Indian tea was enforced by the Chinese, and could be removed by them only.

The more the question is examined, the more plain it becomes that, if the trade were freed, Indian tea must displace China tea in the markets of Tibet. How soon this result would follow upon the removal of the prohibition would depend upon the enterprise of the planters. I observes that Mr. Hennessy, in a note on trade routes and the tea trade of Tibet, based upon information supplied by A—k, comes to the conclusion that Indian tea cannot compete in price with China tea in the Lhassa market. Mr. Hennessy's conclusions appear to be perfectly fair if the accuracy of the data on which they are based could be conceded. Of some of these, however, he speaks with hesitation, and I think I can show not only that they are inaccurate, but that other points have been altogether overlooked by A—k. The argument is that, as carriage by the Changthang route between Darchendo and Lhassa costs almost nothing owing to the "enormous carrying power not only available but even running to utter waste," the price of tea at Lhassa need hardly exceed its price at Darchendo, 890 miles off. The figures given by A—k would show that the best tea is sold at Darchendo for 8 annas a pound, and the worst for an anna and a quarter, and the outside limit of cost of carriage to Lhassa is taken at one rupee per maund, that is 2.25th pie, or less than a quarter of an anna a pound. If these statements were correct then the best China tea could be sold at Lhassa for a little more than 8 annas, and the worst for a little less than an anna and a half a pound. Now, I think that no one reading A—k's report can fail to observe that, admirable as is the scientific part of his work, his observations on commercial questions are extremely scanty and extremely vague. He was at Darchendo for a few days, and at Lhassa for several months. He gives some figures to show the price of tea at the former place, but none to show what is also of importance,—its price at the latter. He actually describes the gates of Darchendo "with doors made of thick boards," but says nothing of the customs duties levied at these gates, at the eastern gate on tea coming in and at the northern and southern gates on tea going out. As a matter of fact every packet of four bricks pays 3/100 of a Chinese ounce of silver (three annas and four pie) on entry and the same duty on exit. Every pound of tea therefore pays 4 pie or one-third of an anna as customs duty, or nearly twice as much as the carriage for 890 miles is estimated to cost.

19. Before I refer to the actual selling price of China tea at Lhassa, I may point out that, against A—k's estimate of 5-1/3 annas for a brick of the worst tea at Darchendo, we have the evidence of a missionary, who resided for some years in the neighbourhood, that the price of a brick of the worst tea at Darchendo is 12-1/2 anas. We have further the export charge for customs duty of 10 pie a brick or 2 pie a pound, which A—k does not refer to. As regards the carriage from Darchendo to Lhassa, it is to be observed that the calculation avowedly proceeds on speculation only. It is assumed that yaks can be hired, as well as fed, for nothing, and that the only expense that need be considered is the food of one man in charge of every 50 yaks, and the wear and tear of accoutrements. I learn, however, from the statements of traders from Lhassa, whom Sarat Baboo has closely interrogated, that, though the tea traders (called Do-pa because they go to Do, the common name for the eastern tract including Amdo, Darchendo, etc.) generally go by the Changlam (or northern road), they have much larger expenses to incur than A—k's estimate would include. Moreover, it will be observed that this estimate takes no account of losses from exposure and from the robbers who are known to infest the route. They have first to purchase their baggage animals at Nag-Chu, which A—k reached in 11 days from Lhassa, and, though yaks feed themselves on a great part of the journey, asses and mules require some grain on pulses. These last animals are sometimes used in preference to yaks because they are able to travel faster and are less liable

to succumb to exposure and fatigue. A trader, who has himself been to Darchendo, has given me the following sketch of a commercial venture undertaken by a Do-pa of his acquaintance. He took two servants and ten yaks to Darchendo by the Chang-lam route. He spent, apart from the sum invested in tea, two *dochhe* (Rs. 250) on the double journey of seven months, including an expensive stay of one month at Darchendo, and he made a profit of Rs. 100 only on the whole transaction. I give these figures for what they are worth, merely to show that the expenses of this expedition of 1,780 miles are not so trifling as has been assumed.

20. I now come to a matter of more practical importance, namely the price at which China tea actually sells at Lhasa. Though A—k expressly mentions the two classes of coarse teas called Chupa and Gyepa, he fails to observe the instructive meaning of the words themselves. *Pa* in Tibetan corresponds to the Hindustani word *walla* for which we have no precise English equivalent. *Chu* means *ten* and *Gye* means *eight*. Chupa simply means "ten walla" and Gyepa "eight-walla." Now it happens that these classes or brick tea are actually used in Tibet as currency. The terms used to describe them merely indicate their conventional value in *tankas* (six annas). The conventional value therefore of a brick (about 5 pounds) of Chupa is Rs. 3-12-0, and a brick of Gyepa is Rs. 3. Besides these, there are fine teas, made up, some in bricks of different sizes, some even in leaf. The first quality of "Duthang," for instance, is sold at Lhassa at 4 srong or Rs. 10 for a brick of 6 pounds, and the second at Rs. 7 for a brick of 5 pounds, or at about Rs. 1-10-0 and Rs. 1-6-0 a pound respectively. I am informed by the merchants that at present the cash price of Chupa varies at Lhasa from 8 to 9 tankas a brick (9-1/2 to 10-1/2 annas a pound), while that of Gyepa varies from 6 to 7 tankas a brick (a little over 7 to about 8-1/2 annas a pound). I can add a curious piece of confirmatory proof. One of my native assistants was presented with a brick of Gyepa tea by the Rajah of Sikkim when I visited Tumlong. He sold this to the coolies when we were in the Lachen valley, and they readily gave him Rs. 2-12-0 for the brick, or 8-4/5 annas a pound. The actual price when payment is made in Indian rupees, or in gold dust, varies at times, but the value of the tea for the purposes of barter is the value expressed by its name. The conventional value of Chupa is therefore 12 annas a pound, and that of Gyepa about 9-1/2 annas a pound. The price actually paid by Gyepa in the Lachen valley was just under 9 annas a pound.

21. In the face of these figures the only question of practical importance that remains, in regard to the price of China tea at Lhassa, is the margin of profit which is allows. If the trade were a monopoly, the present price would be no measure of the price at which the tea could be sold in competition with Indian tea. It may at once be answered that it is not a monopoly. The Chinese officials used, it is said, to get their salaries sent to them in tea on the pretext that no tea could be procured in Tibet: this tea was carried free under *Ilam-yig* (road order) a long the Shung-lam (or Government road), and was afterwards disposed of by them at its conventional value, and of course at an enormous profit. This practice, however,—partly, it is reported, because the villages on the route were becoming deserted in consequence of the perpetual harassment to which the inhabitants were subjected,—has long been stopped. A certain quantity, said to amount to 3,000 mule loads, it still imported annually by the Lhassa Government along the Shunglam, and the people of the villages on the route have to furnish carriage free. But this tea is used to supply the chief officials and the monasteries about Lhasa, and is not sold. The bulk of the trade is carried on by the Do-pa, and no restriction whatever is placed on their operations. I understand that they complain that competition has brought about the

reduction in prices below the conventional value of the bricks and leaves them a very small margin of profit. Some have even abandoned the tea trade and taken to commerce, in their small way, with India. It is quite clear, then, that the prices I have given represent the actual commercial value of the tea at Lhassa. I may add that, as we go westward to Gyantse and Shigatse, the cost of carriage brings the price of the tea nearer and nearer to its conventional value. Every year 300 miles are said to be despatched from Tashi Lunpo to Darchendo to fetch tea for the establishment of the Tashi Lama and the monks. The journey takes nearly eight months. If the Lachen route were opened, Tashi Lunpo would be brought within 15 days, march of Darjeeling.

22. Let us now see what would be the cost of laying down Darjeeling tea at Lhassa. Mr. Hennesay's estimate of the cost of carriage is unduly favourable. He puts it at Rs. 4-9 a maund. This allows for 1-1/2 maunds being carried by a cooly from Darjeeling to Phari, which is taken to be 90 miles. But a Darjeeling cooly will not carry more than one maund on a journey, and the Jeylep pass, which is three days' march this side of Phari, is 96 measured miles from Darjeeling. A pony can carry 1-1/2 maunds to Lhassa in 20 days. The journey would cost Rs. 10, at the rate of 8 annas a day, or 1 anna 4 pie a pound. To be absolutely safe, however, let us take the journey at 25 days and the cost of carriage at 1 anna 8 pie a pound. This would cover the cost of carriage between most of the gardens and Darjeeling. As regards cost of production, it is impossible to estimate the cost of producing the compound of sticks and coarse leaves which, under the destination the Gyepa, now passes current in Tibet for the value of 9 annas a pound. The specimen which I submit herewith will make this clear. I understand, however, that the cost of producing good tea for the English market in the Darjeeling gardens need not exceed 5-1/2 annas a pound. It would be unneccessary to use expensive tea-boxes for packing; but if boxes were used, they would sell in Tibet, where wood is a luxury, for much more than they cost. Doubtless, some system of packing in baskets or in gunny bags would be adopted. Half an anna a pound would be an outside limit of the cost of packing and incidental charges.

23. It comes to this, then, that good Darjeeling tea could be laid down at Lhassa—even on the improbable assumption that the Tibetans would impose an import duty equivalent to that levied by the Chinese at Darchendo—for 8 annas a pound, while the worst China tea sells at an average of about 8 annas, and even the second best quality of China tea sells as high as Re. 1-6 a pound. At Shigatse and Gyantse the cost of Darjeeling tea would be still less, while that of China tea would be still greater. I make no attempt to decide which the planters would find the more advantageous course,—to manufacture brick tea to compete with "Chupa" and "Gyepa," or to send ordinary leaf tea which could far undersell "Duthang" and could be sold at a profit at prices slightly higher than those now prevailing for an immeasurably inferior article. The conditions of the market would soon be discovered if that market were once opened. The figures I have given will show plainly enough how great a field would lie before the Indian product if it were admitted to Tibet.

24. On the question whether the Tibetans would take to Indian tea the evidence is plain enough. Sarat Baboo was given Indian tea at an entertainment at Tashi Lunpo, and he says it was much appreciated. The Jongpen of Kampa repeatedly praised the quality of the tea which I gave him to drink at Gaigong. Tibetan politeness demands that the guest should expressly praise whatever is placed before him by his host. I may note, however, that my friend emptied two cups, while he merely tasted the brandy I gave him, and it is fair to infer that he did really find the tea palatable.

The Jongpens who met Mr. Edgar at the Jeylep liked Indian tea. The Minister at Tashi Lunpo, who has the name of being a connoisseur in tea, drinks Indian tea whenever he can get it, and I have just sent him, through Kamba Jong, a present of some. A Darjeeling merchant, named Rabden, well aware of the profit that would ensue if his venture were successful, tried to smuggle a large quantity of Darjeeling tea into Tibet in the year 1872; but he was detected at Phari, his tea was confiscated and he was imprisoned for three years. The Tibetans tell me that they do not themselves drink the coarse tea sold in the Darjeeling bazar, because it is too bitter. They think that, if it were not fired, it would be more to their taste. Whether it would be necessary to make tea exclusively in bricks for the Tibetan trade is not clear. A Tibetan trader, now in Calcutta, has brought down some green China tea *in leaf* for his own use. These, as I have said above, however, are points which the trade would settle if obstructions were removed. With a large tea-drinking population on one side of the passes and a large production of tea on the other, it cannot be doubted that the producers and consumers would come to an understanding if the opportunity were allowed. I am told that some of the Darjeeling gardens, such as Tukvar and Singell, contain China plants, and they could undoubtedly supply tea such as, at the present moment, the Tibetans require.

25. On the general question of what Tibet would give and take, I cannot do better than quote from a note which Baboo Sarat Chandra Das has prepared for me:

The chief imports of Tibet are cotton cloth, chintz, broadcloth, kinkob, cutlery, indigo, tobacco, copper, pearls, corals, emralds, quick-silver, dyes, sugar, treacle, Ilama and merino cloth and iron. Cotton cloth has the largest demand, the Tibetans of all classes having of late years taken largely to the use of cotton for inner garments, for the lining of their robes and trousers, and for screens and ceilings. Formerly they used to get their supplies from Nepal and China, but now-a-days European cotton cloths from the south have largely arrested the cotton trade of Eastern China, as merchants find it profitless. On account of the dry climate of the country cotton wears as well as the coarse serge, which has the disadvantage of being very rough and heavy. The demand for cotton stuff is really great, and the Nepalese traders sell cotton fabrics at 100 to 150 per cent profit. The extreme dearness is a great hindrance to an increased demand for cotton cloths, as such commodities are thereby brought within the reach of the rich and the luxurious only. The increase of the wool trade will fast increase the demand for cotton in Tibet, as the Tibetans will not care to weave wool into cloth at the extreme disadvantage of selling them below cost price. A thick Bhutia woollen *choga* will sell at one-third the price of the raw wool required to make it. Hence, cotton cloth will fill the Tibetans houses as soon as the exportation of wool increases.

The Napelese merchants generally buy their articles of trade at Calcutta and carry them to Kathmandu for transmission to Lhassa and the interior town of Tibet at great expense of money and time. If they understood the real secrets of commerce, and were induced to bring their goods within the reach of the poorer classes, they could really profit by trade and get opportunities for larger investments of money and for a wider employment of their countrymen.

Broadcloth (of liver, crimson, orange, green, blue, and brown colours) is displacing the Russian broadcloth brought from the North Mongolian frontier. The latter is said to be of better quality, though much more costly than the British Indian broadcloth. But broadcloth stuff, on account of its cheapness, is readily bought by the middle classes, who wear it on state occasions and in making visits to their relations, instead of the durable, but costly *purag* (Tibetan serge of excellent quality).

English inferior broadcloth is esteemed more as an object of luxury than of ordinary use. If traders could be persuaded to sell their goods at a reasonable profit, the demand for broadcloth would be very great. At present well-to-do men in Tibet generally consider broadcloth as an object most suited for presentation to all classes of men. Silk and China satin were formerly fashionable articles for that purpose. Now broadcloth has much superseded their use. The silk and satin presented to men of humbler walks of life do not much benefit them, but broadcloth serves many purposes, as it is easily saleable, may be used as loose upper coats, boot-hose, hats (both for Lamas and females), and various other purposes. The Tibetans are fond of sewing their boot-hoses with broadcloths of different colours with the stripes arranged in rainbow hues. How glad the Tibetan becomes when presented with broadcloth, and what fascinating charm it has over all classes of men, cannot adequately be described in a few words. If Indian traders or the Tibetan merchants could take this stuff to Tibet so as to place it within the reach of all classes of men, the demand for it could not fail to be very high, and its trade lucrative. The Northern Tibetans buy broadcloth from the Mongolians, who bring it from Russian shops in Lower Mongolia. The cost per yard is three to four times the cost of the same article brought to Lhasa from Calcutta *via* Nepal. The Tibetans buy the northern broadcloth under the impression that it is an indigenous product, and therefore a more durable manufacture, being called *sog-po Gontum* i.e. Mongolian broadcloth. Yet the northern merchants, Chinese and Mongols, cannot supply the demand for this dress luxury of the Tibetans by trading in Russian broadcloth. But now-a-days they are getting their mistaken ideas corrected by the Calcutta broadcloth being brought within their reach.

The more we can push on the facilities of trade by the cis-Himalayan passes, by cultivating friendly relations with the Lama Government and by making roads to the frontiers of Tibet, and greater will be progress of southern trade. The Russian trade, as far as the exports to Tibet and Mongolia are concerned, consists of European woollens, cotton cloths, glassware, leather, toys, telescope, and fancy goods, some hard ware, pistols, revolvers, satin, and hides brought from European Russia, Siberia, and North America by way of Kamskatka and Russian America. The coarse Russian broadcloth is much valued by the Tibetans of the middle class, and the finer stuff by the richer classes, both among the clergy and the lay people. Under such circumstances of sufficiently active industry can advantageously be employed to replace the northern traffic by bringing the British Indian articles within the reach of the Tibetans and the Southern Mongolians. The hides are used by the Mongols for making portmanteaus, sacks, tent strings, saddles, and pouches of different shapes. The Tibetans use leather for shoes and saddlery. They make their own portmanteaus with tanned yak skins very rudely. Assam fabrics, raw coarse silk cloth, called *bureah* or *khama* in Tibet, are sought by all classes of men, from the highest to the lowest. The former they use for inner garments and trousers, and the latter serves them as wrappers, like the shawls of the natives of India. The demand for this coarse stuff is incredibly large, but the supply is meagre.

Next in importance and value to the Tibetans is the European cambric called *sook*. Its durability is its great recommendation, and it is used for making trowsers, and occasionally robes for the lay people. It is not so expensive as broadcloth. English velvets and chintzes are also much in demand, the former being used for hats, boots, saddle lining, and the top cover of seats and cushions. They now get the same from China and Mongolia, but the native merchants and the Newars are about to replace that trade by English stuffs from Calcutta. The demand for kinkob and lace from Benares is very great, generally among all classes of men who have any pretension to wealth. The rich line their shoes, boots, coats, outer garments, and hats, the petticoats and jackets of women either wholly or partially, with kinkobs. The high price which the Newars and Kashmiris demand for this article of luxury places it within the reach of a very limited class of men. I cannot describe the earnestness with which many acquaintances and friends asked me to procure them some kinkobs from Benares. They also pointed out the profit that would accrue to me even if I disposed of the same at a comparatively low price, say at 30 to 50 per cent profit. I was really surprised to see that my friends were unable to understand why I disliked fetching them goods like a merchant from the British Indian market. The following colours of European broadcloth, namely, the yellow, orange, crimson, liver, blue and green, are greatly esteemed in Tibet. The clergy are restricted to the use of the first four, the fifth is used by the lay people, and the sixth used exclusively by the females. The English colours are very agreeable to all classes of men according to their faith and taste and are superstitiously admired.

Next in importance to broadcloth is the merino fabric, called *gya-ther*. It is used in entire pieces, slightly sown, of 12 to 16 yards, for the frock-like gowns of the monks, and in pieces of 6 to 8 yards as wrappers. The liver or *gya-mug* colour is eminently suited for clerical costumes. Larger breadths are not much prized, as clothes sewn in numerous patches are prescribed in the sacred books as suited for the clergy.

English and Indian chintzes, though not worn by the Tibetans, and yet largely used for screens, ceilings, and coverings of pictures. Cotton stuffs are now gradually coming into use for the inner garments of priests and ladies. The trousers of the lay people are generally made of blue and white cotton stuffs.

This *khurwas* are used to line the robes of the middle class men. Tents are universally made of cotton stuff, although canvas from Sifan or Silin, which is costly, is preferred by the upper classes. Light canvas brought from Northern Mongolia is of small breadth and less strong than Indian tent canvas. The coarsest kind of borderless shawls are used by the Tibetans who can afford to buy them, and are brought from Ladak and Kashmir through the Nepalese passes.

Tibet has been from time immemorial the principal market for different kinds of precious stones, such as pearls, corals, and amber. The former two are obtained from Nepalese and Kashmir merchants, and the latter from the Ladak and Chinese merchants.

Almost all the females who can afford it buy pearls and coral to adorn their head-dress. The head-dress is the most costly of all the ornaments worn by the Tibetan ladies; its price varying from Rs. 100 to Rs. 10,000. An immense number of pearl strings is used to complete the head-dress of a lady of high rank. The greatest attention is paid to adorning the head by all classes of females, who seem quite indifferent to adorning their persons suitably to their head-dress. The priests who have any pretension to rank and sanctity, as well as well-to-do lay men, carry rosaries made of coral in their hand. The Nepalese merchant have practically the monopoly of the pearl and coral trade. Of late the market has been pretty full; but as good pearls are rare in Lhasa, I was asked by many gentlemen of position and ladies to see if I could fetch them some excellent pearls.

The demand for indigo is always on the increase. Its usefulness as a dyeing material has ever been appreciated in Tibet. All classes of men, except the Lamas, buy indigo in quantities proportional to their requirements. Great landlords invariably maintain manufacturing establishments, and keep the largest supply of indigo.

The costliness of Tibet carpets and rugs is mainly due to the high price of indigo in Tibet. There are numerous dyeing roots and plants that grow on the rocky hills and in the gravelly plateau of Tibet. The present supply, owing to the difficulty of carriage, is very inadequate.

There are no copper mines in Tibet, or at least the people have not been able to discover any which they could work for copper. The Tibetans get large supplies of copper from Nepal and Calcutta. Conveyance from Nepal being very expensive, people now turn to Calcutta as the cheapest market for copper. Almost all sorts of cooking and church utensils are made of copper. The tea-pots, lamp-burners, cooking vessels, water-jugs, images, washing caldrons, the roofing and ornamental spires of temples, are all made of copper plates. For the supply of this useful metal Tibet has been solely dependent on Nepal and Calcutta of late. The Calcutta metal has been declared to be less costly and more easily worked.

Tobacco is largely consumed by the lay people. The women are particularly fond of snuff. Though formerly it was an article of luxury, yet now it has become an article of every-day house consumption. The monks clandestinely smoke tobacco and publicly use snuff when out of the monastery. Rungpore tobacco is much prized in Southern Mongolia, and Chinese tobacco is still in high esteem in Lower Tibet and Upper Mongolia. This is not owing to the superior quality of the Chinese tobacco, but because of the rarity of the article and its high price in the hands of the southern merchants. If steps could be taken to fill the southern markets of Tibet, such as Shiga-tea, Gyang-tse, Lhassa, and Chethang, with tobacco, this drug must find its way to the northern mart of Lower Tibet and Mongolia.

Tibet requires a large number of tropical drugs and spicery; for consumption both for cookery and for the preparation of medicines. In return she exports to India a large number of vegetable and mineral substances, the value of which very few Indian physicians have yet been able to appreciate.

English cutleries are gradually displacing the Chinese, Nepalese, and Bhutea country-made cutleries. At present English knives are beginning to be used instead of the Chinese *gyali* or the chop-sticks. Forks are not valued, but there are few Tibetans who do not buy spoons for their tables. Long needles supply the place of forks in Tibet. While at Gyang-tse I was told by Chanjo Kusho that an ordinary razor (Joseph Rodgers') some eight years ago cost him Rs. 8. He begged me to use his eight-rupee razor in preference to my one, which had cost me only Re. 1-8 at Calcutta. In fact his one was much inferior to my one' but as he had paid Rs. 8 for it, he attached a higher value to it. At present much profit, is derived from the sale of European cutleries, as they are very portable.

Mirrors, tin plates, and chinaware from Canton, are now finding extensive sale in Tibetan markets. The use of ugly wooden cups, such as those made out of maple knots, is fast being superseded by China cups from Calcutta. People consider this a great convenience. The more traders from the south will take chinaware for sale to Tibetan marts, the more will China crockery from Tarchindo and Pekin fall off, and eventually the demand for chinaware from Calcutta will entirely stop the northern trade of Tibet.

The export of Tibetan goods to India, including cis-Himalayan countries, through Nepal, Sikkim and Bhutan, exceeds the imports into Tibet, and compares favourably and hopefully with what formerly existed. Although I have no statistics to bring forward regarding these countries, yet I believe that the information obtained by me is very near the truth, and may have some practical utility, as derived from trustworthy sources.

Tibet gold, obtained as payment for goods by the Newars, is conjectured to be upwards of ten lakhs a year. As the coinage of Tibet is much adulterated, the Kashmiris and Newar merchants sell their goods at a discount over the chief coinage (*tanka*) to provide for the adulteration. When they return to Nepal, they dispose of their silver by exchange for gold or gold-dust. The Nepalese Government having prohibited by law the importation of silver into Nepal, the Newar merchants find it easy to barter in gold, and the Tibet Government naturally yield to the claims of the Newars to leave their silver in Tibet. The coinage of Tibet having no outlet remains in the country, and lessens the extent of annual coinage in the mint. The gold dust and gold pieces annually going out of the country necessitate the further working of the mines, which yield a steady supply. The Newar merchants, who are strictly prohibited from bringing Tibetan, Nepal, or British Indian silver coins to Nepal, carry down gold to dispose off the same with advantage. This saves them much trouble as to the conveyance, security on the way, and time. They refine the Tibet gold-dust, which is usually impure, and gain considerably thereby.

The finest borax, rhubarb, and musk in the world are the exclusive products of Tibet and its frontiers. Much of the first and second is taken to Russia by the Mongolian merchants and by the Chinese merchants to Pekin, and thence by European merchants to Europe and America. The natives of Tibet are ignorant of the great use of these two articles in Europe, and hence we hear so little of rhubarb and borax in the cis-Himalayan trade. Musk and yak-tails have been from time immemorial the renowned articles of Tibetan trade with ancient India. Notices of them are to be found in the travels of Drake, and also in the works of Arrian and Megasthenes. In the sacred books of the Hindu, chowry (yak tail) and musk were the chief articles of Himalayan trade carried on by the Kiratas (the Khumo tribe of Eastern Nepal) and the Bhutans.

All Nepal, Sikkim, Bhutan, Man Twang, Lho Khabra, Daphla country, the Pobo land, Western China, and smaller Mongolia obtain their supply of salt from Tibet. There is an immense salt mine in the Chang district north-west of Lhasa and one month's journey north of Shiga-tse, which furnishes inexhaustible quantities of rocksalt to all Tibet and the neighbouring countries. The Government of Tibet levies no duty on this article, and the Tibetans find it a very convenient commodity to exchange for rice, millet, sugar, and different other products of Nepal or India. I conjecture that about three to four lakhs of rupees worth of salt is annually imported from Tibet into Nepal, and a lakh of rupees worth into Sikkim and Bhutan.

The exports of live-stock, such as sheep, goats, and ponies, are very important in the commerce of Tibet. Their value and growing demand is very marked. I refrain from conjecturing the value of live-stock trade with cis-Himalaya, simply because it is very easy to ascertain it from statistics.

The wool trade (at present of woollens), salt, and live-stock, not to speak of all other minor exports from Tibet, and above all the importation of gold into Nepal, make the exports of Tibet of greater value than the imports from this side of the Himalayas.

III

26. In considering the question of the opening of free commercial relations with Tibet, we have two main factors to deal with—the power of the Chinese, and the influence of the monks of Lhassa. There can be no doubt that, if these two elements were conciliated, the secular Government of Lhassa and the people at large would be glad to see trade and general intercourse established.

27. Of course, the most important is China. However, much we may resent the present policy, and however unreasonable and humiliating we may consider it, we cannot challenge it as an infringement of a right. We ourselves allowed the power of China to become finally supreme in Tibet in 1792, and if our proceedings were the subject of misunderstanding or misrepresentation, it can hardly be said that they did not afford grounds and opportunity for both the one and the other. At any rate, we deliberately abdicated the influence which we had obtained, and might have increased. Since then Nepal, as well as Tibet, has recognized her supremacy, the contracting parties in the Treaty of 1856,—namely "the Chief Sirdars, Bhardars and Lamas of both Governments,"—distinctly declaring that "the Emperor of China is to be obeyed by both States as before." A general authority is claimed even over Sikkim, and the letter of the Ampas to the Maharaja in 1873, regarding the Jeylep road and Mr. Edgar's visit, shows that attempts have sometimes been made to exercise it without much ceremony. And whatever fluctuations Chinese influence in Tibet may have experienced at different times,—with the ebb and flow of popular feeling, the subservience or ambition of different Gesubs, and the long minorities of three Tale Lamas in succession,—there can be no doubt that to-day it is perhaps stronger than it ever was. We have reached one of those periodical crises which events in Tibet appear to bring about in a regularly recurring cycle to give the Chinese opportunities for re-establishing or strengthening their dominion. The murder of one Gesub in 1716; the murder of another, followed by the destruction of the two Ampas, in 1749; the plunder of Tashi Lunpo by the Goorkhas in 1792; the deportation of the Gesub, and the suppression of the Sera monks who supported him, by Ki-Chan in 1844; and how the riot between the monks and the Nepalese in 1888; and the appeal of the Government to China for the deputation of Special Commissioners to keep the former in check,—are all opportunities such as China was eager to grasp in the past, and such as she will not probably forego to-day. Without the permission and countenance of China, no British mission could be sent to, or could hope to reach, Lhasa. But if China's consent and support could be obtained (and this was provided for in the draft of the Chefoo Convention), such a mission, properly conducted, would undoubtedly have an enormous effect in bringing about a good understanding between the Tibetans and ourselves. The few who have been brought into contact with them have found them polite, amiable, hospitable, intelligent, and liberal-minded. This was the experience of Bogle, Turner, Manning, Huc, Gabet and Sarat Chandra Das. I can contribute my own testimony to the same effect. I am satisfied that the Tibetans only require to be spoken fair and treated properly to become our fast friends; and a short visit to Lhasa of Europeans, who might be depended upon to discharge their trust judiciously, would serve to dispel all the clouds of distrust and doubt which past events have gathered about our name. The vast scientific value of such a mission does not require demonstration.

28. It will not be overlooked that there are two Indian products which the Chinese look upon with dislike—opium and tea. As regards opium, it could be made clear that the Tibetans do not consume it, and that only smuggled opium could possibly he carried to China by land at a profit. But if the main line of trade were transferred to Darjeeling, the smuggling of opium would become much more difficult than it is now. The territory of Nepal marches with the opium districts, and it has no interest in the suppression of the smuggling of Indian opium of China; whereas it would be impossible for smugglers to carry on any extensive operations through Darjeeling. Of tea I have spoken above. We have no means of properly estimating the amount of customs duty levies at Darchendo (Ta-tsien-lu). Mr. Hennessy

thinks that the consumption of tea in Tibet is not less than 11-1/2 millions of pounds, and the duty on this, at the rate given above, would be nearly 2-1/2 lakhs of rupees. But this estimate is purely speculative, and there is every reason to suppose that a good part of the amount levied never reaches the Chinese exchequer. As regards the interest of the Lhassa Government in the matter, we only know that the tea they import does not enter the general market, and there seems no reason why they should make any change in their present practice. Whether they would ultimately take to Indian tea is a question which cannot be solved in our present knowledge of the circumstances. There may be political considerations involved with which we are not acquainted. At any rate it is clear that we must secure the countenance of the Pekin Government before we take any active steps to negotiate with the Tibetan authorities at Lhassa. It can be demonstrated that there is already a considerable import of Chinese goods into Tibet through Calcutta, and undoubtedly the superiority of this route over the tedious and dangerous journey of 1,300 miles by land between Canton and Lhassa must, if our policy is adopted, lead to a great increase in the trade. And perhaps, under present circumstances, it would be possible so to present the case to the Chinese that they may be willing to promote our views.

29. I would, therefore, urge that application be made to China for passports and support for a mission to proceed to Lhassa for a specified period, to confer there with the Chinese Commissioners and the Lhassa Government on the admission of Indian merchants to Tibet, and the removal of all restrictions on the free passage of traders by the Darjeeling route. It should be stipulated that the admission of Europeans, except by consent in each case of the Tibetan Government, and on passports issued by them, would be considered outside the scope of the negotiations. Even in Bogle's time, the admission of European was recognized as hopeless—because Chinese influence had become paramount at Lhassa—though Indian merchants were admitted and protected. I think we should largely increase our chances of success if it were made clear, in the first instance, that no such proposal would be made. Our main object is to establish our trade on a sound footing, and to make it the interest of the Tibetans to maintain intercourse with India. This can be done if a mission paves the way, and our native merchants are freely admitted. The admission of Europeans may follow. If it is pressed now, our object will be probably frustrated from the beginning.

Depung	7,700
Sera	5,500
Gahdan	3,300
Tankyaling	600
Checheling	500
Potala	500
Chemeling	300
Chogpoiki	300
Kenduling	200
Meru	200
Total	19,100

30. But, besides the Chinese, we have to take account of the monks who occupy the monasteries in and about Lhassa. The number of monks in each, according to the figures obtained by Baboo Sarat Chandra from the Tibetan records, is given in the margin. Gahdan was founded by the great Tsong-kapa; Depung by Geduntupa, his successor. These monks have always been a power at Lhassa, and have at times shown themselves to be turbulent and unduly. It was they who sacked the houses of the Chinese in 1810, because a Chinese soldier had killed a monk in a scuffle. It was the Sera monks who broke into rebellion in 1844, when Ki-Chan arrested the Gesub, and who compelled the Chinese Ambassador to seek refuge for a time in the house of one of the Kahlons. It was the Depung monks, assisted by those of Sera

and Gahdan, who plundered the shops of the Nepalese in 1883. They seem to represent the national party in permanent opposition to the Chinese, sometimes being headed by the Gesub, as in 1749 and 1844, and sometimes defying both Gesub and Chinese, as in 1810 and 1883. Their attitude towards us would naturally be one of opposition, as it has generally been to the Chinese, not so much on account of bigotry,—for there is very little of this in the country,—as from an apprehension of their power being reduced and their privileges curtailed. There is, however, another motive of jealousy which I suspect had something to do with the attack on the Nepalese in 1883. Some of these monks are very fond of trading, though necessarily they indulge in it in a desultory fashion. In fact, as my lists show, a considerable part of the trade of Lhasa through Darjeeling is carried on by monks who have temporary leave of absence from their monasteries. At the present moment there are monks from Sera and Depung in Calcutta, and I have seen them several times in Darjeeling. They know that their only present competitors in the Indian trade are the Nepalese, and they know that more serious competitors would be found in the Indian merchants if they were admitted. Unless we conciliate their good-will, they will certainly oppose us. But the good-will of the monasteries at large can be acquired by showing them some attention and dealing liberally with them. The Tibetan records are full of instances of the reputation gained by great men by judicious largess to these, the Brahmins of Tibet. As soon as passports from China are received, it would, I believe, have an excellent effect if the rumours now afloat of the respect shown by the British Government to the Tashi Lama's memory were followed by an unofficial communication to the abbots of the three great monasteries, sending them presents, and saying that it was proposed to make substantial gifts to the institutions on the arrival of the mission. The influence of the abbots could certainly be permanently conciliated by an expenditure which would be trifling compared with the importance of the object in view.

31. I need hardly point out the importance of improving the opportunity for further correspondence with Tashi Lunpo, which the letter from the Minister has offered. This has been fully discussed in our letter of 8th instant. The people of the province of Tsang, high and low, have always been friendly to us, and I can say with confidence that my interviews with the Jongpen of Kamba have increased this feeling. Should the application to China for leave for a mission to go to Lhassa fail, I would strongly urge that permission might be sought for a mission to go to Tashi Lunpo to present the congratulations of the Government of India, as soon as the conclusion of the preliminaries connected with the identification of the young Tashi Lama is reported. This would be a precise parallel to Turner's mission in 1784, and it would not fail to produce good results politically and scientifically. Moreover, the Chinese could hardly refuse this request, even if they refused the other; for Colonel Prejvalsky is now travelling in Northern Tibet with two Chinese officers, who are supposed to escort him. It is known that opposition has been fomented at Lhassa with the view of keeping him from reaching the holy city. (This has been reported to me, through Sarat Baboo, by a trading monk of Tashi Lunpo whose home is in Kham where Prejvalsky now is). There would be no fear of any sort of opposition in Tsang if a passport from China were obtained. Our own popularity, the influence of our friend, the Minister, and the fact that the visits was one of respect to Penchen Rimboochay, would secure us a good reception. If, then, the main scheme of a mission to Lhasa fails, I would strongly recommend that his measure at least should be carried out.

32. My visit to the head of the Lachen valley has confirmed me in the opinion that it is desirable to open a road through Sikkim by that route. Even with the roads such as they

are, I found that our duty-paying salt has driven Tibetan salt back three or four marches from Darjeeling, and it would certainly penetrate further if the roads were improved. In the Lachen valley above Lamteng (8,900 feet) the people are extremely well off, with large flocks of sheep and goats and herds of yaks, and excellent crops of potatoes and turnips. They send timber into Tibet and obtain in return tea, salt and barley flour. But though they have constant communication with Tibet by the Kongra Lama pass, they are cut off from Sikkim and Darjeeling for five months of the year owing to the destruction of their temporary bridges and the submersion of the track in places by the rise of the river on the melting of the snows. The road for two marches down the Lachen, from Lamteng to Choongtam,—where it joins the Lachoong and, with it becomes the Teesta,—and then for two more along the Teesta from Choongtam to Sinchik, is very bad and in places descends into the bed of the river. But, except for these four marches, it is possible to take ponies from Darjeeling to the Kongra Lama. If the road were carried along the hillside by blasting (and this would obviate subsequent expenditure on repairs), it would seem, to a non-professional observer, that one suspension bridge only would be required between Lamteng and Choongtam, and this, owing to the narrowness of the stream and the rocks available for supports on both sides, would not be costly. The bridge over the Teesta at Samdong and over the Rungeet would be more expensive. But I cannot doubt that the road would have an important effect in opening up Lower Sikkim and the rich and healthy Lachen and Lechung valleys. I have already referred to what the Jongpen said regarding the obstructions which he is now ordered to place in the way of trade through Kambajong. But if these can be removed, there can be no doubt that a large trade would pass down by the Lachen valley were a proper road available. The fact that the Jongpen was able to meet me at the frontier, notwithstanding two very heavy recent falls of snow, shows that the Kongra Lama pass remains open under very unfavourable circumstances. Immediately beyond it begins the wool country, and Tashi Lunpo itself is only four marches distant. It is very important that he should have a direct road to Tsang and its capital, independent of the circuitous road through Phari Jong, which is in the province of U and under Lhasa. On every ground I recommend that an Engineer be deputed to report upon the probable cost of improving the road and bridging the streams between the Rungeet and the Zemu. From Zemu Samdong to the frontier (three marches) almost nothing is required. He should be instructed to take in hand at once the improvement of the road, where this can be effected with ordinary appliances. I may add that the Maharaja of Sikkim promised me to give every help in the construction of this road and undertook to maintain it on completion. The Lachen people exhibited great joy by being told that such a road was in contemplation, and would help with ordinary labour.

33. My recommendation, then, are—

(1) That application should be made to China for passports and support for a mixed political and scientific mission to proceed to Lhassa for three or four months to confer with the Chinese Commissioners and the Lhassa Government on the free admission of native Indian traders to Tibet and the removal of obstruction on the trade through Sikkim and Darjeeling, it being understood that no proposal for the general admission of Europeans will be brought forward.

(2) That, on passports being received, unofficial overtures be at once made to the abbots of Sera, Depung and Gahdan monasteries with the view of securing their goodwill towards the mission.

(3) That every effort be made to improve the opportunity now obtained for friendly correspondence with the authorities at Tashi

Lunpo and intercourse generally with the province of Tsang; and that, in the event of the negotiations with China for a mission to Lhassa failing, application be made for passports for a small mission to proceed to Tashi Lunpo on the occasion of the identification of the new Penchen Rimboochay.

(4) That an Engineer be deputed to report on the cost of improving the road and bridging the streams between the Rungeet and the Zemu rivers, and to commence work in some parts, in order that permanent communications may be opened with the Lachen valley and the province of Tsang.

Colman Macaulay,

Secretary to the Government of Bengal.

The 19th January 1885.

I append a sketch map which Colonel de Pree, Surveyor-General, has kindly had prepared for me.

[*Report of Mission to Sikkim and the Tibetan Frontier,* 1884.]

3

Residence at Tashilhunpo, and Preparations for Journey to Lhasa

By
SARAT CHANDRA DAS

JANUARY 13—The money we had brought from Darjeeling being almost expended, we were now in the necessity of selling the pearls and gold we had brought with us. I therefore sent Ugyen to the market to inquire of Lupa gyaltsan, with whom we had left some *tolas* of pearls for sale, if he had been able to dispose of them. Lupa gyaltsan told him that he had shown the pearls to a Lhasa merchant, who had not offered more than cost price for them. The market for pearls, he added, was very poor, and we must not expect to realize much profit out of ours for some months to come.

He also told Ugyen that great preparations were being made for the Grand Lama's visit to Lhasa in May, for the ordination of the Dalai Lama. On this occasion the Tashi would have to make return presents and give rewards in money to the various officials and chiefs of Tibet, for which robes, boots, etc., were now being made in great numbers.

January 14—On the way to the market today Ugyen met Lupa gyaltsan, who informed him that some traders from Phagri, Chumbi, and Rin-chen-gang had just arrived, and that, to judge from their conversation, they were not well-disposed towards us. He therefore cautioned Ugyen, so that he might not meet them unprepared. Ugyen, in consequence, first went to the police station and learnt from his friend, the Chinese havildar of Shigatse, who the newcomers were; then he looked them up, and questioned them about the passes to India. They told him they had been able to get here through the Lhasa Government having declared the Phagri pass open. As to the Sikkim rajah coming here, they could give no definite information, though they said there was much talk about his marrying the daughter of a great man of Lhasa.

In the afternoon the minister sent for me, and told me that the boxes containing the lithographic press sent him some months ago had not been opened for fear of small-pox. "I thought the cases contained some miraculous remedies which could neutralize smallpox. One night I smelt some gaseous emanations coming out from the boxes, which I thought contained the germs of small-pox; so I could not sleep that night, so troubled was my mind lest small-pox should attack us." We laughed heartily at his holiness's fancies, and I told him that the vaccine he had asked for was among the things still at the Lachan pass. At last he was convinced of the groundlessness of his fears, and joined with us in laughing at them.

January 15—After breakfast we unpacked in the minister's library the lithogrpahic press, and set it up, the minister taking great interest in the work and assisting me himself.

January 16—After breakfast, which we took with the minister in the west drawing-room of the Phuntso khangsar, he told me that he was most anxious to get the things I had at Lachan. Phurchung was not intelligent enough to get around the Djongpon of Khamba, even if he were provided with the best of passports. He thought it indispensable for Ugyen to undertake the journey to Lachan, especially he had relatives there, a circumstance which would greatly facilitate the accomplishment of the mission.

Ugyen objected to start on such a difficult journey at a season of the year when the cold would be intense and the Kangra lamo pass would be blocked with snow; but he felt, nevertheless, called upon to comply with the minister's request, if he provided him with a proper passport. Not only did the minister promise to give him an excellent passport, but he also said that he would propitiate the gods to the end that they would protect him from dangers from man, beast, or disease, till the first of the third Tibetan moon (end of April, 1882).

When this was settled Ugyen begged the minister to look after me in his absence, and not to allow any injury to be done me on the ground that I was a foreigner. He asked him to give him a letter stating, first, that he (the minister) would see to my welfare, and that I would be in no way molested; second, that on Ugyen-gyatso's return he and I might go on a pilgrimage to Central Tibet; third, that we should be protected in any difficulty which might arise on the score of our being foreigners.

Besides the great importance of obtaining these written assurances from the minister, the production of such a letter by Ugyen, in case of my death during his absence, would relieve him of all responsibility towards our Government.

The minister promised to keep me in his house as a member of his family, to defray all my expenses, and to send me to Lhasa in May with the Tashi Lama's party. Should, however, neither the Grand Lama nor himself go to Lhasa, he would make other arrangements for our pilgrimage there. As to the third point mentioned in the above agreement, he said that he was fully aware when he invited us to come to Tashilhunpo of the responsibility he assumed towards us, and that he would not allow us to be molested by any one during our stay in Tibet.

January 17—The minister went in the morning to Shigatse, to grant absolution to the departed soul of Shang-po, one of the six Tsopon who had been so severely punished by the Chinese authorities on the 13th December last, and who had died from the effects of the flogging then received. We devoted the whole day to the setting up of the lithographic press.

January 18—The minister told Ugyen that Kusho Badur-la, the head of the transportation department, wished to see the pearls we had brought with us. Ugyen did not find him at home, but conversed with his wife, whom he at once recognized, having seen her at Tumlung and Chumbi, she being the elder sister of the present Rajah of Sikkim. She gave him a very kind reception, and talked to him for nearly an hour, treating him to tea and *gya-tug* (vermicelli).

January 19—To-day being the day of the new moon, nearly a thousand beggars lined the road leading from Tashilhunpo to Shigatse, where Lhagpa tsering was distributing alms to them.

At noon Ugyen visited the market-place, where he witnessed a quarrel between a woman and a Khamba over a *tanka'a* worth of *tsamba*, in the course of which the woman challenged the man to take an oath very common in Tibet, namely, that if he told an untruth, he might never see the Grand Lama's face. The people of Khams are a fierce race who infest the solitudes of Tibet, and generally carry on depredations on the isolated villages north of Lhasa. They are a dangerous class.

January 20—Early in the morning we received an invitation to dine with our acquaintance, Lupa gyaltsan. We were told that to-day was the New Year's Day of the working class, and was so observed by all the people of Tibet, with the exception of the clergy.

After breakfast we went to the minister's, and told him the press was ready for working. I asked him to print a very auspicious hymn, that the first fruit of our labour might be a sacred composition. He at once ran to his study and brought a stanza, or *stotra*, composed by the present Grand Lama (of Tashilhunpo?) in honour and praise of the minister. This he copied himself on the transfer paper, and we obtained excellent impressions of it, much to his delight. The stone press" (*do par*) was forthwith given the name of the "miraculous press" (*tul par*).

At three in the afternoon we asked leave to go to Lupa gyaltsan's house, where I had a most hearty reception, he and his wife coming to help me dismount from my pony. We were ushered into a newly finished room on the first floor, where was also his chapel. First *chang* was served, then tea was brought by his daughter, a girl of ten, and the wife placed a wooden bowl filled with *tsamba* and some pieces of boiled mutton on a little table before us. Then Lupa gyaltsan, taking off his turban, asked me to take *sol ja* and consider that I was dining in my own house. Shortly after, Ugyen, in accordance with Tibetan custom, made a short speech exhorting Lupa to always inquire after my health during his absence from Tashilhunpo, and to get for me all such articles of food, etc., that I might want. He thanked him for his kindness, and added that, as Lupa and I were old acquaintances, we should behave to each other as brothers born of the same mother. So saying, he presented him and his wife a rupee and a *khatay* each, putting the coins in their hands and the scarfs round their necks. Ugyen then put a *khatag* around my servant Lhagpa's neck, telling him to serve me ever faithfully. Lupa's daughter, having dressed herself in her gala dress, danced for us and sang a song, first in the Tibetan way, then in the Chinese; she sang also a Chinese song, Lupa accompanying her on the flute (*ling-bu*). After this Lupa's wife sang a song, and then wished us a happy new wear. We then took leave of our hosts, wishing them also a happy new year.

Having inquired if the observance of this day was a purely Tibetan custom, I gathered from their reply that this was the New Year's Day according to the Tibetan custom of the pre-Buddhist period. It is the only remnant of ancient Tibetan custom, as far as I know, which has not been displaced by Buddhism.

January 21—This day was also observed as a holiday by the laity. There were so few persons in the market-place that Ugyen could buy no provisions. The minister graciously insisted that I should take up my quarters in his residence, Puntso Khangsar, where he offered me the library with an attached waiting-room and bathroom.

In the evening Nyima-dorze, the oldest son of the Chyag-dso-pa of Dongtse, came and consulted me about his eyes. On the right one I found that a cataract had formed. I told him I was exceedingly sorry I had no medicines with me to suit the case, but that Ugyen was going to Calcutta as soon as he had obtained a passport, and that he would bring back some drugs with him. He then said that it was this passport that had brought him here to speak to the minister about, and that he believed it would be ready in a day or two.

January 22—I resumed reading English and working sums in arithmetic with the minister. After reading a few lines he turned over the pages of Ganot's 'Physics,' and asked me to explain the diagrams on telegraphy an the camera obscura. He wanted everything explained to him; but, unfortunately for me, I was not myself acquainted with most of the subjects which excited his curiosity. Not prepared to expose my ignorance, I dwelt longer on such questions as I could best explain, and with which I was most familiar; but in spite of all my attempts to evade his inquisitiveness, the shrewd minister gauged me well, and expressed his earnest desire to meet such men as I had described to him, Dr.Sircar and my brother, Navin Chandra, to be.

In the afternoon Nyima-dorje brought the *lam-yig* (passport), and presented it to the minister. We were called in and shown it; but Ugyen disapproved of it, as nothing was said in it of his return journey here, so it was sent back for correction.

January 23—Crowds of visitors came to receive the minister's blessing (*chyag-wang*); among them were many Khalkhas and other Mongols from remote sections of that country. The Khalkhas were introduced by Lobzang Arya, my cook during my first sojourn at Tashilhunpo in 1879, and how a man of standing and elder (*gyer-gyan*) of the Khalkha Kham-tsam. The minister talked with him in Mongolian, after receiving the pilgrims with much kindness.

January 24—Early in the morning I was called by the minister, and found a young monk of the Nyagpa Ta-tsang (a Tantrik school) sitting with him. The minister asked me to examine his eyes, which were a little swollen, telling me at the same time that this young man had served him devotedly during his residence at the Nyag-khang, and was deserving of my care. I gave him a few doses of alum lotion to wash his eyes with, and made him promise to walk round the monastery several times a day whenever it was fair weather.

In the afternoon I lunched with the Tung-chen, and we conversed about the high winds which at this season blow every afternoon. He spoke also of the Phagri pass, and told me that the collector of customs (Serpon) there was a friend of his, and that if Ugyen went to Darjeeling by the Phagri pass, he could give him a letter of introduction to that officer. I thanked him for the kindness, adding that Ugyen preferred the Lachen pass, as he had a passport from the commander of Shigatse which did not extend to Phagri djong.

January 25—The minister told me that in certain stellar maps he had examined he saw that figures were given the different constellations, and that he understood these figures really existed in the sky; so, wishing to see them, he had bought a large telescope at much cost. He did not know, however, how to use it, and was most anxious to have a well-illustrated work on astronomy, that he might know what to look for and where to look for it. He also remembered my saying that the regions of the moon, Saturn, and even of the sun, were visible through the telescope, and he was curious to know what these luminaries contained, for he had hitherto been under the impression that these celestial bodies were angelic luminaries who for the excellence of their moral merits, had been promoted to celestial mansions of different heights, thence to shed on us their radiant luster, and thereby guide all living beings of the earth in the path of *dharma*.

White we were thus talking Nyima-dorje arrived, and presented the passport to his holiness. After perusing it he handed it to me, and I passed it to Ugyen. We found that the commanders of Shigatse (*Dahpan*), in order to prevent the introduction of small-pox, had instructed in it the Djongon of Khamba to examine the contents of our boxes, to prevent contagion being brought into the country in them. This would put the Djongpon in a position to exact from Ugyen any amount of money he might choose; but as it would be inconvenient to wait longer for a corrected *lam-yig*, the minister advised Ugyen to be satisfied with the present one, and to do the best he could with it.

January 26—Ugyen declared that Phurchung's services were absolutely necessary to him, and asked that he be lent to him for six months, adding that without him he would not start on the journey. After breakfast the minister consulted with the Tung-chen and Gopa about keeping me with him. Arrangements were soon made; but they all objected to my keeping Lhagpa as my servant, telling me that a Shigatse man could not be trusted, as they were cunning, deceitful, and faithless. He added that, as he had undertaken to look to my wants and comforts, there was not the least necessity for my keeping a servant at my own expense. Fearing lest he should suspect me of ulterior designs, I at once accepted his decision, though I had hoped, by means of Lhagpa, to keep myself informed of what was going on in the monastery and the town, I myself being practically confined within the walls of the minister's residence, as I was required, according to custom, to wait upon his holiness.

January 27—Ugyen and Phurchung busied themselves in preparing for the journey. The former took a pair of Gyantse blankets and a suit of lambskin clothes, and I gave Phurchung a pair of my own blankets for his use during the journey. They purchased a large quantity of sheep's fat to distribute among the Sikkimese on the way. Dried mutton, *tsamba*, and sheep's fat are the dainties the Sikkimese esteem above all others. They hired four ponies to ride and carry their luggage.

In the evening we were invited to take tea with the minister, when Ugyen took formal leave, making three profound bows to his holiness, and praying that his blessing might always be on him, and that, by the mercy of the sacred Buddhas, he might reach his destination safely.

January 28—To day, the 10th of the 12th moon, was considered a highly auspicious day on which to start for India. At 6 o'clock Ugyen, Phurchung, and I went to the minister's apartment, when his holiness, after a short prayer, wished them a safe and pleasant journey, and placed *khatag* on their necks. At Ugyen's special request I desired Phurchung in a short speech to serve Ugyen as he would serve me, to which he answered, "*La laso, laso*" (yes, sir, yes). Then we returned to the Torgod chyi-khang, our lodging, where, after breakfast, I presented parting *khatag* to my faithful companions. The scene was extremely touching, and they shed tears at leaving me alone. I too, could not suppress my feeling as I exhorted them to take care of themselves in the snows, and to be prepared for heavy snowfalls. They both rode off in high spirits towards Delel.

Shortly after I sent Wang-chyug gyalpo and the minister's page to fetch my clothes, utensils, etc., to my new quarters. They brought some, and told me that my trusted servant, Lhagpa was quietly carrying off my kettles and plates. I immediately went to the Torgod chyi-khang, and asked him to give up the missing articles, but he denied any knowledge of them, though we could see the breast of his gown stuffed out with them, and he insisted the devils (*de*) must have carried them off. I at once sent for the Nyerpa and the Tung-chen. It was impossible, however, to search Lhagpa, so we had to confine ourselves to drawing up a list of the things missing and of the things I had with me; and then, locking the door of my lodgings, the Tung-chen told Lhagpa to return quietly to his house. The Tung-chen smiled at the roguery of my trusted servant, and made me understand that I knew very little about Tibetans, and that I should not have trusted Shigatse people.

January 29—The minister came to my rooms, and insisted on nailing up a curtain, so as to divide the room in two, the books in the northern part, and my seat and bedstead in the southern half of it. He said that such an arrangement was necessary, as the books were of arsenical paper, and I would fall ill if I continually breathed the air of the place. Underneath my room was the cook-room (*sol-tab*) the heat from which kept the library dry and warm. There was but one window, about four feet square, in my room, through which I could see the Nartang hills.

At 9 o'clock breakfast was announced, when the Nyerpa conducted me to the minister's presence. Tea was served me in a pretty china cup, and Kachan gopa brought me a bowl of *tsamba* and a few slices of boiled mutton, and, noticing my difficulty in making dough of the *tsamba* and tea after the Tibetan fashion, took it from me and mixed it himself, twirling the cup on the palm of his hand, and mixing the flour and tea with his forefinger.

In the dining-room there was a parrot lately presented to the minister by the Chyan-dso shar of Tashilhunpo, and a small saffron plant raised from some seed brought from Kashmir. This plant throve well, I was told, but yielded no saffron.

After breakfast I returned to my studies, and with the permission of the minister, commenced a search for Sanskrit books in his library. At noon the cook placed on an earthenware stove near me a pot of steaming tea, and in the afternoon he filled it again. I was told it was injurious to drink cold water; Tibetans very seldom drink it; the laymen quench their thirst with draughts of cold fermented barley liquor (*chang*), and lamas with hot tea.

As the minister, on account of his vows, was debarred from eating in the afternoon, evening, or night, he desired me to take my supper with the secretary; so when the lamp was lighted I went down stairs, and sat gossiping in the kitchen with him.

January 30—To-day I discovered three Sanskrit works written in the Tibetan character. They were the *Kavyadarsha*, by Acharya Sri Dandi; the *Chandra Vyakarana*, by Chandra Gomi; and the *Svarasvat Vyakarana*, by Acharya Ami. I was transported with joy when I saw that they contained explanations in Tibetan.

In the afternoon I showed Sri Dandi's work to the minister, who, to my surprise, was able to give me more information concerning him than I had expected, and he had committed the entire work to memory. "Dandi," he said, "must have lived a thousand and more years ago, for this work was translated into Tibetan by one of the Sakya hierarchies who lived about six hundred years ago, and it is probable that the work was not very new when it came to be known in this country."

January 31—Preparations for the new year's ceremonies now occupy the attention of all classes. Large numbers of men are coming to take the first vows of monkhood, and Kachan Shabdung introduced to-day a number of them to his holiness. The minister's time was largely taken up with these religious duties, and I could not see him for more than ten or twelve minutes. When I withdrew to my room, the astrologer, Lobzang, came to see me; he was busy with the almanac for the new year, and kept turning over its pages to see if there were any mistakes. The minister also had to examine it before submitting it to the Grand Lama.

Lobzang, seeing the lithographic press, was curious to know what "those stones and wheeled apparatus," as he put it, were meant for. He begged me to explain the process of printing, but I evaded his questions, as I had been told not to talk of the press to outsiders.

In the evening the Deba Shika arrived with a large supply of butter and *tsamba*, evidently to be used in the new year's ceremonies.

From this time on I devoted myself to the study of the sacred books and histories of

Tibet, and ceased to keep a regular diary, noting only such things concerning the customs and manners of the country as seemed interesting. When I felt tired of Tibetan I refreshed my mind with the melodious verses of Dandi's *Kavyadarsha*, both in the original and the Tibetan translation, and during my leisure hours I conversed with the Tung-chen, the Nyerpa, and other well-informed men.

The first part of February was very cold; the north wind blew daily, raising clouds of dust in the plain to the west and south of the city. People, however, were busily engaged out-of-doors, gathering fuel and tending cattle; in fact, this is the busiest season of the year, a period of universal merry-making and also of great activity in trade.

The Tibetans, whether monks or laymen, are very early risers. In the monastery the great trumpet (*dung chen*) summoned the monks to the congregation hall for prayers at three in the morning, and those who failed to be present were punished at the Tsog-chen; for, though there is no roll call, yet the absence of a single monk is surely remarked by the provost.

The minister, who frequently peeped into my room to see whether I was studying or no, excused me from early rising on the ground that he often found me up with my books at midnight.

On the 16th I was asked by the Deba Shika to go with him the following day to see the Grand Lama dance, or *cham*. On my observing that I feared the whips of the stage guards (*djim-gag-pa*) if I mixed with the crowd, he promised to have seats reserved for our party.

Early the next morning men and women dressed in their best began streaming into the monastery to see the *cham*. Accompanied by the Tung-chen, the Deba Shika, and a lama friend, we went our way towards the Nyag-khang, in the courtyard of the Tsug-la khang, in which the dances were to begin. On the way we stopped to visit an old chapel containing several inscriptions relating to Gedun-dub, the founder of Tashilhunpo, and the mark of a horse's hoof impressed on a rock, which passers-by touch with their heads.

Then we took our seats on the balcony of the second floor of the Nyag-khang building, and watched the preparations for the dance. Twenty-four sacred flags of satin, with embroidered figures of dragons and other monsters worked in threads of gold, were first unfurled at the top of long and slender poplar poles, and square parti-coloured flags were also hung all around the Tsug-la khang. About a dozen monks wearing coats of mail had masks which, for the most part, represented eagles heads. The dances entered one after the other, and then followed the abbot of the Nyag-pa Ta-tsan, Kusho Yondjin Lhopa by name, holding a *dorje* in his right hand, and a bell in his left. He wore a yellow mitre-shaped cap, with lappets covering his ears and hanging down to his breast. He was tall and fair; he looked intelligent, his manners were most dignified, and he performed his part most cleverly.

After a while the flag-bearers, the masked monks, and all the *cortege* repaired to the great Tsug-la khang of Tashilhunpo, which is about 300 years long and 150 feet broad. Round this courtyard are four-storied buildings with handsome pillared balconies, the Grand Lama's seat being on the western side. The long balconies on the east and south were occupied by the nobility of Tsang, and those on the north by Mongol pilgrims and a number of Shigatse merchants. The abbots of the four Ta-tsan had seats just above the Nyag-pa, who, to the number of fifty odd, and assisted by their Om-dse and the Dorje Lopon, these holding in their hands cymbals and tambourines, went through a short religious service under the direction of the Kusho Yon-djin Lhopa. This latter made during this service peculiar motions with his hands, in which he held, as I have said, a *dorje* and a bell.

When this was over a figure with a dark-coloured mask, and representing the Hoshang Dharma-tala, advanced, and the spectators flung him *khatays*, which his two yellow-faced wives picked up. When these three had left the scene, the four kings of the four cardinal points appeared, dressed in all the wild and barbaric splendour in which such monarchs could indulge. Then came the sons of the gods, some sixty in number, dressed in beautiful silk robes glittering with gold embroideries and precious stones. These were followed by Indian *atsaras*, whose back and bearded faces and uncouth dress excited loud laughter among the crowd. Then appeared four guardians of the graves, whose skeleton-like appearance was meant to remind the spectators of the terrors of death. After this the devil was burnt in effigy on a pile of dry sedge, and with this the *cham* came to an end. While it was in progress incense was burnt on Mount Dolma (Dolmai-ri), behind the monastery, and on all the other neighbouring mountain-tops. I learnt from the Tungchen that there were several books on the subject of these religious dances and music.

The following day (February 18) I went with the Tung-chen for a walk. Proceeding about 300 paces, we came to a flight of stone steps below the western gateway. This latter, which is some twelve feet high and eight wide, has massive doors, which are closed between sunset and sunrise; it is the principal entrance of the monastery. About fifty feet beyond this gate, and on a line with the gilt mausolea of the grand lamas (*gya-phig*), we came to another flight of steps, some of them cut in the rock, which led us to the north-western corner of the monastery and well up the slope of the Dolmai-ri, whence we obtained a good view of the whole of Tashilhunpo monastery, the adjacent villages and mountains.

We now turned to the north-east along a narrow rocky path, which brought us behind the Nyag-khang. I was surprised to notice among the rocks some willows (*chayng-ma*) in flower, and we saw also the impress of hoofs on the rocks, left there, the Tung-chen said, by the chargers of some Bodhisattvas; *rang chyung*, or "naturally produced," the Tibetans say of such marvels. There were several half-starved pariah dogs lying about, who looked at us with sleepy eyes, and the Tung-chen remarked that in all probability they had been sinful *gelong* (monks) in some former existence, and were now expiating their evil deeds. He much regretted that we had not brought some balls of *tsamba* for them.

Some 200 paces farther on in the same direction we came to a huge stone building called Kiku-tamsa. It is about 60 paces in length and 30 in breadth, and I counted nine stories in it. Though it is upwards of two hundred years old, it is still in excellent repair. Captain Turner made a sketch of it in 1783, but he mistook it for "a religious edifice." It is at present used as a godown for dried carcasses of yaks, sheep and goats. Every year, in the latter part of November, all the sacred pictures of the Labrang are hung up on this building for the benefit of the people, who, by touching these paintings with their foreheads, receive the blessings of the gods they represent.

On our way down to the eastern gateway of Tashilhunpo we met two Ladaki Tibetans, who told us that they had just come from the Chang-tang, or the desert in the north-western part of Tibet.

The Tung-chen showed me the Dongtse Kham-tsan, where the people of Dongtse and neighbourhood put up. We also saw a juniper bush planted by Gedun-dub, the founder of Tashilhunpo in which that saintly lama's hair is said to still exist. I had pointed out to me, as we walked along the spacious buildings of the Taisamilng college, the Kyil khang Ta-tsan and the Shartse college.

The descent to the foot of the hill proved very steep, but all along it we found rows of prayer-wheels, which we put in motion as we passed; near the gateway, and beside a *mendong*, there were two dozen of them together.

Passing by the main Mani lha-khang, we reached the eastern gateway of Tashilhunpo. Over it is a notice forbidding smoking within the monastery, for both the red and yellow-hat schools of lamaism strongly denounce tobacco-smoking by monks.

From this gateway a road leads south to the Kiki-naga, where the Grand Lama's mother resides, while another runs westward to the court of the Tashi lama, or Labrang gyal-tsan tonpo.

It was dusk when we had finished our walk around the monastery, and lamps were already burning in many of the houses to bid farewell to the old year.

February 19—New Year's Day—The preparations for the day's celebration commenced before dawn, and the noise of the blowing of the kitchen fires never ceased, as there were many dishes and dainties to be got ready for the dinner the minister was to give to a large party of nobles and incarnate lamas.

When the minister came back from visiting the Grand Lama, he told me that the latter had inquired about me, as he had some translation into Sanskrit which he desired I should make for him. "His holiness," the minister said, "has given me a hundred and twenty titles of chapters of a work he has written, and wishes you to put them into Sanskrit for him." The minister further said that when I had finished this work he would present me to the Grand Lama.

The next day the minister was called to Dongtse by the illness of the Dahpon Phala's wife; his prayers, it was hoped, would restore her to health. About a week after his departure he was suddenly recalled by the Grand Lama, with whom he had, on March 3, a long conference. The Dalai lama's Government had protested against the Tashi lama having taken the vows of monkhood from the Sakhya Pan-chen, a red-hat lama, the hierarch of the Sakhya school. The Dalai lama charged him with encouraging heresy, if not with being a heretic himself. It was for the reason that the Tashi lama had not been invited to ordain the supreme ruler of Tibet, for, belonging to the Gelugpa or yellow-hat school, the Dalai lama could have no connection with the school of which the Sakhya Pan-chen was the chief.

On March 4 the minister ordained some forty monks *gelong*. Formerly the Grand Lama used to perform this ceremony himself, but he has now delegated a large portion of his religious duties, including ordination, to the minister.

Two days after this the minister was again asked to go to Dongtse, as the wife of the Dahpon was still ill, and he (the Dahpon) had orders to proceed at once to Lhasa. The minister asked me if I would accompany him, and I readily assented, as it would enable me to make arrangements for my journey to Lhasa during the next summer.

On March 7 we started, and reached Tashingang the same day. Some of the people we passed were already ploughing, and the trees showed signs of budding.

The next day we reached Dongtse by 4 o'clock in the afternoon. We found the Dahpon's wife, a lady of about thirty, and his sister, Je-tsun Kusho, in the central room of the fifth floor of the castle (*phodrang*).

The Lhacham was dressed in a Mongol robe; on her head was a crown-shaped ornament studded with precious stones and pearls of every size. Pearl necklaces, strings of amber and coral hung over her breast, and her clothes were of the richest Chinese satin brocades and the finest native cloth. The Je-tsun Kusho, an elderly woman and a nun, was dressed very plainly, but, though nuns all shave their heads, she wore all her hair. She belonged, it appears, to the Nyingma school, which allows nuns certain privileges, this one among others.

The following day I prescribed some medicines for Je-tsun Kusho who was suffering from bronchitis, and four days later I administered some to the Dahpon's wife, who had had until then a lama from the Tse-chan monastery attending her. My medicines did her no good, and at this the minister appeared much concerned. I tried a second dose, but with like absence of effect. In fact, the Lhacham felt worse and said that evil stars were in the ascendant in her quarter of the sky (*khams*), and would work her ruin. Some people, she said, insisted she was being persecuted by evil spirits who had followed her here from Tingri (Djong), but she did not believe it; it was the stars which were against her. The minister looked at me and asked me how it was that my medicines were unavailing in the Lhacham's case. In the midst of a dead silence I told him that all the medicines which different persons had administered to the patient were affecting her nervous system, each in a different way. I had heard her say that she had first taken those of a Chinese quack, then those of a Nepalese physician, and lastly the medicines of several learned lama doctors. Under the circumstances I should not have prescribed for her at all, but that as every one had expected me to do something for her, I had ceded to their wishes. It was, however, my opinion that if the Lhacham would be cured, the only medicine she required was no medicine at all.

Under this new treatment, which she promptly adopted, there was a marked improvement in the Lhacham's health within the next ten days. I used frequently to talk with her, and she seemed to entertain a kind regard for me. One day the minister suggested in her presence that it would be a good thing if I could be sent to Lhasa to see the Lord Buddha, the incarnate Shenrezig, the Dalai lama. The Lhacham approved the suggestion, and promised to have me lodged in her residence at Lhasa, and to take me under her protection while there.

On March 23 I left Dongtse for Tashilhunpo. On the way to Tashingang we saw lambs picking the young shoots of grass, and the country folk were busy in the fields with their yaks, which were decorated with red, yellow, blue, and green hair tassels, and collars of coloured wool, and cowries. The farmers hold-certain religious ceremonies on beginning ploughing and on first putting the yokes (*nya-shing*) on their yaks. They also have at this time most amusing ploughing races.

Beyond Norbu khyung-djin we saw, as we rode along, a far off on a slope of rock, incised in gigantic characters, the sacred formulae, *Om vajra pani hum, om wajishvari hum, om ah hum,* etc.

The next day, at 3 p.m., just as we reached the house of the Deba Shika, there was quite a heavy fall of snow. On the 25th we arrived at Tashilhunpo, and I once more took up my interrupted historical studies.

[From *Journey to Lhasa and Central Tibet*, 1902.]

4

'The Younghusband Expedition, an Interpretation'

By

P.L. MEHRA

I

THE STORY of the Younghusband Expedition has never ceased to evoke the interest and excite the curiosity of students of frontier affairs, even in lands far removed from the barren and treeless wastes of Tibet. Today that story has assumed greater significance not for the specialist alone, but even for the layman who finds it exceedingly hard to grasp the meaning of much that has lately passed over this land of mystery and snow that adjoins our northern borders. Any understanding of this border, and its problems, would entail some reasonable familiarity with the aims and objectives visualised—and the results that flowed from the Younghusband expedition. Simply told, the episode is a brief one and relates to the summer of 1903 when Lord Curzon, the then Viceroy and Governor-General of India, chose Major Younghusband to lead a small number of 'frontier diplomats' to negotiate on some trading rights, and settle a few outstanding border disputes, with the representatives of Tibet's god-king and of the Imperial Chinese Resident at Lhasa. The British commercial mission escorted by a couple of hundred well-armed troops penetrated a score of miles into the country to initiate the parleys, and ended finally as a fullfledged military expedition that dictated terms to the battle-worsted Tibetans in the audience-chamber of the golden Potala. This chapter in Indo-Tibetan relations which the baron of Kedlestone thus opened has not yet drawn to its close. In fact it would appear that the (Communist) Chinese invasion of Tibet in 1950, and the more recent agreement signed at Peking between the new masters of Delhi and the Government of Mao Tse-tung are an integral part of the chain reaction that started on its course half a century ago.

Nor could it be maintained that the final word has yet been said on the Younghusband performance at Lhasa. Indeed the treaty which the victorious British commander concluded there marked the beginnings of controversies whose reverberations still fill the pages of learned books and journals. The Curzon-Younghusband team though it has succeeded in persuading a reluctant British Government to sanction the advance to Lhasa, failed woefully in carrying conviction after the initial goal had been reached. The two of them,—'old friends and fellow travellers', to use Lord Curzon's words—had aimed at a political settlement that would have left the British in supreme control, with a territorial and an economic strangle hold over the land which would have been hard to shake. The Conservative Government of Arthur Balfour shrank from the prospect at the very moment of its realisation, and repudiated most of that to which their Commissioner had committed them. There are indeed few instances in history where an expanding imperial system thus deliberately set limits to its expansion, and denied itself the very means whereby it subsisted and flourished.

In the narrative unfolded here an attempt has been made to view the entire sequence of events in the light of an over-all picture of India's landward periphery, with its varied problems, and the political philosophies of the men who conceived, planned and finally executed the mission. Again, the expedition has been viewed not indeed in isolation but as an essential part of the manifold aspects of Lord Curzon's Indian viceroyalty.

II

An important factor that has determined the various problems of India's northern frontier is the geography of the land that lies beyond the Himalayan ranges. Another equally significant factor has been the relative levels of development in the societies of India and the mountain region which conditioned their attitude to the problems of terrain on this frontier. Aside from these, the basic fact of this frontier is the vast expanse of Tibet. To view it in an over-all perspective one might regard undivided India's landward periphery as consisting of two shells: the inner comprising Baluchistan, the North-West frontier tribal area and states, Gilgit and Leh, Sikkim and Bhutan and what comprises the North-East agency (sundering Assam from its neighbours in the north and in the south)—with Nepal occupying a very special position in this "inner" ring. In the "outer" shell Afghanistan and Sinkiang in the west and north-west and Tibet in the north and north-east occupied a highly important and stratègic position. Any understanding of India's land frontiers, and the problems connected therewith, would entail a thorough knowledge of the political geography of these three states vis-a-vis India. Though the first two viz. Afghanistan and Sinkiang, fall outside the scope of this study, one may tarry a while if only to emphasise that alongwith Tibet they present basically the same problem; the survival, to borrow Lord Lytton's picturesque phrase, of earthen pipkins between iron pots. A condition precedent to the survival of such states is that Russia and China in the north should hold apart from India and Pakistan in the south, for in proportion as the iron pots approach each other, the earthen pipkins are endangered. In his Political Testament the Amir Abdur Rehman of Afghanistan, compared his country's plight to that of a swan swimming in a pond with a bear on one bank and a lion on the other. And he counselled his successors for a long time to come to keep to deep water. As for Tibet the late Sir Charles Bell thought her to be an ideal "buffer" and cautioned against either China or Russia dominating her. Much the same holds true in respect of Sinkiang, for she stands at the backdoor of India and Pakistan which is at the same time the front door of the Soviet Union, and at an angle of the hinterland frontier which for centuries has been regarded as the backdoor of China. It would thus appear that a detailed examination of the Tibetan problem in the context, both of its geography and, history would be an aid to a better understanding of all the three countries in the outer periphery.

Tibetans call their country 'Po'. early Arab works referring to it as 'Tobbat', 'Tobbat' and 'Tibat', the word Tibet being a derivation of *To Po* meaning upper Tibet. According to a Chinese authority *To Fan*, or, hinging on a variant on the old pronunciation of the second word, *To Bo*, is the country's Chinese name; To being a phonetic rendering of a Tibetan word for highland, while *Bo* is the name the Tibetans give to themselves. Sanskrit chronicles of the seventh century refer to Tibet as Bhota.

Most of Tibet is a wild, desolate arid waste in the heart of Asia's steepest mountains. It is high plateau, for the most part bleak and barren and cut by mountain chains stretching from

Kashmir to West China; an in hospitable waste of frozen desert. The Tibetan plateau ranges in height from 9,000 to 29,000 feet above sea-level, nearly three-fourth of it lying above 10,000 feet, and in large areas all elevations exceed 16,000 feet. A well known geographer computers that in Tibet, between the Himalayan and the Karokoram ranges alone,there are fifty summits of over 25,000 feet in height. Interspersed with these mountain ranges, however, are small river valleys such as those of the Indus, the Sutlej and the Tsang Po. Except for the valleys most of the country is not habitable, for its unusual elevation, the sharp temperature contrasts between day and night, and lack of adequate water do not encourage settlement—not to mention that even travelling is a hazardous proposition in most parts.

Physically, Tibet has two broad divisions: the Chang Tang, and the rest of the country. The former is the vast, unexplored plateau of north and central Tibet, occupying nearly seventy-five percent of the entire area. Though its means height is approximately 16,000 feet, many of its peaks range above 20,000; the whole area, a desolate and treeless waste, is dependent on the southern region for the barley necessary to feed its domesticated yak. The rest of the country, nearly one-fourth in area may be further subdivided into three regions. One of these, the valley of the Tsang Po and the broken country along the southern border of the Himalayas, is quite a distinct geographical unit. It is the area of Tibet's highest density of population for its fields afford good pasture ground, and the valleys below excellent farming land. The climate here is relatively mild, the winter being no colder than in Peking, and not nearly so cold as in Mongolia. Tibet's main food supply comes from here, her barley and potatoes, beans and vegetables. In parts of the valley where some irrigation has been made possible, wheat and some soft fruit are grown. The second physical subdivision comprises the Tsaidan and the Koko Nor basins in the north-east, and that 'land of great corrosions,' the Kam plains in the east. These are mainly pasture lands where some unirrigated agriculture is also possible. The third area embraces the districts of western or upper Tibet which contain the great mines of Jalung.

To undertake to define Tibet's physical boundaries, and her area and population is no easy task. Thus geographical Tibet also includes what emerged in 1928 as the Chinese provinces of Chinghai and Sinkiang, areas which along with Kansu and Szechwar, have always been regarded by the Tibetans as part of their land. So also a large part of what the Tibetans regard as an integral part of their country is, theoretically at any rate, within Sinkiang. These factors will explain the wide divergences in the estimates regarding her physical measurements. Thus Dr. Richard gives Tibet's greatest length, east-west wide, as 1,240 miles, its greatest breadth, north to south, as 740 miles and the area as 463,320 square miles. In some cases this estimate of half a million square miles just about double itself. Population estimates are also extremely varied. Thus, in 1907 the Chinese Government computed the population at 6,43,000, while 15 years later its figures tell to 1,500,000! This leaves a margin of 5 millions between the lowest and the highest estimates.

Two facts emerge from this necessarily brief survey. At the outset one notices the appalling fact that for its large area the country is for the most part uninhabited. If a compromise figure of 4 millions be accepted for its population and the area be reckoned at 500,000 square miles, the density per square mile does not exceed 8; in the most thickly peopled areas around Lhasa it has been estimated to be 15. This thinness of her population seems to be a matter of concern even to Tibet's new masters. The sparsity, stark as it is, is further accentuated by the large number of monasteries in the country, and their armies of idle monks or lamas. It has been estimated that nearly one Tibetan in every three is a monk, one woman in every fifteen a nun. As if this were not enough the prevalence of polyandry has meant a declining birth-rate. The real working population is thus pitifully small. That will partly explain why Tibet's resources have, to this day, remained completely unexplored and she lives in which Sir Charles Bell calls the 'feudal age'. Until a few years ago she was, as for as transportation went, a country without a wheel—the Tibetan prayer-wheel is, of course, well-known.

The second fact that stands out rather prominently is that this scanty population is largely concentrated in the valley around Lhasa, where some settled agriculture has been possible. Professor Lattimore maintains that nearly five-sixth of the settled area of Tibet is distributed over an arc running from west of Lhasa in the Tsong-po valley around by the east and north-east to the Kansu frontier. The valley is easy of access from the other areas of Tibet and marks as dividing lines between the settled agricultural area surrounding it and the outlying pasture lands. As for its locale in regard to Tibet's principal neighbours, the valley is comparatively distant from the east and north, though relatively closer to the south. Thus, though not ideally situated it has become the real nerve-centre of the country, and the focal point for its main highways. Lhasa, the Mecca of all Tibetans and for many others besides, is situated in the valley and is the seat of the Tibetan Government.

Even the most cursory glance at Tibet's geography, and ours has been a somewhat detailed examination, makes one wonder how the barren and treeless wastes of this high plateau, with a small but shrinking population, living under a medieval if not indeed primitive social system, should have excited the cupidity and invited the wrath of an alien army. This oddity becomes the more striking when one recalls that long and intensive explorations (in the last quarter of the 19th century) in and around Tibet, the Karakorams and the Pamirs had led to the highly satisfying discovery—highly satisfying, that is, for the rival British and Russian imperialism then contending for supremacy in these areas—that no route existed across high Asia which could be used for artillery and wheeled traffic. Nevertheless, what made the land of the lamas important then, as perhaps now, was her geographical location vis-a-vis her huge, populous and powerful neighbours in the south and in the east, and the not very distant yet sprawling landmass of Asiatic Russia that lay to her north and west. These three physical giants of Asia, peripheral to Tibet, have all influenced her past and have to some extent been influenced by it. It may be useful at this stage to attempt a brief historical conspectus of this relationship if only to place the Younghusband expedition in its proper perspective.

III

One of the significant features of Tibet's early contacts with her neighbours is the intimacy and closeness of her ties with India. Even the origins of the Lhasa kingdom which brought about the final political unity of the three distinct yet disparate regions that comprise Tibet can be traced to Indian influences. Thus Tibet's first historical king, the 7th century A.D. Song-tsen Gam-po, is believed to have come from Ladakh, whose proximity to the Indus, and hence Indian influence, is widely accepted. Since Song-tsen Gampo looms rather large in Tibetan annals—he unified the country and is said to mark "the dawn of Tibetan civilisation"—his association with India is not without significance. Another early Indian influence is in Lamaism, which may be regarded as a comingling of the corrupt northern Indian Buddhism of the eighth century with the indigenous Tibetan Bon religion. This admixture owed much to an Indian missionary, one Padma Sambhavan. A Tantrik Buddhist, hailing from

Udhayana in north-western India, Padma Sambhava is one of the patron saints of Tibet, and one of the chief gods of the Red Hat sect, the followers of the original Buddhism of Tibet. In his wake many Indian religious teachers visited the country, the greatest of them being Atisha who came to Tibet in the XI century. The cave where the Indian savant is said to have lived is a few miles outside Lhasa and is still preserved. The Indian 'traffic' to Tibet was by no means a one-way affair for many Tibetan monks travelled in the reverse direction to visit the holy places of Buddhism and maintained close contacts with Indian monasteries in Bengal.

In contrast to the spiritual and cultural influences from India, the Chinese impact on Tibet has been mainly in regard to material things; the habit of drinking tea, the mode of dress of the people, and of furnishings in a Tibetan home. And yet the Mongols and their successors who for long held Tibet as a part of their vast Chinese dominions were responsible for the institutions of the Dalai and the Panchen, a reformed Tibetan church, and the broad outlines of the patron-chaplain relationship that was to subsist for centuries between the rulers of China and the pontiffs of the Yellow Hat in Tibet. That relationship was to undergo many changes during the 18th century principally in the wake of the Chinese armies marching across the land. They came ostensibly to repel the attack of the Mongols from the north and of the Gurkhas from the south yet in reality to tighten the reins of control over the Dalai's domains.

Sandwiched between the Chinese invasions are the early British efforts to open the land of mystery and snow. The aim of Warren Hastings, as of the Hon'ble East India Company which he served, was to find new markets for British goods. It is not unlikely that a vague feeling was also entertained that through 'her little-known backyard' China itself might be made more accessible. Essentially thus the mission of George Bogle and Samuel Turner were essays in commercial diplomacy. That both the envoys of so enthusiastic a sponsor as Hastings failed in their attempts to establish trade-marts, or even to obtain permission for British merchants' access to the lands of the thunderbolt (Bhutan and Sikkim), was due not so much to their want of trying as to the fears and doubts which assailed Tibet's lamas in respect of the dark motives and motivations of the 'firinghies'.

The next hundred years in the story of Britain's repeated efforts to 'open' Tibet are somewhat uneventful. True, the half-eccentric Manning succeeded in reaching Lhasa or the 'brilliant' Colman Macaulay prepared himself, with evident enthusiasm, for leading an official mission. But Manning who went in disguise achieved practically nothing and the 'exigencies of political considerations' led to the countermanding of Macaulay's projected venture. And yet these hundred years witnessed a great change in the over-all picture. The wars with Bhutan and Sikkim in 1861 and 1865 which climaxed the undisputed mastery of the British over the Indian sub-continent seemed further to confirm Tibetan suspicions of British intentions. Nor were the clandestine Indian, explorers—a Nain Singh, a Krishna or a Sarat Chandra Das—sponsored by their British masters and roaming the Tibetan countryside with their sextants and prisms and measured beads designed to allay these fears. Meantime another important factor had been introduced into the situation: a rapid decline in the prestige and authority of the Manchu A'mbans at Lhasa. This decline which reflected the defeats and humiliations of the Middle Kingdom at the hands of the 'foreign devils' synchronised with the emergence of the powerful figure of the 13th Dalai Lama.

The importance of these varied yet inter-related developments came out in sharp relief when the Chinese for, and on behalf of, their wards concluded with the British the Sikkim

Convention of 1890 and the Trade Regulations of 1893. The former sought to define the Tibet-Sikkim boundary, the latter spelled out in detail the trading facilities which British subjects were to enjoy in Tibet. It is significant that the country most vitally concerned in both these arrangements was not a party to either. That perhaps explains much of the subsequent drama ibet's blunt refusal to be bound by any of the stipulations, China's inability to make her do so, and growing British disgust with the resulting situation. Yet despite these frustrations, Lord Elgin's government (in India) displayed a remarkable forbearance with the doings of some fanatical hot-heads across the Sikkim frontier and a sympathetic understanding of the veritable delays and the circuitous diplomacy of the Chinese. Thus the Tibetans simply ignored the agreements, contending that these lacked their consent. In 1895 they occupied certain areas on the Sikkim side of the border, and refused to open Yatung, that 'uninhabited narrow hole in a deep valley', as a trade-mart. In fact the Tibetans built walls on their side to prevent anyone from meeting the British! No wonder that the trade regulations of 1893 though admirable on paper remained a dead letter in practice. Despite these provocations the Indian Viceroy displayed considerable patience; he argued that the Tibetans had a 'reasonable' claim to the areas into which they had moved, that the 1890 treaty did not provide for pillars along the frontier, and that no serious damage had been done to British trade from an undemarcated frontier. While his detractors condemned this policy of 'conciliation' and 'forbearance', his supporters could point to the fact that British trade with Tibet had continued to mount up, that it had actually expanded nearly 500 per cent between 1890 and 1898.

Lord Elgin's policy of patient waiting, however, did not last long. His critics declared it to be totally ineffectual and his successor, who was to play so vital a role in determining the new approach was signally lacking in this admirable quality. Our next preoccupation would be an understanding of Lord Curzon's 'new look' against the background of his early career and of his viceroyalty's manifold problems.

IV

The remarkable change that took place when Lord Elgin handed over the reins of office to his successor Lord Curzon, early in 1899, was nowhere better revealed than in the new Viceroy's approach towards Tibet. From the previous policy of 'patient waiting' there was a sudden shift to one of impatient hurry. It is this violent break with the past, and the developments consequent thereupon, which from the subject-matter of the present study. Before examining these it may be helpful to size up the man who was to play so important a role in the Tibetan drama.

George Nathaniel, 1st Marquess Curzon of Kedleston, was no stranger to India or the East at the time he assumed the Viceroyalty. Years later he confessed that India "haunted him like a passion" even from his infancy. This "fascination and...the sacredness (of India)" had been born of his intense enthusiasm for Britain's vast Asian Empire, "more populous, more beneficient and more amazing" than that of Rome.

Apart from his preoccupation with the Empire which grew with the years, the young Curzon displayed even at Eton a remarkable power of hard work, and a rare maturity of mind. A contemporary, Lord Esther, held that curzon remained to the last an Eton boy, "brilliant, broad-minded, lavish of the endowments...mature at 18." Another epithet that he earned early, and that stuck to him late, was "superior". As a young boy at school he is reported to have displayed a self-confidence which bordered on the boisterous, a remarkable impatience with opposition and an assumption of airs and graces which in an undergraduate democracy seemed to verge on the ridiculous. No wonder, he was the subject of many a doggerel as a student and later, in his long public career, of so much misunderstanding.

Apart from his student days nowhere perhaps is Curzon better revealed than in his early books and travels. The prancing proconsul with a megalomania for territory emerges very clearly from the pages of a "Russia in Central Asia" or of a "Persia and the Persian Question", or of the globe-girdlings which increasingly brought home to him the fascination and the mission of the Empire. Nor could it be sufficiently emphasised that he had been Under-Secretary for India and for Foreign Affairs before he occupied the Viceregal throne. Both facts are of importance. For strange as it may appear one gets the unmistakable impression from the career of the otherwise remarkable man that his mental horizon did not much widen after his late teens. In fact the obsessions of his early school days, confirmed indeed by his travels, were expanded and elaborated in his books even as he continued to wrestle late with some of his early experiences in administration. Thus the proposition, "Are we justified in regarding with equanimity the advance of Russia towards our Indian frontier?", which he debated at Eton while not yet quite twenty continued to form the subject of his serious pre-occupations for the remainder of his long public career. Another early `flame' which has been traced to his youthful years at Oxford was the "Empire". And it is amazing that the almost religious seriousness with which he viewed the duties and responsibilities which it entailed did not diminish even when many an early votary had been disillusioned by the jolts administered by World War I.

Not yet forty, the brilliant, ambitious and—to use an epithet which stuck to him through life—the 'superior' Baron, later Marquess, Curzon of Kedleston stepped into the shoes of the gentle and suave Elgin. Few men could have been better qualified for the Viceroyalty; few indeed could claim his variety of experience and knowledge of Asian problems. India had been the fever and passion of his youth, and India was pivotal to his concept of the Empire. Indeed Curzon thought India was the political pillar and the true fulcrum of Britain's Asiatic dominion. "The secret of the mastery of the world (the Empire of Hindustan)," he wrote in the preface to his "*Problems of the Far East,*" "is, if only they knew it, in the possession of the British people." He was convinced that Britain's position in India gave her certain command of the main land-routes and the railroads that will lay open the Far East in the not distant future. It is necessary to recall that the India but an India that comprised Burma in the east and Aden and the Persian Gulf ports in the west: a "continental order" based on India and extending its authority from Aden to Hong Kong. In fact before he came to rule over the country Curzon had visited India four times, and he knew at first hand most Asian rulers and their countries: he had met the Shah of Persia, the Amir of Afghanistan, the King of Korea, the ruler of Siam (with whom he frequently corresponded), the Emperor of Annam and the King of Cambodia.

It is against this background of the man and his ideas that his handling of the Tibetan question must be considered. Nor should that question be viewed as if in isolation. In fact, there is a close bearing of both the Persian and the Afghan problems on his dealings with Tibet. Lord Curzon's policies in regard to all three were closely akin, for the basic question, as he viewed it, was the same in each case. And this was to check the Russian advance as far away from the Indian glacis, and as effectively, as possible. Another factor that cast a grim and fearful shadow on his Tibetan policy was the growing tension that developed in his relations with his political superiors at home. The battles which he fought with them, and the 'victories' which he claimed to have scored left a deep cleft that grew deeper as the years rolled by. Thus between 1899 and 1902 his relations with India Office cooled appreciably. In the earlier year he had more or less openly defied Lord Salisbury's instruction as regards the Sultan of Oman by dispatching a naval squadron from Bombay and obtaining from the ruler a public rescission of this concession to the French under threat of a direct bombardment of his palace. In the latter year he solicited the King's direct intervention after the Secretary of State and the Cabinet had refused his suggestion that the Imperial Durbar (of 1903) should be associated with a Royal proclamation of some tax relief. In between the two episodes there were others—his ruthless condemnation of the institution of the Presidency Governors, his demand that the expense of Indian representatives at the King's coronation should be borne by HMG, the Indian Councils' criticism of the Viceroy's appointment of the Policy Commission, and of his projected educational reforms—and they all served to leave a very unhappy impress on the relations between London and Calcutta.

In analysing Lord Curzon's approach towards Tibet two distinct stages are readily discernible. The watershed is provided by the despatch of January 8,1903. In the early part of his viceroyalty Curzon, abandoning the policy of forbearance and conciliation, had tried a direct approach to the master of the Potala. China was ignored and the Tibetan pontiff reminded of the seriousness of the British intent. Curzon who had condemned the old approach as both "unproductive and inglorious," insisted that his "new look", to borrow a somewhat over-worked yet significant phrase, was designed to achieve "results".

The Viceroy's preliminary sizing up of the problem, made not long after he assumed office, provides the key to his thinking on the subject. In this he suggested,

That Yatung, on the Tibet side of the frontier, which under the Regulations of 1893 had been fixed as a post for Indian trade "can never be expected to be a real mart." To counter this he was prepared to cede to the Tibetans land in the neighbourhood of Giagong (which they "are so desirous of retaining") if P'hari, further up in the Chumbi valley, be thrown open to trade without any restrictions. The Viceroy also suggested, and this is significant, that there be an option of sending a British official to visit P'hari and to reside there—"if this should prove desirable."

That negotiations with the Chinese Resident are not likely to prove fruitful. "We seem....to be moving in a vicious circle. If we apply to Tibet we either receive no reply, or are referred to the Chinese Resident." And if the Chinese Resident is approached, "He excuses his failure by his inability to put any pressure upon Tibet." In a letter to Lord George Hamilton a week earlier the Viceroy has described the position regarding China as "most ignominious" and the use of the Chinese Amban as intermediary, "an admitted farce."

Born of his impatience with the Chinese "farce", Lord Curzon was thus suggesting a straight and direct approach to the Tibetans, accompanied by a broad hint regarding a British official visiting and residing in Tibet—"if this proves desirable." The Secretary of State's reaction was very favourable in regard to the first suggestion, though he doubted the "expediency" of the second. He feared it might cause "complications", and even delay the settlement of the "essential" part of the negotiations.

The correspondence that ensues is concerned largely with the implementation of the policy enunciated in this initial exchange. The Bhutan vakil in Lhasa, one Kazi Ugyen, was approached for an informal approach to the Dalai. He was armed with the promise that the Tibetans would be "liberally" rewarded for any rights which they might concede in the

Chumbi valley. This mission however, proved a failure and the viceroy making another effort entrusted a personal letter to a Chaktar Urkh, one of the two governors of Western Tibet. Here too keen disappointment awaited Lord Curzon, for six months later the Viceroy's letter was returned unopened. The Governor protested that "in the face of regulations against the intrusion of foreigners into Tibet" he had not dared to send it to Lhasa. Still undaunted, and now for the third time, the Viceroy had another try at it. Kazi Ugyen who was paying a visit to Lhasa was entrusted with a letter in which the Indian potentate warned the Tibetan pontiff that if his (Lord Curzon's) overtures failed, his government "must reserve the right to take such steps as may seem to them necessary and proper. In his despatch to Lord George Hamilton he advocated the adoption of "some practical measures" if his attempts should fail.

Outside the formality of a State paper Lord Curzon had shown his exasperation in a personal letter to the Secretary of State a few months earlier. He confessed therein that he felt completely outraged by the fact that the Dalai had assumed towards him an attitude of contemptuous silence, that in returning his letter unopened he, the all-powerful Viceroy, had been treated as "the pettiest of petty potentates." And he ended, "It is really the most grotesque and indefensible thing that at a distance of a little more than 200 miles from our frontier, this community of unarmed monks should set us perpetually at defiance." One wonders if Kazi Ugyen's warning to the Dalai that "should the Viceroy in Calcutta lose patience, it will not end well for you," or his description of the reigning (Indian) Grand Mogul as "the greatest official under the King" was inspired?

What were the Home Government's views on so strong a plea for an "altered policy," or the urgent adoption of some "practical" measures? The Secretary of State did indeed lack the vigour and fire of Curzonian rhetoric, but his arguments did not lack force. He conceded that relations with Tibet had not been satisfactory and that in such a case "you would be justified in adopting strong measures." But having said that he marshalled argument upon argument against any precipitate move. Thus he reminded the Viceroy that Tibet was "politically subordinate" to China; that the difficult nature of the country would make any military operations hazardous; that the Viceroy's ceaseless pressure for closer relations would be likely to increase "distrust of our intentions" and that any precipitate action "would be viewed with much disquietude and suspicion." He ended by warning the Viceroy against taking any steps "that may involve a risk of the complications that I have indicated."

V

Nowhere perhaps was the gap that lay between the Viceroy's viewpoint and that of the Home Government laid bare more vividly than here. Curzon had always regarded it as axiomatic that where diplomacy failed there was no alternative except to resort to force. As he put it baldly: "Nothing can be or will be done with the Tibetans until they are frightened. I should at once move a few men up to the frontier." This indeed was the basic assumption behind his plea for an "altered policy." For the authorities in London, nurtured in the tradition of the cool and dispassionate Salisbury, what they could not secure by diplomacy they were, usually, willing to forego. The divergence in outlook had been patent from the day the Hon'ble George Nathaniel Curzon was sworn in as the old phlegmatic Salisbury's Under Secretary for Foreign Affairs. And Lord George Hamilton's warnings were not, one would suppose, designed so much to carry conviction as to restrain his over-zealous lieutenant.

The Tibetans, it seemed, were playing into his hands too, for the Viceroy's second letter to the Dalai was now returned unopened, the Dalai protesting that he could not enter into any communication before first consulting his Council and the Ambans. Weighing different alternatives for putting future relations on a "more satisfactory footing", the Viceroy rejected one of a complete trade embargo. A second one, of occupying the Chumbi valley, "was not proposed at present." It is significant that the Viceroy did not reject it out of hand. What did he advocate? He proposed that the Political Officer in Sikkim tour along the frontier, that he erect boundary pillars wherever these be necessary or desirable, that grazing grounds which the Tibetans might have occupied at Giagong or elsewhere be cleared, or fees charged for violations. Mr. Claude White, the Political Officer, was to have on his tour an escort of one company of Gurkhas, with another in reserve. The Viceroy was persuaded that his suggested course of action had advantages: if the Tibetans did not resist, the Convention would be observed, if they did by impeding the Political Officer's approach, by endeavouring to assert Tibetan claims to Giagong or by destroying boundary pillars they would have only themselves to blame for the clash that "may result". Maintaining that these were "the minimum" proposals that he could recommend Lord Curzon emphasised that if the Tibetans showed an attitude of permanent hostility he would seriously advocate an occupation of the Chumbi valley until they agreed to a diplomatic conference at Lhasa!

Another part of Lord Curzon's despatch deserves close scrutiny. While maintaining that the isolationism of the Tibetans was "not difficult to comprehend", he felt it was incompatible either with proximity to the territories of a great civilized power, or with due respect for the stipulations into which the Chinese Government had entered on their behalf. The situation, he felt, was the most "extraordinary anachronism of the 20th century" and must be brought to an end with as little delay and commotion as possible since there were factors in it "that might at a later date invest the breaking down of these unnatural barriers with a wider and more serious significance."

What was the Viceroy's veiled reference to? "Factors in the situation" which were likely to invest the problem with a "wider and more serious significance?" That Lord George Hamilton acquiesced so readily in the Viceroy's proposed course of action would seem to confirm the existence of these "factors". In fact the land of the lamas was fast becoming a hot-bed of intrigue and the sprawling mass of Czarist Russia was casting some dark shadows across the Potala. We may at this stage turn to this part of the story for it profoundly influenced all subsequent developments in Lord Curzon's Tibetan policy.

Few can read Lord Curzon's despatches on Tibet in 1901-1902 without being struck by his restlessness on the unsatisfactory nature of India's relations with Tibet. We have already adverted to his insistence that more "practical" measures were necessary in place of the old policy of watchful waiting, and we have noticed that the Home Government opposed though it was to his views, did finally concur in some of his suggestions. In fact not a little of the Viceroy's exasperation with the Tibetan situations arose out of this weird phenomenon: that while the Dalai-Lama sent accredited "diplomatic missions" accompanied by autographed letters to the Tsar of Russia, the Indian potentate who rated himself no less important a Grand Mogul was treated with ill-concealed contempt. His sealed letters, sent by special messengers, addressed to "the Illustrious Dalai Lama, Supreme Pontiff of the Great Buddhist Church were returned unopened on the lama plea that the Dalai was barred communication with the outer world. For not only was there increasing evidence of Russian intrigue but perhaps a growing suspicion that the 13th reincarnation of Chen-rezi was fomenting it. Apart from the Dalai whom his principal biographer has rated a "unique world figure", a Russian Buriat monk, one Aguan

Dorjieff, played an important part in this drama. A word in regard to them may not be out of place here.

Any detailed reference to the institution of the Dalai Lama may not be possible in this brief survey. It may suffice here to recall that the office of the Dalai goes as far back as the close of the 14th century, that it was the third of the line who converted Mongolia, that the "Great Fifth" was received by the Chinese Emperor in Peking as if he were an independent sovereign, and that today it is the 14th reincarnation of the first who is the spiritual head of the Tibeto-Mongolian world. Our narrative, however, is concerned with the present Dalai's predecessor: Nag Dang Lo-Sang Theedan Gyarso Gyon Rimboochay, to give him his full name, or perhaps more simply the 13th Dalai Lama. In the long and chequered story of the reincarnations of the Tibetan Gods, and for all the 37 summers of his adult life, he exercised the full temporal and spiritual authority vested in his high office. Few before him exercised such powers and though political prophecy is at best a hazardous preoccupation it does not appear likely that any of his successors would achieve that distinction either.

The 13th Dalai was born in June 1876 in a family of ordinary peasants in the province of Tak-po, which lies to the south-east of Lhasa, a few days' journey from the capital. His discovery was a particularly clear one, nor were there any rival candidates. And since the divine indications in his case were so unmistakable, the Tibetan Government refused to make use of the Golden Urn—a proof also perhaps of the weakening of the Manchu-Chinese overlordship. The date shows that this would coincide with the declining prestige of the Manchu Empire because of the Taiping Rebellion and the defeat in the war with Britain and France in 1861. Having been chosen, the young Dalai, hardly two years of age, was brought to Lhasa. His enthronement, however, had to await the confirmation of the Emperor which took nearly a year and was not celebrated until 1879.

A young Dalai's life is certainly not enviable. Separated from is parents, denied any playmates, encaged within the high walls of the Potala—as though a prisoner—and surrounded by austere looking monks the young child grows up in very much of an abnormal atmosphere. From an early age reading and writing are stressed as also long meditations. The young 13th went through the same mill. His biographer records that his life was deeply secluded and his bane, "study and study and study in the subtleties of the complicated religion!" As he grew up many obstacles were strewed across his path. The young Dalai's Regent who was the head of the Ten-gye-ling monastery in Lhasa had employed his own brother as Chief Minister. The two of them with the help of a third, who was the abbot of a monastery, concocted a plot aiming at the young ruler's life. Great was the horror and indignation with which the discovery of this plot was greeted. The conspirators, when unmasked, were visited with exemplary punishments—the legacy of the bitterness thus generated persisting even to this day. Thus it was later noticed that the monks of the Ten-gyeling always aided and abetted the Chinese armies whenever they appeared in Lhasa. At that time they started a prophecy that the 13th Dalai was the last of the line: "another way of saying that he was a sham reincarnation."

Apart from this plot, which must have shaken the young ruler violently, there was the important fact that he was an eye-sore to the Chinese. We have already noticed that the Golden Urn was not used at the time of his selection. No wonder that the Manchu Emperor took well-nigh a year to accord approval to his enthronement. Equally the failure of this Regent's plot also denoted a growing weakness of Chinese authority. For usually it was a common Sino-Tibetan effort made for a common cause. One need hardly add that the

Chinese were always averse to having a Dalai exercising both spiritual and temporal authority. The 13th, however, had cleared his path, and though entitled to succeed to the sovereignty of Tibet at 18 (17, by our reckoning for the Tibetans take into account both the year of birth as also the current year), he actually did not take over until two years later. And when he did take over he realised that his limitations were of an extreme character. As he confessed to Bell.

> "I came into power when I was 20 years old, but I did not know at all how to govern a country. For the first five or six years it was very difficult.....However within ten years I had, in some degree, improved the Government.

Ambitious—how ardently had he wished to take over control of worldly power—extremely hard-working (the shades of Kedleston!) the Dalai's early problems were to check the power of those who had been, for so long, used to exercising it. One of his first acts was to "crack" down on the monks whose rule of Lhasa during the days of the Great Prayer Festival meant considerable lawlessness. He also quietly, but successfully, scotched an attempt by the Chinese Amban to appoint one of his proteges as a Minister in the Tibetan Cabinet.

While in domestic matters the young Dalai seemed gradually to be mastering the difficulties facing him, his handling of Tibet's foreign relations showed neither firmness, nor yet any maturity. That the Chinese control had weakened was patent enough and the Dalai was sufficiently shrewd to ensure that it did not raise its ugly head again. His dealings with India and Russia, however, were not marked by any adroitness. As for the former it appears the clandestine missions sponsored by the authorities in India in the nineteen eighties had frightened the Tibetans. Later the stories of Christian missionaries and the long drawn out conflict over the Sikkim frontier must have added to this initial fright and distrust. To the Tibetans, and their ruler, it seemed equally certain that the British were intent to destroying their freedom and their faith. A disagreeable and an aggressive people who must be kept out at all costs!

[From *Journal of Indian History*, August 1955.]

5

The Unveiling of Lhasa

By

EDMUND CANDLER

THE CONDUCT of Great Britain in her relations with Tibet puts me in mind of the dilemma of a big boy at school who submits to the attacks of a precocious youngster rather than incur the imputation of 'bully'. At last the situation becomes intolerable; and the big boy, bully if you will, turns on the youth and administers the deserved thrashing. There is naturally a good deal of remonstrance from spectators who have not observed the by-play which led to the encounter. By sympathy must be sacrificed to the restitution of fitting and respectful relations.

The aim of this record of an individual's impressions of the recent Tibetan expedition is to convey some idea of the life we led in Tibet, the scenes through which we passed, and the strange people we fought and conquered. We killed several thousand of these brave, ill-armed men; and as the story of the fighting is not always pleasant reading; I think it right before describing the punitive side of the expedition to make it quite clear that military operations were unavoidable—that we were drawn into the vortex of war against our will by the folly and obstinacy of the Tibetans.

The briefest review of the rebuffs Great Britain has submitted to during the last twenty years will suffice to show that, so far from being to blame in adopting punitive measures, she is open to the charge of unpardonable weakness in allowing affairs to reach the crisis which made such punishment necessary.

It must be remembered that Tibet has now always been closed to strangers. The history of European travellers in Lhasa forms a literature to itself. Until the end of the eighteenth century only physical obstacles stood in the way of an entry to the capital. Jesuits and Capuchins reached Lhasa, made long stays there, and were even encouraged by the Tibetan Government. The first Europeans to visit the city and leave an authentic record of their journey were the Fathers Grueber and d'Orville, who penetrated Tibet from China in 1661 by the Sining route, and stayed in Lhasa two months. In 1715 the Jesuits Desideri and Freyre reached Lhasa; Desideri stayed there thirteen years. In 1719 arrived Horace de la Penna and the Capuchin Mission, who built a chapel and a hospice, made several converts, and were not finally expelled till 1740. The Dutchman Van der Putte, first layman to penetrate to the capital arrived in 1720, and stayed there some years. After this we have no record of a European reaching Lhasa until the adventurous journey in 1811 of Thomas Manning, the first and only Englishman to reach the city before this year. Manning arrived in the retinue of a Chinee General whom he had met at Phari Jong, and whose gratitude he had won for medical services. He remained in the capital four months, and during his stay he made the acquaintance of several Chinese and Tibetan officials, and was even presented to the Dalai Lama himself. The influence of his patron, however, was one strong enough to insure his safety in the city. He was warned that his life was endangered, and returned to India by the same way he came. In 1846 the Lazarist missionaries Huc and Gabet reached Lhasa in the disguise of Lamas after eighteen months 'wanderings' through China and Mongolia, during which they must have suffered as much from privations and hardships as any travellers who have survived to tell the tale. They are received kindly by the Amban and Regent, but permission to stay was firmly refused them on the grounds that they were there to subvert the religion of the State. Despite the attempts of several determined travellers, none of whom got within a hundred miles of Lhasa, the Lazarist fathers were the last Europeans to set foot in the city until Coloned Younghusband rode through the Pargo Kaling gate on August 4,1904.

The records of these travellers to Lhasa, and of others who visited different parts of Tibet before the end of the eighteenth century, do not point to any serious political obstacles to the admission of strangers. Two centuries ago, Europeans might travel in remote parts of Asia with greater safety than is possible to-day. Suspicions have naturally increased with our encroachments, and the white man now inspires fear where he used only to awake interest.

The policy of strict exclusion in Tibet seems to have been synchronous with Chinese ascendancy. At the end of the eighteenth century the Nepalese invaded and overran the country. The Lamas turned to China for help, and a force of 70,000 men was sent to their assistance. The Chinese drove the Gurkhas over their frontier, and practically annihilated their army within a day's march of Khatmandu. From this date China has virtually or nominally ruled in Lhasa, and an important result of her intervention has been to sow distrust of the British. She represented that we had instigated the Nepalese invasion, and warned the Lamas that the only way to obviate our designs on Tibet was to avoid all communication with India, and keep the passes strictly closed to foreigners.

Shortly before the Nepalese War, Warren Hastings had sent the two missions of Bogle and Turner to Shigatse. Bogle was cordially received by the Grand Teshu Lama, and an intimate friendship was established between the two men. On his return to India he reported that the only bar to a complete understanding with Tibet was the obstinacy of the Regent and the Chinese agents at Lhasa, who were inspired by Peking. An attempt was arranged to influence the Chinese Government in the matter, but both Bogle and the Teshu Lama died before it could be carried out. Ten years later Turner was despatched to Tibet, and received the same welcome as his predecessor. Everything pointed to the continuance of a steady and consistent policy by which the barrier of obstruction might have been broken down. But Warren Hastings was recalled in 1785, and Lord Cornwallis, the next Governor-General, took no steps to approach and conciliate the Tibetans. It was in 1792 that the Tibetan-Nepalese War broke out, which, owing to the misrepresentations of China, precluded any possibility of an understanding between India and Tibet. Such was the uncompromising spirit of the Lamas, that, until Lord Dufferin sanctioned the commercial mission of Mr. Colman Macaulay in 1886, no succeeding Viceroy after Warren Hastings thought it worth while to renew the attempt to enter into friendly relations with the country.

The Macaulay Mission incident was the beginning of that weak and abortive policy which lost us the respect of the Tibetans, and led to the succession of affronts and indignities which made the recent expedition to Lhasa inevitable. The escort had already advanced into Sikkim, and Mr. Macaulay was about to join it, when orders were received from Government for its return. The withdrawal was a concession to the Chinese, with whom we were then engaged in the delimitation of the Burmese frontier. The display of weakness invited the Tibetans to such a pitch of vanity and insolence that they invaded our territory and established a military post at Lingtu, only seventy miles from Darjeeling.

We allowed the invaders to remain in the protected State of Sikkim two years before we made any reprisal. In 1888, after several vain appeals to China to use her influence to withdraw the Tibetan troops, we reluctantly decided on a military expedition. The Tibetans were driven from their position, defeated in three separate engagements, and pursued over the frontier as far as Chumbi. We ought to have concluded a treaty with them on the spot, when we were in a position to enforce it, but we were afraid of offending the susceptibilities of China whose suzerainty over Tibet we still recognised, though she had acknowledged her inability to restrain the Tibetans from invading our territory. At the conclusion of the campaign, in which the Tibetans showed no military instincts whatever, we returned to our post at Gnatong, on the Sikkim frontier.

After two years of fruitless discussion, a convention was drawn up between Great Britain and China, by which Great Britain's exclusive control over the internal administration and foreign relations of Sikkim was recognised, the Sikkim-Tibet boundary was defined, and both Powers undertook to prevent acts of aggression from their respective sides of the frontier. The questions of pasturage, trade facilities, and the method in which official communications should be conducted between the Government of India and the authorities at Lhasa were deferred for future discussion. Nearly three more years passed before the trade regulations were drawn up in Darjeeling—in December, 1903. The negotiations were characterized by the same shuffling and equivocation on the part of the Chinese, and the same weak-kneed policy of forbearance and conciliation on the part of the British. Treaty and regulations were alike impotent, and our concessions went so far that we exacted nothing as the fruit of our victory over the Tibetans—not even a fraction of the cost of the campaign.

Our ignorance of the Tibetans, their Government, and their relations with China was at this time so profound that we took our cue from the Chinese, who always referred to the Lhasa authorities as 'the barbarians'. The Shata Shape, the most influential of the four members of Council, attended the negotiations on behalf of the Tibetans. He was officially ignored, and no one thought of asking him to attach his signature to the treaty. The omission was a blunder of far-reaching consequences. Had we realized that Chinese authority was practically non-existent in Lhasa, and that the temporal affairs of Tibet were mainly directed by the four Shapes and the Tsong-du (the very existence of which, by the way, was unknown to us), we might have secured a diplomatic agent in the Shata Shape who would have proved invaluable to us in our future relations with the country. Unfortunately, during his stay in Darjeeling the Shape's feelings were lacerated by ill-treatment as well as neglect. In an unfortunate encounter with British youth, which was said to have arisen from his jostling an English lady off the path, he was taken by the scruff of the neck and ducked in the public fountain. So he returned to Tibet with no love for the English, and after certain courteous overtures from the agents of 'another Power,' became a confirmed though more or less accidental, Russophile. Though deposed, he has at the present moment a large following among the monks of the Gaden monastery.

In the regulations of 1893 it was stipulated that a trade mart should be established at Yatung, a small hamlet six miles beyond our frontier. The place is obviously unsuitable, situated as it is in a narrow pine-clad ravine, where one can throw a stone from cliff to cliff across the valley. No traders have ever resorted there, and the Tibetans have studiously boycotted the place. To show their contempt for the treaty, and their determination to ignore it, they built a wall a quarter of a mile beyond the Customs House, through which no Tibetan or British subject was allowed to pass, and, to nullify the object of the mart, a tax of 10 per cent on Indian goods was levied at Phari. Every attempt was made by Sheng Tai, the late Amban, to induce the Tibetans to substitute Phari for Yatung as a trade mart. But, as an official report admits, 'it was found impossible to overcome their reluctance. Yatung was eventually accepted both by the Chinese and British Governments as the only alternative to breaking off the negotiations altogether.' This confession of weakness appears to me abject enough to quote as typical of our attitude throughout. In deference to Tibetan wishes, we allowed nearly every clause of the treaty to be separately stultified.

The Tibetans, as might be expected, met our forbearance by further rebuffs. Not content with evading their treaty obligations in respect to trade, they proceeded to overthrow our boundary pillars, violate grazing rights, and erect guard-houses at Giagong, in Sikkim territory. When called to question they repudiated the treaty, and said that it had never been shown them by the Amban. It had not been sealed or confirmed by any Tibetan representative, and they had no intention of observing it.

Once more the 'solemn farce' was enacted of an appeal to China to use her influence with the Lhasa authorities. And it was only after repeated representations had been made by the Indian Government to the Secretary of State that the Home Government realized the seriousness of the situation, and the hopelessness of making any progress through the agency of China. 'We seem', said Lord Curzon, 'in respect to our policy in Tibet, to be moving in a vicious circle. If we apply to Tibet we either receive no reply or are referred to the Chinese Resident; if we apply to the latter, he excuses his failure by his inability to put any pressure upon Tibet.' In the famous despatch of January 8, 1903, the Viceroy described the Chinese suzerainty as 'a political fiction,' only maintained because of its convenience to both parties. China no doubt is capable of sending sufficient troops to Lhasa to coerce the Tibetans. But it has suited her book to maintain the present elusive and anomalous relations with Tibet, which are a securer buttress to her western dependencies against encroachment than the strongest army corps. For many years we have been the butt of the Tibetans, and China their stalking horse.

The Tibetan attitude was clearly expressed by the Shigatze officials at Khamba Jong in September last year, when they openly boasted that 'where Chinese policy was in accordance with their own views they were ready enough to accept the Amban's advice; but if this advice ran counter in any respect to their national prejudices, the Chinese Emperor himself would be powerless to influence them.' China has on several occasions confessed her inability to coerce the Tibetans. She has proved herself unable to enforce the observance of treaties or even to restrain her subjects from invading our territory, and during the recent attempts at negotiations she has to admit that her representative in Lhasa was officially ignored, and not even allowed transport to travel in the country. In the face of these facts her exceedingly shadowy suzerainty may be said to have entirely evaporated, and it is unreasonable to expect us to continue our relations with Tibet through the medium of Peking.

It was not until nine years after the signing of the convention that we made any attempt to open direct communications with the Tibetans themselves. It is astonishing that we allowed ourselves to be hoodwinked so long. But this policy of drift and waiting is characteristic of our foreign relations all over the world. British Cabinets seem to believe that cure is better than prevention, and when faced by a dilemma have seldom been known to act on the initiative, or take any decided course until the very existence of their dependency is imperilled.

In 1901 Lord Curzon was permitted to send a despatch to the Dalai Lama in which it was pointed out that his Government had consistently defied and ignored treaty rights; and in view of the continued occupation of British territory, the destruction of frontier pillars, and the restrictions imposed on Indian trade, we should be compelled to resort to more practical measures to enforce the observance of the treaty, should he remain obstinate in his refusal to enter into friendly relations. The letter was returned unopened, with the verbal excuse that the Chinese did not permit him to receive communications from any foreign Power. Yet so great was our reluctance to resort to military coercion that we might even at this point have let things drift, and submitted to the rebuffs of these impossible Tibetans, had not the Dalai Lama chosen this moment for publicly flaunting his relations with Russia.

The second Tibetan Mission reached St. Petersburg in June, 1901, carrying autograph letters and presents to the Czar from the Dalai Lama. Count Lamsdorff declared that the mission had no political significance whatever. We were asked to believe that these Lamas travelled many thousand miles to convey a letter that expressed the hope that the Russian Foreign Minister was in good health and prosperous, and informed him that the Dalai Lama was happy to be able to say that he himself enjoyed excellent health.

It is possible that the mission to St. Petersburg was of a purely religious character, and that there was no secret understanding at the time between the Lhasa authorities and Russia. Yet the fact that the mission was despatched in direct contradiction to the national policy of isolation that had been respected for over a century, and at a time when the Tibetans were aware of impeding British activity to exact fulfilment of the treaty obligations so long ignored by them, points to some secret influence working in Lhasa in favour of Russia, and opposed to British interests. The process of Russification that has been carried on with such marked success in Persia and Turkestan, Merv and Bokhara, was being applied in Tibet. It had long been known to our Intelligence Department that certain Buriat Lamas, subjects of the Czar, and educated in Russia, have been acting as intermediaries between Lhasa and St. Petersburg. The chief of these, one Dorjieff, headed the so-called religious mission of 1901, and has been employed more than once as the Dalai Lama's ambassador to St. Petersburg. Dorjieff is a man of fifty-eight, who has spent some twenty years of his life in Lhasa, and is known to be the right-hand adviser of the Dalai Lama. No doubt Dorjieff played on the fears of the Buddhist Pope until he really believed that Tibet was in danger on an invasion from India, in which eventuality the Czar, the great Pan-Buddhist Protector, would descend on the British and drive them back over the frontier. The Lamas of Tibet imagine that Russia is a Buddhist country, and this belief has been fostered by adventures like Dorjieff, Tsibikoff, and others, who have inspired dreams of a consolidated Buddhist church under the spiritual control of the Dalai Lama and the military aegis of the Czar of All the Russians.

These dreams, full of political menace to ourselves, have, I think, been dispelled by Lord Curzon's timely expedition to Lhasa. The presence of the British in the capital and the helplessness of Russia to lend any aid in such a crisis are facts convincing enough to stultify the effects of Russian intrigue in Buddhist Central Asia during the last half-century.

The fact that the first Dalai Lama who has been allowed to reach maturity has plunged his country into war by intrigue with a foreign Power proves the astuteness of the cold-blooded policy of removing the infant Pope, and the investiture of power in the hands of a Regent inspired by Peking. It is believed that the present Dalai Lama was permitted to come of age in order to throw off the Chinese yoke. This aim has been secured, but it has involved other issues that the Lamas could not foresee.

And here it must be observed that the Dalai Lama's inclination towards Russia does not represent any considerable national movement. The desire for a rapprochement was largely a matter of personal ambition inspired by that arch-intriguer Dorjieff, whose ascendancy over the Dalai Lama was proved beyond a doubt when the latter joined him in his flight to Mongolia on hearing the news of the British advance on Lhasa. Dorjieff had a certain amount of popularity with the priest population of the capital, and the monks of the three great monasteries, amongst whom he is known to have distributed largess royally. But the traditional policy of isolation is so inveterately ingrained in the Tibetan character that it is doubtful if he could have organized a popular party of any strength.

It may be asked, then, What is, or was, the nature of the Russian menace in Tibet? It is true that a Russian invasion on the North-East frontier is out of the question. For to reach the Indian passes the Russians would have to traverse nearly 1,500 miles of almost uninhabited country, presented difficulties as great as any we had to contend with during the recent campaign. But the establishment of Russian influence in Lhasa might mean military danger of another kind. It would be easy for her to stir up the Tibetans, spread disaffection among the Bhutanese, send secret agents into Nepal, and generally undermine our prestige. Her aim would be to create a diversion on the Tibet frontier at any time she might have designs on the North-West. The pioneers of the movement had begun their work. They were men of the usual type—astute, insidious, to be disavowed in case of premature discovery, or publicly flaunted when they had prepared any ground on which to stand.

Our countermove—the Tibet Expedition—must have been a crushing and unexpected blow to Russia. For the first time in modern history Great Britain had taken a decisive, almost high-handed step to obviate a danger that was far from imminent. We had all the best cards in our hands. Russia's designs in Lhasa became obvious on the part of the Tibetans, and provocation such as would have goaded any other European nation to a punitive expedition years before. We could go to Lhasa, apparently without a thought of Russia, and yet undo all the effects of her scheming there, and deal her prestige a blow that would be felt throughout the whole of Central Asia. Such was Lord Curzon's policy. It was adopted in a half-hearted way by the Home Government, and eventually forced on them by the conduct of the Tibetans themselves. Needless to say, the discovery of Russian designs was the real and prime cause of the despatch of the mission, while Tibet's violation of treaty rights and refusal to enter into any relations with us were convenient as ostensible motives. It cannot be denied that these grievances were veiled enough to justify the strongest measures.

In June, 1903, came the announcement of Colonel Younghusband's mission to Khamba Jong. I do not think that the Indian Government ever expected that the Tibetans would come to any agreement with us at Khamba Jong. It is to their credit that they waited patiently several months in order to give them every chance of settling things amicably. However, as might have been expected, the Commission was boycotted. Irresponsible delegates of inferior rank were sent by the Tibetans and Chinese, and the Lhasa delegates, after some fruitless parleyings, shut themselves up in the fort, and declined all intercourse, official or social, with the Commissioners.

At the end of August news came that the Tibetans were arming. Colonel Younghusband learnt that they had made up their minds to have no negotiations with us *inside* Tibet. They had decided to leave us alone at Khamba Jong, and to oppose us by force if we attempted to advance further. They believed themselves fully equal to the English, and far from our getting anything out of them, they thought that they would be able to force something out of us. This is not surprising when we consider the spirit of concession in which we had met them on previous occasions.

At Khamba Jong the Commissioners were informed by Colonel Chao, the Chinese delegate, that the Tibetans were relying on Russian assistance. This was confirmed later at Guru by the Tibetan officials, who boasted that if they were defeated they would fall back on another Power.

In September the Tibetans aggravated the situation by seizing and beating at Shigatze two British subjects of the Lachung Valley in Sikkim. These men were not restored to liberty until we had forced our way to Lhasa and demanded their liberation, twelve months afterwards.

The mission remained in its ignominious position at Khamba Jong until its recall in November. Almost at the same time the expedition to Gyantse was announced.

In the face of the gross and deliberate affront to which we had been subjected at Khamba Jong it was now, of course, impossible to withdraw from Tibetan territory until we had impressed on the Lamas the necessity of meeting us in a reasonable spirit. It was clear that the Tibetans meant fighting, and the escort had to be increased to 2,500 men. The patience of Government was at last exhausted, and it was decided that the mission was to proceed into Tibet, dictate terms to the Lamas, and, if necessary, enforce compliance. The advance to Gyantse was sanctioned in the first place. But it was quite expected that the obstinacy of the Tibetans would make it necessary to push on to Lhasa.

Colonel Younghusband crossed the Jelap la into Tibet on December 13, meeting with no opposition. Phari Jong was reached on the 20th, and the fort surrendered without a shot being fired. Thence the mission proceeded on January 7 across the Tang Pass, and took up its quarters on the cold, wind-swept plateau of Tuna, at an elevation of 15,300 feet. Here it remained for three months, while preparations were being made for and advance in the spring. Four companies of the 23rd Pioneers, a machine-gun section of the Norfolk Regiment, and twenty Madras sappers, were left to garrison the place, and General Macdonald, with the remainder of the force, returned to Chumbi for winter quarters. Chumbi (10,060 feet) is well within the wood belt, but even here the thermometer falls to 15° below zero.

A more miserable place to winter in than Tuna cannot be imagined. But for political reasons, it was inadvisable that the mission should spend the winter in the Chumbi Valley, which is not geographically a part of Tibet proper. A retrograde movement from Khamba Jong to Chumbi would be interpreted by the Tibetans as a sign of yielding, and strengthen them in their opinion that we had no serious intention of penetrating to Gyantse.

With this brief account of the facts that led to the expedition I abandon politics for the present, and in the succeeding chapters will attempt to give a description of the Chumbi Valley, which, I believe, was untrodden by any European before Colonel Younghusband's arrival in December, 1903.

I was in India when I received permission to join the force, I took the train to Darjeeling without losing a day, and rode into Chumbi in less than forty-eight hours, reaching the British camp on January 10.

(1905)

6

The Journey to Tibet

By

CLEMENTS R. MARKHAM

I

FROM TASSISUDON TO PARI-JONG

WHILE I was at Tassisudon an insurrection broke out in favour of Deb Judhur, the former chief; and the disturbance which this occasioned protracted my stay. The malcontents, after a fruitless attempt on the place of Tassisudon, seized Simptoka, a castle in its neighbourhood, in which they found arms and ammunition.

There are no cannon in this country. The castles are built on eminences, with lofty and thick walls which have loopholes; the windows are high, project out, and are provided with heaps of stones to throw upon assailants. The doors are strong and secured by bars of iron; the entrance to some of them is by a covered way, defended by towers; and they want but the mote and the bridge to resemble the Gothic castles of our ancestors. There are only two ways of reducing them—by fire or by famine. The first appears easy enough, for as there are no arches, the roofs and floors are all of wood. But Simptoka having been built by Deb Seklu, a very popular Rajah, and being full of furniture and effects belonging to the government, it was resolved to blockade it. Troops were accordingly collected from the distant provinces, and three of the roads were stopped up. The fourth, however, was still open. The Deb Rajah's force increased every day. Deb Judhur's party saw no prospect of assistance; and after a siege of ten days they abandoned Simptoka, and being favoured by moonlight, escaped over the mountains into Teshu Lama's country.

I left Tassisudon on the 13th of October, 1774, the day of their retreat, in company with Mr. Hamilton; Mirza Settar, a native of Kashmir, who had joined me from Rangpur, and spoke the language of this country; the Tibetan Paima, a messenger of Teshu Lama, who had been sent for me; and a servant of the Deb Rajah, who was to attend me to the borders of his country.

Our way was by Rinjipu, commonly called Paro-gaund. The direct road is over the mountains, and we were to have travelled over it, escorted by a guard. This, however, was now unnecessary, and we took the low road along the banks of the Chinchu. It was the same by which we had come from Buxa-Duar. We passed Simptoka, and came up with a party of the Deb Rajah's men. They halted at a little village, and their leader sent for us. He had formerly been Kalling, or secretary, to the Deb Rajah, and had been lately promoted to the office of Donnai, or Head Dewan. He enjoys the first place in the chief's favour, and his sagacity and superior abilities entitle him to it. In anything that relates to the government of his own country, he might be pitted against many a politic minister. As a philosopher, he would twist him round his finger. Of a trust, an ounce of mother-wit is worth a pound of clergy.

The Donnai was sitting on the ground surrounded by his men. He gave me part of his carpet. We had a dram of whisky. He told me of the escape of the insurgents from Simptoka; that he was in pursuit of them by the foot of the mountains, while another detachment had taken the upper road. As soon as we left him, I saw a village on the top of the mountain in flames: it was a punishment for its attachment to the Deb Judhur.

A soldier in Bhutan is not a distinct profession. Every man is girt with a sword, and trained to the use of the bow. The hall of every public officer is hung round with matchlocks, with swords and shields. In times of war or danger, his servants and retainers are armed with these; the inhabitants, assembled from the different villages, are put under his command, and he marches in person against the enemy. The common weapons are a broadsword of a good temper, with shagreen handle; a cane-coiled target, painted with streaks of red; a bow formed of a piece of bamboo; a quiver of a junk of the same tree, the arrows of reeds, barbed, and often covered with a poison said to be so subtile that the slightest wound becomes mortal in a few hours. Some few are armed with a pike. They put great confidence in firearms; but are not so cunning in the use of the matchlock, as of their ancient weapons, the sword and the bow. Their warlike garb is various and not uniform. Some wear a cap quilted, or of cane and sugar-loaf shape, with a tuft of horse-hair stained; others, an iron-netted hood, or a helmet with the like ornament; under these they often put false locks to supply the want of their own hair, which among the tribe of Bhutanese is worn short. Sometimes a coat of mail is to be seen. In peace as well as in war, they are dressed in short trousers, like the Highland philabeg; woollen hose, soled with leather and gartered under the knee; a jacket or tunic, and over all two or three striped blankets. Their leaders only are on horseback, and are covered with a cap, rough with red-dyed cowtails. They sleep in the open air, and keep themselves warm with their plaids and their whisky. When they go to war or to an engagement, they whoop and howl, to encourage each other and intimidate the enemy. They are fond of attacking in the night time. As to their courage is battle, those can best speak who have tried it. I saw only some skirmishes.

We arrived at Lumbolong towards night, the 14th of October. Our room was like a large warehouse, supported by posts. A fire was lighted upon a stone in the middle, and as there are no vents, we suffered as much from its smoke as we benefited by its heat. For want of a more polite entertainment, I sent for some women who had come with the baggage, and had a Bhutan song. There is no giving a description of it; and as I know nothing of music, I could not take it down. It is more like church chimes than anything else. Some of the notes are lengthened out as long as the breath will last, and people used to climbing mountains are far from being short-winded. A battle with fists between our guide and the landlord—the second I have seen here. What a contentious place is Lumbolong!

We left it the next morning, and continued to descend the Chinchu, till it is joined by the Pachu, near Paku. Here we crossed it, and entered the narrow valley through which this last runs rapidly. The mountains along which we passed are bare and rocky, and there are no houses to be seen except the dwellings of some fakirs. On the opposite side is a village, and some wheat fields.

A heavy shower of snow had fallen two days before we left Tassisudon, and the tops of all the mountains were white with it. The Bengalis, when they got up in the morning, were much surprised at the sight of it. They inquired of the Bhutanese, who told them it was white cloths, which God Almighty sent down to cover the mountains and keep them warm. This solution required, to be sure, some faith; but it was to them just as probable as that as glass, and be able to walk across a river. When different climes exhibit such incredible phenomena to the inhabitants of other countries, why should not the accounts of travellers be treated with indulgence, and even the adventures of Sinbad the Sailor be read with some grains of allowance?

We arrived at Essana after midday on the 15th of October. This is a village situated in a small but fruitful valley. Everybody was busy with the harvest. As soon as a field of rice is ripe the water is drained off, and the stream that supplied it diverted into a different channel. It is then cut down with teethless sickles, and is either placed against the narrow ridges which surround the fields and separate them from each other, or it is laid flat upon the stubble-ground. In a few days it is built up in little rocks, regularly, but without being bound. From, these it is taken down; a beam is raised breast high, and supported upon two posts; under it a large mat is spread, and the men and women, leaning upon it, tread out the rice with their feet. A different method is used with the wheat, which is bearded. It is tied up in small sheaves. In some places (Kepta) they separate the grain from the straw by burning it; in others (Tassisudon) they thrash it out with flails. The wheat is reaped in the beginning of June.

In all these different occupations of husbandry the heavy burden lies upon the fair sex: they have a hard lot of it. Besides all this, the economy of the family falls to their share. They have to dress the victuals and feed the swine. They are not much troubled indeed with washing or scrubbing: the fashion of the country renders this quite unnecessary. But not unfrequently one sees them with a child at the breast, staggering up a hill with a heavy load, or knocking corn, a labour scarcely less arduous. And with all this bitter draught they appear to have few of those sweetenings which might render it more palatable. They have none of the markets, fairs, churches, and weddings of England; they have none of the skipping and dancing of France; they have none of the devotion of the lower people in other Roman Catholic countries; they have none of the bathings, bracelets, ect., of the Bengali; and yet I know not how it comes to pass, but they seem to bear it all without murmuring; and, having nothing else to deck themselves with, they plait their hair with garlands of leaves or twigs of trees. The resource of a light heart and a sound constitution are infinite.

Proceeding up the Pachu, we arrived at Rinjipu, the capital of province, on the 16th of October. I was lodged in a long hall adjoining the temple. The palace is a miniature of Tassisudon. The valley is large, well cultivated, and filled with detached villages. In one of these there is a bazaar, the only one I believe in the country, and two Kashmiri houses; but there is no calling it a town.

The government of Paro-gaund is the most important under the Deb Rajah. The person who now holds it is a cousin of Lama-Rimboche, who, upon the late revolution, laid aside the habit of a fakir, which he had assumed under the former administration, and returned to worldly affairs. His jurisdiction is very extensive. Besides the districts from which he takes his title of Paro Penlop, the governments of Dalimkotta, Lukhi-Duar, Chamurchi-Duar, and all the districts towards the Murungs are under him. He has the power of life and death in his hand. He repairs once a year to Tassisudon, and pays a fixed annual revenue to the Deb Rajah; but delivers in no account of his administration. He retains, however, his office only during pleasure, and a mandate from the presence reduces him to the level of other subjects.

The revenue of Paro-gaund, as well as of most of the interior districts, is paid chiefly in grain, horses, blankets, etc., and the money come principally from Lukhi-Duar, Buxa-Duar, and other Duars or outlets into the low country. But I must not here pretend to give particulars.

I was waked in the morning with the firing of guns and the war whoop. I thought we had not yet done with our fighting; but it turned out to be only the head of a rebel, which they were carrying into the palace in procession, with a white handkerchief as a flag before it.

I stayed two or three days at Paro-gaund; visited the Penlo; received a reinforcement of blankets from him, and continued my journey on the 19th October. I also received a visit from the Donnai.

We were obliged to make short journeys on account of the coolies. We stopped at Duko-jong on the night of the 20th, and were lodged in the castle, romantically enough situated on the top of a mount. Under most of the windows are hives of bees in the open air. They have cold quarters of it.

Our next stage was Chanon, which we reached on the 21st. It consists of four or five houses on the banks of the Pachu, surrounded with turnip fields, for which alone it is famous.

The road from Tassisudon had been pretty level; we could ride most part of the way. Our next stage was extremely steep; keeping close to the Pachu, which dashes over rocks, wet with its spray. One place was very picturesque. High perpendicular rocks were overhead. The Pachu, now reduced to a large stream, running rapidly by: on the other side a high round mountain, covered with silver firs and pines, intermixed with other trees, red, yellow, and all those colours with which a natural wood is variegated towards the close of autumn. The summits of the hills were white with snow. When we got up to the highest part of the road, we found the sides of the mountains entirely bare, owing, I suppose, to their being exposed to the north wind. We met a flock of sheep, the first we had seen; small, with good wool. We met also droves of cow tailed cattle; they are used as beasts of burden, and were then carrying skins, with the wool upon them, to Paro-gaund, where the coarse blankets are mostly manufactured. They were almost all black, very rough, uncouth make, a large hump, short legs, and the large bushy tail for which they are noted.

There are no inhabitants at Gaissar, a place we arrived at on the 22nd of October. There is only a low house, like a stable without doors. We were obliged to bring our provisions and fuel from the last stage. We required it all to keep as warm. The hills all about were covered with snow; and to mend the matter, a heavy shower of it came in the night time.

This was all frozen in the morning, and most of our road to Pari-jong was covered with snow. When we got down the hill to the Pachu, we found the stones and bridges hanging with icicles. There were no houses to be seen, and only some herds of cattle feeding on the sides of the valley, which was bounded on the northwest by a hill between two moderate mountains. On reaching the top we found six heaps of stones with banners. They serve to mark the boundary between the Deb Rajah's country and that of the Lama, which now lay before us; plain and open to the north; hilly to the west; behind, to the east and south, mountains. I arrived at Pari-jong on October 23.

I found the Bhutanese, who was down in Calcutta, waiting for me. I have dismissed the Deb Rajah's servant, and am to proceed towards Shigatze in a day or two.

II

FROM PARI-JONG TO DESHERIPGAY

The first object that strikes you, as you go

down the hill into Tibet, is a mount in the middle of the plain. It is where the people of Pari-jong expose their dead. It happened, I hope not ominously, that they were carrying a body thither as we came down. Eagles, hawks, ravens, and other carnivorous birds were soaring about in expectation of their prey. Every village has a place set apart for this purpose. There are only two exceptions to it. The Lamas are burnt with sandal-wood, and such as die of the smallpox are buried, to smother the infection; so that three of the five kinds of funerals (and I know no more) which the inhabitants of this world use are known to the people of Tibet.

As we advanced a little farther, we came in sight of the castle of Pari-jong, which cuts a good figure from without. It rises into several towers with the balconies, and having few windows, has the look of strength; it is surrounded by the town. The houses are of two low stories, flat-roofed, covered with bundles of straw, and so huddled together that one may chance to overlook them. There is little to be said for them. The ceilings are so low, that I have more than once been indebted to the thickness of my skull; and the beams being very short, are supported by a number of posts, which are little favourable to chamber-walking. In the middle of the roof is a hole to let out the smoke, which, however, departs not without making the whole room as black as a chimney. This opening serves also to let in the light; the doors are full of holes and crevices, through which the women and children keep peeping. I used to give them sugar-candy, and sometimes ribbons; but I brought all the children of the parish upon my back by it. The straw upon the top keeps the house warm. The same style of architecture prevails in the villages upon the road. It has a mean look after the lofty buildings in the Deb Rajah's country; but having neither wood nor arches, how can they help it?

There is no walking out after it is dark, on account of the number of dogs which are then let loose; they are of the shepherd breed, the same kind with those called Nepal dogs, large size, often shagged like a lion, and extremely fierce.

The two Lhasa officers who have the government of Pari-jong sent me some butter, tea, etc., the day after my arrival; and, letting me know that they expected a visit from me, I went. The inside of the castle did not answer the notion I had formed of it. The stairs are ladders worn to the bone, and the rooms are little better than garrets. The governor was dressed in a russet coloured tunic of coarse woollen, and a linen cloth folded and laid upon his bare head. The other, who I understand is a sort of judge, was clad in coarse black cloth. They were seated beside one another upon carpets. The etiquette is much the same as with the Dewans at Tassisudon.

Four score of Deb Judhur's people had taken refuge in this fort. The Deb Rajah sent to demand them, but they were not given up. The conversation which passed on that occasion was, I am told, as full of the principles of government and the law of nations, as it is had been conducted by Grotius and Puffendorf.

Pari-jong stands in a confined plain, entirely surrounded by hills and mountains, except to the north-east, which allows that ruffian wind free entrance. It is on every account abundantly bleak, and bare and uncomfortable.

My friend Paima was considered here as a great man, and all Teshu Lama's vassals endeavoured by their presents and attention to secure his interest of court. His levees were crowded with suitors; and the night before our departure he invited all his friends, and gave them a grand entertainment. I knew nothing of this, and sent for him to play a game at chess. My servant found him dressed out in the governor's *khilat*, seated under a piece of green silk for a canopy, surrounded by all the peasants and peasants' wives, singing, dancing, and drinking, and as great as a prince.

It was, therefore, the morning of October 27, 1774, before we set out. Our party was now considerably increased by the accession of Paima and six other of Teshu Lama's servants. Everybody was mounted on horseback; the horses being all geldings, low sized, and quiet, hardy, ill-dressed, unshod. Having got clear of all the dogs and of all the beggars at Pari-jong, we journeyed slowly over the plain.

One of Paima's servants carried a branch of a tree with a white handkerchief tied to it. Imagining it to be a mark of respect to me and my embassy, I set myself upright in my saddle; but I was soon undeceived, for after stopping at a tent to drink tea with the abbot of a monastery in the neighbourhood of Pari-jong, subject to Teshu Lama, we rode over the plain till we came to a heap of stones opposite to a high rock covered with snow. Here he halted, and the servants gathering together a parcel of dried cow-dung, one of them struck fire with his tinder-box, and lighted it. We sat down about it, and the day being cold, I found it very comfortable. When the fire was well-kindled, Paima took out a book of prayers; one brought a copper cup, another filled it with a kind of fermented liquor out of a new-killed sheep's paunch, mixing in some rice and flour, and after throwing some dried herbs and flour into the flame, they began their rites. Paima acted as chaplain. He chanted the prayers in a loud voice, the others accompanying him, and every now and them the little cup was emptied towards the rock. About eight or ten of these libations being poured forth, the ceremony was finished by placing upon the heap of stones the little ensign, which my fond imagination had before offered up to my own vanity. The mountain to which this sacrifice was made is named Chumalhari. It stands between Tibet and Bhutan, and is generally white with snow. It rises almost perpendicular like a wall, and it attended with a string of smaller rocks, which obtain the name of Chumalhari's sons and daughters.

As the water of the Ganges, or of some refreshing brook, is considered holy among the sun-scorched Hindus, so rocks and mountains are the objects of veneration among the Lama's votaries. They erect written standards upon the tops of them, they cover the sides of them with prayers formed of pebbles, in characters so large "that those that run may read," and like the Jews of old, when they went a whoring after strange gods of the heathen, they get themselves up into high places.

The plain over which we had to ride is covered with gravelly sand. It produced nothing but some tufts of withered grass, which afforded a scanty subsistence to the herds of cattle. The sides of the hills to the westward are perfectly bare; they appear like rocks over which the sand and stones had been heaped, leaving here and there the sharp points jutting out; beyond these you see the high mountains in the Demo Jong country, among which, I imagine, is the snowy hill seen from Dinajur and other plains in Bengal. For several days the country bore the same bleak and barren aspect, answering to Churchill's description:

> *"Far as the eye can reach no tree is seen,*
> *Earth clad in russet scorns the lively green."*

The plain cause of this poverty of soil is that God Almighty has so ordered it; but a much more ingenious reason may be drawn from the following circumstances.

The coldness of the climate renders fuel a very essential article, and as no wood is to be had, the Tibetans are obliged to use cowdung, which is carefully gathered from the fields. This is built up in a circular form, or put into a pot with a hole in the bottom. It makes a cheerful ardent fire when well-kindled, and the people are abundantly skilful in the art of managing it, which my own ill success has often shown me to be a very difficult science.

We arrived at Tunno, our next stage, about three o'clock. Some of my servants who walked were so tired that they were brought home on peasants' backs, as I had not been able to find horses for them all. I next day got cow-tailed bullocks, but the Hindus would not ride on them because if any accident should happen to the beast while they were on him, they would be obliged, they said, according to the tenets of the Shaster, to beg their bread during twelve years, as an expiation for the crime. *Memo*—Inconvenient carrying Hindu servants into foreign parts.

Our road next day (October 28) led us along the banks of the lake called Sham-chu Pelling. It is fed by a large mineral stream, which issues out of the side of a mountain, and extends about eighteen miles from the north to south. It was half frozen over, and well stocked with wild ducks and geese. We also met with some hares, and a flock of antelopes, besides a herd of wild animals called kyangs, resembling as ass, and which I shall afterwards have occasion to describe more particularly.

We should have had excellent sport, but for my friend Paimas scruples. He strongly opposed our shooting, insisting that it was a great crime, would give much scandal to the inhabitants, and was particularly unlawful within the liberties of Chumalhari. We had many long debates upon the subject, which were supported on his side by plain common-sense reasons drawn from his religion and customs; on mine, by those fine-spun European arguments, which serve rather to perplex than convince. I gained nothing by them, and at length we compromised the matter. I engaged not to shoot till we were fairly out of sight of the holy mountain, and Paima agreed to suspend the authority of the game laws, in solitary and sequestered places.

The religion of the Lamas is somehow conneeted with that of the Hindus, though I will not present to say how. Many of their deities are the same; the Shaster is translated into their language, and they hold in veneration the holy places of Hindustan. In short, if the religion of Tibet is not the offspring of the Centoos, it is at least influenced by them. The humane maxims of the Hindu faith are taught in Tibet. To deprive any living creature of life is regarded as a crime, and one of the vows taken by the clergy is to that effect. But mankind in every part of the world too easily accommodate their consciences to their passions, and the Tibetans find no difficulty in yielding obedience to this doctrine. They employ a low and wicked class of people to kill their cattle, and thus evade the commandment. The severe prohibition of the Hindus in regard to eating beef is likewise easily got over. The cows of Tibet are mostly of the bushy-tailed kind, and having therefore set them down as animals of a species different from the cow of the Shaster, they "eat, asking no questions for conscience' sake." The general principle by which they determine the degree of culpability in depriving an animal of life is very ingenious. According to the doctrine of transmigration, there is a perpetual fluctuation of life among the different animals of this world, and the spirit which now animates a man may pass after his death into a fly or an elephant. They reckon, therefore, the life of every creature upon an equal footing, and to take it away is considered as a greater or smaller crime, in proportion to the benefit which thereby accrues to mankind. According to this doctrine, "the ox who clothes the ground in all the pomp of harvest, the sheep who lends them his own coat, and yields them milk in luscious streams," are slaughtered without mercy; while the partridge and wild duck enjoy the protection of government, and the trout lives secure and unmolested to a goodly old age. The musk goat is condemned, on account of its perfume. The deer and the hare are tried on a double charge, and suffer for their skin as well as their flesh. But I am following out disquisitions foreign from my journey.

A stream of water falls from the Sham-chu into the Calo-chu Lake, which extends about ten miles east and west. A large village, named Caloashur, stands upon the bank of it, and another stream runs from it northwards. We kept close to this stream for several days: it falls into the Tsanpu Shigatze, turning many mills on its way. These are constructed on the simplest plan: a duct is cut in the same manner as in Europe; but the wheel, instead of being perpendicular, is horizontal, and turns the upper millstone, which is fixed to its axle, without any other machinery. There are also several bridges on this river, but very different from the wooden ones we met with among the mountains. They are walls, with breaks or openings to let the water through, which are covered with planks or large flags. In the Deb Rajah's country they choose the narrowest part of the river to throw over a bridge: here they take the broadest.

Our route continued almost due north through valleys little cultivated and bounded by bleak and barren hills, between whose opening we saw distant mountains covered with snow. Here and there we saw a few houses, with some spots of rushy ground, or of brown pasture, but not a tree or a plant was to be seen, and the number of ruinous houses and deserted villages rendered the prospect more uncomfortable. At Kanmur a few willows were planted round the village. We were lodged in the temple at the top of the house, which is generally the best apartment. Towards evening we had a visit from a priest who resides at Giansu, on the part of Teshu Lama, and began on acquaintance which we had afterwards abundance of opportunity to improve. He was dressed in a lay habit, consisting of a red broadcloth tunic, with a cap turned up with furs. He sat about an hour with us, and applied to Mr. Hamilton about medicines.

This village is subject to Lhasa. The house in which we lodged had lately changed its inhabitants. Of fifteen persons who formerly lived in it every one had died last year of the small pox.

As we generally set out by sunrise, we arrived early at our stages. Dudukpai, the next village, which belongs to Teshu Lama, had also a good many willows about it. The people were all busy building and stacking their straw, and were singing at their work. Our landlords' family seemed to be one of the happiest in Tibet. The house belongs to two brothers, who are married to a very handsome wife, and have three of the prettiest children I ever saw. They all came to drink tea and eat sugar-candy. After nigh came on, the whole family assembled in a room to dance to their own singing, and spent two hours in this manner with abundance of mirth and glee. I would stop to describe, but I shall have an opportunity afterwards, and am now going to discuss a philosophical and much more important subject.

The inhabitants of Tibet seem to be of a distinct race from those in the Deb Rajah's country. It struck me on my arrival at Parijong, and every day's journey has served to confirm it. The latter were the most robust and well-built race I ever saw. I cannot say so much for the former. Their strength, too, is in the same proportion; any burden with which the one will climb the steepest mountains, must be diminished fully a third to be carried by the other on level ground. One might seek for the cause of this in the difference of soil and climate. I will endeavour to account for it on another principle, because it may throw some light on the way of life among each people.

Labour certainly renders a man strong; *caeteris partibus*, a blacksmith or a carpenter will be stronger than a tailor or a barber. I have already mentioned the toilsome life of the Deb Rajah's subjects. The nature of this country exposes its inhabitants to no such hardships. The hills, although in many places abundantly steep and high, are so bare and sterile that they are left in a state of nature. The valleys only are cultivated, and the roads lead through them, which cuts off all climbing of mountains. Goods are chiefly carried on bullocks and asses; the corn is trod out by cattle and ground by water-mills, and the country producing no forests the inhabitants are freed from the hard labour of hewing down trees, and transporting them from the tops of mountains.

But however this easy life may contribute to render the men less robust, it has evidently a very favourable effect upon the women, who are certainly more delicate and joyous than their neighbours; and this freedom from intensive labour gives likewise to the whole body of the people more time for gossiping and other sociable amusements, which soften this heart and cheer the temper. This also, together with other causes which it is needless to mention, renders the Tibetans much better bred and more affable than their southern neighbours, and the women are treated with greater attention. In the Deb Rajah's country, whatever a countryman saves from his labour is laid out in adorning his sword with silver filigreework, or buying a square box which contains a little gilt image, and is buckled to his back. Here it is bestowed on purchasing coral and amber beads, to adorn the head of his wife. The head-dress of the women is extremely neat and becoming. I have elsewhere described it. But the dirtiness of their hands and faces (many of which deserve a better fate) is a point which, as I cannot attempt to excuse, my partiality to the Tibetans will not allow me to enlarge upon.

I must except, however, our landlady, who kept herself and her family as neat as a Dutch woman, and, saving her black eyes, she had something the look of one.

The first part of our ride next day, the 2nd of November, was through the same bleak country we had hitherto met with; but the valley in which Giansu stands is extensive, well-cultivated, and full of whitened villages. The hills on each side draw close towards the north; between them rises a high and almost perpendicular rock, upon the top of which stands Giansu Castle. It is formed of many walls and turrets. The tower, is built at the foot of the rock on the east side; on the west; it is washed by the river, beyond which a monastery and village are built on the declivity of a mountain. Altogether it makes a fine prospect.

Towards evening we arrived at our quarters, about three miles short of Giansu. They belong to the priest who paid us a visit on the road. The house is surrounded with willows and other trees. It has a number of small windows, and the roof is adorned with little ensigns and written banners. We were lodged in the temple, which was full of painted chests, matchlocks, bows, cushions and other lumber. One corner was hung with mythological paintings, and below a parcel of little gilt cross-legged images, with a lamp burning before them, from which, as all the family are gone to bed, I have taken the liberty to steal some oil in order to finish this account, hoping that it will not be imputed to me as a sacrilege.

This evening the Gosain, who was down in Calcutta, arrived with three of the Lama's servants. Our host arrived in the morning. He had applied to Mr. Hamilton about an inveterate complaint, and I tarried a day on purpose. He is an elderly man, of gentle and modest manners. He sat with me most of the afternoon, and I am sure I drank above twenty cups of tea. As I had waited upon the Lhasa officers at Pari-jong, I offered a visit to those at Giansu, but it was declined on the pretence of one of them being absent.

On our journey next day we passed through the town of Giansu, and under the castle. The streets are narrow, and the houses as I have before described them. Crowds of people assembled to look at us. These exhibitions were very irksome at first, but I have grown to be accustomed to them. I have remarked that we are much more stared at and run after in towns than in villages, and in villages than in solitary houses. Curiosity, perhaps, although natural to mankind, and however the seeds of it may be implanted in them, requires, like music, to be cultivated. It gathers strength from being exercised; it languished and lies asleep when there are no objects to engage its attention.

We met with no more ruinous houses. The villages came now to be more numerous; and the low lands in the valleys, though light and sandy, were covered with barley stubble. We arrived at our stage in good time; and having nothing else to fill up my paper with, will beg leave to give a description of a Tibetan churn. I have often admired the construction of the Bengal ones. I think in this country, however, they have improved on them. The barrel which contains the milk is put on the ground; the strap has two cross boards at bottom. It is put into the barrel, and the lid, with a hole for it to pass through, is fastened on; a thong of leather is then put twice round the staff, and the ends being brought over a small roller (which is supported horizontally by, and turns round between, two posts) are tied to two foot-boards, one end of them raised about six or eight inches from the ground, the other resting upon it. On this a man stands, and moving his feet alternately up and down, twists about the staff in the churn with great velocity and much satisfaction. If I could draw I would give a plan of it, but I cannot.

I met here also with a machine for cutting straw for cattle, but it is not worthy of description. As I remember what a great discovery the cutting of straw was considered in England, I mention it only to show that nations undervalued by Europeans can, without the assistance of Royal Societies, find out the useful arts of life, and for the rest, whether they be of advantage to mankind or otherwise is a question above my reach.

We proceeded next morning, November 5, along the banks of the river, now considerably increased. We saw a good many villages at a distance, and at length came in sight of Painam, a castle built on a rock. The situation is a good deal similar to that of Giansu, but I think finer; the towers are more regular. Under the rock there is only a village. Deb Judhur passed the night in our neighbourhood, on his way to Giansu, where he was afterwards confined.

The valley to the north of Painam was by far the most populous I had yet seen. The villages stand very thick. A small town called Ghattong is built on the side of one of the hills, and the houses being all whitened make a good appearance. We had hitherto kept in the road towards Shigatze, but we now turned to the east, and took that of Chamnamring, in the neighbourhood of which Teshu Lama has for some years resided, on account of the smallpox which lately raged in Tibet. After passing the valley we had to ascend some hills by a difficulty and stony path, then to descend, and then ascend again, after which we had a view of the Tsanpu, running eastwards. When we had got half-way down the hill we stopped at a single house, where we took up our quarters for the night.

On our way over these hills we met with a flock of sheep, which had come from the Dospa country (Tushkhind) with a cargo of salt, and were then returning from Giansu, loaded with barley and wheat. They were of a large breed, with horns extended horizontally. There were about twelve hundred of them, and each sheep carried two bags of grain, which might be about twenty or twenty-five ponds. They were very obedient to their drivers' whistles, and if any of them happened to get out of the road were easily brought back by the shepherds' dogs.

There are a great many rushy fields in the neighbourhood of the place where we stopped. Mr. Hamilton had good shots at four hares, but his fowling-piece was bent and he missed them.

On the 7th of November, after descending an easy hill, we arrived on the banks of the Tsanpu. It is here about the breadth of the Thames at Putney. The channel is not fordable. Having drank some of its water, washed my hands and face, and thrown a rupee into it, we embarked in the ferry-boat, of which there are several in this place. They are in the shape of an oblong square, about twenty-five feet long and broad. The bottom is a float of thick planks, closed in by perpendicular walls to the height of about four feet, with an opening on each side, cut down to about two feet, which serves for the entrance. The whole is bound together with bars of iron, and painted white. At each end of the boat is a white ensign about a foot square. This large hulk is moved by an oar on each side, which are pulled by two men, pushed by another standing opposite of them, and drawn by a woman, who holds a rope fastened to the end of the oar which is in the water. It is managed at the stern by one man with a large headed oar. In our boat there were twenty-three persons, seven horses, one cow-tailed bullock, and fourteen asses, besides baggage. As the river is far from being rapid, we crossed it without losing much ground. Large herds of bullocks and flocks of sheep were waiting on each side for a passage. There is another kind of boat used in the summer time for transporting goods. It is made of hides, about eight feet long, four broad, and two deep the ribs of willow poles. There were none afloat, but we saw many of them upon the bank keel up, and one end being raised a little they thus serve for a habitation.

After crossing the river we rode northwards over a large sandy bank, which is overflowed in the rainy season, and entered a valley which opens upon the Tsanpu. We had fine sandy roads here, and I ran some races with Purungir. The Tibet ponies are much swifter and better blood than I expected. We took up our quarters at a monastery in a small village. The abbot was a short, sickly looking man, but courteous and hospitable. His dinner was just ready, and he sent us a couple of joints of most excellent mutton.

In the afternoon we walked out, and sat down on the banks of the rivulet which runs through the valley, and while we were looking at some dromedaries, a gylong or priest came up to us, and sat down beside us. The few words of the language which I was master of were little able to support a varied and entertaining conversation. I understood, however, the priest's caution against sitting on the ground and in the sun. He was dressed in the habit peculiar to his order, which I have already described; but it had seen many years' service, and was now threadbare. He had thrown off his hose to wade the river, when our snuff-box attracted his notice. Upon this, he loosened a wallet which hung at his back, and after turning over some books of prayers, a yellow cloth coat lined with lambskin, a small parcel of tobacco, and another of tea, he came to a bundle of incense papers, and having presented four of them to Mr. Hamilton, claimed some snuff in return. This exchange being made, and having taken leave by a salutation of thumbs, which is the sign of the superlative degree of comparison, he laid his bundle and hose upon his back, and, wading the river, continued his journey.

The lower gylongs here are not so well off as in the Deb Rajah's country; they are a much more numerous body, and the lamas having engrossed all authority into their own hands, the priests particularly the inferior ones, are without the political consequence enjoyed by the elergy in the neighbouring kingdom.

We set out early in the morning, and travelled northwards along the banks of the rivulet. We passed opposite to Teshu-tzay, where the Lama received his birth, and at length came in sight of Chamnamring, a castle belonging to Lhasa, situated upon the top of a hill, with a small town under it, built in the form of a square, and enclosed within walls. Having forded the river, we entered a little cross valley, where we stopped to drink tea at some tents prepared for us, and having received with handkerchiefs from a Gosain sent with inquiries by Teshu Lama, we proceeded to Desheripgay, a small palace in which the Lama resided.

[From *Narratives of the Mission of George Bogle to Tibet, and of the Journey of Thomas Manning to Lhasa,* 1879.]

7

Lhasa and its Mysteries

By

L. AUSTINE WADDELL

LHASA THE FORBIDDEN

"IN THE heart of Asia lasts to this day the one mystery which the nineteenth century has still left to the twentieth to explore—the Tibetan oracle of Lhasa."

—*Curzon.*

"In the year of the Wood-Dragon (1904 A.D.) the first part of the year protects the young king; (then) there is a great coming forward of robbers, quarreling and fighting, full many enemies, troublous grief by weapons and such like will arise, the king, father and son will be fighting. At the end of the year a conciliatory speaker will vanquish the war."

—*Tibetan Prophecy from Almanac for the Wood Dragon Year* (1904 A.D.)

Wreathed in the romance of centuries, Lhasa, the secret citadel of the "undying" Grand Lama, has stood shrouded in impenetrable mystery on the Roof-of-the World, alluring yet defying our most adventurous travellers to enter her closed gates. With all the fascination of an unsolved enigma, this mysterious city has held the imagination captive, as one of the last of the secret places of the earth, as the Mecca of East Asia, the sacredotal city where the "Living Buddha," enthroned as a god, reigns eternally over his empire of tonsured monks, weaving their ropes of sand like the schoolmen of old, or placidly twirling their prayer-wheels, droning their mystic spells and exorcising devils in the intervals of their dreamy meditations. But now, in the fateful Tibetan Year of the Wood-Dragon, the fairy Prince of "Civilisation" has roused her from her slumbers, her closed doors are broken down, her dark veil of mystery is lifted up, and the long-sealed shrine, with its grotesque cults and its idolised Grand Lama, shorn of his sham nimbus, have yielded up their secrets, and lie disenchanted before our Western eyes. Thus, alas! inevitably, do our cherished romances of the old pagan world crumble at the touch of our modern hands!

How the astrologers of Tibet were able to predict this distressful storm which was in store for their country, so long before it happened, and to specify that it should occur exactly in this very year, is amazing. Certain it is, that the prophetic words heading the foregoing page, and here reproduced from their original, were copied out by myself, about a year before our expedition was ever heard of, from a Tibetan manuscript almanac for this ill-starred year of the Wood-Dragon, of the fantastic calendar of the Lamas. In view of this adverse prophecy staring them in the face, the poor Tibetans, so deeply influenced at all times by superstition, are much to be admired for their patriotism and fanatical loyalty to their priest-god, in desperately rushing headlong upon a conflict which, even in their ignorance of our overwhelming strength, they knew was already doomed by their own oracles to be a hopeless contest, in which Tibetan exclusivism was fighting its death struggle.

The inaccessibility of Lhasa has been due to part to the well-nigh unsurmountable natural barriers which seclude that city behind the most stupendous mountains in the world, and to the extreme difficulty of journeying within the country of Tibet itself, owing to the enormous elevation averaging 12,000 to 15,000 feet above the sea-level, and the absence of all facilities for travel. But the chief cause has been the political barriers raised by its monks, the Lamas, who are at the same time the rulers, the priests, and the merchants of the country; and who, prompted by their own commercial and clerical self-interest, and their dread of losing their advantageous monopoly by the introduction of Europeans and their methods, have struggled and striven by every means in their power to preserve their isolation. Suspicious of all strangers, and ever on the alert, they blocked all avenues of approach to their country, and unflinchingly opposed all intruders, repelling them by armed force if necessary. In this way, such daring travellers as Colonel Prjevalsky in 1872-1879, Count Szechenyi in 1880, Mr. Rockhill, the great Tibetan scholar, in 1889 and 1892, M. Bonvalot and Prince Henry of Orleans in 1889, Captain Bower in 1891, the ill-fated M. Dutreuil de Rhins in 1893, Mr and Mrs. Littledale in 1895, and Dr Sven Hedin in 1901—all of these explorers, after braving unparalleled dangers in the attempt, had to confess to having failed to penetrate beyond the mere outskirts of the central province, and not within a week's journey of Lhasa. As a result of this forcible exclusion from the populous central tracts, the narratives of these travellers are mainly geographical, and contain, with the exception of Rockhill's, little information about the life and notions of the people.

Nor was the jealousy of the Lamas directed against Europeans only. All natives of India, whether Buddhists or not, except a few well-known merchants from Nepal and Ladak, were equally excluded and prevented from crossing the frontier, in accordance with the standing order of the Emperor of China, as conveyed to the missionary M. Huc half a century ago, which prescribed that "no Moghul, Hindostani (Indian), Pathan or Feringhi (European)" should be admitted into Tibet.

It resulted from this exclusive policy that when the British Government wished, in view of possible contingencies, to get a trustworthy map of the great unknown territory of the Land of the Lamas which for so many hundred of miles marched with the frontiers of India, it had to employ as its secret surveying spies, for the most part Tibetans, who had settled on our side of the Himalayas as naturalised British subjects, and whose Mongoloid features assisted in their disguise. Of this class were the famous surveying "Pundits" Nain Singh and "A-K", trained and sent out into unknown Tibet by Colonel Montgomery of the Indian Survey in 1866 and subsequently; and to these survey spies we are indebted for most of our knowledge of the map of Tibet. These gallant exploring pundits, both of them naturalised Tibetans from the North-western Himalayas of Kumaon, after being thoroughly trained to survey-work—to the use of the prismatic compass to plot out routes, understand maps, read the sextant, recognise the fixed stars, use the boiling-point thermometer for altitudes, etc.—they proceeded, in the guise of merchants, risking their lives in the event of detection, to traverse Tibet in all directions and map it out in secret. In this adventurous enterprise they displayed wonderful courage and resource in evading and overcoming suspicion.

The former pioneer explorer, Nain Singh, disguised as a merchant of Ladak, reached Lhasa through Nepal in 1866, and was the first to fix the latitude and longitude of the Forbidden City. Again, eight years later, in 1874, he revisited that place from Ladak by way of the great gold-mine region, in both cases making wide traverses and curves across the country. He did most of his surveying under cover of his prayer-wheel and rosary. When he saw anyone approaching he at once began to twirl his prayer-wheel, and as all good Buddhists whilst doing that are supposed to be absorbed in religious thoughts, he was very seldom disturbed. His prayer-wheel, instead of the usual prayer-scrolls, contained long slips of paper for recording the compass-bearings of places, and the number of paces between towns, etc.; and afterwards, as it was always exempt from customs-house examination, it secreted a compass. His rosary, instead of the usual one hundred and eight beads, was made up of one hundred as counters for his paces—at every hundred paces he dropped a bead. On his visit to the Grand Lama, in a batch of pilgrims, he was much exercised lest His Holiness, who is credited with knowing the secrets of all hearts, should penetrate his disguise; but the pundit put on a bold face and passed this ordeal successfully.

The latter explorer, Krishna, who is a well-educated gentleman and a personal friend of mine, is officially known as "A-K" by reversing the initials of his name. He did even better work, the best of all these native explorers. He, too, visited Lhasa twice, the second time in 1878, and cross-quartered Tibet, up to the borders of Mongolia, China, and Burma, with such remarkable accuracy that, when his figures were calculated out in Calcutta, they fitted in almost exactly with those of the Russian observer, Colonel Prjevalsky, at their points of contact in Mongolia, this agreement being the more surprising when we consider that their routes extended across many hundreds of miles of the most difficult country in the world. Captain Ryder of the Royal Engineers also informs me that he recently tested several of A-K's road-measurements in South-eastern Chinese Tibet by wheel-cyclometer and found that A-K's measurement by paces was marvellously accurate. The other most famous Tibetan surveying spies are Lama Ugyen Gyatsho and Kuntup, both naturalised British Tibetans of the Sikkim or Darjeeling border of Tibet.

Even such men were repeatedly stopped as suspects, and as they procured this geographical information at the risk of their lives, they have mostly been rewarded with pensions and grants of land.

The geographical knowledge thus bravely procured by these Tibetans agents of the British Government, combined with the route-surveys across the outer ranges by Mr Rockhill and the few Europeans above-named, has already filled up most of the map of Tibet, the basis of which was the old "Lama Survey" of the Jesuits, under that most active of Chinese Emperors, Kangshi, in 1717.

A very few Indians also have gained entry into Tibet, during the past century, and even into its sacred capital, in the guise of Tibetans, which their swarthy skin renders somewhat easy. Thus Babu Sarat Chandra Das of Bengal contrived to get into Tibet from our frontier town of Darjeeling, over a quarter of a century ago, in disguise as the Tibetan companion of the surveying Lama, Ugyen Gyathso; and he was also smuggled into Lhasa for a few days as a feigned Tibetan monk by a Lama friend of Ugyen Gyatsho. The terrible penalty, however, paid by Ugyen's old Lama friend for being a party to the impersonation by which this Bengali procured entry into Lhasa is horrible to relate, and throws a lurid light on the savage inhumanity of Buddha's so-called vice-regency on earth. I heard the story several years ago from eye-witnesses, and from the lips of my friend the Tibetan governor of Lhasa himself, who shed tears of emotion as he related it to me. This beloved old Lama was one of the chief monks of the western capital of Tibet at Tashilhumpo, who have practically nothing whatever to do with the political government of the country, which is in the hands of the Lhasa Lamas. He bore the high title of "Minister" or *Seng-chen*.

As he was anxious to learn the language of India, the native country of Buddha, he asked Ugyen Gyatsho, on the occasion of one of his visits to Tibet, to bring with him next time he returned an Indian to teach him this language, and he would arrange to have him passed secretly through from the Darjeeling frontier. In this way Sarat C. Das, who happened at that time to be at Darjeeling as a vernacular teacher in the school there, got to Tashilhumpo, and after a few months there he begged the Lama, in return for his services, to get him a sight of Lhasa. After much importunity the Lama consented, and persuaded his nephew, the governor of Gyantse, to whom he disclosed the Babu's disguise, to take the Babu there for a few days in the retinue of his wife. When, over a year later, it leaked out at Darjeeling that this good-hearted old Lama had assisted an Indian to get into Lhasa, even for a few days, notwithstanding his high position, next in rank only to the Grand Lama himself, and of such sanctity that he was esteemed to be an incarnation of a divinity, and the bodies of his predecessors for three generations were all enshrined in gilded tombs in the Grand Lamasery, where they were objects of worship by swarming pilgrims—nevertheless, when it transpired that he had assisted Sarat Chandra to get into Lhasa, he was denounced from Lhasa as a traitor, he was dragged from his high office by the fanatical Lamas of Lhasa to that sacred city, and there beaten daily in the public market-place, and afterwards ignominiously murdered, with his hands tied behind his back. His body, denied its place amongst his predecessors, was thrown into a river to the east of Lhasa, and his reincarnation was abolished for ever by the Grand Lama, who exercises dominion over the soul as well as the body, although, curious to relate, a child which was born immediately after the murder, and who is now an inmate of one of the monasteries, bears on his body the peculiar mark of being a reincarnation of this Lama, namely, the absence of a left knee-cap, which is an extraordinarily rare abnormality. The ruin thus brought about by the Babu's visit extended also to the unfortunate Lama's relatives, the governor of Gyantse (the Phala Dahpon) and his wife (Lha-cham), whom he had persuaded to befriend Sarat C. Das. These two were cast into prison for life, and their estates confiscated, and several of their servants were barbarously mutilated, their hands and feet were cut off and their eyes gouged out, and they were then left to die a lingering death in agony, so bitterly cruel was the resentment of the Lamas against all who assisted the Babu in his attempt to spy into their sacred city, which resulted in practically no addition to our knowledge of that city beyond what was already recorded by the native survey explorers.

Of Asiatic outsiders, other than Indians, a few Russian survey spies, of late years, have added considerably to our knowledge of the Forbidden City. One of the best known of these is M. Tysbikoff, who brought back, in 1902, photographs of that city. The last of all these Asiatic foreigners who contrived to enter Lhasa was the Japanese priest, Kawaguchi, and he had to flee for his life in May 1902, when his disguise and nationality were discovered. In revenge, several of his friends amongst the monks in the Sera monastery where he lodged in Lhasa have been imprisoned, and some, it is reported, had their eyes gouged out by order of His Holliness the Grand Lama.

Contrary to the general popular belief, quite a number of Europeans succeeded in reaching Lhasa in former days during the past three centuries; and, though never welcomed, they were permitted to reside their for varying periods of months and years. Most of them were devoted Roman Catholic missionaries, and the meager accounts they have left us, industriously collected by Sir Clements Markham merely served to whet our curiosity for more.

The first European to set foot in Lhasa

seems to have been Friar Odoric, who is believed to have reached that sacred city about the year 1330 A.D. on his way overland from China. Nearly three centuries elapsed before another European followed him, this time also from the China side. The Austrian Jesuit, Grueber, accompanied by the Belgian Count Dorville, made his way from China to Lhasa on foot in 1662, and remained there for two months and passed out by Nepal; the only extant sketch of the Grand Lama's palace, until a few years ago, was made by the former of these two travellers. They did not see the Grand Lama, as they refused to prostrate themselves before him. They were followed, in 1706, by the Capuchin Fathers Joseph do Asculi and Francisco de Tour, and, in 1716, by the two Jesuits Desideri and Freyre, who travelled from Delhi *via* Kashmir and Leh. Desideri undertook this daring journey and settled at Lhasa in the hope of converting the Tibetans to Christianity. He remained there thirteen years, when he was recalled by the Pope and prevented returning on account of complaints made against him by Capuchin monks who had found their way to Lhasa shortly after him from Patna in India *via* Nepal, and established there a rival mission. The chief of these Capuchins was Horace della Penna, with no less than twelve others, of whom at least four reached Lhasa *via* Nepal in 1719, and established there a mission which lasted more or less continuously for *nearly half a century* in that city. They were, in 1724, allowed to build a chapel in Lhasa, which the Grand Lama, who held many friendly arguments with these fathers, himself visited, and was deeply impressed by what he saw there. Horace returned to Rome in 1735 for reinforcements, and the Pope sent out with him, in 1738, nine more, *also letters to the Dalai Lama*, and Grand Lama of Lhasa. They reached that city in 1740, and remained there for twenty years more, when they were expelled through the influence of the Chinese political Resident, and were forced to retire with their converts to Nepal. From here, driven out a few years after by the barbarous Goorkhas at their cruel invasion of that country, they settled in British territory at Bettiah in Bengal on the borders of Nepal, where I visited this mission in 1880, and heard for the first time of its chequered and romantic history. Its Tibetan work was not abandoned, and thus has given rise to the paradox that the "Vicar Apostolic of Tibet," who is still nominated at Rome up to the present day, unable to find a footing in Tibet, is forced to live on the borderland in China to the east, or in British territory in the Darjeeling district to the west of the closed land.

No Englishmen ever saw Lhasa up till the present year, except one, about a century ago, if we do not admit the doubtful case of Moorcroft. This one was Thomas Manning, of the Chinese branch of the old East India Company's Service. He was a friend of Charles Lamb, himself also of the same Company's office in London. Manning, fascinated by the romantic accounts of China and its mysterious dependency Tibet, determined to devote his life to exploring these regions. His friend Lamb tried to dissuade him from what he termed "foolish" purposes. "Believe me," writes Lamb, "tis all poets' invention. Pray try and cure yourself. Take hellebore. Pray to avoid the fiend. Read no more books of voyages, they are nothing but lies." But Manning was resolved, and entered the Chinese branch of the Company's service to acquire the Chinese language and the knowledge of the customs of the people necessary for his plan of travel. After three years at Canton he proceeded to Calcutta, in 1811, for official assistance in his enterprise; but the red-tapeism of those early days, discouraging the employment of anyone outside its own clique, however specially fit, denied him help of any kind, and would not even grant him any credentials. Depressed by this official neglect, he nevertheless bravely set out alone; and in the guise of a Chinese physician, enduring endless hardships, made his way through Bhotan to Lhasa. He resided in that city some months, and had several friendly interviews with the Grand Lama there till he was finally arrested by the Chinese and deported back to India. Thence he returned to China by the way he came; but disgusted with the official treatment he withheld the report on his travels, and even related his experiences to no one, and left only a few jottings in a rough diary.

Manning's first interview with the Grand Lama is recorded in some detail, and the glimpse thus obtained lent some colour to the popular belief in the supernatural character of this sacred personage, who just before Manning's visit had "transmigrated" into the body of a princely young child.

"This day (17th December 1811) I saluted the Grand Lama! Beautiful youth. Face poetically affecting; could have wept. Very happy to have seen him and his blessed smile. Hope often to see him again," and Manning goes on to relate:—

> "The Lama's beautiful and interesting face and manner engrossed almost all my attention. He was at that time about seven years old, had the simple and unaffected manners of a well-educated, princely child. His face was, I thought, poetically and affectingly beautiful. He was of a gay and cheerful disposition, his beautiful mouth perpetually unbending into a graceful smile which illuminated his whole countenance....He enquired whether I had not met with molestations and difficulties on the road, to which I promptly returned the proper answer. I said that I had had troubles, but now that I had the happiness of being in his presence they were amply compensated, I thought no more of them. I could see that this answer pleased both the Lama and his household peoples." On Manning being asked if he had any request to make: "I begged of the Grand Lama to give me books respecting his religion and ancient history, and to allow me one of his learned Lamas who understood Chinese to assist and instruct me." This request was only very partially complied with, a promise being made that copies would be prepared and delivered afterwards.

This unfortunate child died a few years afterwards, assassinated, it is believed, by his regent in his intrigues to retain the sovereign power for sometime longer in his hands.

Previous to Manning, only two parties of Englishmen had ever set foot in Tibet, though neither of them reached Lhasa. They were the emissaries of Warren Hastings, the first and greatest of our governor-generals of British India. This far-sighted administrator, who did so much to transform the trading East India Company into a sovereign power and source of strength to England, had strong geographical instincts. In the same year in which he assumed office, he caused a survey of his territory to be made, resulting in the celebrated map of Rennel, the first fairly correct map of India. In the same year he tried to bring the Land of the Lamas into friendly and commercial intercourse with the plains of Bengal. For this purpose he established a great fair under the mountains at Rangpur, below Bhotan and taking advantages of a letter he received from the Grand Lama of Western Tibet, interceding for Bhutanese raiders, he despatched; in 1774, a mission to the Grand Lama, consisting of Mr. Bogle, a magistrate, and Dr A. Hamilton of the Indian Medical Service, in the hope of opening up new trade. This mission was well-received in Western Tibet, but was not allowed to go on to Lhasa; nor did it succeed in negotiating any commercial treaty. Still, it was a great thing to have opened up amicable relations with Western Tibet, and to cement the friendship still further, Warren Hastings established a Tibetan temple at Howrah in Calcutta, and he seized the opportunity of the death of this friendly Lama of Tashilhampo in Western Tibet to send another mission to congratulate the new Lama upon his "reincarnation"—for the Tibetans believe that their great Lamas never die, but on their apparent death merely transmigrate into the body of a newly-born child. This mission of congratulation was despatched in 1783, under Captain Turner, a relative of Warren Hastings, as Bogle had meanwhile died. Captain Turner seems to have been not a little impressed by the halo of supernatural dignity and decorum surrounding this infant, though one cannot help feeling that the irony of the following passage of diplomatic history is at least as remarkable as its official adroitness.

"On the morning of the 4th December (1783) the British envoy had his audience and found the child then *aged eighteen months* seated on a throne with his father and mother on his left hand. Having been informed that though unable to speak he could understand, Captain Turner said: `The Governor-General on receiving the news of your decease in China was overwhelmed with grief and sorrow, and continued to lament your absence from the world until the cloud that had overcast the happiness of your nation was dispelled by your reappearance; and then, if possible, a greater degree of joy had taken place than he had experienced grief on receiving the first mournful news. The Governor anxiously wished that you might long continue to illumine the world by your presence, and was hopeful that the friendship which had formerly subsisted between us would not be diminished, but rather than it might become still greater than before; and that by your continuing to show kindness to his fellow-countrymen there might be an extensive communication between your votaries and the dependents of the British nation.'

"The infant looked steadfastly at Captain Turner with the appearance of much attention, and nodded with repeated slow motions of the head as though he understood and approved every word. His whole attention was directed to the envoy and, he conducted himself with astonishing disunity and decorum. He was the handsomest child Captain Turner had ever seen."

But this mission also failed to reach Lhasa, or to secure any commercial treaty, owing to the hostility of the Chinese Resident at Lhasa, who, it was alleged, caused the following letter to be sent by the Regent of Lhasa to the friendly Lama of Western Tibet. He had heard, he wrote, "of two Feringhi (Europeans) having arrived in Tibet with a great retinue of servants; now the Feringhi were fond of war, and after insinuating themselves into a country raised disturbances and made themselves master of it; and as no Feringhis had ever been admitted into Tibet he advised the Tashilhumpo Lama to find some method of sending them back"; and the Emperor of China, he added, forbade the admittance of all Feringhis.

Another Englishman, Dr Moorcroft, is alleged to have reached Lhasa in 1826 and to have remained there for many years, although another account asserts that he died in 1826 before reaching Lhasa. Dr Moorcroft had a remarkable career. He devoted himself to the commercial exploitation of Ladak and North-Western Tibet, chiefly as a source of breeding horses for the Indian Government, but, as in the case of Manning, his request for official recognition in dealing with these far-off countries, was rigorously refused. Even when, undeterred by his want of official standing, the chiefs of Ladak, whose confidence he had won through his unique intimacy with the people, made him their medium of an offer of their allegiance to the Indian Government, this offer was peremptorily refused, with the result that the Sikhs took over Ladak, and it afterwards passed with Kashmir to the Raja of the latter country and so was lost to us. Moorcroft disappeared soon after, and the story which M. Huc heard in Lhasa from the lips of Moorcroft's servant, and also from several Tibetan officials, of his master's long residence in that city in the disguise of a Kashmir merchant, is quite possible.

"The servant's story, which was confirmed by other people in Lhasa, was: Moorcroft arrived from Ladak at Lhasa in the year 1826 with his Ladak servant; he wore the Musulman dress and spoke the Persian language, expressing himself in that idiom with so much facility that the Kashmirians of Lhasa took him for one of their countrymen. He hired a house in the town, where he lived for twelve years with his servant Nishan, whom he had brought from Ladak, and who himself thought that his master was a Kashmirian. Moorcroft had purchased a few herds of goats and oxen, which he confided to the care of some Tibetan shepherds in the gorges of the mountains about Lhasa. Under the pretext of inspecting his herds, the feigned Musulman went freely about the country, making drawings and preparing his geographical charts. At last, having dwelt for twelve years at Lhasa, Moorcroft took his way back to Ladak, but whilst in the province of Nari (or Hundesh in North-Western Tibet) he was attacked by a troop of brigands, who assassinated him. The perpetrators of this murder were pursued and arrested by the Tibetan Government, who recovered a portion of the property of the English traveller, among which was a collection of geographical designs and charts. It was only then and upon the sight of those objects that the authorities of Lhasa found out that Moorcroft was an Englishman."

The last Europeans to enter Lhasa were the two French Lazarist priests MM. Huc and Gabet. They went, in 1845, to inspect the new diocese of the Vicar Apostolic of Mongolia, which the Pope had just created. They arrived in the sacred city on 29th January 1846, and sojourned there about a month, when they, like the missionaries before them, were expelled by the Chinese resident Minister, who cunningly persuaded the Lama that their spiritual power would be overthrown by the rival creed of the Christian missionaries; though the real reason was believed to be retaliation for China's defeat at that time in the opium war.

There is, indeed no doubt that China has all along persistently exercised her suzerainty over Tibet to encourage the Lamas to exclude Europeans from the country, lest her own commercial advantages and political prestige should suffer. China's suzerainty dates only from 1720 A.D., when she stepped in with an army, on the invitation of one of the rival factions of monks at Lhasa, to put down a civil and religious war there. On restoring order, the emperor Kangshi established at Lhasa for the first time two Chinese mandarins as political agents or *Ambans*—of whom we have heard so much lately—with large powers and a suitable force for their protection. Up to this time Tibet, though paying nominal tribute to China, was practically independent. As an indemnity, China also retained a large slice of the richest part of Eastern Tibet.

Still tighter did China draw her hold over Tibet to the express exclusion of Europeans, when the Emperor Chenlung (famous for his artistic porcelain) had to send an army to drive the Goorkhas out of Tibet in 1792. In that year the freebooting Goorkhas attracted by the reports of the immense riches of the great monastery of Western Tibet which Bogle and Turner had visited, sent an expedition to plunder it. The panic-struck monks appealed to the Chinese emperor, whose army routed the Goorkhas, drove them over the Kirong Pass (about 16,000 feet above the sea), and pursuing them into Nepal, inflicted on them a humiliating defeat near their capital (Kathmandu). As the Chinese general reported that the Goorkhas had been assisted by British officer (which, however, was not a fact), China thereupon established the forts at Phari and other places along the Indian frontier to bar all ingress from that side.

Since our Sikkim-Tibet war of 1888, the Chinese have aided the Tibetans in making exclusion still more absolute.

My own private attempt to reach Lhasa

from the Nepal side, in the summer of 1892, in the disguise of a Tibetan pilgrim, with surveying instruments secreted in prayer-wheels, hollow walking-sticks, and false-bottomed baskets, was frustrated of the unfortunate circumstance that the Raja of our protected Himalayan state of Sikkim, to the east of Nepal, on the intrigues with the Tibetans having been discovered, escaped with all his valuables into Tibet, at the very time and by the very same track, *via* Tashiraka, which I had selected. Thereupon that track, thus favoured by the Raja in his unplanned' excursion, the only one at all promising for my purpose, was so rigorously watched by both Nepalese and Tibetans that my small party was detected. In the passes remote from the central province I found it was possible to evade the frontier guards so as to march for several days in the interior, always shifting camp after dark to circumvent spies and robbers. In this way on two occasions I penetrated to the source of the Sutlej river in North-Western Tibet, but when discovered and stopped I had of course to return to avoid political complications.

To escape detection was well-nigh impossible for a European, as every headman of every village in Central and Western Tibet has for many years been held responsible by the Lhasa Lamas, under penalty of death, that no foreigner should pass though or receive shelter in his village. The headman passed on this threat and responsibility to each villager. Thus every Tibetan watched and prayed so keenly into the personality of all travellers, that our Tibetan survey spies were constantly stopped on suspicion. Even the Mongolian-featured Kawaguchi was frequently suspected—"You are not what you pretend to be," said one of his inquisitive companions; "I am inclined to think you are in Englishman in disguise. If you are not actually English, I am sure you are a European of some sort." Nevertheless, as there was an off-chance of escaping detection, I was willing to take it, notwithstanding that my movements at Darjeeling were watched by resident Tibetan spies, and a description of my appearance sent to Lhasa. In this latter was the reference to blue eyes, which puzzled Dr Sven Hedin as to why his Tibetan captors should search for this particular feature in his face.

The almost insuperable obstacles thus raised against entry to any part of Tibetan proper, even far outside the charmed Lhasa, seems to have led many European travellers of late years to extend the limits of the magical term "Tibet" so far northward as to include the whole of that vast uninhabitable desert the "Changthang" which lies between inhabited Tibet and the Kuen Lun wall of the lofty plateau overlooking the lowlands of Central Asia; although neither this no-man's-land itself nor its approaches are held by the Tibetans, nor by anyone to "forbid" the way for hundreds of miles. One result of this has been to convey the false impression to the public that Tibet is a vast desert plain, bleak, barren and treeless, which we shall see is widely different from the reality.

This isolation of Lhasa, maintained for so many centuries, has resulted in that city becoming the centre of the most extreme form of priest-government the world has ever seen, and had led its esoteric priest-king, in his luxurious, self-centred leisure, to arrogate to himself the position of a divinity. He is adored as a manifestation of the Divine Being who has taken an undying form upon the earth—a supernatural condition which has exercised over European minds a weird fascination.

[From *Lhasa and its Mysteries*, 1905.]

8

Lhasa

By

PERCEVAL LANDON

BEFORE taking up again the story of the Expedition I propose to sketch the internal affairs of Lhasa for the last few years with somewhat greater detail than before. The key to the situation in Tibet, which was not becoming desperate, is to be found in the deliberate and steady determination of the Tibetans to do away with the Chinese suzerainty. This is a policy of long standing. Thirty-five years ago the spirit of independence was already abroad in Tibet, and there was a recognised progressive party, headed by no less a dignitary than the treasurer of Gaden monastery. Under the old regime, as is well-known, a consistent policy of regency, made possible only by the equally systematic assassination of each successive young Grand Lama before he reached the age of eighteen, resulted in a continual regency, and therefore also a continual opportunity for the assertion and re-assertion of the Chinese suzerainty, for no regent could be appointed without the sanction of the Chinese Emperor. The very election of the Dalai Lama himself was theoretically subject to the approval of Peking, but this prerogative was seldom, or never, exercised. In other parts of his dominions the Chinese Emperor made undoubted use of his rights. At Urga, a new Taranath Grand Lama, the third in importance in the Buddhist world, was on one occasion, peremptorily disqualified by his majesty on the grounds that his immediate predecessor had been a turbulent and seditious fellow, and that there was no good ground for supposing that he had been reincarnated in any human being. Against this the good people of Mongolia entered a violent protest. They said that such a contention cut at the root of their religion, and so much trouble did they give that eventually the Emperor compromised; he said that as the monks of Urga had chosen a Mongolian to be their chief he would allow the election to stand, but that on no account thenceforward was a reincarnation to take place in the body of a Tibetan. The descent of the spirit is thus regulated to-day. Again it is necessary to remind the European reader with a sense of humour that these apparent absurdities are the source of very real and often very bitter political feeling in the Far East, and that the application of European habits of thought to these circumstances can only result in a total misapprehension of the whole situation. The Tibetans see no absurdity in situations thus created at a time when in other ways their national aspirations were shaping a shrewd and Occidental policy.

The leader of the party died indeed before achieving success, but it is worth notice that in the election of the present Dalai Lama, in 1874, a change, directly attributable to the dead reformer's personality, was made in the devolution of the spirit of Avalokiteswara. In the old days the names of all babies born at the time of the assassination of the previous Dalai Lama were written on slips and put into a golden urn, which, it is reported, levitated itself and thrice cast forth the slip of paper bearing the name of the chosen child. This miracle is supposed to have been somewhat assisted by the writing of the same name upon every slip, and it was to guard against any such political manipulation of this all-important choice that a new plan of selection was then adopted. Acting upon the counsel of the chief magician of Nachung Choskyong, the discovery of the new Dalai Lama was entrusted to the pious clairvoyance of the Shar-tse Abbot of Gaden. This man, acting upon instructions, went to the Chos-kor Plain, to the east of Lhasa and there on the surface of the Muli-ding-ki lake the new reincarnation was seen in his mother's lap upon a lotus flower. After a brief search for mother and child, Tubdan Gyatso, the present pontiff, was found at Paru-chude in the district of Tag-po. This method of choosing a successor to the divine authority checkmated the ordinary intrigues by which family influence as well as official guardianship secured to the Chinese suzerain no small voice in the acts of the doomed child's government. The last regent, as has been said, was chosen from Gaden though he also had some connection with the Kun-de-long in Lhasa.

Eighteen years afterwards, when, under other circumstances, his life would have been brought to a sudden conclusion, Tubdan Gyatso was spared. This has been attributed by some to the unrest prevailing during our troubles with India at that time; the treaty was then actually in process of construction in Calcutta, and it is very likely that the recent war with ourselves had suggested to the shrewder Tibetans that the time had come finally to take their affairs into their own hands. China had been of no use to them in their dispute with India, and to have 'reincarnated' the Dalai Lama at that moment meant a repetition of the usual opportunity for the exertion of Chinese influence which would have been peculiarly inopportune and even disastrous. He was therefore allowed to survive maturity, but only as a religious pontiff, the temporal power remaining in the hands of the regent. But as soon as the treaty was signed the last vestige of Chinese influence in Tibet was thrown off by a *coup d'etat*, in 1895, strangely resembling that of King Alexander of Servia under similar circumstances, Tubdan Gyatso declared himself temporal sovereign as well as religious autocrat, cast the regent into prison and poisoned him almost immediately.

Such was the position in 1901. There were at this time three important men in Lhasa: the Dalai Lama, Dorjieff and the 'Premier'—the Shata Shape. The last of the triumvirate was a man who had been brought into prominence some years ago by an unfortunate incident in Darjeeling. The story is well-known: a Tibetan was ducked in the fountain for insolence displayed by him or by one of his countrymen towards an Englishwoman in a rickshaw. The man's rudeness did not, perhaps, justify so drastic a punishment, but it was not altogether unnatural, and it was our misfortune rather than our fault that we thus incurred the perpetual and bitter hatred of the man, who, in the course of a few years, was destined to become prime minister of Tibet; for the victim was no other than the Shata Shape, then exiled and under a temporary cloud. He never forgot or forgave, and it is not surprising that when the opportunity presented itself he flung himself heart and soul into the change of policy advocated by Dorjieff. Sufficient reference has already been made to the career of Dorjieff; of the Dalai Lama, we only know from Chinese sources that he is a headstrong and somewhat conceited man, not without strength of character, but intolerant of restraint in any form. Physically he is a tall and powerfully built man with unusually oblique eyes.

Opposed to them stood the various representatives and delegates of the ruling priestly caste, greatly swayed by the traditional respect and homage which the Grand Lama's position inspires in the least dutiful of his subjects, but stubbornly refusing to depart from their ancient principles and the policy of seclusion which had stood Tibet and themselves in good stead for so long. In all else the Dalai Lama was able to have his way, but neither the introduction of a Russian protectorate, nor the presence of Russian representatives in Lhasa, would the Tsong-du tolerate in any form whatever, or for an instant. To neither side were the claims or the opinions of the Chinese of the slightest moment. The return of Dorjieff in December with the unofficial understanding between Russia and Tibet was, therefore, the inauguration of a difficult period for the Dalai Lama.

The existence of this understanding was fact that he could neither openly avow nor, on the other hand, entirely conceal. The solemn anti-foreigner covenant, signed by the Tsong-du, was obstinately pleaded by the opposition and nothing could be done. The Dalai Lama changed his methods. Not for a moment did he abandon the policy which promised to secure for himself and for his country the apparently gratuitous protection of Russia and freedom from the ever-present dread of the English; and he did not attempt to conceal his not unnatural dislike for the shortsighted policy of the Tsong-du, by which he now found himself as much thwarted as by any possible interference of China. But in their existing mood it was impossible to coerce the members of the National Council, so for the future he determined to use the wide powers he was able to wield without reference to it, and he believed that their scope was extensive enough to carry through his matured Russophile policy, not so much by the deliberate choice of the Tsong-du, as of necessity, and he set himself determinedly to bring about that necessity. This was no easy task. There was no trouble then with India, and the self-confident Tibetans attached small value to any inducements that Russia could hold out. Tibet had succeeded easily in regaining her independence of China, and could conceive no reason for putting herself again under obligation to any man. But with shrewder foresight the Dalai Lama saw that some such protection from the north or from the south was ultimately inevitable. He chose to make a truce with Russia. Apart from the practical inducements offered by Dorjieff, it must be remembered in his choice of an ally that he was acting upon a principle well-known in the East. Long before his days the worn out shoes and mouldy bread of the men of Gibeon had persuaded Joshua that it was safe to make a treaty of peace with so distant a tribe. The moral effect of an alliance with either was, as he knew well, a guarantee for the non-interference of the other. Now India is but a fortnight away, while Russia, by the quickest route is full four months' journey distant.

So soon, therefore, as he could make the Tsong-du recognise the necessity for outside support, he knew that the assistance of Russia, as being the more distant friend, would, as a matter of course, be preferred by it to the traditional and imminent menace of Indian influence. He set himself to bring this recognition about, and it was clear that if friction could in some way be established in his relations with India, he would have gone far towards obtaining his end. In achieving his purpose, he had neither scruples nor difficulty. Reference has been made before to the policy of aggression he adopted, but the acts may be briefly recapitulated here. The frontier regulations of Sikkim were violated in a flagrant manner; the grazing rights near Giao-gong were encroached upon in a way which he was well aware we could not much longer suffer. A customs house and a barrier were actually erected and occupied, and British subjects kept out by force from a small portion of the British Empire. Eventually the arrival of a letter from Lord Curzon, in the middle of 1902, offered him an opportunity he was not slow to use. The letter was returned unopened, without apology or comment of any kind.

Such, it will be remembered, was the situation immediately before the arrival of the mission at Kamba jong.

Under this new regime the Tsong-du were little consulted. It was Tubdan's intention to use them after wards, but rather for the mere purpose of ratifying an inevitable policy than of asking them their opinion upon its wisdom. No definite, information of their attitude seems to have been sent to Russia. Rifles were from time to time received and stored at Norbuling under the Dalai Lama's personal supervision, and Dorjieff continued to distribute small but valuable European-made gifts among the leading men of Lhasa. The action of the Indian Government in sending Mr. Claude White to enforce the rights of the Sikkimese over their grazing grounds was interpreted by the Grand Lama as an act of poverty hostility, and was used to hasten the catastrophe—all the more readily, perhaps, because of the repeated warnings of the old Amban Yu-Kang that the Tibetan policy with regard to the English was both foolish and *ultra vires*: his protests were, however, consistently and insolently ignored. At last, however, it seems that the Shata Shape recoiled before the lengths to which the Dalai Lama, now utterly in the toils of Dorjieff, was prepared to go, the exact circumstances of their quarrel are not known, but it is clear that in 1903 the Shata Shape was deposed from office and thrown into prison; where, I believe, the unfortunate man remains. The story of this incident is not without interest.

We get glimpses of the internal affairs of Lhasa about this time, which reveal sufficiently clearly the chaos which was then reigning. To any demur on the part of his colleagues in the government, the Dalai Lama opposed ill temper instead of argument, and soon made the unfortunate discovery that the slightest threat of resignation from temporal affairs—which one might have supposed to be no unwelcome idea to his harassed colleagues—speedily reduced the most insubordinate member of the Tsong-du to submissiveness.

But the dissatisfaction of Tibet with the Russophile tendencies of the Grand Lama could not thus be checked, and the co-operation of England and China in the advance of the Mission to Kamba jong was a rebuff for the Grand Lama that could not be misinterpreted. The great astrologer of Tibet, the Lama of Re-ting, was asked about this time to interpose the influence of the stars against the encroachment of the British. It is remarkable that in his answer he makes the definite charge that the troubles from which Tibet was suffering were due to the fact that bribes of European money had been unlawfully accepted by Tibetan officials.

On the 3rd or 4th of October, it was asserted that 150 Russian rifles were brought to the Potala by Dorjieff. At this time the latter's influence reached its highest point, and it was regretfully admitted in Lhasa that even the Shapes themselves were obliged to curry favour with him to get anything done or even listened to by the Dalai Lama. About this time, owing to the direct intervention of Dorjieff; the Dalai Lama took the arbitrary and high-handed step to which we have referred. On the 13th of October he sent for and imprisoned at Norbu-ling the four ministers of state and the representatives of the Three Monasteries. He accused the Shata Shape of having taken bribes; the other members were charged with having concealed from the Dalai Lama important facts connected with the boundary dispute, with having taken money from Ugyen Kazi on the occasion of the presentation of an elephant, with being behindhand in their biennial reports, and, in general, with disobedience to his Holiness, and with attempting to carry on the business of the country contrary to his intentions and orders. In order to carry through this *coup-de-main*, he once again threatened to resign and adopt the meditative life unless his action were endorsed. He was completely successful.

Almost the last act of these unhappy men was a refusal to attend the annual review on the plain between Sera and Lhasa on the day when the Emperor of China is customarily saluted by obeisance made towards the east. It is probable that they refused to attend this yearly ceremony in order to avoid offending either the Emperor or the Dalai Lama, either by abandoning or persisting in the old custom which the latter seems now to have forbidden for the future, and it is not without significance that, in order to save themselves from internal treachery, the four deposed Shapes had bound themselves by an oath to stand or fall together.

The points were put upon the i's of the situation by the remark of the Amban's about this time even if ambassadors were sent to meet the British at any point, and even if they succeeded in coming to an agreement, the Tsong-du would refuse to ratify the treaty. Of the four Shapes or Kalons, the monk official Te-kang the Shata Shape and Sho-kang were the more responsible and respectable officers; the last, by name Hor-kang, a man of somewhat weak character, who had been in office but four months, committed suicide almost immediately in terror. Their places were taken by the Ta Lama, as ecclesiastical member, the head of the house of Yutok, the Tsarong Depen and the Tsechung Shape; none of them, with the exception of the Yutok Shape, of any social position or strength of mind.

The Ta Lama, whom we repeatedly met at one time or another, was a gentlemanlike old priest, verging on his second childhood and incapable of keeping his attention fixed on any subject for more than a minute or so at a time. The Yutok Shape was a phlegmatic fatalist who seemed fully aware of the impossibility of doing anything for the country with the scanty authority he possessed. The other two were negligible quantities and were clearly appointed for the sole purpose of allowing a freer hand to the Dalai Lama's personal eccentricities. With this ramshackle government the affairs of Tibet were carried on; every now and then the Amban, who had already received notice of his dismissal, tried, in a weak manner, to settle the matter by a personal appeal to the Grand Lama or the Tsong-du, but the treatment of the Mission at Kamba jong is witness enough to the small importance that was attached to Chinese representations at this period. In December 1903 the Shapes, by instruction of the Dalai Lama, definitely refused transport to the Amban. This, by preventing his approaching Colonel Younghusband, was tantamount to an active refusal to allow China to interfere in any way. It was the last straw; he angrily demanded that their refusal to obey the orders of the Chinese Emperor should be set down in writing. It was probably somewhat to his surprise the Dalai Lama instantly acquiesced and assumed full responsibility for the action. Tibet had decided to act as an independent kingdom, and as soon as the gauntlet had been thrown down, troops were moved out from Lhasa along the southern road to Phari. Yu-kang then rather weakly offered to pay his own transport expenses, but this was as steadily refused as before. For sometime now the Amban had been unable to obtain an answer from the Dalai Lama even to questions wholly unconnected with the dispute with ourselves; from this moment he was an insignificant and ultimately a disgraced man.

The arrival of the new Amban, Yu-tai, was about the time announced from Chyando, and Yu-kang made his preparations to return. His degradation was no loss to us. He had been acting upon the confidential orders of Yung-lu for many years and undoubtedly supported the Tibetans in their refusal to negotiate with the English, relying upon assurances received from Yung-lu that Lhasa would be occupied by Russian troops in the spring of 1903. This corroborates Dorjieff's boast, and our minister in Peking obtained from Prince Ching an admission that he had heard the report. Nor when pressed did the Russian minister in Peking deny that there was a certain *rapprochment* 'on religious grounds'; but Yung-lu's death shortly afterwards and the first rumblings of the Japanese war cloud effectually held the hand of Russia. The Dalai Lama therefore found himself in the position of having paved the way for advances on Russia's part from which nothing was to be expected, while from our side he could only await that demand for satisfaction and a clearer understanding which he had himself deliberately provoked.

By this time even the pious citizens of Lhasa were grumbling against their divine ruler. They whispered that the Potala Lama, as he is not infrequently called in Lhasa, after having murdered the regent the Tibet and imprisoned the Shapes, was about to consummate his folly by losing the country itself as well. The wildest confusion prevailed in official circles; no man trusted his nearest friend; the Amban, trying perhaps to retrieve his credit at the last moment, appears now and then in a whirl of fussy and impotent ill temper, making demand that his master must be obeyed that transport must be provided for him, that the La-chung men must be released at once. No one paid him the slightest attention, and at last he seems to have subsided upon receipt of an unpleasant communication from Peking, intimating that his punishment would be decided upon after he had returned; and this is the end of Yu-kang.

Meanwhile the new Amban was slowly making his progress towards Lhasa. He had started in November, 1902, and fifteen months seems an inordinate time for even a Chinese official to take in covering the distance which separates Lhasa from Peking. He had asked for an escort of 2,000 men to accompany him, but as a matter of fact he found it difficult to provide for the needs of the bare hundred whom he was allowed to take. He had been selected for the post because he was the brother of Sheng-tai who had concluded the unfortunate treaty of 1890, and it was regarded as only fitting and just by the Oriental mind that the harm done by one member of a family should be rectified by another. On his way he met Mr. E. Nicholls, an American, at Ta-chien-lu, the frontier city, where he seems to have spent sometime in extracting money from the Chinese prefect and the Tibetan "gyalpo" alike. He seems to have asserted his intention of restoring Chinese authority, and he admitted no sympathy with the Tibetan desire for seclusion, arguing that it Sze-chaun was open to foreigners there could be no reason why the pretensions of the Tibetans should be permitted for a moment. He moved on to Batang for the same dubious purposes that had detained him at Ta-chien-lu.

On the 12th of February, the belated official reached Lhasa and assumed the reins of government. Later in the same month Dorjieff's influence began to wane. The intrigues with Russia had been overdone and were the common talk of the town. It was known and widely resented that the Dalai Lama had sent back to St. Ptersburg a Buriat who had come to Dorjieff, bringing with him a large sum of money. Moreover, the new Amban, whatever his moral deficiencies, had at least some energy at first. He tried to carry things with a high hand, and one of his first action was severely to censure the inaction of a Chinese representative, who had been ordered south to confer with Younghusband; he seems also to have given our Kamba jong acquaintance, Ho, a bad quarter of an hour on the ground that he had misappropriated Government money. A week after his arrival he made an official visit to the Dalai Lama, and for three hours attempted to bring him to reason; it was not, however, of much use, and on his return to the Residency the Amban set himself to the re-organisation and reform of the military arrangements in Tibet so far as the Chinese soldiery was concerned. On one point at least he failed as completely as his predecessor; he, too, first requested and finally demanded that he should be allowed transport to go to Tuna to meet

Younghusband, or Yun-hai-phun, as they transliterated the name. This the Dalai Lama courteously but firmly refused. At a subsequent visit the Amban seems to have moderated his tone, but to no effect; the Dalai Lama again cheerfully accepted the responsibility for every obstacle that was placed in the way of the Amban's intended journey, and refused to permit the strengthening of the Chinese garrisons at the frontier and in Lhasa. The mood of the Tibetans at this period was anything but conciliatory. The Tongsa Penlop, who had written offering his services as mediator once again, was told that only after a retreat to Yatung and payment of damages for our trespass at Phari would the question of negotiation be opened.

But the display of temper was not confirmed to officials. About this time levies from the province of Kams were called up, but they refused to come, alleging that no proper rations had been served out to them; a promise of proper supplies (which, by the way, was never performed) induced them to send about a thousand men for the defence of Lhasa, but in other parts of the country the demands of the Dalai Lama were met with a blank refusal. Upon the top of this came the news of the disaster at Guru and of our occupation of Gyantse jong. The discontent redoubled. Dorjieff felt that, now or never, the time was come for action if he wished to save his life. He seems to have argued to himself that if a successful attack could be made upon the small British garrison at Chang-lo, time would be gained and his policy justified, for the moment at least. On the other hand, if such an attack were unsuccessful his own liberty and even his own life would be in danger; he therefore planned and ordered the attack on the Mission post on May 5th, and straightway fled the country, posting north along the Sining highway, and ultimately branching off along the Urga road.

About this time the Tsarong Depen asked that troops should be sent to Nagartse to oppose the advance of the British troops. He especially objected. It is said, to the English habit of taking photographs. The Pro Penlop in Bhutan was stealthily approached by the Dalai Lama, at the same time with the object of inducing the Bhutanese, in the absence of the Tongsa Penlop, to destroy the British lines of communication, and a second messenger was sent in haste to Russia as the former envoy had not returned.

High officials now began to talk among themselves almost without concealment of the foolishness of the Dalai Lama, but no one dared to say much to him. The news that Russia was getting the worst of it in Korea had reached Tibet. A report of the fight on the Karo la was received with consternation in Lhasa, but the Grand Lama merely observed that it was time to send forward the Golden Army and, if necessary, all the male inhabitants of Lhasa also. The rumour that Gyantse jong had been retaken and the British garrison there exterminated to a man helped to restore public confidence a little, and about the same time a letter of sympathy came from Bhutan causing disproportionate satisfaction. It is significant that the Chinese Amban refused to believe in the killing of even a couple of Chinese at Dzara during the Karo la fight, pointing out that the England had not killed one of his countrymen throughout the expedition, and bluntly declaring his belief that these two had been assassinated there by Tibetans.

Such, then, was the position until the middle of July, when the Dalai Lama heard that Gyantse jong had been again recaptured and that the English were on the point of starting for Lhasa. He lost no time. Disguised in the plain dirty crimson of a common monk the mortal body of Tubdan Gyatso fled away from his ancient residence and hallowed cathedral in Lhasa, carrying within him the incarnate soul of Avalokiteswara. He set his golden feet along the Nakchu-ka road and never looked back till he was eight days journey from the capital. With him went the Chief Magician, he who many years ago had helped to place Tubdan upon the throne, and in later years had foretold only too truly that the "year of the wood dragon" (i.e., 1904) would spell disaster for Tibet. These two men at the present moment are at Urga, where a religious jehad is being organised, and it is quite clear that no finality in our relations with Tibet can be secured until they are persuaded of the foolishness of opposing the rights of India, or until, as is far more likely, they have been quietly put out of the way by the hierarchs whose ancient regime they have so rudely offended.

As to the negotiations which we had so far vainly endeavoured to begin, it should be remembered that the terms which Colonel Younghusband was instructed to demand from the Tibetans were in themselves neither burdensome nor indeed as heavy as we had a right to demand. Briefly stated, they included a demand that the frontier should be rectified, that an indemnity should be paid of an amount and in a manner to be subsequently decided, that foreign political influence should be totally excluded from Tibet and that no concessions for mines, railways on telegraphs should be granted without the knowledge and the assent of the Indian Government. Trade markets were to be established at Gyantse and Gartok, a place far on the road from Shigatse to Leh, and another clause permitted trade from India to pass freely along any existing highway of commerce. A Resident in Gyantse was to be appointed, but no representative of British interests, political or commercial, was to be posted at Lhasa. As a guarantee for the payment of the indemnity the Chumbi Valley was to be occupied by the British. The suzerainty of the Chinese was frankly recognised throughout the document, and it need hardly be said that Russia was not referred to. Colonel Younghusband had frankly expressed his opinion that it would be cheaper and more effectual in the long run to have a Resident in Lhasa and if the Government had not committed themselves to an opposite policy by their promises to Russia it is possible that this suggestion, which, to some extent commended itself to Lord Curzon also, might have been adopted. We shall see later the actual course of negotiations and the form which this treaty eventually assumed. For the moment it is only necessary to remember that Lord Curzon's absence from India on leave from the end of April to the beginning of December, placed him somewhat at a disadvantage. He has, however, in the fullest manner, acknowledged his indebtedness to Lord Ampthill, Governor of Madras and acting Viceroy of India during Lord Curzon's furlough, for the steady way in which the policy, which had been begun and shaped by himself, was consistently pressed forward by his successor. The latter, who was thus in office during the actual advance to Lhasa and the signing of the treaty, is a man of capacity far beyond his years. Difficult as his opinion was—and the difficulty was added to by the ultimate uncertainty prevailing as to the length of his tenure of office—it was universally recognised that he had dealt with a new and increasingly difficult situation with firmness and restraint, and the Home Government regarded themselves as under a deep obligation to him.

One advantage of the sending of the expedition has been, as Lord Curzon is probably very well aware, that public attention has now been definitely drawn to a matter which had been allowed to be shelved almost too long. However, much some of the less responsible members of the Opposition in England may regret it, it cannot again seriously be contended by them that our position on the northern frontier of India was this time safe. I have referred to the warnings that reached Lord Curzon of the gradual insinuation of Russian influence at Lhasa, and the expedition proved conclusively that those rumours considerably underestimated the importance of the occasion. There is no reason in the world why Russia should not obtain a predominating influence in Lhasa except the plain one that it is incompatible with our own clearly recognised interests. If such a consideration is held not to have justified the sending of the Mission, there is little more to be said, but to those who recognise the importance of safeguarding our Indian frontiers without possibility of mistake, a few more considerations as to the policy to be observed in the future with regard to Tibet may here be offered.

To begin with, we have discovered for the first time the true nature of southern Tibet. It is far from resembling the dreary waterless deserts of the north, so well-described by Sven Hedin and others, and it must also be admitted that it in no way substantiates the impression left upon the mind by the reports sent in by the secret surveyors. Apart from the fact that the native of India has no eye for the beauties of nature, and would as soon make a day's journey across a desert as a park, it must be remembered that the very manner in which these invaluable men were obliged to carry out their work precluded the possibility of much observation. To go on walking from day to day, intent only upon counting every footfall and faithfully registering the hundreds and the thousands upon a Tibetan rosary, naturally debars a traveller from such observations as would have suggested to the Indian authorities both the stored up and the potential wealth of the great alluvial river-flats of southern Tibet.

I do not know that there are many feats in the world of adventure, endurance and pluck that will compare favourably with that of the Indian native entrusted with the work of secret exploration in Tibet. In the first place it must be remembered that to secure the brains necessary for the work a class of native has to be employed which, by tradition at least, is not the pluckiest in the peninsula. The wonder therefore is doubled when one remembers the splendid work of such men as Krishna (better known as A.K.) or Kuntup (K.P.), for the moral courage needed to persist in an enterprise like this can hardly be overestimated. The men employed are of necessity entirely without companions and without resources; they are engaged upon one of the most hazardous occupations that remain in the world, that of a spy in a barbarous country, and should they fail for one minute in all those months and years of exile, they know that no mercy will be extended to them; and I think it but fair to add that not one of the them would in any emergency betray the Government whose servant he is. There is known case of a man who actually consented to be betrayed by his colleague as a spy in order that one at least of the two might be able to escape and bring back to India the priceless notes and calculations collected during a year of travel. For three years Kintup was sold into slavery and endured it without complaining.

But this is not all; a life of exploration, apart from the dangers and hardships of it, is one of unremitting toil; the mere physical endurance needed to travel in this brain-benumbing way, counting each step, hardly daring to raise the eyes from the track at one's feet lest a number should be missed, or lest suspicion should be aroused, is incredible. One man measured the length of the Ling-kor, the road round Lhasa, by counting the prostrations necessary, afterwards solemnly repeating the whole process over a measured mile. Another man is known to have travelled 2,500 miles, counting every footstep over mountain ranges. Atma Ram did the same thing in one of Captain Bower's expeditions for a distance of 2,080 miles. Nain Singh counted his steps from Leh to Assam—look at it on the map. When the story of Asian exploration is finally and worthily written, the work of these lonely spies, twirling incessantly within their wheels rolls of blank paper instead of prayers which are laboriously and minutely filled up night after night with the day's observation, must receive a place of honour second to none. Hurree Chunder Mookerjee in "Kim" is a character, drawn, I believe, immediately from the record of Krishna's work.

To return to the question of protecting the northern frontier of India. It seems a fair estimate that, so far as supplies are concerned, a force of a hundred thousand men could without difficulty rely upon the produce of the luxuriant valleys of the Tsang-po and the Nyang chu. It was no friend of England's who remarked that the natural frontiers of India were less the Himalayas than the impenetrable deserts which lie a hundred miles north of Lhasa, and it is a serious consideration for us that if Russia's influence should ever predominate in Lhasa, the actual ground to be fought for, diplomatically or otherwise, is that which lies across the barrier formed by the Himalayas. The advanced base, whether of the defending or of the encroaching force, must lie in these valleys. If the fertile fields of southern Tibet cannot enter into the calculations of an invading nation, that nation will have to rely upon the trans-Siberian railway as its base, and I need hardly say that this is tantamount to ridiculing the whole danger of invasion through Tibet. Such, baldly stated, is the situation.

To secure immediate access to this glacis of granaries is the obvious policy for the British Government to pursue, and it cannot be said too insistently that the recognition of this necessity in no way whatever involves interference with the internal affairs of Tibet. As to a protectorate, the very idea of undertaking responsibility for an additional eighteen hundred miles of frontier is ridiculous. This, however, is a different matter. To secure the advantage there is little constructive work needed. An alternative route to the prohibitive hardships of the Natu la is now being surveyed along the valleys of the Di chu and the Ammo chu. It is proposed to push rail-head from some point on the line in the neighbourhood of Dam dim as far up the lower slopes of the Himalayas as is feasible without a rack, and then to construct a cart road, with an easy gradient, along the valley to the head waters of the Di chu, crossing into Bhutanese territory near Jong-sa, and at a height of 9,000 ft., overpassing at its lowest point the great mountain wall which here hems in the right bank of the Ammo chu. From this height there is almost a level run into Rinchengong. Once in the Chumbi Valley the difficulties of a second expedition will have been largely overcome, for even as these volumes are published the road from Rinchen-gong to Kamparab is receiving the last touches from the engineers who have worked on it so long. From Kamparab there is a level natural road which has been steadily used throughout the present expedition for wheeled traffic as far as Kang-ma. The road is practicable for carts for a few miles further still, and the construction of the road I have mentioned over the Jongsa la would enable stores, unloaded at rail-head, to be carried, without bulk broken, on wheeled carts to within thirty miles of Gyantse itself. It is hardly necessary to comment upon this. We have, I repeat, no wish in the world to interfere with Tibet so long as Tibet does not imperil our tranquillity in Bengal. While we ourselves seek no exclusive rights in the country, we have at the same time no intention of allowing any other power to secure them. So long as the Tibetans cordially co-operate with ourselves in excluding foreign political influence, so long will we assist them to the best of our power by doubling the existing barriers along the common frontier. But it must be patent to the shallowest that the simple laying of this road will in future put us in a position to insist, should our friendliness be insufficient to win the loyalty and good faith of the hierarchy of Lhasa. It is but bare justice to credit Captain O'Connor with the original suggestion of its construction in any practicable form.

Inseparable from this cart road is the

question of trade. Elsewhere I have referred to the staple products of the country. On our side it seems clear that tea is beyond all competition the chief export from India which the Tibetans would buy profusely and with gratitude should the opportunity be fairly presented to them. But a curious and unfortunately not an extraordinary thing is the unwillingness of the Darjeeling tea planters to recognise the real necessities of the case. They are ready to supply their ordinary tea in its ordinary form to any extent, but they seem quite unwilling to manufacture the tea in that shape in which alone the Tibetans recognise the article. I believe that after some pressure the institute of planters in the Darjeeling district have sent two men to the Chinese tea fields to learn the method of making bricks of tea, such as the Tibetans require, but it seems strange that it should have required an expedition to teach them such an obvious act of commercial prudence.

This, then, is in brief the truth about our future relations with Tibet, and in whatever terms the treaty now signed may eventually be ratified the fact remains unalterable, that by the simple construction of a road the northern frontier of India can now be safeguarded at an expense which is ridiculously small in comparison with the millions lavished on the north-west, and one which by sheer encouragement of trade will be recouped within ten years. Roads are the great pioneers of peace, and those who know their north-west frontier best will be the first to admit the almost instant results of their construction even in the most hostile districts. But the matter may safely by left in the hands of Lord Curzon.

[From *Lhasa—An Account of the Country......in the Year* 1903-4.]

9

A Visit to the Tashi Lama

By
CHARLES BELL

IN THE autumn of 1904 Captain O'Connor visited Shigatse from Gyantse and made the acquaintance of the Tashi Lama, thus renewing in person the friendship which had been interrupted since the time of Warren Hastings, more than a hundred years before. In the winter of 1905 the Tashi Lama, with the Tongsa Penlop of Bhutan and the Maharaja of Sikkim, came to India. He was received by the Prince of Wales, witnessed a review of 70,000 troops at Rawal Pindi, and visited the sacred places of Buddhism.

Mr. White went to England for four months in September 1906, and I was then recalled from my Indian district to take up his work during his absence. This now included Tibet and Bhutan in addition to Sikkim.

The Tashi Lama sent me a warm invitation to visit him at his seat at Tashi-Ihunpo, and the Indian Government permitted me to accept this. Mr. Dover, the State Engineer in Sikkim, accompanied me. Shigatse, the second town in Tibet, is situated only half a mile from Tashi-Ihunpo, a monastery containing four thousand monks. Our way from Gyantse lay down the broad valley of the Nyang Chu past the Dong-tse monastery, where a high Incarnate Lama was done to death, in the old unfriendly days, for sheltering Sarat Chandra Das; then past Nor-bu Kyung-tse and other prosperous villages till we came to the valley of the Tasang-po. My welcome at Shigatse was hearty in the extreme. It commenced thirteen miles outside the town with the arrival of high officials bringing silk scarves of welcome. Farther on, officers invited me to a large tent erected by the roadside, where Tibetan tea and other light refreshments were provided. By the time we reached Shigatse our cavalcade was large and picturesque, for in the wonderful clearness of the Tibetan atmosphere the coloured silks and brocades of the Tibetan nobility show to great advantage. I was lodged in the villa belonging to the King of Shigatse, the Tashi Lama's brother. Here further presentations took place. Bags of rice were brought for myself and my servants, barley and peas for my ponies and mules, and scarves of welcome multiplied more and more. A guard of Tibetan police, holding whips with short stocks and long, workmanlike thongs, kept off the curious.

My visit lasted for a week. There is no need to describe it here in detail. The main point is that the Tashi Lama and his people, whose friendship Captain O'Connor had already gained, showed the utmost friendliness to myself as the agent of the Indian Government.

On the day following our arrival I called on His Holiness. Mr. Dover and I were ushered through successive rooms, up dark, steep staircases, worn and slippery from the feet of countless pilgrims. Very impressive was the reception by the enthroned Incarnation of 'The Buddha of Boundless Light' in the dim, pillared hall. After giving our scarves of greeting we were led to seats on his right hand, while his Ministers stood on his left, and farther off priests intoned solemn chants suitable to the occasion.

But though the official calls of greeting and farewell were of interest and showed the friendliness prevailing, my two private calls showed this still more clearly. These took place in a beautiful, secluded pavilion, surrounded with water, and standing in the park of the Lama's country seat on the outskirts of the town. Here no curious ear could listen to what passed between us, and the conversation ranged over many subjects.

The Lama is fond of animals, and has a creditable menagerie in his park. He is interested in most novelties Producing a modern rifle with telescopic slight, he asked me to explain its mechanism. But his interest centred chiefly on the political situation. He had accepted the Indian Government's invitation to visit India, depending on their support if his acceptance should subsequently lead him into trouble. This Chinese were regaining power in Tibet, and he feared their reprisals. Would our Government come to his aid if necessary? I gave him such comforts as my instructions allowed, and it is probable that my visit to Shigatse helped in some degree to preserve him from untoward consequences. He feared also the Tibetan Government at Lhasa. Our Government had fought with Lhasa, but showed friendliness to Tashi-lhunpo, and the enmity of his own Central Government was, therefore, inevitable. The latter suspected that Tashi-lhumpo aimed at soliciting the help of Britain to obtain independence from their rule, and thus to divide and weaken Tibet as a whole.

As regards China, our Government was saved by the subsequent outbreak of the Chinese revolution. As regards Lhasa, the cordial relations with the Central Government, which was afterwards established, enabled me to tender advice in the right quarter, thus helping to prevent reprisals and to promote the unity of Tibet.

Truly the Tashi Lama has a wonderful personality. Somewhat short in stature, with a fair and healthy complexion, the smile with which he regards you is touched with the quiet saintliness of one who prays and works for all mankind, but it is at the same time the smile of a friend who takes a personal and sympathetic interest in your own concerns. It is not surprising that he should be loved by his people. It is good that there is such a man in Tibet; it is good that there are such men in the world.

It would not, however, be correct to assume that, while the Dalai Lama takes a large share in politics, His Holiness of Tashi-lhunpo is entirely engrossed in things spiritual. For he too has his worldly dominion, though it is far smaller than that of the Dalai and is under the Dalai's overlordship. The Tashi Lama has temporal power over three districts, of which Shigatse is not one, for the Central Government see the advantage of having their own officers there to watch events at Tashi-lhunpo. When the occasion seemed to demand it, the Tashi Lama has made diplomatic moves, unknown even to his Chief Minister, by acting through an aide-de-camp or other personal attendant.

Between Lhasa and Tashi-lhunpo, as mentioned above, there is a deep and abiding jealousy, but Tibetans will tell you that the Grand Lamas themselves are untouched by feelings of antagonism, which are kept alive by the subordinates on both sides. In common with most Orientals, Tibetans have indeed the habit of blaming ministers rather than rulers when things go wrong. But it does seem to me also that the rivalry is stronger among the subordinates. The Grand Lamas, being deeply imbued with religion, are able to rise to some extent above feelings of personal jealousy. And the Tashi Lama, with the lesser worldly interests, is able to devote himself almost entirely to his spiritual duties. 'As to my part,' wrote a former Tashi Lama to Warren Hastings a hundred and fifty years ago, 'I am but a religious devotee, and it is the custom of our sect, with the rosary in our hands, to pray for the welfare of all mankind, and for the peace and happiness of the inhabitants of this country.' So it is in the main at this time also. And the Tashi Lama reaps his reward in the love and reverence with which his people regard him. When he came back from India, men as well as women literally wept with joy at his safe return, though the Tibetan does not weep easily.

The monastery of Tashi-lhunpo with its four thousand monks is a town in itself, surrounded by a wall. Built on the slope of a rocky spur, its tall houses rise one above another, facing south across the plain. Through them runs a line of five strong, impressive buildings, each like the other, and surmounted by gilded roofs of Chinese design, which dazzle your eyes in the morning sun. These are the mausolea of the five departed Tashi Lamas, the present Lama being the sixth. While the exteriors of these mausolea are dazzling, their interiors also are surprinsingly beautiful, that of the first Lama being especially fine. Even after the lapse of so many years a vision still remains with me of altars, fully but tastefully equipped with cups of solid gold and silver, of corals, turquoises, and other precious stones, some of these even let into the floor, and behind the altar in each case a pyramid, some twenty-five feet high, adorned with gold, silver, and precious stones. On the top of the pyramid is an effigy of the deceased Lama. Vases of old porcelain and cloisonne complete the picture. No garishness is here, but a beautiful, harmonious design.

A visit to the Tashi Lama's metal factory found only some thirty artisans at work. They were engaged in turning out five hundred images of the god, Tse-pa-me, 'Eternal Life,' the distribution to various monasteries throughout Tibet. Another day I went over the monastery with its printing establishment at Na tang, seven miles out of Shigatse, along the road to Sakya. Thirty-three monks are employed in the printing establishment, which is said to be the largest in Tibet. The letters are carved on heavy rectangular blocks of wood, which are arranged on high racks in the rooms assigned to them, and numbered alphabetically. The printing is done rapidly. Three monks work together, one taking the impressions, another handing the paper, and the third looking after the blocks. The paper is manufactured from the bark of one of the species of *Daphne* plant (*Edgeworthia Gardneri*) and comes mostly from Bhutan. During my visit three copies were being made of the Teng-gyur, the great Commentary on the Lamaist Scriptures. It consists of some two hundred and twenty volumes; the Scriptures themselves, known as the Kang-gyur, being contained in preferably one hundred and eight volumes, though often in about one hundred only. The number one hundred and eight is sacred to Tibetans, and happy is the man who lives to be a hundred and eight years old, attaining the perfection of old age! The memory of a Tibetan friend of mine, who is said to have died at this age, will long be treasured among his descendants and their neighbours.

The Tashi-lhunpo monastery has its own printing place, but it is on a much smaller scale than the one at Na-tang. The other chief printing place is at Der-ge in eastern Tibet. There the blocks are of metal, and the impressions are said to be clearer than those at Na-tang.

The fort at Shigatse is of especial interest, for it is said to have been built by the celebrated king of Tsang, who defeated the last king of Sitya Dynasty in 1635, but was himself subdued a few years later by Gushi Khan, the Mongol, who installed the fifth Dalai Lama on the Tibetan throne. The people of Shigatse claim that the present form of the famous Potala, the

Dalai Lama's Palace at Lhasa, was copied by the Chief Minister of the fifth Dalai Lama from the Shigatse fort. Tradition ascribed the power of this king of Tsang to the fact that his mother was a demon, and many are the stories told of the cleverness and trickery which enabled him, a young groom in the stables, to rise to supreme power in the Tsang province.

It was during this visit to Shigatse that I was introduced to a curious Tibetan custom. Letters from the Tashi Lama would be brought by his servants, who would bring at the same time a verbal message from His Holiness. The letter was invariably the most important part of the communication and frequently modified the terms of the letter. Later on I found this custom to be common among high Tibetan officials. Fear that the letter may be seen by the Chinese or other unfriendly persons has given rise to the practice. Sometimes Europeans travelling in Tibet have been shown letters issued by those in authority to Tibetan officials, enjoining the latter to help the traveller. But difficulties appear and the instructions in the letter do not seem to be obeyed, in the spirit at any rate. The reason is that instructions of a very different nature have been conveyed verbally.

Another way of sending secret messages is to write them on wooden tablets. These are dispatched by a trustworthy servant, who can erase them immediately in the event of danger. The Tibetan tablets consist of five or six thin and narrow strips of wood bound together in an outer cover.

On the 6th November 1906 I paid my farewell call on the Tashi Lama, and at his request went round to see him privately afterwards. He gave me a photograph of himself, coloured by a Tibetan artist. At its foot he wrote his name and titles in golden letters and affixed his seal. As a rule he makes one of his officers write his signature, for he considers his own handwriting to be inferior. A neat handwriting is ranked as a matter of the highest importance in Tibet.

Following night His Holiness, the Ministers and other leading officials, accompanied by two hundred soldiers, fled towards India, taking their seals of office with them. Twelve hours later, at Chak-sam, they reached the Tsangpo, the great river forty miles from Lhasa. On the further side they left the soldiers to hold back the pursuing Chinese soldiery as long as possible. The Tibetans did so, killing a good many of the pursuers, and then dispersed across the country.

Nine days after leaving Lhasa, the Dalai Lama and his following rode into safety across the Sikkim frontier. The distance travelled was two hundred and seventy miles, with three high passes and a broad river to cross. A few days later he arrived in Darjeeling. For the Lama himself and his elder Ministers, accustomed to travel in leisurely luxury, it was a remarkable achievement.

In defence of their proceedings the Chinese Foreign Office pointed out that the Indian Government had blamed them in the past for failing to make the Tibetan Government observe treaty engagements and had in consequence, in 1904, dispatched the Expedition to Lhasa. The Government of China had accordingly sent their troops to secure the observance of treaty obligations, to protect the trade marts, and to maintain peace and order. The Expedition which Lord Curzon and the British Government dispatched and withdrew in 1904 was clearly the cause of the Chinese advance. But it was hard on Tibet, and subsequently disastrous to the Chinese themselves, that the latter should have carried it forward in such a tactless and savage manner. It is curious that one Asiatic race should not know how to treat another, allied to it more or less by the strong ties of race and religion. But the history of all Asia abounds in such instances. Perhaps the explanation, partly at any rate is that Asiatic Governments have not yet learnt and inwardly digested the value of tolerance as an art of Government—of tolerance, that is, in the things that really matter. And thus it has fallen out that the white foreigner has spread over Asia, giving to her people something that they cannot give to each other.

[From *Tibet—Past and Present*, 1924.]

10

A Visit to a Tibetan Country Seat

By

CLEMENTS R. MARKHAM

ON THE 11th of March, 1775, the Pyn Cushos were to set out for their country seat, about two days, journey from Teshu Lumbo, and asked me to accompany them. I was glad of an opportunity of varying the insipid scene, and applied for the Lama's permission, which he readily granted me. We set out about midday. I carried with me only one Hindustani servant, resolving to live like a Tibetan. The Pyn Cushos had about a dozen servants. We arrived towards evening at a village, in the valley through which runs the Tsanpu, and took up our quarters in the head man's house. After drinking tea, dinner was brought in. A cup of hashed mutton, not unlike a greasy curry, another of boiled rice, a third of raw beef beat into a jelly, and highly seasoned with salt, turmeric, and other spices. It is far from unsavoury, when one can get the better of European prejudices. There were also a joint of mutton well boiled, and another just scorched on the outside but raw within. It requires no conjuring to find out on which I made my dinner. There is no such thing as two people cutting from the same joint of meat, or helping themselves from the same plate, so that a separate set of the above dishes was served up to each. After this we had fruits and sweetmeats, and, the Pyn Cushos having lent me a pipe, we sat down to smoke. We then adjourned to a small garden, to shoot arrows. A tent was pitched with a black clot at some distance. Such as hit the bull's eye had a handkerchief given them. I also received one, though unmeritedly. Night came on. We returned and sat down about a goodly fire, new kindled in the middle of the room, spending a couple of hours in singing, drinking *chang*, playing upon the guitar, or at chess. Mr. Hamilton and I then retired to another apartment, where a supper was prepared for us, as if we had not tasted meat that day; but afraid that we would not relish Tibetan victuals, the Pyn Cushos had ordered their servants to ask our people about our usual food, and had prepared some eggs, fish, and roasted fowls.

Next morning we get up before day, and found the Pyn Cushos ready to sit down to breakfast, upon tea and cold mutton. As I can always eat at any hour of the day or night, I did not fail to partake with them. After this we had the ceremony of the master of the house presenting us with fruits, sweetmeats, and carcasses, and having settled all this in due form, we set out on our journey. Having ridden about an hour we reached the bank of the Tsanpu. The boats were all on the other side, and the river covered with shoals of snow-mixed ice. We had to wait here a couple of hours. There was a tent with tea prepared for us, and I spent part of the time in sliding on the ice, with which a neighbouring pool of water was covered. As soon as we were ferried over, we mounted our horses and rode cheerily up the sandy bank of the Tsanpu, stopping twice at tents prepared for us, to refresh ourselves with tea and mutton. In the afternoon we came to the foot of a mountain covered with red ochre, and dedicated to some wrathful deity. Here the Pyn Cushos set up the branch of a tree, with a white handkerchief fastened to it. The Tsanpu at this place forms a large sheet of water immediately below the road. You have a view of its winding for a great way up and down, and the prospect would be very fine if there was anything besides bleak bare hills to look at. The winds in this valley are very strong, often carrying up the dust in columns to a great height, or forming it into hills of sand. Turning to the right we entered the valley where the Pyn Cushos' estate is situated, and stopped at some tents set up by a servant of Gesub Rimboche, who has the care of a house belonging to that minister. Among the rest of our entertainment were excellent mutton puffs, a dish which I had not before seen. Ascending the valley we arrived at Rinjaitzay Castle about an hour after it was dark, having, by our stopping and tea drinkings, taken a complete day to perform a journey which might easily be done in six hours.

I was lodged in the room of the church, which is generally the best in the house. As the Pyn Cushos, particularly the youngest, are keen sportsmen, it was hung round with matchlocks, bows and arrows, swords, shot-bags, etc., and one part of the wall was covered with Chinese paper-hangings. After presenting me with loads of fruit, they brought in supper, which made the sixth time that I had seen meat that day.

During the five or six days we spent at Rinjaitzay, the Pyn Cushos entertained us in the most hospitable manner, omitting nothing that could contribute to our amusement. They made parties on horseback, shooting matches with bows and matchlocks; they caught and bagged hares, for us to see them retaken by the greyhounds; partridges and other game for us to eat, and one day we went out with the nets to catch musk goats. This requires a more particular description.

After riding about three miles from Rinjaitzay, we stopped at a tent and sat there two hours while the servants went up the hills to reconnoiter. I confess I did not much conceit this method of hunting in a tent, and formed no favourable presage of our sport. At length I prevailed on the younger brother to set out, and letting loose the dogs we rode along the sides of the hills, but without seeing anything except a covey of partridges; and although the Pyn Cushos make no bones of shooting when by themselves, they were afraid that some of the Lama's people who accompanied me might mention it at Teshu Lumbo, and so get them into a scrape.

At length, when we were about to return, one of the servants came with the news of having found a musk goat asleep in a quarry. The dogs were immediately tied up. The people with the toils went along the side of the mountain, and above the place where the game lay, while we followed slowly after. The toils are made of cords, formed into a number of nooses hung close to one another, on a rope which is extended at about three feet from the ground, and supported by rods stuck in the earth at intervals of about ten or twelve feet. There is another row of nooses similar to this placed parallel to it, and at the distance of about five feet. When these double toils were set all round one side of the quarry, and at about a gunshot from it, we spread ourselves encircled the other side, and with shouts and stones at length awakened the musk from his profound sleep. As soon as he got upon the brow of the hill, he boundingly made towards the toils, and having twice attempted to leap over them, thrust his head into one of the nooses. When we came up to him he was quite breathless with struggling, and all the skin, which is very tender, was torn off his neck with the cord. We carried him home and put him into a closet adjoining to my room; but he died before morning.

The musk is about the size of an antelope, but without any horns. The bag of perfume for which it is famous is produced only in the male, who is also of a colour more dark than the female, and distinguished by two tusks which fall perpendicularly from his upper jaw. The hair is speckled yellow and brown at the point, and resembles the fledges of a quill almost as much as hair. It has an amazing strong attractive quality, like amber, and sticks to your fingers so that it is difficult to shake it off. The skins of the musks which I have seen in the Deb Rajah's country are much darker than those in Tibet; they approach almost to black. The common way of killing the musk is by matchlocks and bows and arrows. It is sadly persecuted by the peasants about the beginning of winter, and numbers of them seek protection on the privileged mountains behind Teshu Lumbo.

The partridges are considerably smaller than those in England. Regarding their taste I cannot say anything, for the cook allowed three, which Mr. Hamilton one day shot, to fly away some hours after they were dead; and those which the Pyn Cushos now caught for me were so tame, it would have been a sin to kill them; so I set them at liberty, which was considered by the Lama's servants to be a very pious action. As to the Pyn Cushos, they are little scrupulous about this or any venial sin, and, as long as it comes not to the knowledge of the Lama, will do anything you like.

The Pyn Cushos keep a large parcel of all kinds of dogs at Rinjaitzay, and some of them, particularly Shamo, are great favourites. There is also a wolf chained at their foot of the stair, a tiger cat fastened to a stone on the leads, besides other animals.

After supper everyone retired to his room and went to bed, thinking no evil. But about the middle of the night we were alarmed with a dreadful barking and howling among the dogs, which soon brought all the family together upon the leads; Mr. Hamilton and I in our shirts, the rest with only a blanket wrapped round them, it being the custom for the Tibetans, both men and women, to sleep naked. There was no light but starlight; the noises still continued. Some said it was thieves; but as I could not think anybody would be so wicked as attempt to rob the Lama's family, I had nothing for it but to conclude it was the devil. In the meantime a most extraordinary yelling began just under our nose, which being totally different from anything I had ever heard, would certainly have served to confirm my notion, had not the whole family, to my utter astonishment, burst out into a fit of laughing; and, Paima having managed to light a lamp with his tinder-box, we had the satisfaction to see Mr. Wolf, whose breaking loose had occasioned all this disturbance, pinned down by the tiger cat, with her claws fixed in his cheeks. And so, having remanded him into confinement, each of our motley group, after looking a little at one another, returned laughing to bed.

Early in the morning we took leave of our hosts, set out from Rinjaitzay, and reached Teshu Lumbo at night, by excusing myself from stopping to drink tea at various places, and pushing through a great whirlwind of dust towards the end of our journey. At night the palace and all the town were illuminated, in honour of the last Teshu Lama. It is reckoned very unlucky if the lamps should be blown out, and yet they were blown out upon this occasion. However, the sons of men can easily find salvos for anything. A few extraordinary prayers, or one or two solemnities, avert the evil.

In the morning my friend Debo Dinji Sampu came to see me. He looked more thoughtful than usual; and after we had drank dish of tea and exchanged a pinch of snuff, he told me the cause of it—that he was appointed Governor of Janglache, a castle of some consequence, about three days higher up the Tsanpu. I congratulated him on his good fortune; but it would not do. He said to me: "I know that many people would solicit this office, the obtaining of which gives me so much uneasiness; but I have from my youth continued with the Lama. I have never been employed on any public business; I am not used to writing, and have had no practice in accounts. I shall have a vast deal to do in my new employment; I know not well how to set about it, and am afraid of getting into a scrape." As the Christian virtue of humble mindedness is so rare, I could not help being pleased to meet with it in a Pagan. What I said to encourage Debo Dinji produced, as often happens, no effect; and he wanted me to apply to the Lama that he might accompany me, at least to Tassisudon; but he would not allow me to mention it as his desire, and I could not do it else. Soon after he set out for his government, having first taken leave of me, and presented me with some purses of gold dust and a white handkerchief at parting. I felt not the same heart's liking for the priest who succeeded to the honour of bringing me rice and tea in the morning, as I had for Debo Dinji. He afterwards was sent by the Lama to attend me to Tassisudon, and fell a sacrifice to a strange climate.

Some Chinese merchants came to Teshu Lumbo to buy lamb skins, and a Kashmiri brought one of them to see me. From his manners I thought he must be a little man. His cap was faced with black lamb skins; but as I understood the Lama did not wish me to have any connection with him, I sent him away. I did not find him near so white as I expected.

I was invited to pass the afternoon at the Sopon Chumbo's where I was treated with all the things I have so often repeated, set off with the most easy and entertaining conversation. The manners of the Tibetans are in general very engaging; but Sopon Chumbo, by travelling through Tatary and China, and by a long residence at the Court of Peking, has improved upon them.

I now seldom stirred out of my room, being employed from morning to night in translating some papers which the Lama gave me about Tibet.

The severity of the winter was now passed; the ice melted faster than it froze; the weather in the heat of the day was very comfortable, and I began to turn my views towards Bengal.

The Teshu-tzay Killadar's family had left us, and Durjay Paumo had set out for her convent. The Pyn Cushos were returned to Teshu Lumbo, but it was only to escort their mother and sisters to Teshu-tzay. I this day took leave of Chum Cusho and the two nuns, not without many blessings and much advice from the old woman, and many promises to the nuns of writing to them and sending them lories and looking glasses. My parting with the Pyn Cushos was a harder task. I never could reconcile myself to the thoughts of a last farewell, and however anxious I was to return to Bengal and to the world, I could not take leave of my Tibetan friends with indifference, and would not find little satisfaction in repeating the circumstances of it.

The last days of my stay at Teshu Lumbo were taken up with these ceremonies; all my acquaintance in the palace coming to me with pots of tea, little presents, kind looks, and kind expressions.

[From *Narratives of the Mission of George Bogle to Tibet and of the Journey of Thomas Manning to Lhasa,* 1879.]

11

Residence at Lhasa

By
SARAT CHANDRA DAS

PRECEDED by Pador carrying his long lance and by Tsing-ta driving the pack-pony, we entered the city. The policemen (*korchagpa*) marked us as new-comers, but none of them questioned us. My head drooped with fatigue, my eyes were hidden by dark goggles, and the red pagri around my head made me look like a Ladaki. Some people standing in front of a Chinese pastry shop said, as I passed, "Look! there comes another sick man; small-pox has affected his eyes. The city is full of them. What an awful time for Tibet!"

After a few minutes' ride we came to the Yu-tog zamba, a short stone bridge with a gate, where a guard commanded by a lama is stationed, which examines all passers-by to ascertain the object of their visit to the city. To the great delight of my companions, who had been most anxious about my getting over the bridge, we passed by without a question being asked us.

Near the bridge I noticed the *doring*, a monolith on which is an inscription in Tibetan and Chinese. Though a thousand years old, the stone has been but little affected by the weather, and the characters can be easily read. The monolith I took to be between eight and ten feet in height, and it stands on a low pedestal.

At the Yu-tog zamba the city proper begins. The street on both sides was lined with native and Chinese shops; in front of each was a pyramidal structure, where juniper spines and dried leaves obtained from Tsari are burnt as an offering to the gods.

Coming to the street of the south of Kyil-khording, we found on either side of it Nepalese shops several stories high, also Chinee ones, where silk fabric, porcelain, and various kinds of brick-tea were exposed for sale.

A lama guided us from this street to the Bangye-shag, a castle-like building three stories high, the residence of Sawang Phala, the husband of my protectress, the Lhacham. Leaving me at the postern gate, my two companions went in and presented the lady with a *khatag*, and she directed them to take me to Paljor rabtan, a building belonging to the Tashi Lama, where all officers and monks from Tashilhunpo find lodgings when in Lhasa, and where we would be given accommodations.

The gateway of Paljor rabtan was about eight or nine feet high and five feet broad, and from the lintels fluttered fringes about a foot and a half broad. Two stout flag-poles 20 to 25 feet high, carrying inscribed banners stood on either side of it. Ascending a steep staircase, or rather a ladder, we came to a verandah, opposite which was a pretty glazed house, the dwelling of the *khang-uyer* (or "housekeeper") and were soon given by him a room to lodge in; and served with tea and *chang* by an old woman. From the window of our room we could see the *damra*, or grove of poplars and willows in a marshy bit of land adjacent to the Tangyeling monastery, and further west shone the lofty gilt spires of Potala.

May 31—The heavy shower which had fallen last evening cleared up the atmosphere, and the gilt domes and spires glittering in the morning sun filled me with delight, and I had difficulty in subduing my impatience to visit all the monuments now before me, and of which I had dreamed of for so many years. At 7 o'clock Pador brought me a port of tea prepared in the house of the water-carrier; but, instead of butter, tallow had been used in its preparation, and I could not swallow it; but we managed, after a while, to make some in our own room. shortly after Tsing-ta came in, bringing a pair of rugs, two cushions, and two little tables he had borrowed at the Bangyeshag. He had also an invitation from the Lhacham to visit her in the afternoon.

Having shaved and donned my lama costumes and goggles, we started for Bangyeshag, which was about a mile from our lodgings. Most of the shops we saw were kept by Kahsmiris, Nepalese, or Chinese; the Tibetan ones were few and poorly supplied.

Bangyeshag is a lofty, flat-roofed stone building with two large gateways. The ground floor is used as storerooms and quarters for the *amlas* as retainers of the Phala estates. The beams, the cornices, as also the window-frames, are painted red; a few of the windows have a little pane of glass in them, but most of them are covered with paper. On reaching the second floor, the Lhacham's maids (*shetama*) greeted me most kindly, and insisted on my taking a cup or two of tea, after which they led me to her ladyship's room, where, taking off my hat, I presented her a visiting scarf (*jadar*) and a piece of gold of about a *dzo* weight. Making motion to one of her maids to present me a scarf, she kindly wished me welcome (*"Chyagpeb nang chig, Pundib la"*), and bade me take a seat (*"Pundib la, shu dang shag, shu, dang shag"*). After conversing with her a while about my recent illness, and telling her of the kindness of the Dorje Phagmo, that merciful Lady of the Lake to whom I owe my life, I took my leave and returned home.

June 1—June 1 is the holiest day of the year, *saga dawa*, the day of the Buddha's *nirvana*, and incense was burnt on every hilltop, in every shrine, chapel, lamasery, and house in or near Lhasa. Men, women, and children hastened to the sacred shrine of Dyil-khording (or Jo khang, as it is commonly called), to do *puja* to the Jo-vo ("Lord Buddha") and obtain his blessing. All carried in their hands bundles of incense-sticks, bowls of butter, and *khatag* of all sizes and qualities. Our fellow-lodgers went with the rest, calling at my room on the way out, and in a short time we also joined the crowd.

A broad street runs in front of the Jo khang, and the road which comes from the Pargo kaling gate terminates on its western face, and here grows a tall poplar said to have sprung from the hair of the Buddha. Beside this is the ancient stone tablet erected by the Tibetans in the ninth century to commemorate their victory over the Chinese, and which gives the text of the treaty then concluded between the Emperor of China and King Ralpachan.

The magnificent temple engrossed, however all my attention. In front of it is a tall flag-pole, at the base of which hang two yak-tails, some inscriptions, and a number of yaks and sheep-horns. In the propylon of the chief temple (*Tsang khang*), the heavy wooden pillars of which are three to four feet in circumference, and about twelve feet high, upwards of a hundred monks, were making prostrations before the image of the Lord (*Jo-vo*) on a throne facing the west. This famous image of the Buddha, known as Jo vo rinpoche, is said to have been made in Magadha during the lifetime of the great teacher. Visvakarma is supposed to have made it, under the guidance of the god Indra, of an alloy of the five precious substances, gold, silver, zinc, iron, and copper, and the "five precious celestial substances," probably diamonds, rubies, pais-lazuli, emeralds and *indranila*.

The legend goes on to say that the image was in the first place sent from India to the capital of China in return for the assistance the Emperor had given the King of Magadha against the Yavanas from the west. When the Princess Konjo, daughter of the Emperor Tai-tsung, was given in marriage to the King of Tibet, she brought the image to Lhasa as a portion of her dowry.

The image is life-size and exquisitely modelled, and represents a handsome young prince. The crown on its head is said to be the gift of Tsong-khapa, the great reformer. The Kunyer said that the image represented the Buddha when at the age of twelve; hence the princely apparel in which he is clothed and the dissimilarity of the image to those seen elsewhere. On the four sides of it were gilt pillars with dragons twined around them, supporting a canopy. On one side of the image of the Buddha is that of Maitreya, and on the other that of Dipankara Buddha. Behind this, again, is the image of the Buddha Gang-chan wogyal, and to the right and left of the latter those of the twelve chief disciples of the Buddha.

We were also shown the image of the great reformer, Tsong-khapa, near which is the famous rock, called *Amolonkha,* discovered by Tsong-khapa. On this rock is placed the bell with a gem in the handle, supposed to have been used by Maudgalyayana, the chief disciple of Buddha.

After the image of the Buddha, the most celebrated statue in this temple is that of Avalokiteswara with the eleven faces (Shen-re-sig chu-chig dzal). It is said that once King Srong-btsan gamblo heard a voice saying that if he made a full-sized image of Shenrezig, all his wishes would be granted him; so he constructed this one, in the composition of which there entered a branch of the sacred Bo tree, some soil of an island in the great ocean, some sand from the River Nairanjana, some *gosirsha* sandalwood, some soil from the eight sacred places of India, and many other rare and valuable substances. All these were first powdered, then, having been moistened with the milk of red cow and a goat, made into a paste and moulded into a statue. To give it additional sanctity, the king had a sandalwood image of the god brought from Ceylon put inside of it.

This statue is also known as the "five self-created" (*nya rang chyung*); for the Nepalese sculptor who made it said that it had sprung into shape rather than had been moulded by him, and it is further said that the souls of King Srong-btsan gambo and his consorts were absorbed in it. It occupied the northern chapel in the temple, and is surrounded by the images of a number of gods and goddesses.

In the outer courtyard of the temple is a row of statues, among which is that of King Srong-btsan gambo and various saints and Pundits. On the porch of the Tsang-khang are images of the Buddhas of the past, present and future. Innumerable other highly interesting images and votive offerings were shown us, among which I will mention a hundred and eight lamps made out of stone under Tsong-khapa's directions.

Among the other objects of interest shown us was a stone slab (*Padma pung-pa*) which King Srong-btsan gambo and his wives were wont to use as a seat when taking their baths, and a life-size statue of Tsong-khapa surrounded by images of gods, saints and worthies. In the room where these statues are seen, and which is closed by a wire lattice, is also a famous image of the god Chyag-na dorje (Vaj-rapani). When the iconoclast King Langdarma began persecuting Buddhism, he ordered this image to be destroyed. A valet tied a rope around its neck to drag it from the temple, but he suddenly became insane, and died vomiting blood, and the image was left undisturbed.

In the outer court, or *khyamura*, is the image of the god Tovo Metsig-pa, by whose power the invading armies of China were routed in the war which immediately followed the death of King Srongbtsan gambo. Near it are statues of the king and his two consorts, and some huge yak-horns, of which the following anecdote is told to inquisitive pilgrims by the temple servants (*kunyer*). Ra-chung-pa, a disciple of the great saint Milarapa, had been to India, and had there studied under the most learned masters all the mysteries of the faith, and had returned to Tibet filled with pride over his knowledge. Travelling to Lhasa with his master, they reached the middle of the desert called Palmoi-paltang, when Milarapa, who knew of the conceit of his disciple and wished to teach him a lesson, ordered him to fetch him a pair of yak horns lying near by. But Rachung-pa said to himself, "The master wants everything he sees. Sometimes he is as fretful as an old dog, at other as full as childish fancies as an old man in his dotage. Of what possible use can the horns be to him; he can neither use them for food, drink, nor clothing?" Then he asked the sage what he proposed doing with them. "Though it is not possible to say what may occur," replied Milarapa, "they will certainly be of use sometime or other;" and he picked them up himself and carried them along.

After a while a violent hailstorm overtook the travellers, and there was not so much as a rat-hole in which they could find shelter. Ra-chung-pa covered his head with his gown, and sat on the ground till the storm had passed by. When he searched for the lama, he could see him nowhere; but he heard a voice, and, looking about, lo! there was Milarapa seated inside one of the horns. "If the son is the equal of the father, then," said the saint, "let him seat himself inside the other horn;" but it was too small to even serve Rachung-pa for a hat. Then Milarapa came out of the horn, and Ra-chung-pa carried them to Lhasa, and presented them to the Jo-vo.

After visiting all the ground floor we climbed up to the second and third stories, where we were shown a number of other images, among which I noticed that of Paldan Ihamo. By the time we had seen all the images we had exhausted our supply of butter, for Pador had put a little in every lamp lighted that day in the chapels. Those before the image of the Jo-vo were of gold, and each must have held ten or twelve pounds of butter.

By the time we reached our lodgings I was completely worn out, and passed the rest of the day in my rooms or on the housetop, the view from which always charmed me, especially when the rays of the setting sun shone brightly on the gilded domes of the temples and palaces.

I was much troubled, in my mind by hearing from tsing-ta that small-pox was raging in town, even the keeper of our house, his wife and children, were down with the disease, and in every dwelling in the neighbourhood some one was ill with it.

On the following morning (June 2), after an early breakfast, I went to visit the famous shrine of Ramoche, carrying, as on the previous day, bundle of incense-sticks, some butter and *khatags*. We took a horribly muddy lane, where heaps of filth emitted a most offensive odour; then turning northward, we crossed the Potala road at the north-west corner of the Tomse-gang, as the Kyil-khording square is commonly called, and passed by the lofty Wangdu *chorten*, which was built to bring under the power (*wang*, "power" *du*, "to subjugate") of Tibet all the neighbouring nations. This spot is also called Gya-bum gang, for it is said that once during the Ming dynasty of China 100,000 (*gya-bun*) Chinese troops camped (*gang*) on the plain to the north of this *chorten*. Other accounts explain this name by saying that in the war with China, after the death of King Srongbtsan gambo, 100,000 Chinamen were killed in a battle near this spot.

A few hundred paces beyond this place we reached the gate of Ramoche, the famous temple erected by the illustrious Konjo, daughter of the Emperor Tai-tsung, and wife of King Srong-btsan gambo. It is a flat-roofed edifice three stories high, and has a wide portico. At the front of the building there is to be seen a very ancient inscription in Chinese, giving probably the history of the building of the temple. The image of MiKyod dorje (Vajra Akshobhya), brought here by King Srong-btsan's second wife, a Nepalese princess, is of undoubted antiquity, even though the face of the statue is covered with gilding.

In the northern lobby are heaps of relics—shields, spears, drums, arrows, swords, and trumpets, and in a room to the left of the entrance, and shut in by an iron lattice, are a few very holy images. With the exception of a very small gilt dome built in Chinese style, I saw nothing strongly indicative of that description of architecture, and, taking it all together, Ramoche fell for short of the preconceived idea I had formed of it.

Lay monks, or Serkempa, usually perform the services held at Ramoche, and half a dozen of them and a *kunyer* (sexton) live in the upper stories of the temple.

As we left the temple we were met by a party of singing beggars, who followed us to our house clamouring for *solar*, or alms; finally we sent them off with a *karma*, or the value of two annas. Had we given more we would have been persecuted by numerous other parties of these pests.

June 3—A lama of Khams whom I had met at Tashilhunpo, came to see me to-day. He told me that he was waiting for nine loads of silver from Tshilhunpo, on the arrival of which he would leave for Western China, coming back to Lhasa next March or April. I had heard at Tashilhunpo that he had a caravan of 700 mules, and carried on trade between Darchendo and Lhasa. The Pomda Lama was a man of gigantic stature, something over six feet, well proportioned, and of great strength; he was well-known to brigands, and none dared molest him. My further acquaintance with him confirmed me in the opinion I have formed of the Khambas. Though they are wild, they are devoted friends, and when once one becomes intimate with one of them, he will be faithful to the end.

I heard to-day the following story about the famous Regent Tsomoling and his social reforms: Once there came to Lhasa a lama pilgrim from Tsoni, an Amdo, and he was admitted into the Sera convent, where he studied under a learned Mongol lama. After a few years the Amdo lama's tutor returned to his home, and on parting he left his pupil a couple of earthen pots, a *khatag*, and a bag of barley, the most valuable things he possessed, as he told him. The pupil, disappointed with these gifts, carried the pots to the market and sold them for half a *tanka*, with which he bought butter that he put in the lamps burning before the great image of the lord (Jo-vo), praying that if he ever became Regent of Tibet, he might be after to reform the social customs of the country.

In the course of time he rose to the dignity of a teacher in his convent; then he became its abbot, or *khanpo*; and finally he rose to the rank of regent. One of the first acts of his administration was to expel all public women from Lhasa, and to compel all women to cover their faces with a coating of catechu, so as to hide their comeliness from the public view. Women were also made to wear a bangle cut out of a conch-shell on their right wrist, by which they could be held when arrested. From his time also dates the use by women or aprons (*pang-den*) and of the present style of headdress, or *patug*. The old style of *patug* is now only worn by the wives (or Lhachma) of the Shape (ministers). He was the first of the Tsomoling lamas, and his reincarnations still inhabit the lamasery of that name behind Ramoche.

One June 4 I again visited the Jo khang. After paying reverence to the Jo-vo and circumambulating his sacred throne, the *kunyer* poured some holy water (*tu*) into my hand from a golden vessel. In a little *chorten* in one of the chapels on the south side of the temple is kept a statue of red bell-metal, or *li-mar* made so says tradition, in the days of King Kriki, when men lived 20,000 years. For many centuries it was kept by the kings of Nepal; but when a princess from that country married King Srong-btsan gambo, she brought it to Tibet, and placed it in this temple, where it is the object of constant worship.

But perhaps the most revered of all the images in the Jo Khang, exclusive of that of the Jo, is that of Paldan Ihamo (Srimati devi). The terrifying face of the goddess is kept veiled, but the *kunyer* uncovered it for us. This terrific goddess is regarded as the guardian of the Dalai and Tashi lamas. The chestnut-coloured mule she rides, the offspring of a red ass and a winged mare, was given her by the goddess of the sea. The saddle she sits on is the skin of an ogre, and the bridle and crupper are vipers. Kya dorje gave her dice with which to play for lives, and the ogres, or Srinpo, presented her a string of skulls, which she holds in her left hand, and the goblins that haunt graveyards gave her corpses, on which she feeds. In her right hand she holds a club given her by the god Chyagna-dorje. Twas in such fearful attire that she waged war against the foes of Buddhism, and became the greatest of all its guardian deities.

The chapel of Paldan Ihamo in overrun by mice, so tame that they crawled up the *kunyer's* body. They are supposed to have been lamas in former existences. On one of the walls we saw a painting made with the blood of King Srong-btsan.

As we were walking home I saw some men hawking books, and told them what works I would buy it they could but procure them for me. They promised to bring them to me shortly.

The excellent brick-tea (*du tang-nyipa*) which I had brought from Tashilhunpo was now exhausted, and I was reduced to drinking a miserable quality known as *qua-pa. Du tang*, or first-quality tea, is more highly flavoured than the quality I liked, but it was too strong for me.

Tea was introduced into Tibet earlier than the tenth century, but it only became of universal use from the time of the Sakya hierarchy and the Phagmodu kings. During the early part of the Dalai Lama's rule the tea trade was a government monopoly, and since the beginning of the present century, though nominally open to every one, the trade is practically in the hands of the officials.

Some notes on the mode of selection of incarnate lamas may not be out of place here. It used to be customary when selecting incarnate lamas to either decide by throwing dice or by some other trial of luck, or by taking the opinion of the College of Cardinals; but that method not giving perfect satisfaction, it was decided that the candidates should undergo certain examinations, which, together with the hints thrown out from time to time by the defunct incarnation as to where and when his successor would be found, helped in the determination of the lawful reincarnation.

From the middle of the seventeenth century down to 1860, when the Dalai Lama, Tinle-gyatso, was chosen, the rightful reincarnation of a defunct saint was found out by the use of the golden jar, or *ser-bum*.

Three years after the death of an incarnate lama the names of the different children, who it was claimed were his reincarnation, were taken down. These names, in the case of the Dalai or Tashi Lamas, were sent to the regent for examination, after which the president of the conclave, in the presence of the Regent and the ministers, enclosed in *tsamba* balls slips of paper, on each of which was written the name of a candidate. In other *tsamba* balls were slips on which was written "yes" or "no", as well as some blank slips. All these were put together in a golden jar, which was placed on the altar of the principal chapel of Lhasa, and for a week the gods were invoked. On the eighth day the jar was twirled round a certain number of times, and the name which fell out three times, together with a pellet in which was a slip inscribed "yes", was declared the true reincarnation. Those who were sent to bring the reincarnated saint to Lhasa or Tashilhunpo submitted him to certain trials; as, for example, picking out from a number of similar objects the rosary, the rings, cup, and mitre of the deceased lama.

In 1875, a year after the death of the Dalai Lama Tinle-gyatso, the regent and the College of Cardinals consulted the celebrated Nachung Chos-gyong oracle about the Dalai's reappearance, and the oracle declared that the reincarnation could only be discovered by a monk of the purest morals. It required, again, the supernatural powers of the oracle to find the future discoverer of the Grand Lama; he was the Shar-tse Khanpo of Gadan, a lama of great saintliness and profound knowledge. The oracle further stated that he should go to Choskhor-gya, as the reincarnation was to be found somewhere near Kong-po. The Khanpo went there accordingly, and sat in deep meditation for seven days, when, on the night of the last day, he had a vision and heard a voice which directed him to repair to the Mu-li-ding-ki tso (lake) of Choskhor. Awakening from his sleep, the Khanpo went to the lake, where, on the crystal surface of the water, he saw the image of the incarnate Grand Lama seated in his mother's lap, and his father fondling him. The house, its furniture, all was shown him. Suddenly the image disappeared, and he set out at once for Kong-po. On the way he stopped in Tag-po at the house of a respectable and wealthy family, and at once he recognized the child and all the images seen in his dream. He promptly informed the Government at Lhasa, and the regent and the cardinals came to Tag-po and took the child, then a year old, and its parents to the Rigyal palace, near Lhasa. This child, now aged ten, is called Nag-wang lo-zang tubdan gya-tso "the Lord of speech, the mighty ocean of wisdom."

The reason why the golden jar was not used for finding this reincarnation was because of the apprehension that the Dayan Khanpo's spirit—he had but recently died, and had been violently opposed to the Dalai lamas and their form of government—might be able to cause a wrong name to be drawn from the jar.

June 5—Early this morning I was invited to dine with the Lhacham at Bangye-shag. I was received most graciously, and was led by the Lhacham to her drawing-room, a room about 16 feet by 12, facing the south and on the third story of the building. There were in it two Chinese chests of drawers, on top of which were a lot of porcelain cups; Chinese pictures—picnics and dancing most of them represented—covered the greater part of the walls; the ceiling was of Chinese satin, and thick rugs of Yarkand and Tibetan make covered the floor. Well-polished little tables, wooden bowls for *tsamba*, and some satin-covered cushions completed the furniture of the room.

After conversing for a while and drinking a few cups of tea, the Lhacham withdrew, and one of her maids showed me the rooms in the mansion. The furniture was much the same as that in the Lhacham's room, only of inferior quality and ruder make. The walls were painted green and blue, with here and there pictures of processions of gods and demons, and the beams of the ceiling were carved and painted. The doors were very roughly made and without panels; the windows were covered with paper, with a very small pane of glass fitted in the middle of each. There were no chimneys in any of the rooms, but earthenware stoves, or *jala*. In a few of the rooms flowers were growing in pots.

Returning to the Lhacham's room, dinner was served me at noon, and while I ate she asked me many questions concerning the marriage laws of India and Europe. When I told her that in India a husband had several wives, and that among the Phyling a man had but one wife, she stared at me with undisguised astonishment. "One wife with one husband!" she exclaimed. "Don't you think we Tibetan women are better off? The Indian wife has but a portion of her husband's affections and property, but in Tibet the housewife is the real lady of all the joint earnings and inheritance of all the brothers sprung from the same mother, who are all of the same flesh and blood. The brothers are but one, though their souls are several. In India a man marries well several women who are strangers to each other." "Am I to understand that your ladyship would like to see several sisters marry one husband?" I asked. "That is not the point", replied the Lhacham. "What I contend is that Tibetan women are happier than Indian ones, for they enjoy the privileges conceded in the latter country to the men."

June 7—My two men had heard from Gadan Tipa, a soothsayer, that they would be stricken with small-pox if they ventured to go to Samye, and they besought me to give up the idea; but I declared emphatically my resolve to visit that famous lamasery, and also that of Gaden.

On June 8 I again visited the Jo khang. The numerous wooden pillars supporting the second story are among the most remarkable things in this temple. The largest of these have capitals with sculptured foliage, and are called *ka-wa shing-iho chan*. At their base are buried, it is said, great treasures of gold and silver. Other pillars, with dragon-heads as capitals, have hidden under them charms against devils, for curing diseases, and for keeping off and thwarting the evil designs of the enemies of Buddhism and of the government of church. Other pillars, again, called *seng go-chan*, "having lions' heads as capitals," have concealed under them many potent charms (*yang-yig*) to insure bounteous crops.

Under floor of the Lu-khang are many charms and precious things wrapped in snow-fox or snake-skin. These, it is supposed, preserve the flocks and herds of Tibet. Beneath the image of Dsambhala is hidden in an onyx box some *tag-sha* which preserves the precious stones, the wool, the grain, and the other riches of the country.

Among the other objects of special sanctity, I was shown in the passage for circumambulating the temple a cavity in the rock where neither moss nor grass grow; it is said to keep back the waters of the Kyi chu from invading the Jo khang.

June 9—I went out walking to-day in the direction of Ramoche. On the streets I met numerous bands of *ragyabas*, or scavengers, wandering from place to place, clamouring for alms from every newcomer or pilgrim they saw. If no attention is paid to them, they thrust their dirty hats in the stranger's face and lavish insults on him; and if he take offence, they reply, "Why, my lord, this is not insolence; we are but saluting you!"

These *ragyabas* of Lhasa form a guild. Persons convicted of any crime, or vagabonds, are usually sent back to their native villages, there to work out their sentence; but when the authorities cannot learn whence they come, they are handed over to the chief of the *ragyabas*, who receives them into his guild. Besides begging, the *ragyabas* cut up the corpses which are brought to the two cemeteries of Lhasa, near which they live, and feed them to vultures and dogs. A *ragyaba* may not show his wealth, however, great it be; the walls of their houses must be made with horns of sheep, goats or yaks, the convex sides turned upwards.

At present the chief of the *ragyabas* is a man of about fifty years, called Abula, he wears a red serge gown and a yellow turban. Cursed is the lot of the *ragyabas*, and twice cursed is Abula, if a day passes without a corpse being brought to the cemetery; for people believe that if a day passes without a death it portends evil to Lhasa.

In connection with the erection of Ramoche, it is said that the princess who had it built discovered that the spot on which the temple was erected was in communication with hell, and that there was a crystal palace inhabited by the Nagas deep in the earth underneath this place.

Among the most remarkable relics preserved in this temple, and which I had not had time to examine on my first rather hurried visit, I now noticed one of Dolma made of turquoise, and which is said to render oracles, one of Tse-pa-med, made of coral, and one of Rin-chen Khadoma in amber, and a number of others of jade, conchshells and *mumen*, besides many jars and bowls of jade and gold.

In the afternoon I called on the Lhacham, and was sorry to learn that her second son had small-pox. I told her how disappointed I was at not having been able to get even a glimpse of the Kyabgong, the "lord protector" of Tibet, the Dalai Lama. "Alas!" I added, "I have not acquired a sufficient moral merit in former existence to be able to see Shenrezig in flesh and blood!"

"Do not be cast down, Pundib la; though it is not an easy matter for even the Shape and nobles of Tibet to see the Dalai Lama, I will arrange an audience for you."

Early the next day a gentleman (*ku-dag*), who was a Dungkhor of Potala, called on me, and said that the Kusho Lhacham of Phala had arranged with the Donyer chenpo of Potala for an audience for me with the Dalai Lama, and that I must get ready as soon as possible.

Swallowing breakfast as quickly as possible, I put on my best clothes, and had hardly finished when the Dungkhor Chola Kusho, accompanied by a servant, arrived. Having provided myself with three bundles of incense-sticks and a roll of *khatag*, we mounted our ponies and sallied forth. As we crossed the doorway we saw a calf sucking, and several women carrying water. My companions smiled, and Chola Kusho remarked that I was a lucky man, as these were most auspicious signs.

Arriving at the eastern gateway of Potala, we dismounted and walked through a long hall, on either side of which were rows of prayer-wheels, which every passer-by put in motion. Then, ascending three long flights of stone steps, we left our ponies in care of a bystander—for no one may ride further—and proceeded towards the palace under the guidance of a young monk. We had to climb up five ladders before we reached the ground floor of Phodang marpo, or "the Red palace," thus called from the exterior walls being of a dark red colour. Then we had half a dozen more ladders to climb up, and we found ourselves at the top of Potala (there are nine stories to this building), where we saw a number of monks awaiting an audience. The view from here was beautiful beyond compare: the broad valley of the Kyi chu, in the centre of which stands the great city surrounded by green groves; the gilt spires of the Jo-khang and the other temples of Lhasa, and farther away the great monasteries of Sera and Debung, behind which rose the dark blue mountains.

After a while three lamas appeared, and said that the Dalai Lama would presently conduct a memorial service for the benefit of the late Mru Ta Lama (great lama of Meru gomba, and that we were allowed to be present at it. Walking very softly, we came to the middle of the reception hall, the roof of which is supported by three rows of pillars, four in each row, and where light is admitted by a skylight. The furniture was that generally seen in lamaseries, but the hangings were of the richest brocades and cloths of gold; and church utensils were of gold, and the frescoing on the walls of exquisite fineness. Behind the throne were beautiful tapestries and satin hangings forming a great *gyal-tsan*, or canopy. The floor was beautifully smooth and glossy, but the doors and windows, which were painted red, were of the rough description common throughout the country.

A Donyer approached, who took our presentation *khatag*, but it held back, at the suggestion of Chola Kusho, the present I had for the Grand Lama; and when I approached him I placed in his lap, much to the surprise of all present, a piece of gold weighing a *tola*. We then took our seats on rugs, of which there were eight rows; ours were in the third, and about ten feet from the Grand Lama's throne, and a little to his left.

The Grand Lama is a child of eight with a bright and fair complexion and rosy cheeks. His eyes are large and penetrating, the shape of his face remarkably Aryan, though somewhat marred by the obliquity of his eyes. The thinness of his person was probably due to the fatigue of the Court ceremonies and to the religious duties and ascetic observance of his estate. A yellow mitre covered his head, and its pendant lappets hid his eyes; a yellow mantle draped his person, and he sat cross-legged with joined palms. The throne on which he sat was supported by carved lions, and covered with silk scarfs. It was about four feet high, six feet long, and four feet broad. The State officer moved about with becoming gravity: there was the Kuchar Khanpo, with a bowl of holy water (*tu*), coloured yellow with saffron; the Censor-carrier, with a golden censor with three chains; the Solpon chenpo, with a golden teapot; and other household officials. Two gold lamps, made in the shape of flower vases, burnt on either side of the throne.

When all had been blessed and taken seats, the Solpon chenpo poured tea in his Holiness's golden cup, and four assistants served the people present. Then grace was said, beginning with *Om, Ah, Hum,* thrice repeated, and followed by, "Never losing sight even for a moment of the Three Holies, making reverence ever to the Three Precious Ones. Let the blessing of the Three Konchog be upon us," etc. Then we silently raised our cups and drank the tea, which was most deliciously perfumed. In this manner we drank three cupfuls, and then put our bowl back in the bosoms of gowns.

After this the Solpon chenpo put a golden dish full of rice before the Dalai Lama, and he touched it, and then it was divided among those present; then grace was again said, and his Holiness, in a low, indistinct tone, chanted a hymn, which was repeated by the assembled lamas in deep, grave tones. When this was over, a venerable man rose from the first row of seats and made a short address, reciting the many acts of mercy the Dalai lamas had vouchsafed Tibet, at the conclusion of which he presented to His Holiness a number of valuable things; then he made three prostrations and withdrew, followed by all of us.

As I was leaving, one of the Donyer chenpo's (or chamberlain) assistants gave me two packets of blessed pills, and another tied a scrap of red silk round my neck—these are the usual return presents the Grand Lama makes to pilgrims.

As we were going out of the hall, we were met by Chola Kusho's younger brother, a monk in Namgyal Ta-tsan, the monastery of the palace, and in his and his brother's company I visited the palace, and learnt from them much relating to the history and the traditions of the place.

We first visited a chapel where is an image of Shenrezig with eleven heads and a thousand arms, an eye in the palm of each of his hands. Near it is an image with four arms, also many small gold *chorten* and objects in bronze. Next I was led to a hall where there is an old throne, opposite which are images of King Srongbtsan, his two consorts, his minister Tonmi Sambhota, General Gar, and Prince Gungri gung-btsan. Leaving this room, we went to the great hall where Nag-wang lob-zang, the fifth Dalai Lama, used to hold his court. Old paintings, supposed to be indestructible by fire, representing King Srong btsan's family, Shenrezig, and the first Grand Lama, hung from the pillars, and several images, among which one of sandalwood representing Gon-po, may be seen here.

We were then led to the hall where the Desi Sangye-gyatso used to hold his councils. Here also is the tomb of the first Dalai Lama. It is two-storied, and the dome is covered with thin plates of gold. The Dalai's remains are entombed with many precious things, and the sepulcher is ornamented with various objects of the richest designs and most costly materials brought hither by devotees. This tomb is called the Dsambling gyan, and is the prototype of the tombs we saw around it containing the remains of the other incarnations of the Dalai Lama; but these are all smaller than it.

After visiting these halls we descended to the Namgyal Ta-tsan. The architecture of the Phodang marpo embarrassed me greatly, the halls and rooms being piled up story on story. The stonework was beautiful, but it is so poorly drained that in many places the odours are stifling.

Entering a small room, the cell of our guide, we were given seats and served with tea and a collation. Shortly after we started home, having expressed in the warmest terms our thanks to Chola Kusho and his brother for their kindness. We followed the *ling-khor*, as the road which encircles Lhasa is called. On the way we passed a small grove where is the elephant-shed, the solitary occupant of which—a present from the Rajah of Sikkim—was standing in a barley patch near by. Further on we came to a place where the corpses of the townspeoples are fed to pigs, whose flesh by the way, is said to be delicious. Near here are numerous huts of Ragyabas.

In the evening a drove of donkeys loaded with *tsamba* and butter arrived from Gyantse, and I was distressed to learn that my friend the minister had small-pox. My men again began pestering me to return to tsang, alleging as a pretext that I might be of assistance to the minister, and I finally prepared to go to him, especially as the donkey-men said he had expressed a desire to have me near him.

On June 11 I went to see the Lhacham, thanked her for having obtained for me an audience of the Kyab-gong Rinpoche, and spoke to her about my intention of setting out for Dongtse. She advised me to leave at once, as small-pox was raging at Lhasa; her two sons now had it, and from her appearance I feared that she was about to fall ill of the same disease.

Returning to our lodgings, I despatched Tsing-ta to her to ask a loan of 200 *tankas*. The sum was brought me in the evening by her maid Apela, and the Lhacham also sent me provision for the journey and feed for the ponies.

[From *Journey to Lhasa and Central Tibet*, 1902.]

12

Lhasa and its Vanished Deity

By
EDMUND CANDLER

THE PASSAGE of the river was difficult and dangerous. If we had had to depend on the four Berthon boats we took with us, the crossing might have taken weeks. But the good fortune that attended the expedition throughout did not fail us. At Chaksam we found the Tibetans had left behind their two great ferry-boats, quaint old barges with horses' heads at the prow, capacious enough to hold a hundred men. The Tibetan ferrymen worked for us cheerfully. A number of hide boats were also discovered. The transport mules were swum over, and the whole force was across in less than a week.

But the river took its toll most tragically. The current is swift and boisterous; the eddies and whirlpools are dangerously uncertain. Two Berthon boats, bound together into a raft, capsized, and Major Bretherton, chief supply and transport officer, and two Gurkhas were drowned. It seemed as if the genius of the river, offended at our intrusion, had claimed its price and carried off the most valuable life in the force. It was Major Bretherton's foresight more than anything that enabled us to reach Lhasa. His loss was calamitous.

We left our camp at the ferry on July 31, and started for Lhasa, which was only forty-three miles distant. It was difficult to believe that in three days we would be looking on the Potala.

The Kyi Chu, the holy river of Lhasa, flows into the Tsangpo at Chushul, three miles below Chaksam ferry, where our troops crossed. The river is almost as broad as the Thames at Greenwich, and the stream is swift and clear, the valley is cultivated in places, but long stretches are bare and rocky. Sand-dunes, overgrown with artemisia scrub, extend to the margin of cultivation, leaving a well-defined line between the green cornfields and the barren sand. The crops were ripening at the time of our advance, and promised a plentiful harvest.

For many miles the road is cut out of a precipitous cliff above the river. A few hundred men could have destroyed it in an afternoon, and delayed our advance for another week. Newly-built sangars at the entrance of the gorge showed that the Tibetans had intended to hold it. But they left the valley in a disorganized state the day we reached the Tsangpo. Had they fortified the position, they might have made it stronger than the Karo la.

The heat of the valley was almost tropical. Summer by the Kyi Chu River is very different from one's first conceptions of Tibet. To escape the heat, I used to write my diary in the shade of gardens and willow groves. Hoopoes, magpies and huge black ravens became inquisitive and confidential. I have a pile of little black notebooks I scribbled over in their society, dirty and torn and soiled with pressed flowers.

For a picture of the valley I will go to these. One's freshest impressions are the best, and truer than reminiscences.

Nethang.

In the most fertile part of the Kyi Chu Valley, where the fields are intersected in all directions by clear-running streams bordered with flowers, in grove of poplars where doves were singing all day long, I found Atisa's tomb.

It was built in a large, plain, barn-like building, clean and sweet-smelling as a granary, and innocent of ornament outside and in. It was the only clean and simple place devoted to religion I had seen-in-Tibet.

In every house and monastery we entered on the road there were gilded images, tawdry paintings, demons and she-devils, garish frescoes on the wall, hideous grinning devil-masks, all the Lama's spurious apparatus of terrorism.

These were the outward symbols of demonolatry and superstition invented by scheming priests as the fabric of their sacerdotalism. But this was the resting-place of the Reformer, the true son of Buddha, who came over the Himalayas to preach a religion of love and mercy.

I entered the building out of the glare of the sun, expecting nothing but the usual monsters and abortions—just as one is dragged into a church in some tourist-ridden land, where, if only for the sake of peace, one must cast an apathetic eye at the lions of the country. But as the tomb gradually assumed shape in the dim light, I knew that there was someone here, a priest or a community, who understood Atisa, who knew what he would have wished his last resting-place to be; or perhaps the good old monk had left a will or spoken a plain word that had been handed down and remembered these thousand years, and was now, no doubt, regarded as an eccentric's whim, that there must be no gods or demons by his bomb, nothing abnormal, no pretentiousness of any kind. If his teaching had lived, how simple and honest and different Tibet would be to-day!

The tomb was not beautiful—a large square plinth, supporting layers of gradually decreasing circumference and forming steps two feet in height, the last a platform on which was based a substantial vat-like structure with no ornament or inscription except a thin line of black pencilled saints. By climbing up the layers of masonry I found a pair of slant eyes gazing at nothing and hidden by a curve in the stone from gazers below. This was the only painting on the tomb.

Never in the thousand years since the good monk was laid to rest at Nethang had a white man entered this shrine. To-day the courtyard was crowded with mules and drivers; Hindus and Pathans in British uniform ; they were ransacking the place for corn. A transport officer was shouting:

'How many bags have you, babu?'

'A hundred and seven, sir.'

'Remember, if anyone loots, he will get fifty *beynt*' (stripes with the cat-o'-nine-tails).

Then he turned to me.

'What the devil is that old thief doing over there?' he said, and nodded at a man with archaeological interests, who was peering about in a dark corner by the tomb. 'There is nothing more here.'

'He is examining Atisa's tomb.'

'And who the devil is Atisa?'

And who is he? Merely a name to a few dry-as-dust pedants. Everything human he did is forgotten. The faintest ripple remains to-day from that stone cast into the stagnant waters so many years ago. A few monks drone away their days in a monastery close by. In the courtyard there is a border of hollyhocks and snapdragon and asters. Here the unsavoury guardians of Atisa's tomb watch me as I write, and wonder what on earth I am doing among them, and what spell or mantra I am inscribing in the little black book that shuts so tightly with a clasp.

Toilung.

To-morrow we reach Lhasa.

A few hours ago we caught the first glimpse of the Potala Palace, a golden dome standing out on a bluff rock in the centre of the valley. The city is not seen from afar perched on a hill like the great monasteries and jongs of the country. It is literally 'hidden.' A rocky promontory projects from the bleak hills to the south like a screen, hiding Lhasa, as if Nature conspired in its seclusion. Here at a distance of seven miles we can see the Potala and the Lamas" Medical College.

Trees and undulating grounding shut out the view of the actual city until one is within a mile of it.

Tomorrow we camp outside. It is nearly a hundred years since Thomas Manning, the only Englishman (until to-day) who ever saw Lhasa, preceded us. Our journey has not been easy, but we have come in spite of everything.

The Lamas have opposed us with all their material and spiritual resources. They have fought us with medieval weapons and a medley of modern firearms. They have held Commination Services, recited mantras, and cursed us solemnly for days. Yet we have come on.

They have sent delegates and messengers of every rank to threaten and entreat and plead with us—emissaries of increasing importance as we have drawn nearer their capital, until the Dalai Lama despatched his own Grand Chamberlain and Grand Secretary, and, greater than these, the Ta Lama and Yutok Shape, members of the ruling Council of Five, whose sacred persons had never before been seen by European eyes. Tomorrow the Amban himself comes to meet Colonel Younghusband.' The Dalai Lama has sent him a letter sealed with his own seal.

Every stretch of road from the frontier to Lhasa has had its symbol of remonstrance. Cairns and chortens, and *mani* walls and praying-flags, demons painted on the rock, writing on the wall, white stones piled upon black, have emitted their ray of protest and malevolence in vain.

The Lamas knew we must come. Hundreds of years ago a Buddhist saint wrote it in his book of prophecies, Ma-ong Lung-Ten, which may be bought to-day in the Lhasa book-shops. He predicted that Tibet would be invaded and conquered by the Philings (Europeans). When all the the true religion would go the Chang Shambula, the Northern Paradise, and Buddhism would become extinct in the country.

And now the Lamas believe that the prophecy will be fulfilled by our entry into Lhasa, and that their religion will decay before foreign influence. The Dalai Lama, they say, will die, not by violence or sickness, but by some spiritual visitation. His spirit will seek some other incarnation, when he can no longer benefit his people or secure his country, so long sacred to Buddhists, from the contamination of foreign intrusion.

The Tibetans are not the savages they are depicted. They are civilized, if medieval. The country is governed on the feudal system. The monks are the overlords, the peasantry their serfs. The poor are not oppressed. They and the small tenant farmers work ungrudgingly for their spiritual masters, to whom they owe a blind devotion. They are not discontented, though they give more than a tithe of their small income to the Church. It must be remembered that every family contributes at least one member to the priesthood, so that, when we are inclined to abuse the monks for consuming the greater part of the country's produce, we should remember that the laymen are not the victims of class prejudice, the plebeians groaning under the burden of the patricians, so much as the servants of a community chosen from among themselves, and with whom they are connected by family ties.

No doubt the Lamas employ spiritual terrorism to maintain their influence and preserve the temporal government in their hands ; and when they speak of their religion being injured by our intrusion, they are thinking, no doubt, of another unveiling of mysteries, the dreaded age of materialism and reason, when little by little their ignorant serfs will be brought into contact with the facts of life, and begin to question the justness of the relations that have existed between themselves and their rulers for centuries. But at present the people are medieval, not only in their system of government and their religion, their inquisition, their witchcraft, their incantations, their ordeals by fire and boiling oil, but in every aspect of their daily life.

I question if ever in the history of the world there has been another occasion when bigotry and darkness have been exposed with such abruptness to the inroad of science, when a barrier of ignorance created by jealousy and fear as a screen between two peoples living side by side has been demolished so suddenly to admit the light of an advanced civilization.

The Tibetans, no doubt, will benefit, and many abuses will be swept away. Yet there will always be people who will hanker after the medieval and romantic, who will say: 'We men are children. Why could we not have been content that there was one mystery not unveiled, one country of an ancient arrested civilization, and an established Church where men are still guided by sorcery and incantations, and direct their mundane affairs with one eye on a grotesque spirit world, which is the most real thing in their lives—a land of topsy-turvy and inverted proportions, where men spend half their lives mumbling unintelligible mantras and turning mechanical prayers, and when dead are cut up into mincemeat and thrown to the dogs and vultures?'

To-morrow, when we enter Lhasa, we will have unveiled the last mystery of the East. There are no more forbidden cities which men have not mapped and photographed. Our children will laugh at modern travellers' tales. They will have to turn again to Gulliver and Haroun al Raschid. And they will soon tire of these. For now that there are no real mysteries, no unknown land of dreams, where there may still be genii and mahatmas and bottle-imps, that kind of literature will be tolerated no longer. Children will be sceptical and matter-of-fact and disillusioned, and there will be no sale for fairy-stories any more.

But we ourselves are children. Why could we not have left at least one city out of bounds?

Lhasa,
August 3.

We reached Lhasa to-day, after a march of seven miles, and camped outside the city. As we approached, the road became an embankment across a marsh. Butterflies and dragon-flies were hovering among the rushes, clematis grew in the stonework by the roadside, cows were grazing in the rich pastureland, redshanks were calling, a flight of teal passed overhead ; the whole scene was most home-like, save for the bare scarred cliffs that jealously preclude a distant view of the city.

Some of us climbed the Chagpo Ri and looked down on the city. Lhasa lay a mile in front of us, a mass of huddled roofs and trees, dominated by the golden dome of the Jokhang Cathedral.

It must be the most hidden city on earth. The Chagpo Ri rises bluffly from the riverbank like a huge rock. Between it and the Potala hill there is a narrow gap not more than thirty yards wide. Over this is built the Pargo Kaling, a typical Tibetan chorten, through which is the main gateway into Lhasa. The city has no walls, but beyond the Potala, to complete the screen, stretches a great embankment of sand right across the valley to the hills on the north.

Lhasa,
August 4.

An epoch in the world's history was marked today when Colonel Younghusband entered the city to return the visit of the Chinese Amban. He was accompanied by all the members of the mission, the war correspondents, and an escort of the two companies of the Royal Fusiliers and the 2nd Mounted Infantry. Half a company of mounted infantry, two guns, a detachment of sappers, and four companies of infantry were held ready to support the escort if necessary.

In front of us marched and rode the Amban's escort—his bodyguard, dressed in short loose coats of French gray, embroidered in black, with various emblems; pikemen clad in bright red with black embroidery and black pugarees; soldiers with pikes and scythes and three-pronged spears, on all of which hung red banners with devices embroidered in black.

We found the city squalid and filthy beyond description, undrained and unpaved. Not a single house looked clean or cared for. The streets after rain are nothing but pools of stagnant water frequented by pigs and dogs searching for refuse. Even the Jokhang appeared mean and squalid at close quarters, whence its golden roofs were invisible. There was nothing picturesque except the marigolds and hollyhocks in pots and the doves and singing birds in wicker cages.

The few Tibetans we met in the street were strangely incurious. A baker kneading dough glanced at us casually, and went on kneading. A woman weaving barely looked up from her work.

The streets were almost deserted, perhaps by order of the authorities to prevent an outbreak. But as we returned small crowds had gathered in the doorways, women were peering through windows, but no one followed or took more than a listless interest in us. The monks looked on sullenly. But in most faces one read only indifference and apathy. One might think the entry of a foreign army into Lhasa and the presence of English Political Officers in gold-laced uniform and beaver hats were everyday events.

The only building in Lhasa that is at all imposing is the Potala.

It would be misleading to say that the palace dominated the city, as a comparison would be implied—a picture conveyed of one building standing out signally among others. This is not the case.

The Potala is superbly detached. It is not a palace on a hill, but a hill that is also a palace. Its massive walls, its terraces and bastions stretch upwards from the plain to the crest, as if the great bluff rock were merely a foundation-stone planted there at the divinity's nod. The divinity dwells in the palace, and underneath, at the distance of a furlong or two, humanity is huddled abjectly in squalid smut-begrimed houses. The proportion is that which exist between God and man.

If one approached within a league of Lhasa, saw the glittering domes of the Potala, and turned back without entering the precincts, one might still imagine it an enchanted city, shining with turquoise and gold. But having entered, the illusion is lost. One might think devout Buddhists had excluded strangers in order to preserve the myth of the city's beauty and mystery and wealth, or that the place was consciously neglected and defaced so as to offer no allurements to heretics, just as the repulsive women one meets in the streets smear themselves over with grease and cutch to make themselves even more hideous than Nature ordained.

The place has not changed since Manning visited it ninety years ago, and wrote:- 'There is nothing striking, nothing pleasing, in its appearance. The habitations are begrimed with smut and dirt. The avenues are full of dogs, some growling and gnawing bits of hide that lie about in profusion, and emit a charnel-house smell ; others limping and looking livid; others ulcerated; others starved and dying, and pecked at by ravens ; some dead and preyed upon. In short, everything seems mean and gloomy, and excites the ideal of something unreal.' That is the Lhasa of to-day. Probably it was the same centuries ago.

Above all this squalor the Potala towers superbly.

Its golden roofs, shining in the sun like tongues of fire, are a landmark for miles, and must inspire awe and veneration in the hearts of pilgrims coming from the desert parts of Tibet, Kashmir, and Mongolia to visit the sacred city that Buddha has blessed.

The secret of romance is remoteness, whether in time or space. If we could be thrown back to the days of Agincourt we should be enchanted at first but after a week should vote everything commonplace and dull. Falstaff, the beery lout, would be an impossible companion, and Prince Hal a tiresome young cub who wanted a good dressing-down. In travel, too, as one approaches the goal, and the country becomes gradually familiar, the husk of romance falls off. Child Roland must have been sadly disappointed in the Dark Tower ; filth and familiarity very soon destroyed the romance of Lhasa.

But romance still clings to the Potala. It is still remote. Like Imray, its sacred inmate has achieved the impossible. Divinity or no, he has at least the divine power of vanishing. In the material West as we like to call it, we know how hard it is for the humblest subject to disappear, in spite of the confused hub of traffic and intricate network of communications. Yet here in Lhasa, a city of dreamy repose, a King has escaped, been spirited into the air and nobody is any the wiser.

When we paraded the city yesterday, we made a complete circuit of the Potala. There was no one, not even the humblest follower, so unimaginative that he did not look up from time to time at the frowning cliff and thousand sightless windows that concealed the unknown. Those hidden-corridors and passages have been for centuries, and are, perhaps, at this very moment, the scenes of unnatural piety and crime.

Within the precincts of Lhasa the taking of life in any form is sacrilege. Buddha's first law was, 'Thou shalt not kill; and life is held so sacred by his devout followers that they are careful not to kill the smallest insect. Yet this palace, where dwells the divine incarnation of the Buddhist, the head of the Bhuddist Church, must have witnessed more murders and instigations to crime than the most blood-stained castle of medieval Europe.

Since the assumption of temporal power by the fifth Grand Lama in the middle of the seventeenth century, the whole history of the Tibetan hierarchy has been a record of bloodshed and intrigue. The fifth Grand Lama, the first to receive the title of Dalai, was a most unscrupulous ruler, who secured the temporal power by inciting the Mongols to invade Tibet, and received as his reward the kingship. He then established his claim to the godhead by tampering with Buddhist history and writ. The sixth incarnation was executed by the Chinese on account of his profligacy. The seventh was deposed by the Chinese as privy to the murder of the regent. After the death of the eighth, of whom I can learn nothing, it would seem that the tables were turned : the regents systematically murdered their charge, and the crime of the seventh Dalai Lama was visited upon four successive incarnations. The ninth, tenth, eleventh, and twelfth all died prematurely, assassinated, it is believed, by their regents.

There are no legends of malmsey-butts, secret smotherings, and hired assassins. The children disappeared; they were absorbed into the Universal Essence; they were literally too good to live. Their regents and protectors, monks only less sacred than themselves, provided that the spirit in its yearning for the next state should not be long detained in its mortal husk. No questions were asked. How could the devout trace the comings and goings of the divine Avalokita, the Lord of Mercy and Judgment, who ordains into what heaven or hell, demon god, hero, mollusc, or ape, their spirits must enter, according to their sins?

So, when we reached Lhasa the other day, and heard that the thirteenth incarnation had fled, no one was surprised. Yet the wonder remains. A great Prince, a god to thousands of men, has been removed from his palace and capital, no one knows whither or when. A ruler has disappeared who travels with every appanage of state, inspiring awe in his prostrate servants, whose movements, one would think, were watched and talked about more than any Sovereign's on earth. Yet fear, or loyalty, or ignorance keeps every subject tongue-tied.

We have spies and informers everywhere, and there are men in Lhasa who would do much to please the new conquerors of Tibet. There are also witless men, who have eyes and ears, but, it seems, no tongues.

But so far neither avarice nor weightlessness has betrayed anything. For all we know, the Dalai Lama may be still in his palace in some hidden chamber in the rock, or maybe he has never left his customary apartments, and still performs his daily offices in the Potala, confident that there at least his sanctity is inviolable by unbelievers.

The British Tommy in the meanwhile parades the streets as indifferently as if they were the New Cut or Lambeth Palace Road. He looks up at the Potala, and says: 'The old bloke's done a bunk. wish we'd got 'im; we might get 'ome then.'

Lhasa,

August-.

We had been in Lhasa nearly there weeks before we could discover where the Dalai Lama had fled. We know now that he left his palace secretly in the night, and took the northern road to Mongolia. The Buriat, Dorjieff met him at Nagchuka, on the verge of the great desert that separates inhabited Tibet from Mongolia, 100 miles from Lhasa. On the 20th the Amban told us that he had already left Nagchuka twelve days, and was pushing on across the desert to the frontier.

I have been trying to find out something about the private life and character of the Grand Lama. But asking questions here is fruitless; one can learn nothing intimate. And this is just what one might expect. The man continues a bogie, a riddle, undivinable, impersonal, remote. The people know nothing. They have bowed before the throne as men come out of the dark into a blinding light. Scrutiny in their view would be vain and blasphemous. The Abbots, too, will reveal nothing ; they will not and dare not. When Colonel Younghusband put the question direct to a head Lama in open durbar, 'Have you news of the Dalai Lama? Do you know where he is? 'The monk looked slowly to left and right, and answered, ' I know nothing.' The ruler of your country leaves his palace and capital, and you know nothing? 'The Commissioner asked. 'Nothing,' answered the monk, shuffling his feet, but without changing colour.

From various sources, which differ surprisingly little, I have a fairly clear picture of the man's face and figure. He is thick-set, about five feet nine inches in height, with a heavy square jaw, nose remarkably long and straight for a Tibetan, eyebrows pronounced and turning upwards in a phenomenal manner—probably trained so, to make his appearance more forbidding—face pock-marked, general expression resolute and sinister. He goes out very little, and is rarely seen by the people, except on his annual visit to Depung, and during his migrations between the Summer Palace and the Potala. He was at the Summer Palace when the messenger brought the news that our advance was inevitable, but he went to the Potala to put his house in order before projecting himself into the unknown.

His face is the index of his character. He is a man of strong personality, impetuous, despotic, and intolerant of advice in State affairs. He is constantly deposing his Ministers, and has estranged from himself a large section of the upper classes, both ecclesiastical and official, owing to his wayward and headstrong disposition. As a child he was so precociously acute and resolute that he survived his regent, and so upset the traditional policy of murder, being the only one out of the last five incarnations to reach his majority. Since he took the government of the country into his own hands, he has reduced the Chinese suzerainty to a mere shadow, and with fatal results to himself, consistently insulted and defied the British. His inclination to a rapprochement with Russia is not shared by his Ministers.

The only glimpse I have had into the man himself was reflected in a conversation with the Nepalese Resident, a podgy little man, very ugly and good natured, with the manners of a French comedian and a face generally expanded in a broad grin. He shook with laughter when I asked him if he knew the Dalai Lama, and the idea was really intensely funny, this mercurial, irreverent little man hobnobbing with the divine.' I have seen him,' he said, and exploded again. 'But what does he do all day?' I asked. The Resident puckered up his brow, aping abstraction, and began to wave his hand in the air solemnly with a slow circular movement, mumbling' *Om man Padme om'* to the revolutions of an imaginary praying-wheel. He was immensely pleased with the effort and the effect it produced on a sepoy orderly.' But has he no interests or amusements?' I asked. The Resident could think of none. But he told me a story to illustrate the dullness of the man, for whom he evidently had no reverence. On his return from his last visit to India, the Maharaja of Nepal had given him a phonograph to present to the Priest-King. The impious toy was introduced to the Holy of Holies, and the Dalai Lama walked round it uneasily, as it emitted the strains of English band music, and raucously repeated an indelicate Bhutanese song. After sitting a long while in deep thought he rose and said he could not live with this voice without a soul; it must leave his palace at once. The rejected phonograph found a home with the Chinese Amban, to whom it was presented with due ceremonial the same day.' The Lama is *gumar,*' the Resident said, using a Hindustani word which may be translated, according to our charity, by anything between' boorish' and 'unenlightened.' I was glad to meet a man in this city of evasiveness whose views were positive, and who was eager to communicate them. Through him I tracked the shadow, as it were, of this impersonality, and found that to many strangers in Lhasa, and perhaps to a few Lhasans themselves, the divinity was all clay, a palpable fraud, a pompous and puritanical dullard masquerading as a god.

For my own part I think the oracle that counselled his flight wiser than the statesmen who object that it was a political mistake. He has lost his prestige, they say. But imagine him dragged into durbar as signatory, gazed at by profane eyes, the subject of a few days' gossip and comment, they sunk into commonplace, stripped of his mystery like this city of Lhasa, through which we now saunter familiarly, wondering when we shall start again for the wilds.

To escape this ordeal he has fled, and to us, at least, his flight has deepened the mystery the envelops him, and added to his dignity and remoteness ; to thousands of mystical dreamers it has preserved the effulgence of his godhead unsoiled by contact with the profane world.

From our camp here the Potala draws the eye like a magnet. There is nothing but sky and marsh and bleak hill and palace. When we look out of our tents in the morning, the sun is striking the golden roof like a beacon light to the faithful. Nearly every day in August this year has opened fine and closed with storm-clouds gathering from the west, through which the sun shines, bathing the eastern valley in a soft, pearly light. The western horizon is dark and lowering, the eastern peaceful and serene. In this division of darkness and light the Potala stands out like a haven, not flaming now, but faintly luminous with a restful mystic light, soothing enough to rob Buddhist metaphysics of its pessimism and induce a mood, even in unbelievers, in which one is content to merge the individual and become absorbed in the universal spirit of Nature.

No wonder that, when one looks for mystery in Lhasa, one's thoughts dwell-solely on the Dalai Lama and the Potala. I cannot help dwelling on the flight of the thirteenth incarnation. It plunges us into medievalism. To my mind, there is no picture so romantic and engrossing in modern history as that exodus, when the spiritual head of the Buddhist Church, the temporal ruler of six millions, stole out of his palace by night and was borne away in his palanquin, no one knows on what errand or with what impotent rage in his heart. The flight was really secret. No one but his immediate confidants and retainers, not even the Amban himself, knew that he had gone. I can imagine the awed attendants, the burying of treasure, the locking and sealing of chests, faint lights flickering in the passages, hurried footsteps in the corridors, dogs barking intermittently at this unwonted bustle—I feel sure the Priest-King kicked one as he stepped on the terrace for the last time. Then the procession by moonlight up the narrow valley to the north, where the roar of the stream would drown the footsteps of the palanquin-bearers.

A month afterwards I followed on his track, and stood on the Phembu Pass twelve miles north of Lhasa, whence one looks down on the huge belt of mountains that lied between the Brahmaputra and the desert, so packed and huddled that their crests look like one continuous undulating plain stretching to the horizon. Looking across the valley. I could see the northern road to Mongolia winding up a feeder of the Phembu Chu. They passed along here and over the next range, and across range after range, until they reached the two conical snow-peaks that stand out of the plain beside Tengri Nor, a hundred miles to the north. For days they skirted the great lake, and then, as if they feared the Nemesis of our offended Raj could pursue them to the end of the earth, broke into the desert, across which they must be hurrying now toward the great mountain chain of Burkhan Buddha, on the southern limits of Mongolia

Lhasa.

August I9.

The Tibetans are the strangest people on earth. Today I discovered how they dispose of their dead.

To hold life sacred and benefit the creatures are the laws of Buddha, which they are supposed to obey most scrupulously. And as they think they may be reborn in any shape of mammal, bird, or fish, they are kind to living things.

During the the morning service the Lamas

repeat a prayer for the minute insects which they have swallowed inadvertently in their meat and drink, and the formula insures the rebirth of these microbes in heaven. Sometimes, when a Lama's life is despaired of, the monks will ransom a yak or a bullock from the shambles, and keep him a pensioner in their monastery, praying the good Buddha to spare the sick man's life for the life ransomed. Yet they eat meat freely, all save the Gelug-pa, or Reformed Church, and square their conscience with their appetite by the pretext that the sin rests with the outcast assassin, the public butcher, who will be born in the next incarnation as some tantalized spirit or agonized demon. That, however, is his own affair.

But it is when a Tibetan dies that his charity to the creatures becomes really practical. Then, by his own tacit consent when living, his body is given as a feast to the dogs and vultures. This is no casual or careless gift to avoid the trouble of burial or cremation. All creatures who have a taste for these things are invited to the ceremony, and the corpse is carved to their liking by an expert, who devotes his life to the practice.

When a Tibetan dies he is left three days in his chamber, and a slit is made in his skull to let his soul pass out. Then he is rolled into a ball, wrapped in a sack, or silk if he is rich, packed into a jar or basket, and carried along to the music of conch shells to the ceremonial stone. Here a Lama takes the corpse out of its vessel and wrappings, and lays it face downwards on a large flat slab, and the pensioners prowl or hop round, waiting for their dole. They are quite tame. The Lamas stand a little way apart, and see that strict etiquette is observed during the entertainment. The carver begins at the ankle, and cuts upwards, throwing little strips of flesh to the guests ; the bones he throws to a second attendant, who pounds them up with a heavy stone.

I passed the place to-day as I rode in from a reconnaissance. The slab lies a stone's-throw to the left of the great northern road to Tengri Nor and Mangolia, about two miles from the city.

A group of stolid vultures, too demoralized to range in search of carrion, stood motionless on a rock above, waiting the next dispenser of charity.

A few ravens hopped about sadly : they, too, were evidently pauperized. One magpie was prying round in suspicious proximity, and dogs conscious of shame slunk about without a bark in them and nosed the ground diligently. They are always there, waiting.

There was hardly a stain on the slab, so quick and eager are the applicants for charity. Only a few rags lay around, too poor to be carried away.

I have not seen the ceremony, and I have no mind to. My companion this morning, a hardened young subaltern who was fighting nearly every day in April. May, and June, and has seen more bloodshed than most veterans, saw just as much as I have described. He then felt very ill, dug his spurs into his horse, and rode away.

[From *The Unveiling of Lhasa,* 1905.]

13

Tibet the Mysterious

By

THOMAS HOLDICH

I

[Early Tales about Tibet—Conformation of Tibetan Plateau and its Mountain Barriers—Routes into Tibet—North-western Routes—Leh, Shipki, and Niti Passes—Sikkim Passes—Eastern Routes—Ta-chien-lu—Routes from the North.]

THROUGH ALL the ages Tibet has held a paramount position amongst those regions of the world which have been popularly invested with a veil of mystery because they are inaccessible and unknown.

Tibet is so isolated, so lofty, so irresponsive to outside influences has held herself so far apart from the meddling interference of the busy, commercial world, as to provoke the enterprise of generations of speculative geographers, who, accepting *"omne ignotum pro magnifico,"* have startled the world with small instalments of truth surrounded by wide embroideries of decorative fancy. One of the earliest, if not quite the first, of these Tibetan romances dates from the days of Herodotus, nearly five hundred years before our era. When all the writings of the great "Father of history" can be carefully examined by the light of modern research, it will be found that his general accuracy is indisputable. His knowledge of Asiatic geography and his care in collating such evidence as may be gathered from the earliest of classical "travellers' tales" testifies to the possession by him of considerable analytical faculty and discernment. To one particular tale at any rate he gives a cautious admission of probability, but by no means a cordial assent. It was said that in the extreme northwest of India there existed a race of enormous ants, fierce and powerful, whose peculiar mission in life was the digging out of gold. Traders, mounted on swift camels, occasionally succeeded in seizing the gold which was accumulated in heaps by these excavating ants, and then rode rapidly away, pursued by other ferocious guardians of the soil who slew them if they caught them. Amongst all the ludicrous exaggerations of ancient classical tradition relating to India, this one story evinces a remarkable tenacity of existence. It is repeated in every tale of the East that is told by compilers and adventurers before the days of Herodotus, and is only doubtfully regarded by him as pure fiction. It was not until, in recent years, the trans-Himalayan explorers of the Indian Survey recorded their experiences that any light could be thrown on its origin. These explorers, making their way painfully over the terrific altitudes which intervene between India and western Tibet, reached at length the gold-mining districts which lie beyond the mountains on the great western plains. Here they discovered the Tibetan workman delving for gold after a fashion of his own. The intense cold and the fierce winds of the highlands compelled him to grovel on the ground enfolded in a thick, black blanket, whilst he dug, or scratched, painfully and slowly at the alluvial soil with the end of the first tool available to his hand, which was usually the horn of the Tibetan antelope. To all appearance he was a rough imitation of a huge horned ant grubbing up the auriferous soil and piling it in heaps for subsequent washing. Guarded by immensely powerful dogs (whose ferocity even to this day is a byword amongst travellers in Tibet), he has pursued his unenviable calling from those very early days until now, hardly improving his processes, making but slight impression and shallow indentations in the soil, and probably leaving behind two-thirds of the gold which it contains. Here, then, according to Sir H. Rawlinson, is the solution of the mystery that surrounded that particular tale ; and it is but one illustration of the perceptive faculty possessed by Herodotus that he should consider it worthy of record.

Hardly anything of note concerning Tibet occurs in the works of medieval geographical writers and compilers. The huge, great central upheaval south of the Gobi depression extending along the whole length of the Himalayas (which form its southern buttress or revetment through which the great natural staircases lead upwards to the plateau from the plains), geologically coeval with the Himalays of the Northwest, but never by countless ages than those of the East, has ever been a barrier against the ever-recurrent tides of human movement southwards. No medical trade routes ever crossed Tibet from the north. Along the length of the intervening plains of Chinese Turkestan they ran westward from China till they touched the central barrier (the Taurus of the Classics), which is the eastern wall of the Pamirs. They then diverged northward, or twisted over the Pamir region to Badakshan and the Oxus, but they ever avoided Tibet. The countless tides of Central Asian emigration (Aryans, Skyths, Mongols, etc.), when they overflowed into India, passed by way of Badakshan and the Hindu Kush—never across Tibet. No Chinese Pilgrim seeking knowledge at the fountain-head in northern India ever traced his way across the Tibetan uplands from the plains of western China and Kashgar, although he often selected a straighter route than that of Mongol invaders. Avoiding the central Pamir region and Tibet by crossing the Hindu Kush near its northeastern base by either the Wakjir or Baroghel pass, he entered the valleys of Gilgit and Chitral in order to make his way over routes incredibly rough and difficult to the ancient Gandhara—the seat of all that was most sacred to Buddhism in the extreme northwest of India. The great rolling Tibetan highlands have thus played a most important part in the history of Asiatic migration. They have been the natural buffer-land between Central Asia and India, covering so wide a space of the northern frontiers of India, that the only mountain gateways that have ever been opened from the north into the rich sunlit plains of the peninsula are to be found beyond them, and within the comparatively restricted length of the mountain borderland which stretches between Karachi and the Kohistan of Kabul. Who shall say how much the wealth of India, depending on the accumulation of centuries of patient industry and taken from her own prolific soil, owes to the Tibetan barrier. For countless ages, ere there was added to the world a southern zone of communication represented by the ocean and ocean-going ships, that wealth has been protected by mighty land barriers. For ages, when adventurous and mobile forces bred in the eastern steppes of high Asia, hardened and trained to the exercises of war, found power to traverse the huge continent which contained them,—westward to Europe or southward to Cathay,—and pillage the stores accumulated in the cities of the unwarlike working races of a softer and more genial world, it was only from the west and by very narrow ways that they could touch India. Truly they made good use of their opportunities when they found them, but it is worthy of record that the fiercest and most devastating hordes of all the countless nomads who poured out of Asia from age to age—the Mongols—only made India the scene of their destroying migrations when they could turn the western flank of the Himalays. They never crossed the Tibetan Chang.

The great corrugated uplands of Tibet, seamed with ridges of high altitude, inhospitable, bleak and desolate, though they be, do not in themselves, however, present any insurmountable difficulty to geographical exploration.

The chief obstacles to Tibetan exploration have ever been the mountain barriers which surround the plateau, rather than the plateau itself. These mountain systems on all sides of Tibet are massed into a series of gigantic walls, the ranges and ridges of which are not fashioned as long spurs reaching out from the highlands and gradually diminishing in altitude till they fade into the plains below, enclosing long sloping valleys which would answer the purpose of ramps or shelving approaches to the heights ; but they are folded range after range in gigantic altitudes (higher than the ranges of the plateau), forming a rough but readily recognisable system of parallel flexures flanking the general edge of the central Tibetan upheaval.

Tibet may be described as a huge pear-shaped formation, with the small end of the pear attached to the southeastern corner of the Pamirs at the point where the Kashmir hinterland, from the heights of the giant Muztagh range, looks northward over the sources of the rivers of Chinese (or eastern) Turkestan. The Muztagh range might almost be called the stem of the pear, the narrow end of the pear gradually widening out therefrom being appropriately known as Little Tibet. Little Tibet is politically an outlying province of Kashmir. As the Northern side of the pear-shaped formation curves boldly eastward it is represented by the border mountain systems of Kuen Lun, Altyn Tagh, Nan Shan, etc., which, following each other in succession, carry the northern boundary of Tibet to the province of Kansu of China. where exactly Kansu ends and Tibet begins is a matter rather of conjecture than political certainty; but for the purposes of description we will consider all the country south of the Altyn Tagh and the Nan Shan ranges to be Tibet. To the north of these ranges is the comparatively low-lying region of Chinese Turkestan, with abundant fertility about its western extremity and along the edges at the foot of the mountains, and a sand-strewn desert in its midst, hiding the remains of those cities which have been made known to us by the researches of Sven Hedin and Stein. Throughout the Kuen Lun series of mountain systems there is a certain structural similarity. The main ranges are folded in vast anticlinals parallel to the edge of Tibet and to each other, ridge upon ridge, like a series of walls. It is not to-be supposed that the simplicity of this description is readily to be recognised in the mountain masses themselves. There is the usual complexity of subsidiary spurs and more or less isolated massifs, of geological faults, and inconceivably rough foothills, which present to the eye the appearance of mountain features without arrangement and without plan. Nevertheless there is (as there is in the Himalayas) an underlying structural basis which marks them rather as successive walls of the plateau than as direct extensions from it.

The result is extreme irregularity in the main lines of drainage which cut their way through-passages transverse to the walls, following the weakest lines of resistance (or, it may be, retaining a primeval course during the upheaval of the mountain masses) till they reach the plains. Not only are the valleys which form the natural approach to Tibet from the north thus liable to narrow restricted gorges and desperately rough intervals where they break across or through a ridge, but they are lengthened inordinately between the plains and the plateau. These main lines of approach (so far as they are known) will be described hereafter.

On the east, at the broad end of the pear-shaped plateau, the mountains of the Kansu border curve round southward (allowing the head-waters of the Hoang Ho of China to pass through them as they curve), and gradually merge into a fairly well-defined north to south range which figures on the map as Sifan. Here, within the limits of Tibet, there occurs the commencement of a most remarkable orographical feature. Range after range striking outwards from the plateau follows the same curving course from southeast to south, bending in orderly procession like the waves of the sea, deepening their valleys and steepening their sides as they proceed southwards, till the whole-southeastern world of Tibet is but a succession of mountain waves whose forest-crested summits gradually reach southwards into Burma. Down the deep troughs of these southeastern valleys of Tibet flow the waters of several of the most important rivers of Asia. The Di-chu (or Yang tsi) is the outermost, with a course of eight hundred miles ere it passes the Tibetan frontier. The Mekong, the river of Siam, and the Salwin, one of the two great rivers of Burma, lie within the Yang tsi and parallel to it. Recent evidence points to the fact that the Irawadi, the next great Burmese river, does not rise far, if at all, within the Tibetan border.

It is the contiguity of these intervening ranges, the difficulty presented by a succession of rugged mountain walls, which proves to be the great barrier between Tibet and China on the east.

But while approach directly from the east is rendered almost impossible by this geographical distribution of ridge and valley, the same distribution rather favours approach from the south east, i.e., from the province of Yunnan is China,or from Burma, Thus there is a route from Yunnan which takes advantage of the Di-chu (Yang tsi) River valley. It is marked by the trade centre of Batang.

In more irregular but still recognisable form the curving structure of the mountain system continues over the intervening space westwards till it determines the bend of the river Brahmaputra, which changes its direction as it flows from Tibet into Assam, and thus rounds off, as it were, the eastern end of the Himalayas. The irregular trans-Brahmaputra hills, through which runs a part of the southern boundary of Tibet, are drained by one or two minor rivers which join the Brahmaputra from the east. They are supposed to be within the sphere of British political influence, but they are practically beyond it, and through their valleys, owing to the fierce and irreconciliable nature of the tribes which people them (Abors, Mishmis, etc.), no right of way to Tibet has ever been established. It may be that eventually it is here that we shall find that open door which, leading upward by paths indicated by geographical structure as the easiest, will reach the cultivated lands of eastern Tibet (and ultimately the plateau) by a route involving no high passes and no long detours. The Brahmaputra marks the natural gateway of the hills. Westward of the Brahmaputra, to the extremest point of the Kashmir stem of the pear-shaped plateau, are interposed the great Himalayan barriers, which are perhaps the most effective barriers of all.

The structural relationship of the Himalayan ranges the south of Tibet is very similar to that of the mountains on the north. Throughout their whole length, from the great bend of the Indus (where that river leaves the longitudinal valleys of its upper reaches to break transversely across the ridges as it seeks its way to the plains) to the great bend of the Brahmaputra (where that river is forced into a curving deflection from its Tibetan channels), through fifteen hundred miles of mountains, there runs a dominant water-parting, or backbone to the whole system. This is set back from the plains of India at a distance of about one hundred miles. It is on this divide that the magnificent array of highest snowcapped peaks is to be found, from the giants of Kashmir to the groups of pinnacles about Everest and Kanchenjanga. It is the "snowy range" par excellence, and seen from Himalayan hill stations. We are not quite sure what becomes of it through the unexplored regions of Nepal, but it apparently loses its continuity as a district. The general trend or axis of this great curving divide determines the shape of the southern edge of the Tibetan plateau. Infinitely higher that the plateau, it is yet but part of that procession of mountain walls which form its southern support Northward it overlooks the plateau; southward it overlooks the apparently confused and tangled mass of lower subsidiary ranges which fill up the intervening one hundred miles between itself and the plains of India. But there is no real structural confusion about these minor ridges and ranges. Most of them maintain a parallel formation of ridge and valley to the snowy range. This is very observable in the extreme northwest, and is recognisable throughout the Himalayas in spite of the maze of spurs and offshoots which tend to disguise the fundamental design. North of this range there is a minor (yet still gigantic) subsidiary and parallel wall (enclosing a space of upland waste about thirteen thousand feet above sea level) which overlooks the great troughs where the Indus, the Sutlej, and the Brahmaputra collect their forces. The Sutlej and the Indus flow westward by separate routes to India. The Brahmaputra flows eastward through southern Tibet till it is turned in its course by the eastern walls of the plateau and forced through the Dihang gorges into upper Assam. "On the north of the Himalayan wall rise the Karakoram and Gangri mountains, which form the immediate escarpment of the Tibetan tableland. Behind the Gangris on the north the lake-studded plateau of Tibet spreads itself out at a height averaging fifteen thousand feet. Broadly speaking the double Himalayan wall rests upon the low-lying plains of India, and descends north into the river trough beyond which rises the Tibetan plateau. Vast glaciers, one of which is known to be sixty miles in length, move their masses of ice downward to the valleys. The higher ranges between India and Tibet are crowned with eternal snow. They rise in a region of unbroken silence like gigantic frosted fortresses, one above another, till their white towers are lost in the sky." (*W.W. Hunter*).

Yet another river besides the Sutlej, the Karnali, one of the largest affluents of the Ganges, breaks through the Himalayas between the arms of the Indus and Brahmaputra. The Karnali is a Nepalese river, and its upper course is therefore but indifferently known. There is no doubt, however, that its sources lie beyond the Himalayas.

The Indus rises on the slopes of Kailas, the sacred mountain, the Elysium or Siva's Paradise of ancient Sanskrit literature. Its long and comparatively straight course from its source at sixteen thousand feet above the sea, through channels running northwest through gigantic mountains, is often comparatively placid. It flows over broad gravely beds, gathering strength as it flows, for five hundred miles ere it plunges into the gorge of Iskardoh, which is said to be fourteen thousand feet in sheer depth. The Sutlej rises on the southern slopes of Kailas. It flows no longer from one of the sacred lakes of Manasarawar, famous in Hindu mythology. Abandoning its ancient cradle in Rakhas-Tal, it now issues from the foothills of Kailas. It cuts its way from birth through a vast accumulation of deposits by a deep gully between precipices of alluvial soil, and finally pierces the Himalayas by a gorge with mountains rising to twenty thousand feet on either side. This is in the region of the famous Shipki pass, where the Tibetan outposts hold the frontier.

The traveller who wishes to traverse the wide desolation of the Tibetan plateau has a considerable choice of routes. From north, south, east, and west explorers and adventurers have tackled the problem of reaching the capital of the country, Lhasa, and with about equal want of success. The northern routes from the plains of Chinese Turkestan which have been exploited by Prejevalski, Sven Hedin, Deasy, Stein, Littledale Bonvalot, and others are distinctly the most difficult and unpromising, partly because it is necessary to reach the plains of Kashgar before attempting them—and this in itself is no mean performance ; partly because these northern routes lead to the wildest and most desolate uplands of all the desolate field which Tibet presents. These are Russian routes, inasmuch as they lead direct from the Russian Asiatic borderland of Chinese, Turkestan, and they are long routes bristling with all the formidable barriers that a bleak and immensely high mountain system can set in their way ere the dreary open steppe is attained at altitudes which are considerably greater than those of southern Tibet. Russia is shut off from the capital of Tibet by natural barriers which are infinitely greater than those which present themselves on the side of India. Geographically, Lhasa, and all of Tibet which holds promise of future civilised development, is within the meshes of the broad network of hinterland communication which is cast from India or from China, and never could be attached to a direct northern system by any, but the weakest of geographical ties. There is nevertheless a bond of religious and commercial union between Russia and Tibet which is maintained by a much-traversed route on the northeast,-a long route and an important one,—about which there is more to be said hereafter.

These northern routes will be considered in connection with those explorations which led to their discovery.

From the south Tibet is approached by the Sutlej opening through the Himalayas and by a group of passes leading from Kumaon. There are also routes about which we know little leading direct from Nepal, but the principal (because the most direct and the nearest) group of trans-Himalayan passes into Tibet are those which traverse the valleys of Sikkim and Bhutan.

On the east one or two routes are well-known, amongst them one which from prehistoric days has been the main and the best-trodden route from China to Lhasa, i.e., that which cuts the boundary at the frontier station of Ta-chien-lu (Darchendo). This indeed not only connects Pekin with Lhasa, and is historically responsible for the great movement of the Chinese race westward which ended in the conquest of Tibet, but it stretches its length (as will be explained more fully) to Kashmir and India, and must rank as one of the greatest of Asiatic trade routes.

The routes into Tibet from the northwest diverge from Leh, the capital of Ladak, and many a traveller has started from the quaint Buddhist town in search of adventure in the trackless Tibetan plateau land. Ladak is the extreme outlying, uptilted province of Kashmir, and the modern road between Srinagar (the capital of Kashmir) and Leh is a well-laid-out route two hundred and forty miles in length,—frequently traversed, but involving some formidable passes. Leaving behind him the sombre shade of the thick pine woods of the Sind valley, the traveller encounters the main orographical line of division between Kashmir and Tibet at the point marked by the well-known Zoji La pass,—a pass which is typical of many other Himalayan passes, where the cutting back of the southern stream at its head has tended to obliterate the steep slopes of the northern side. A sharp ascent of two thousand feet from the south, zigzagging up the face of a precipitous slope, flanking a narrow and steep-sided gorge, leads over the pass to an open and apparently level valley, partly blocked with debris and talus, where it is difficult to determine in which direction the stream runs.

Approaching it from the Tibetan side, the great traveller Sven Hedin calls it "the worst pass I have ever seen," although its altitude (not more than eleven thousand five hundred feet) is low compared with many which he must have previously encountered in Tibet. But he crossed it on the 9th of January, when the pass is usually closed by winter snow.

Beyond the Zoji La the road drops into the Indus basin, and is within the limits of Ladak (or Little Tibet), which geographically and climatically belongs rather to Tibet than to Kashmir. Hugging the river banks (but one hundred and fifty feet above it), it passes through some of the grandest of trans-Himalayan scenery. Near Leh the Indus is walled in between tremendous precipices, where it has literally carved a way for itself through the mountains. Its dark green waters flow in tranquil silence through broad reaches, or break up in thundering cataracts where the channel contracts. Occasionally the sunlight finds a way through the deep-shadowed cliffs overhanging its southern banks, and then it strikes the surface into emerald patches, and sends long, slanting shafts into the glistening depths. It is a weird, wild scene, a fit introduction to a weird and wild country. Yet there are broken spaces of cultivation where apricot and apple orchards hide the dwellings of as cheery hearted a population of mountaineers as is to be found in the wide world. The Ladaki lives to laugh, and, living (as he frequently does) a life in which the carrying of loads seems to be the fundamental object of existence, he nevertheless succeeds in securing for himself a fair share of that happiness which knows no fixed geographical limits.

Leh is the market town, the commercial centre of western Tibet. The town climbs up the side of a hill, as do most Tibetan towns, and the general look of it, flat-topped as to roofs and sloping as to walls, is almost Chinese in effect; but it lacks the grace of Chinese outline. As usual, a monastery dominates the town with high splay-footed walls, perforated by perpendicular rows of windows (or openings) marking successive flats. Red and white against a brown background of rugged hills is the prevailing colour scheme; the air is dry and dusty, with the clear but wintry light of all north Indian highland places. Leh is distinctly Tibetan. There is none of the airy grace of the rickety buildings which overlook the Jehlam at Srinagar. It is substantial, square built, and somewhat heavy—like the Tibetan himself. But it is a busy town, and caravans are constantly coming and going in its market-place.

From Leh into the Tibetan plains there is but one recognised road, and that road crosses the Chang La (seventeen thousand six hundred feet) within fifty miles of Leh. Still following the right bank of the Indus for a space, amidst scattered evidences of the Buddhist faith (kists covered with stone slabs stretching their length for hundreds of feet along the river side, and repeating with monotonous reiteration the Buddhist formula "Om mane padme hum)," the road diverges suddenly eastward from the village of Sakti, and climbs the Chang La. It is not such a formidable pass as its altitude might lead one to expect, as the snow is usually less here than on the outer Himalayan ranges of similar altitude. The vapour-bearing currents from the southwest lose their moisture on the outer Himalayan heights, where snow is precipitated in vast quantities. Tibet is on the whole remarkably free from snow. The Chang La is occasionally passable all through the winter, but it is precipitous and difficult to climb,—"nothing but blank walls of bare, gray rock," says Sven Hedin. However, he crossed on the 18th of December without any mishap. From the pass the road drops eastward to the Shyok valley (where is Tanksi, with its picturesque monastery of Jova perched on a detached crag), and then rises over the intervening eastern water parting, and drops to the head of the Pangong Lake. Here commences Tibet proper, and from here the recognised caravan roads southeast to Rudok, or by the northern shores of the lake to Gangra, have not always been those selected by adventurous explorers for the purpose of crossing the Tibetan Chang when they designed to leave their tracks on the map of the interior. Here we leave it. Beyond this point the road to Lhasa is an explorers' route, of which we possess but a scanty descriptive outline, although it is one of the great highroads of Asia. From Srinagar to the Tibetan frontier it is the best known of all approaches to Tibet.

Next in order eastward amongst Himalayan approaches are the Shipki and the Niti routes, which are familiar enough to residents in Simla or Naini Tal, but are, nevertheless, but seldom traversed by any of them. Everyone who has visited Simla knows the highroad to Mahasu and Narkanda. The view of the northern mountains from Narkanda, forty miles from Simla, is the most striking view of Himalayan scenery that is to be obtained anywhere near Simla, a town which is not well-placed for landscape effects. The sense of astonishment inspired by the magnificent wall of snow-capped mountains towering over the shadowed depths of the Sutlej valley is intensified by the dramatic suddenness with which a sharp bend in the road reveals the vision. So far the great central trade route to Tibet (which this well-engineered road was designed to be) has only carried one along the crests of subsidiary spurs overlooking east and west, long waving lines of green and purple hills spread abroad in infinite variety of light and shade, and chequered with patches of forest and terraced field. The rhododendrons and blue pines and silver oak of Simla have gradually given place to firs and green oak, and long, straight-stemmed pines standing thickly and darkly in the lower depths; but there has been no view of the majesty of eternal snow and glacier till we reach Narkanda.

At Narkanda one suddenly faces a stupendous range, and looks through a vast space of the uplifted mountain side, slung, as it were, midway between unknown depths below and the bright glory of snow outlines clear cut against the azure sky above.

From Narkanda the road dips into the depths of the Sutlej valley, passing under the shadow of gigantic pines, thickly burdened with ferns and moss, till the river itself is touched and the road commences to cling to it. It then follows the Sutlej valley to the main pass on the Tibetan frontier at Shipki, but it is no longer a road of the same class as that which connects Simla with Narkanda. As a Tibetan trade route the road is a failure, but there is a very large local traffic upon it, due to the development of villages and cultivation in the valleys near Simla, which is largely dependent on local means of supply for wood and vegetables. Once in Tibetan territory this route follows the southeasterly course of the Sutlej to its source near the Rakhas-Tal, the westernmost of the twin lakes of Manasarawar. About midway it passes through the Tibetan town of Totling, where there is a monastery, and which is a not unimportant centre of road communications in connection with the gold fields of the west.

Farther east again we find a group of passes connecting Kumaon with Tibet to the north of Almorah,—the Mana, Niti, Milam, Darma (Langpya La), and Byans (Mangohang La), all forking off from the upper tributaries of the Alaknanda affluent of the Ganges. The Mana (eighteen thousand five hundred feet), which is at the head of the Badrinath stream, leads directly northward to Totling on the Sutlej. The altitudes of the Niti and the Milam are not well-determined, but they cannot be much less than that of the Mana on the west. All these passes appear to be over eighteen thousand feet. Across the Milam there is still some traffic in gold-dust and borax, which is brought across the Himalayas on the backs of sheep, which (in spite of certain objections on the part of the lamas at Lhasa) still continue to be beasts of burden in southern Tibet. They travel remarkably well, and keep their condition under under circumstances which would prove fatal to the condition of mules. They take back to Tibet cooking-utensils, pots, pans, and earthenware, but naturally no very bulky merchandise can be transported over the rugged mountain tracks in this way.

The Karnali, or Gogra, River, rising near the sources of the Sutlej and Indus, also affords a trans-Himalayan passage; but it leads through a maze of mountains to the same focus on which the more western routes converge, and has apparently no separate trade outlet of its own on to the Tibetan plateau. All these routes practically centre on the same point,—the twin lakes of Manasarawar in the southern Tibetan district of Nari Khursam, or Hundes, which lie below the sacred peaks of Kailas. The great alluvial plain of Nari Khursam divided by the gorge of the Sutlej River is a sort of landing in the Tibetan staircase. In its midst Totling is the chief place of importance, as we shall see further on. Beyond it are infinite mazes of mountains still intervening between the landing and the rugged plateau land, but there are no more Himalayas. The farther mountains are but lofty incidents of the great central table-land.

About the passes from Nepal to Lhasa we know exceedingly little, although Nepal was the connecting link of the Tibetan missions with India in the beginning of the eighteenth century. Nepal still maintains a formal recognition of Chinese suzerainty, and from Kathmandu there issues a periodic procession of priests and high military functionaries bearing tribute to Pekin. The procession moves by way of Lhasa, and strikes straight into Tibet. Presumably it crosses the main Himalayas by a pass which was used by an Indian explorer in 1867, who made his way direct from Khatmandu into the valley of the Yeru Tsanpo (Brahmaputra), to the well-known monastery of Tadum. Aided by the disguise of a pigtail and a false bottom to his box of merchandise, this explorer crossed by the No-La (sixteen thousand six hundred feet), at the head of a western affluent of the Gandak River of Nepal, and thence made a most eventful journey through Tibet. It is from such sources that we derive all our geographical knowledge of the most important part of Tibet, i.e., the southern districts which lie immediately north of the Himalayas and are watered by the great Yeru Tsanpo. Doubtless the Gandak affluents draining down the rugged sides of the main range afford opportunities for the passes than that of the No-La. The Kirong, the Jong-ka-jong, and the Kuti, north of Khatmandu, surmount the main Himalayan water- parting at points which can hardly be twenty-five miles south of the Yeru Tsanpo. Nepal has hitherto been a forbidden land to Europeans. Europeans have seen most of Tibet, traversed it from north to south and from east to west ; but no European ever made close acquaintance with Nepalese topography until Captain Wood was permitted to fix the position of Mount Everest from points of observation near Khatmandu in 1904. It is impossible to say exactly by what passes the Chinese invaded and conquered that country. It is, however, certain that they must be fairly easy and accessible.

The most significant groups of passes leading from India into Tibet is that of Sikkim, connecting the basins of the Tista and of the Ammu Chu (river of Assam) with the valley of the Tsanpo near Lhasa.

Two or three routes into Tibet diverge from our railway base at Siliguri on the eastern frontier. One is carried by the mountain railway line to Darjeeling; and from Darjeeling as his base the traveller (such travellers as Dr. Weddell, Mr. Douglas Freshfield, and the Bengali pundit, Chandra Das, etc.) descends into the Tista valley, and makes his way by an easily recognisable, but occasionally difficult, route along the Lachen affluent of the Tista and over the Kamba La or Kangra pass (sixteen thousand six hundred feet) to Kamba Jong. Kamba Jong is separated from the trade and religious centre of Shigatze on the Tsanpo by cross-country roads, for the most part not better and no worse than the ordinary unmade country tracks passing through the uncultivated areas of India, but with one or two crossings of mountain passes *en route.* Or, instead of following up the Lachen affluent of the Tista, the traveller may take the Lach-lung affluent to the Donkia pass (eighteen thousand one hundred feet) and strike into the road to Gyangtse. This route, however, involves five or six crossings of intermediate passes before reaching Gyangtse, and although such passes are not formidable, they are obstructive. By far the most direct route to Gyangtse and Lhasa is that which was followed by the Tibetan mission under Colonel Younghusband. From Siliguri a cart road runs by the Tista valley to Kalimpong, just below Darjeeling, and thence diverges to the northeast over a series of ascents and descents for forty-two miles to Gnathong (twelve thousand feet), and on to the "smooth and easy" pass called Jelep La, which divides the basin of the Tista (or Sikkim) from the upper basin of the Ammo Chu (or Chumbi), which is Tibet. At this point only Tibet drives a wedge southward into the body of the Himalayas. The valley of the Ammo Chu formerly belonged to Bhutan, but Tibet has recently asserted the right of occupation, and it is here that her troublesome intrusions into British territory necessitated the campaign of 1888, which succeeded in driving the Tibetan rabble over the Jelep La into Chumbi, from whence they came. Chumbi is said to be a delightful country. It has been called the Engadine of the Himalayas, and it is doubtless a pleasant offset to the wintry regions which lie above and beyond it. Pari, in the upper valley, is a town of about three hundred houses, protected by a fort. According to one authority, it is "abundantly bleak and bare," being four thousand feet higher than the Chumbi town (ten thousand feet), and not far below the Tang La pass, over the principal Himalayan water divide between the Tsanpo and the Ammo Chu. But Hooker describes it as an important trade entrepot, where tobacco fruit, and cloth from Bhutan are found, together with vegetables, cattle and fish. Customs are collected here by Tibetan officials. The Tang La, above Pari (fifteen thousand seven hundred feet), is an exceptionally easy pass for the Himalayas. From it northward there runs rivulet which, swelling into a stream and finally developing into a full-grown river, flows almost directly northward through an open and gently rounded plain to Gyangtse and the Yeru Tsanpo. There is not a pass to bar the way nor a serious physical obstacle to contend with, as far as Gyangtse. It is, *par excellence*, the great central route across the breadth of southern Tibet,—that part of Tibet which, being within the Brahmaputra basin, is in true geographical affinity with India in spite of the intervening Himalayan wall. The journey from the Indian frontier to Lhasa may be made in a fortnight over fairly good country roads and through tracts which are partially cultivated. From the north,—From Kashgar or the frontier of Chinese Turkestan to Lhasa,—it is a journey of months across a wild and desolate table-land, the horrors of which have been described to us by Sven Hedin Bower, Prijevalski, and others, presenting an aspect of Tibet which has little in common with the Tibet of the upper Brahmaputra.

Whilst the gates of Tibet have ever been jealously guarded against European advance from the west or south, and the wild, bleak wind-swept plains and rocky defiles of the northwest, added to the desolation of dreary steppes, stretching in stone-strewn monotony for hundreds of miles, have effectually hindered the progress of trade developments in these directions through all historic times, it has not been the same on the east or the northeast. From the west, in spite of all obstacles, a certain amount of intermittent trade has always filtered through Leh, or over the passes of Kumaon to India, owing chiefly to the fact that gold and borax are easily transportable commodities; but the main trade of Tibet has always run China-wards. Gold, even from the extreme western fields near the Kashmir border, has been carried in far larger quantities to Pekin, over a distance of three thousand miles, than it ever has to Leh, which is hardly three hundred miles from the centre of the western mining districts. The Sikhs, by way of Kashmir, and the Mongols, from the north, have alike attempted the conquest of Tibet with no substantial commercial profit ; but the Chinese from the east have swamped the country with most practical results. With a loose and elastic system of administration, which leaves both the spiritual and temporal government of Tibet almost untouched, and interferes not at tall with the customs of the people, the Chinese hold on Tibet has yet been of very solid advantage to China. Trade and commerce either follow the flag, or precede it, and most of the material comforts and luxuries of the few centres of semi-civilisation which Tibet possesses are the direct result of Chinese military enterprise. Tea, for instance, of a specially inferior quality, made as much from refuse as from the actual leaf, and cemented with rice water into the form of hard unpromising bricks, is imported in immense quantities from China, and, strange to say, it fully meets the requirements and the taste of a people who do not appreciate Indian tea. Nearly all this eastern trade now flows through the one centre on the eastern frontier called Darchendo in the older maps, or, more correctly, Ta-chien-lu in the never ones.

From western and southwestern China the approaches to Ta-chien-lu are through a mountainous region by tracks which follow the main courses of the upper affluents of the Yang tsi king in the province of Ssu-chuan. From the Min river affluent, which drains a busy and populous centre of Chinese industry, a tributary called the Tung leads upwards to the frontier at Ta-chien-lu ; another affluent flowing south, itself a feeder of the Yalung, defines a route which connects Ta-chien-lu with the frontiers of the province of Yunnan. There are no very high passages; no enormous altitudes to be dealt with on these two Chinese roads, which enclose between them a vast mountain tract inhabited by the independent Lolos. They are routes full of the interest of human activity and of magnificent scenery ; and about them one of the most fascinating stories of travel ever written has been given to the world from the pen of M.E. Colborne Baber, once secretary to the Chinese legation at Pekin. It is indeed a matter of deep regret that the mysterious visions which haunt the mist-clothed Mount Omi at the junction of the Tung and the Min (to use the Jesuit name for a river which is not known locally as the Min) are found too far from the borders of Tibet to be included with due propriety in the stories of Tibetan exploration. There is no enchanted Omi amidst the bleak desolations of Tibetan highlands. No emanation from the aureole of Buddha, seen as a "golden sunlike disc enclosed in a ring of prismatic colours more closely blended than the rainbow," ever cheers the hearts of the saints at Lhasa. Omi is Chinese, and but serves to emphasise the fact that of all the roads that run to Lhasa, that which approaches from the east is certainly the most fascinating by reason of the glory of its scenery, if it is not also the greatest by reason of its trade.

Ta-chien-lu is a picturesque mountain town, not more than eight thousand four hundred feet above sea level, and it constitutes the doorway into a corner of Tibet which is by far the richest in cultivation, the best in climate, and possibly the most productive in mineral wealth. The town lies "at the western end of a very narrow valley, so narrow indeed that for miles together it has no floor but the path and the torrent, which, after fifteen miles of cataracts, plunges into the Tung at Wa-Ssu-Kou; a mere gorge, in short, between two spurs of the snowy range over which the Che-to road passes."

Bower calls Ta-chien-lu a " pestilential spot," but this estimate of its salubrity is probably based more on the well-known want of sanitation which pervades all Asiatic hill towns than on any known condition of climate. Other travellers are more or less reticent. From Ta-chien-lu the great trade route rises to the elevation of thirteen thousand four hundred feet at Litang, between the Di chu and its Tung affluents, ere descending again to Batang, which is in the actual valley of the Di chu (or Kin sha, or Yang tsi). Batang is only eighty-one hundred feet above sea level, and from here the Tibetan highroad, crossing a narrow intervening divide, drops into the valley of the Nam chu, or Mekong River, which it follows to Chiamdo at a high level on the left bank where "travelling is not difficult" but "the people are given to much thieving." The narrow troughs (rather than valleys) which enclose the waters of the upper Yang tsi, the upper Mekong, and the Giama Nu Chu (which is now believed to be the upper Salwin River) are amongst the most populous and best-developed valleys of eastern Tibet. Their contiguity to the main trade route and their comparatively low elevation combine to render them prosperous , and it is here if anywhere that the future prospect of economic value in regard to mineral wealth appears to be most promising. It is therefore a matter of interest to note that this is a part of Tibet which might be reached from India with comparative facility and without encountering a rigorous climate by other routes than those of China. Following up the Lohit Brahmaputra to the northeast from the head of the valley of Assam, a forest track runs for one hundred and twenty miles to Rima, the capital of the Zayul district. From Rima routes diverge to the northeast and the northwest. Either route must inevitably encounter a high watershed between the basins of the upper Salwin and the Dibang affluent of the Brahmaputra, before descending into the valley of the former river, and it is probable that the passes over this intervening ridge would not be lower than the fifteen thousand feet average of the Tibetan plateau. But the route would not be long,—from eighty to one hundred miles from Rima to the Salwin, and perhaps seventy more to the China route near Batang. This is, however, conjecture, or hitherto the irrepressible hostility of the mountain tribes people of Upper Assam has proved an insuperable bar to successful exploration. Between the Brahmaputra and the Salwin, across the two hundred miles of intervening mountains, in the hidden depths of which are born the infant streams which swell the waters of the mighty Irawadi, no geographer has ever yet penetrated. It will not always be so. Upper Assam may yet point the way from India to northwestern China.

Setting aside for the present certain routes through Bhutan to Lhasa, we may note that there are yet other ways into Tibet (highways in the literal sense of the word) than those of the west and south and east, and by these other ways adventurers have reached the plateau from the north. By the northeast passage (a passage of primary importance) that grand explorer of Russian nationality, Prjevalski, and his lieutenant Roborovski, penetrated southwards to the sources of the Hoang Ho, the Yellow River of China. That way too came the American Rockhill, and the Frenchman Bonvalot (only a little more to the west). Sven Hedin, prince of Swedish travellers, with Carey and Dalgleish, Stein, Littledale, and Deasy, have all passed the northwestern hills,—so there is no lack of record. Not one of them ever reached Lhasa. Tibetan prejudice against travellers was too much for them. But they all scaled the northern walls of Tibet, and we know that there is not one, but several, recognised passes from the lowlands of Chinese Turkestan to the highlands of the plateau, which even in their rough condition of natural obstructiveness are yet passable for horses and camels. The point to be noted in connection with these northern passes is that they are not, and they never can be important trade routes.

The geographical conformation of the Tibetan plateau itself forbids it. It is not the passes themselves which are the obstacle. It is the great central region of lake-splashed upland—one huge, bleak wilderness of inhospitality-which intervenes between them and the warmer more genial (comparatively genial) districts of the Brahmaputra basin, wherein are all the great villages and trade centres of Tibet. This is the real obstacle, and has ever been so. No artificial efforts of man will ever contend against the giant distributions of nature in these uplands. The general outline of these distributions will be dealt with later. At present my object is to prove that the outside fringe of the veil of mystery which overhangs Tibet has been lifted on all sides of the plateau. It may well be doubted whether any further explorations will reveal to us more important breaks in the border line of mountain wall than those which we already know. If roads are to be made, we know where they must be made. It concerns us now, geographically, to consider what there is on the plateau when once it is reached ; and this we can best do by the light of such revelations as the Tibetan explorers of all nationalities have given us in the records of their wandering from the earliest ages.

II

Geological Evolution—The Chan Tang and Northern Tibet—Valleys of the Indus and Brahmaputra—The Fanglam Trade Route—Eastern Tibet—The Rivers of China and Burma—the Southern Zone-Climate.

So unique is the position of Tibet that a short description of its physical characteristics is almost essential to a comprehension of successive methods of exploration.

It seems probable that the primeval forces which first upheaved this gigantic excrescence on the face of earth gave it an axis running from west to east, which approximates to the position of the northern water parting or rim of the Indian hydrographic basin.

The plateau elevation culminates on this central line at an altitude of seventeen thousand six hundred feet about the seventy-ninth meridian. From this central line the uplands slope away on all sides—to about thirteen thousand feet towards the east and to eleven thousand in the southern zone, i.e., the basin of the Yero Tsanpo. A secondary axis of upheaval is sometimes recognised in the Kuen Lun mountain system on the northern edge. Modern Indian geologists are disposed to associate the upheaval of Tibet with that of the great trans-Indus table-lands of Baluchistan and Afghanistan on the west, with the northwestern Himalayas on the south, and the northern Burmese mountains on the east ; that is to say, they consider it to be very much more recent than the central portions of the Indian peninsula, or of the Himalayas to the northeast of India. This contention appears to be justified by the discovery of certain forms of fossils indicating the existence of life which has nowhere been found in the great highland steppes of the Asiatic continent, or in the broad expanse of the ancient beds of Central India. In later ages there must have accumulated on these heights as vast superincumbent mass of ice and snow, burying Tibet as effectually as Greenland is buried at the present moment, grinding down the mountain ranges to their present comparatively insignificant level, and spreading the debris of them in vast accumulations of detritus over the face of the table-land.

The next process was the recession of the ice, the gradual withdrawal of glaciers, the formation of lakes,—of lakes innumerable,-which in their turn have, for the most part, dried up and disappeared, leaving traces of their ancient beds behind them, spreading far afield from the present limited dimensions of such relics as remain. There may have been more than one or two glacial epochs, for all we know. There probably have been cycles of accumulation and disappearance; but it seems certain that during all these untold ages the process of gradual upheaval has been continuous, and with the advance of scientific investigation it will probably be proved to be still in action. When man made his first appearance we need not ask but there can be no reasonable doubt that the Tibetan is the latest survival of the ancient Turko-Mongol stock which once prevailed through all high Asia. The Tibetan came from the northeast in a purely Mongol form, and later from the southeast,—from Burma and Assam in the form of the Tibeto-Burman of modern ethnology, who aforetime occupied a great part of northern India.

The valley of the Brahmaputra, of the Subansiri and of those eastern affluents of the Brahmaputra which are separated from the sources of the Irawadi only by the narrow Patkoi range, were once the main avenues of approach to Tibet. It is worth nothing that the Tibetan himself claims descent from the monkey.

The boundary limits of Tibet and the ways which cross the surrounding borderland of mountains have already been indicated. Within the limits of the recognised Tibetan frontier we have three great physical divisions of vastly elevated plain which it is important to distinguish from each other. There is (i) the great northern plateau flanked by the Kuen Lun and the steppes of Tsaidam, which we know as the Chang tang (the "Northern Plain"). This is the region of highest elevation, too high and too cold for anything but pastoral use, where salt lakes are scattered at intervals amidst vast sterile flats, where grass is scanty and trees are absolutely wanting. It is sparsely inhabited by Mongolian nomads. Intensely cold (yet occasionally baked by more than summer heat under the summer sun), wind-swept, storm-beaten, and barren, it is perhaps the most inhospitable region in the Asiatic world. Its average elevation is about fifteen thousand feet above sea level, and above this again rise the crests of intersecting ridges of rounded outline which seam its surface in every direction, and increase the altitude by two thousand or three thousand feet. Rivers rise in the Chang and flow northward through the Kuen Lun range (and its extensions eastward) to the plains of Chinese Turkestan; the Kiria is perhaps the best known of them. Somewhere on the southern edge of the Chang is the water divide of India. No one has defined its exact geographical position. Some of the gigantic lakes of Central Tibet may possibly be within the Indian basin, but of many of them it is known that they have no outlet. These lake regions form the pasture lands of the Bod-pa nomads.

The Chang is the true Tibetan bulwark of the Indian frontier. It is impassable for large bodies of people, and has proved to be almost impassable for small companies.

The second physical division of Tibet includes the upper valleys of the Indus and Brahmaputra and their affluents, some of which are large rivers, e.g., the Kyichu, on which stands Lhasa. At the parting of the waters where the Indus, the Sutlej, and the Brahmaputra divide to the west and east, southern Tibet is high (fifteen thousand five hundred feet) ; but for three hundred miles to the northwest (following the Indus), and for seven hundred miles to the southeast and east (following the Brahmaputra), the level gradually diminishes to about thirteen thousand feet near the Ladak frontier, and eleven thousand feet on the Brahmaputra south of Lhasa. There is no sudden fall ; the descent is gradual, and the great rivers often flow in broad shallow reaches over smooth beds. This is the land of the Bodyul, or settled inhabitants of Tibet. Here are tracts that contain valleys warm enough for cultivation; these the Tibetans call "rong" (a ravine or narrow cleft in a hill), which word is more particularly applicable to the lowest and warmest valleys which produce crops twice in the year.

"The alluvial beds in the valleys are composed of debris of the surrounding rocks, laid out in horizontal deposits, which in course of time have become furrowed into gigantic ravines, with a succession of narrow terraces forming steps on each flank. It is on the existing lower alluvial beds that cultivation is carried on in plots which are usually well-watered and very fertile. The sharp needle peaks which are highest of all and bare of soil, but covered with perpetual snow, are met with most frequently in tracts of rong, and the rounded hills coated with grass to altitudes sometimes exceeding sixteen thousand feet in parts of Chang tang. The forest-clad mountain tracts which are occasionally met with occur chiefly in the rong. The general direction of hill and mountain chains is east and west, but northwest and southwest in western Tibet, where they are most irregular,—northeast and southwest in the province of U, and north and south in eastern Tibet. " Thus writes General Walker (late Surveyor-General of India), as the result of observations made chiefly by the native surveyors of his department.

The upper Indus valley contains some notable towns which are local centres of trade, such as Gartok, Demchok, etc., and is not devoid of the softer beauty of lower Himalayan scenery beneath the stupendous cliffs and crags of the ranges stretching north of Kailas. The Manasarawar lakes and the pasture lands which border them are the western Tibetan shepherds' paradise,—a paradise set amidst a vast stony wilderness. In the valley of the upper Brahmaputra, where the yellow glacial streams pour down from the outer Himalayan wall, or the clear flow of currents from the central lakes join the main stream, there is a gradually increasing extent of cultivation and human habitation. Fine monasteries exist at intervals, great clusters of square-cornered white buildings clinging to the hillsides overlook the valley between Tadum and Shigatze.

Although there is not a town in Tibet that would rank as second class in India, there are imposing collections of stone-built, white-faced houses dominated by ever-prevalent monastic buildings, which are quite equal in the scale of township with the secondary towns of Afghanistan or Baluchistan ; and indeed are not unlike the townlets that may be seen clinging to the spurs of the Hindu Kush north of Kabul. Tadum, Janglache, and Shigatze are the most important towns west of Lhasa.

Throughout the length of this southern region of Tibet there stretches a very remarkable trade route called the Junglam. From Leh it runs west of the Pangong lake to Rudok, the western frontier town of Tibet. Thence it crosses a breadth of the Chang tang lake region till it touches the upper Brahmaputra at its sources on the Mariam Ga (fifteen thousand five hundred feet),—the meridional water parting between the Indus and the Brahmaputra. Twice it crosses the Yero Tsanpo (upper Brahmaputra) by bridge or ferry, and passing midway through Shigatze is carried by a southerly detour to Gyangtse and Lhasa.

Within this stretch of nine hundred miles there are twenty-five staging places from twenty to seventy miles apart, with accommodation for about two hundred men. The road is generally well-defined, loose stones are cleared away in the defiles, and piles of stones with flags on sticks guide the way through the open stretches of table-land. East of Lhasa it runs to Chiamdo (the capital of the Kham province,—a garrison town), to Batang, Litang, and Ta-chien-lu on the Chinese frontier. It is the official post-road between Kashmir and Pekin, traversable at all seasons of the year by mounted men, and is probably the most remarkable (as it is the most elevated) postal highway in the world.

The third great physical division of Tibet comprises the eastern mountains and valleys. From the desolate steppes of Tsaidam on northeast to the rim of the Brahmaputra basin north of Lhasa, the eastern edge of the great central Chang tang forms an orographical feature which is of vast importance in the physical conformation of eastern Asia. Here arise innumerable rivulets which gather their infant forces together to form the first affluents of the great rivers of China, of Siam, and of Burma. The Hoang Ho (Yellow River) finds its source in the Oring Nor lake (or group of lakes) to the southeast of the great Koko Nor, and curving eastward and northward through the country of the Sifan (the western barbarians of China), till it approaches within one hundred miles of the southeastern corner of the Koko Nor, it takes its way as a full-grown river through northern China to the Pacific. To the west of the sources of the Yellow River rise those of the next great river of China, the Yang tsi king. The position of the extremest west of those sources which contribute uninterruptedly to the Di chu (the upper Yang tsi) is not exactly known, but it must be east of the route followed by Sven Hedin in his last adventurous journey into Tibet from the north. It will probably be found about the meridian of 91° east longitude. Flowing southeast, and separated from the upper Hoang Ho by the Baian-Kara-ulla range, it curves southward in about the same meridian (100° East Lon.) that the Hong Họ curves northward, admitting of the rise of another great river (the Nag-chu) between them. The Nag-chu eventually joins the Yang tsi when the latter finally assumes its eastern course through the width of China to the Pacific. Next to the Di-chu the Nam-chu (upper Mekong) starts from this same meridional divide, but probably from sources not so far west as the Di-chu, and follows a course which throughout Tibetan territory is almost parallel to that of the Di-chu. Finally, a fourth great river, the Salwin, a river of Burma, is represented by the Giama-Nu-Chu, which, gathering together many affluents from the highlands to the northeast of Lhasa, follows a course parallel to the Nam-chu and the Di-chu, curving gradually southward. Parallel to the Giami-Nu-Chu (but separated therefrom by a breadth of from four hundred to five hundred miles of mountains) is the Brahmaputra River, which bends from its easterly course through southern Tibet to pass southeastward through Himalayan gates to thc valley of Assam. This broad intervening space belongs to the Brahmaputra basin. Some very important valleys of no great elevation (Poyul, Zayul, etc.) drain into the Brahmaputra within it, being separated by a lofty divide from the narrow valley of Giama-Nu-Chu, or Salwin, to the east. It is a very remarkable feature in Asiatic orography which thus presents itself. First, the Brahmaputra, maintaining its general characteristic of a wide basin with important affluents converging on to the main stream up to the point where it emerges into the plains of Assam ; beyond this, overlooking the sources of these converging affluents, a containing mountain chain, distinct and apart from the Himalayan system, rounding off the heads of shelving valleys which slope westwards to the Brahmaputra, and dominating an eastern structure of enormous parallel mountain folds which enclose between their successive crests the deep troughs of some of the greatest rivers of Asia.

So close set are the successive ridges and ranges which part the Salwin from the Mekong, and the Mekong from the Yang tsi, that, at a point level with the head of the Assam valley one hundred miles would bridge them all. The Irawadi river of Burma is now supposed to rise to the southeast of this eastern extension of the Brahmaputra basin, amongst the wild hills which lie between the head of the Assam valley and Burma.

In the future of Tibetan commercial policy it is eastern Tibet which will prove to be the most important division, for it is the division of Tibet which contains the greatest present wealth and the greatest promise for the future, Travellers leaving the cold altitudes of the Chang behind them and descending gradually through the long narrow valleys towards the Chinese frontier are never weary of recounting the delightful change of climate and scenery which they encounter. There are magnificent forest-clad slopes beneath the snow-clad crests of the main ridges; there are thousands of well-watered, well-cultivated, and well-populated valleys hidden away amongst the folds of the main chains. The large and better-known valley, such as Darge on the Di-chu, or Chiamdo on the Nam-chu, are prosperous, populous, and priest-ridden ; the lesser-known valleys, such as Poyul and Zayul, are reported to be the centres of Tibetan art and industry. The whole region is full of unexploited mineral wealth, and, like western China, which it so greatly resembles, is bound to prove eventually an important factor in the world's economy. Two great trade routes run through this country, which are sufficiently described elsewhere. One (the Janglam) connects Lhasa with Ta-chien-lu and China; the other follows approximately (in several alternative loops) that line of water division in which the Chinese rivers rise, and connects Lhasa with the Koko Nor and Sining fu in the province of Kansu. Both lead to Pekin eventually, but the most important at present is the Ta-chien-lu route, which absorbs the greater part of the Tibetan trade.

Before describing in detail the progress of recent Tibetan exploration, the reader would do well to recall and fix in his mind the relative position of certain geographical (or strategical) points, which may be called obligatory points for the understanding of the value to be attached to individual lines of research. On the extreme west is Leh, the capital of the farthest outlying province of Kashmir-Ladak.

From Leh the southern valley regions of Tibet can be approached either by passing through Rudok at the southeastern extremity of the Pangong lake or by passing up the affluents of the Indus. It is equally possible to reach the northern Chang from Leh ; and thus Leh figures as the principal focus, or point of departure, for those explorers who make Kashmir their base. On the south Tibet is approached more directly either by the Kumaon group of passes, by Nepal, by Sikkim, or by Bhutan, the most direct route to the heart of the southern provinces at Lhasa being by Sikkim and the valley of Chumbi. On the east it is well to note the position of Ta-chien-lu,—the Chinese frontier trading-post. It is by this route that Tibet has been finally conquered, and by this route Tibet now maintains by far the greater part of its trade connections with the outside world. On the northeast the position of Sining fu and the Koko Nor region are of great political importance. This marks the line of route between Manchuria and Lhasa via Mongolia or China, and although the Mahommedan rebellions have temporarily thrown it out of popularity, it is still a great highway of pilgrimage,—the channel by which Lhasa maintains its supremacy in the Buddhist world amongst the far-off peoples of Mongolia and western China. The influence of Lhasa southward terminates abruptly at the Himalayan wall. Northward and northeastward it reaches to the farthest limits of Asiatic civilisation, and it is to four hundred millions of people in the far East what Mecca is to the Mahommedan world of the West. On the north the bleak desolation of the mountain barriers which shut off the lowlands of Chinese Turkestan from the highlands of the Chang tang (as well as the breadth of the Chang tang itself) admits of no base which is ever likely to be of the least importance for the support of either political, commercial, or military enterprise. It is southern and northeastern Tibet, not northern, with which the world will interest itself hereafter.

The southern zone of Tibet, which includes the true Bod-land, is divided into four provinces; viz., Nari on the west, Kham (otherwise Do Kham) on the east, and in the centre Tsang (adjoining Nari) and U (adjoining Kham), these two provinces being known conjointly as Utsang. A considerable belt of the central country is known as Hor. Nari includes Ladak and Balti, which are now part of Kashmir, but which are frequently spoken of as Little Tibet, as well as the districts of Khorsum and Dokthol, the latter being conterminous with western Nepal, and both being under the Lhasa Government.

Nari has only been partially explored by European travellers, the upper valleys of the Sutlej and Indus, the Manasarawar lake region, and the sources of the Brahmaputra and Karnali alone being accessible. Eastwards from Nari, the Dokthol country and the Utsang provinces (economically the most important in high Tibet) were originally explored by the native staff of the Survey of India; they have now been partially surveyed by officers attached to the Younghusband mission, and geographically they may the said to constitute the best-known part of Tibet. There are still, however, some important valleys watered by tributaries of the Brahmaputra flowing from the east into the central channel of the river (where it follows a southerly course to Assam) which are an absolute *"terra incognita"* so far as their topographical structure is concerned. The valleys of upper Zayul and Poyul are within the pale of Tibetan administration. Lower Zayul is almost certainly outside that pale, and is occupied by independent and barbarous tribes—Maris, Abors and Mishmis—who acknowledge no authority. The elevation of lower Zayul is not more than four thousand feet, and the climate of these lowlands is so repugnant to the Tibetan highlander that lower Zayul is regarded and utilised as a penal settlement. We are not even absolutely certain that we are correct in uniting the Giama-Nu-Chu with the Salwin. So great an authority as General Walker considers that the body of water contained in the Salwin at the farthest north point to which it has been explored from the Burmese side is not sufficient to warrant the inflow of so large a river as the Giama-Nu-Chu, and that the latter is really and affluent of the Irawadi and not of the Salwin. Native reports however make the Giama-Nu-Chu and the Salwin one and the same river, and this is probably correct. We have at any rate some interesting geographical problems yet to solve in these regions, and they all lie near to our own border.

A prevalent misconception about Tibet is that the climate is so rigorous and the cold so intense that European existence in the country would be sustained with difficulty. It is true that very severe cold is encountered on the lofty passes leading into Tibet, but so far as the southern regions of the plateau are concerned—the valley of the Brahmaputra and the eastern valleys of affluents of the Chinese rivers—no such extreme of temperature is to be feared. The climate is dry, and snow seldom lies long in the plains beyond the Himalayan barrier. Even in winter the streams of the Brahmaputra basin are not always frozen. Two crops a year are raised on the cultivated areas of the lower valleys—such as Shigatze and Gyangtse, or in the Kyichu. Climate and temperature depends more on geographical position than on mere altitude, and the latitude of the Brahmaputra valley is low and its position sheltered. No vast plains of sand stretch their length across its flanks to send scorching blasts across in summer, or the freezing winds of the Turkestan "shamshir" in winter. Under normal circumstances the climate of southern Tibet (at eleven thousand five hundred feet) is delightful in summer, when " the land is covered with vegetation, streams flowing in every valley, and all nature bright, sparkling and fresh." Even in winter, when snow and frost claim the land as their own, there is general movement throughout the country. It is then that the roads and rivers are rendered passable by ice to the trade caravans of the north and east. At Lhasa the mean temperature observed by Indian surveyors is thirty-six degrees Fahrenheit in February and March, and sixty-one in June and July. In the eastern valleys the climate is Himalayan in character, and its degrees of salubrity are more or less dependent on altitude.

I have been cautious in dealing with map altitudes which have been determined by means of barometrical observations. No such observations are trustworthy at such elevations, and they may very easily be in error by five hundred feet more or less. We now have certain accurately determined trigonometrical results from the observations of Major Ryder, and his assistants with Sir Frank Younghusband's mission in southern Tibet, where it is no longer necessary to depend too closely on the results obtained by native explorers.

III

Short Outline of Tibetan History—Introduction of Buddhism—Struggles with China and Mongol Interference—Growth of Lamaism—Chinese Administration.

An uninterrupted tale of exploration in the wilderness of Tibet, devoid (as Tibetan tales mostly are) of the stirring incidents of personal adventure, would prove but flat and unprofitable reading if they did not lead to a position from which we may form a fair estimate of the present status of Tibetan nationality, and make a rough forecast of the possible future of Tibet in the world of political strategy. But it would take too much space to consider in detail the opinions expressed by each individual traveller and to compare their impressions seriatim. It will be more useful to gather them at once into one collective whole, and to give a short summary of the existing form of government in Tibet and of its evolution, before we follow further the lines of modern exploration. We shall at least incidentally explain the position of some of those Tibetan functionaries with unpronounceable names who are so frequently referred to in the records of Tibetan travel.

The history of Tibet is the history of a country which, like India, has never lately been able to claim an integral nationality amongst the nations of the world. Foreign domination, either in Mongol or Chinese form, is invariably to be recognised, and it need be no matter of surprise to us if Tibetan traditions point to a final domination which is neither Mongol nor Chinese, but European. We are indebted to Prinsep, Kosma de Coros, Schlagentweit, and Sarat Chandra Das for the earliest records which may be called historical, including lists of kings dating from legendary beginnings (about the fifth century B.C.) to the end of the monarchy in 914 A.D. Throughout these legendary beginnings there runs a sort of traditional recognition of dual form of government for Tibet, Spiritual and temporal,—a form of administration akin to that of Rome, and one which finally found expression in Lhasa with the evolution of the Dalai Lama and his regent.

The aboriginal Tibetans appear to have been a savage and warlike people who invaded China and upper Burma with success, and even dictated terms of peace to the Chinese government. It was from China that the first principles of civilisation crept across the mountains to Tibet, coincident which the introduction of Buddhism by the young Chinese wife of the Tibetan King Srong-than-gumpo. She was the daughter of the Chinese emperor, and was received in marriage by the king after his successful invasion of China in the year 640 A.D. She found a useful ally in the Nepalese wife of the same monarch, and the two ladies worked together in harmony to lay the foundation of one of the mightiest religious institutions that the world has ever seen. King Srong-than-gumpo. (converted to Buddhism by his wife) founded Lhasa, and and Lhasa has ever since been the pivot of Buddhist thought and Buddhist faith for all eastern Asia. It has been as the holy of holies, the dwelling of the ark of the covenant, to one- third of the human race. It is so still. If ever England aspires to be a Buddhist power she must reckon first with Lhasa.

The Buddhism then introduced into Tibet

was supported by books and relies collected from India, and two great monasteries (Labrang and Rinpoche) were founded. But Indian Buddhism had long lost the grand simplicity of ifs principles. This had disappeared with the invasion of the Huns about the beginning of our era. Fa Hian (the Chinese traveller) found the doctrines of the " Great Vehicle" (sometimes called the Skythic form of Buddhism) in full force at Peshawur in the fifth century A.D. "Saints and angels sprang into existence, and grew and flourished till the Buddhist sky was full of them" (says Prof. Rhys Davids). Then the animism of the barbarous Huns was revived, with debasing beliefs in charms and ceremonies. The Tantra system, which was started at Peshawur in the sixth century A.D. was nothing better than witchcraft and sorcery. The Buddhism of Tibet thus partly derived from India did not supplant the older forms of Tibetan demonology till King Kir Song de Tsan reigned over the land (A.D. 740-786). It was then that true religion was acknowledged by ecclesiastical historians to be firmly established, and the Samye monastery was founded to contain the books collected from India. King Kir Song de Tsan is reckoned in Buddhist records to be the most illustrious and the most pious monarch who ever reigned over Tibet. It is worth nothing that the son of this king was one of the greatest socialists in history. He enacted that all men should be equal ; he compelled the rich to share their riches with the poor he favoured an absolutely equal distribution of all the comforts and conditions of life. This was indeed the attainment of a high ideal—but it did not answer. In a very short time his people by the natural force of personal idiosyncrasy returned to their former condition of inequality, and after repeating the experiment three times he gave it up. The wise men of Tibet said it was due to a survival of inequality in methods of existence during former lives.

In the early years of the ninth century a severe struggle with China took place, and thereafter throughout a period of intricate history, struggles with Mongols from the north and with China on the east were periodic. Nothing stands out very clearly after the break up of the Tibetan monarchy into four provincial kingdoms about the end of the tenth century, until the arrival of the celebrated Indian Buddhist Atisha, who settled in the great lamaserai of Thoding in Ngari. He introduced books and education and some of the element of astronomical science in 1026, and he was probably the first of the great priests whose authority became paramount in the country. He put the whole Tantra system into the background and resorted again to first principles. For three hundred years a purer form of Buddhism maintained its ground, whilst priests and lamas multiplied exceedingly, until the Mogul Emperor Kublai Khan (son of Genghis Khan) invested the high priest of the red-cap sect with sovereign power over the thirteen provinces of U and Tsang (which comprise Tibet proper), Together with Kham and Amdo, in 1252. This was a complimentary exchange for the kindly offices of the abbot in crowning him emperor of the widest empire the world has ever seen. For four centuries more the lamas of the Sakya monastery remained spiritual rulers of Tibet, temporal authority being exercised by regents whom they appointed.

Meanwhile, a new and powerful sect had arisen in Tibet. Modern lamaism (defined by Prof. Rhys Davids as "the union of ethical and metaphysical ideas with a hierarchal system and temporal sovereignty at Lhasa") may be said to have been founded by the great reformer Tsong kapa (the Luther of Tibet) in 1390. By 1410 there were three huge monasteries and thirty thousand disciples to testify to the activity of the reformation. In all respects Tsong kapa appealed to first principles, following Atisha, and pleading for the re-establishment of ancient customs. It was he who founded the custom of an annual week of fasting and prayer in which churchmen and laymen alike take part and which is described by the Jesuit missionary Huc. He never disputed the authority of the red-cap Sakya lamas. His sect is known to this day as the"yellow" or "orange" sect, from the colour of the robes its disciples wear. By the middle of the fifteen century the yellow caps were paramount, and a dual spiritual authority was established over Tibet at Lhasa and Tashilumpo.

When the Mongol dynasty of China ceased, that of the Mings yet further enlarged the authority of the Tibetan rulers and recognised the chief lamas. The failing power of the Mings in China favoured the interference of the Mongols in Tibetan affairs again, and a Tartar invasion occurred in the middle of the seventeenth century, which partially ended the Sakya red-cap rule and established that of the rising yellow caps. The fifth of the grand lamas of the reformed faith appears to have been a man of great strength of character and much diplomatic ability. According to Weddell he made excellent use of the opportunity afforded by the incident of the Tartar irruption, and with the assistance of the Tartar prince wrested the temporal authority out of the hands of the red-caps, and established himself as the first Dalai (or Tale) Lama of Tibet,—practically uniting in his person the offices of high priest and king, although a Tartai prince was nominally installed as king at Lhasa. The word "Dalai" appears to be merely the Mongolian rendering of his name (Vast as the Ocean).

He then set about establishing for himself and his successors a divine origin, based on a book of "revelations" which he "discovered," proving that all grand lamas were incarnations of the Great King Srong-tsan-gumpo, and enforcing his claims and his creed with such strong measures that the Jesuit missionary Grueber calls him "devilish God the Father who puts to death such as refuse to adore him." He however recognised the Grand Lama of Tashilumpo (Shigatze) as the reincarnation of a Pseudo-Buddha, second only to himself in spiritual significance, and thus founded the present recognised system of a dual spiritual rule in Tibet. The theory of reincarnation in infant form was not introduced into practice till later, and it was the cause of so much friction between rival sects as to lead to another Tartar invasion in 1717, when Lhasa was taken by storm.

Then the Emperor of China intervened with a powerful army. He ejected the Tartars, established the succession of the Dalai Lama by re-births, and curtailed his power at the same time. Two Ambans (or Ambassadors) were then appointed, with a Chinaman as regent or king. The "King" was murdered by the Dalai Lama in 1727, and the inevitable Chinese reprisals included the transfer of temporal power to a "mayor of the palace," one Miwang, of whom we shall hear more from the Capuchin fathers of the Tibetan missions, whom he befriended for years. A massacre of the Chinese in 1749 led to another punitive expedition (which will be referred to later), and from this time Chinese influence has been paramount in Tibet, until it was discredited by the late war. Latterly the present Dalai Lama, assisted by the young "national" party, has openly defied Chinese authority and has declared himself pro-Russian.

We may note here that the present Dalai Lama is the thirteenth in succession ; that he has reached the mature age of thirty (his four predecessors having died or disappeared about the age of eighteen) ; and that he shows every disposition to follow the dictates of a headstrong will under Russian influence. There is a popular saying in Lhasa, referred to by one of the native explorers of the Indian Survey forty years ago, that the thirteenth Dalai Lama will be the last.

Briefly we may indicate the chief features of present Tibetan administration.

The Ambans appointed by China are responsible for the foreign and military government of the country, leaving civil and religious administration in the hands of the Tibetans. They are appointed for three years only. Subordinate to them at Lhasa and Shigatze are two chief commandants and two paymasters of the Chinese army. These, with three subordinate commanders at Lhasa, Shigatze, and Dingri (on the Nepal frontier), and three non-commissioned officers complete the entire administrative staff of China. It is not a large one. The whole force of Chinese troops in the country does not exceed forty-five hundred men distributed between Lhasa, Shigatze, and the Nepalese frontier. The chief civil authority in Tibet is invested in the head of the Tibetan hierarchy,—the Dalai Lama (gyal-rinpoche),—who resides in the far famed Potala at Lhasa. Nominally equal to him in rank, but in reality secondary in authority, is the Panchen rinpoche, or Grand Lama, who resides at Tashilumpo, near Shigatze; and there is in the far Mongolian distance (directly under Russian influence) a third Grand Lama of Tibet, known as the Bogda (himself an "avatar"), the supreme pontiff of the Lamaistic church, who resides at Urga. This spiritual dignitary is really of older creation than the Dalai Lama, for his office was founded when the Mongol dynasty in China finally disappeared. The authority of the Dalai Lama is unquestioned. His decision is final, and he is only questioned in cases of emergency. His powers are transmitted to a special officer nominated by the Chinese government, who is called by various names. He is the Gyalpo, or regent (when the Dalai Lama is a minor), or Nomokhan (Mongolian),—the " king of the law," and he is frequently referred to in books of travel as the "king." He is traditionally selected from the four head lamas of the monasteries of Chomoling, Kondoling, Tangialing, and Chajoling, each one of whom is an "avatar," i.e. he is reincarnated at death in the body of an infant. Equal in rank to the Nomokhan near Lhasa. But he is not an "avatar." Next to him is the Lama Guru or chaplain of the Dalai Lama, who (like the Deba Lama of Galdan) is the subject of Chinese nomination.

China thus preserves a careful supervision over the religious element in the Tibetan government. The Nomokhan rules with the help of a council of five ministers representing the financial, judicial, revenue, and home departments, with a Lama for ecclesiastical affairs. The four provinces. Nari, U, Tsang, and Kham, are each under a Kablon, or governor, assisted by a competent staff. Outside these provinces are several minor "kings," or Gyalpos, and within them there are four principalities directly under Chinese authority. These are Dyag and Chiamdo on the east, Tashilumpo, and Sakya Kongma to the southwest of Tashilumpo. In the east the principalities of Darge and Ta-chien-lu (amongst others) are more or less directly under the China. The remarkable feature about this form of government is the maintenance of Chinese authority throughout so vast a country with the assistance of so small a military force. China was till lately nominally dominant everywhere, holding the keys of all important position in Tibet, and regulating all important appointments. Lately, the authority of the Amban has been set aside without difficulty when convenient to the Tibetan rulers to dispense with it. Tibet has assumed a new and stronger position of independence since the result of the late Chinese war have discredited the power and prestige of China; and doubtless Chinese diplomacy sometimes finds it convenient to shift the responsibility of action on the Tibetan shoulders whenever such action might jeopardise her friendly relations with foreign powers whom she has reason to respect.

Such a government presents unusual difficulties to political negotiation. A nebulous responsibility in the councils of Tibet has hitherto baffled our efforts at establishing a definite basis for the opening of trade and free intercourse with the rich and promising valleys of southern and eastern Tibet. The Tibetan government has throughout all historical negotiations treated the Indian government with the contempt which is always shown by the semi-barbarous and ignorant tribespeople of the India frontier towards a power whose reluctance to use force is attributed to weakness. We may perhaps hope for a stronger position in future, but it will—depend on some outward and visible sign of our authority at Lhasa.

[From *Tibet, the Mysterious*, 1906.]

14

General Report by Mr. Bogle on his Return from Tibet

By
CLEMENTS R. MARKHAM

To the Hon. Warren Hastings. Governor-General, & c.

Hon. Sir,—The commission for opening a free intercourse between the inhabitants of Bengal and Tibet with which you were pleased to entrust me being now finished, I beg leave to lay before you an account of the course and issue of my negotiations.

But as the state of the countries which I lately visited is little known, it may not be improper to premise some circumstance regarding their situation and government. In doing this, however, I shall endeavour to avoid entering into those minute details which might swell this address to an improper length.

The range of mountains which stretches from the Murung country to the banks of the Brahmaputra and the north-east frontier of Bengal is inhabited by a people known in Bengal by the name of Bhutanese. These mountains are divided by glens or deep valleys, with rapid rivers running through them. They are covered with the loftiest trees, and the snow lies upon the tops of some of them all the year round. The valleys and least steep parts of the mountains are cultivated, producing wheat, barley, and rice, sufficient not only for the support of the people, but even to form a considerable article in their commerce with their northern neighbours .

About two hundred and sixty years ago, this country, which I shall distinguish by the name of Bhutan, is said to have been united under one government by Noanumgay, a disciple of the Lamas of Tibet. Before that time it was parcelled out among a number of petty and independent chieftains, who were engaged in perpetual wars and commanded fierce and barbarous vassals. Noanumgay, by forming laws and introducing religion, in concurrence with other causes, rendered the people obedient to a strict and regular administration. He was reverenced by his subjects during his lifetime as a great Lama, and is still worshipped by his descendants. His fame, however, is confined to Bhutan, and his spirit is considered only as an emanation from the pontiffs of Tibet.

Upon his death his soul was supposed to be divided into equal portions, and to animate three different children, who were regarded as Lamas, and the supreme power was jointly vested in them, assisted by the clergy, to whom they owed their elevation. The same ingenious device furnished them with successors, and this form of government still continues. One of these Lamas, named Lama Giassa-tu, died about twelve years ago, and the person into whom his soul passed is not yet discovered; another, Lama Shabdong, is a boy seven years of age, so that the whole authority of this priestly government at present resides in Lama Rimboche. The executive administration is entrusted to an elective officer, styled Cusho

Debo, who is known in Bengal by the name of the Deb Rajah.

The abilities of Deb Judhur, the last person who held this office, enabled him to render himself independent of the Lamas and the clergy, and he ruled Bhutan during five years with an absolute sway; but the oppression of his government, his violent measures in regard to Bahar, and the unfortunate war with the English in which this engaged him, afforded the clergy an opportunity of deposing him, of driving him into exile, and of electing a new chief in his stead. Upon this revolution Lama Rimboche came to be considered as supreme, and regained that authority in the government to which by the ancient constitution he thinks himself entitled.

The kingdom of Bhutan is far from being populous. The natives in the interior part of the country are generally above the middle size, of robust and muscular make, and of a light copper complexion. They are of a hasty and quarrelsome temper, and addicted to the use of spirituous liquors. Theft and robbery, except in time of public disturbances, are little known. The higher class of people are formal and ceremonious in their manners, fond of long speeches, and although often acute and judicious in the affairs of their own state, yet having almost no intercourse with strangers are reserved and difficult in business.

The country is defended by the inhabitants, who are all trained to the use of the bow or of the matchlock, and its steep mountains and arduous roads, leading over precipices and covered with thickets, form a barrier which an enemy might find it difficult to surmount.

The revenue of Bhutan is paid chiefly in rice, butter, and other articles, which are consumed by the priests and servants of government, or hoarded up in storehouses. The low countries which they possess on the borders of Bengal yield some money, and the custom by which upon the death of a public officer his estate escheats to the government, opens another source of revenue. But the people, although enjoying all the necessaries of life, are possessed of little wealth, and indeed, have little occasion for it. The taxes upon the inhabitants are light; their possessions are hereditary; they hold their lands upon military tenures, being bound to fight, to carry burdens, and to perform other services for the government.

The kingdom of Tibet lies to the northward of Bhutan. The frontier town is Pari-jong. Tibet is called by the natives Pu—pronounced as in French. Tibet is full of mountains, inferior in height to those in the Deb Rajah's country, through they take their rise from a more elevated plain, which are intermixed with more extensive valleys. As Bhutan is the most woody country I ever saw, Tibet is the most bare and unsheltered; except in the neighbourhood of villages, a tree is seldom to be seen. The hills are covered with sand, stones and gravel. The soil of the villages, though poor, is rather better, and produces, with good management, wheat , barley, and some peas, but no rice.

The climate is extremely cold; the lakes and rivers are covered with ice. The thermometer, in the month of December, at Chamnamring, which is in latitude 31, 39, and about half a degree to the northward of Lhasa, used sometimes to be within 3° of the bottom of the scale, or 29° under freezing point; and even in the middle of April, and in a more southern situation, heavy showers of snow fell and standing water froze. The great elevation of the country above the sea, and the northerly winds which blow over Tatary, probably occasion this severity in the climate.

The Tibetans are of a smaller size and of a make much less robust than their southern neighbours. Their complexion is naturally as fair as the people in the south of Europe, and many of them have colour, some are quite ruddy : they are of a mild and cheerful temper. The higher rank of people at the Lama's court are polite, and entertaining in conversation, with which they never mix any compliments or flattery.

Tibet was formerly independent, being governed by a succession of hereditary kings. About sixty years ago the ministers, conspiring together, put their king to death and assumed the administration into their own hands. Mewan Cusho, his cupbearer, escaped towards Ladak, and having spent some years in engaging the interest of the neighbouring chiefs, returned with a powerful army, defeated the ministers, and engaged, in consideration of protection, to hold his crown under the Emperor of China. After a wise and prosperous reign of thirty years he was succeeded by his son Wang Cusho.

The Lamas had long before this established themselves and their religion in Tibet. By the liberality or superstition of its kings, or by their influence with the Tatars, who often invaded the country, they procured grants of lands and villages, where they founded temples and monasteries. They were considered as sovereiga pontiffs, and adored as God's viceregents. Pilgrimages were made to them from different parts of Tatary, offerings of considerable value were presented to them, but they enjoyed not that degree of temporal power which the imprudence of Wang Cusho enabled them to obtain.

The tyranny and oppression of his administration, the murder of his brother, and above all his intention of becoming independent of China, were represented by the Dalai Lama in the strongest colours to the Court of Peking, which accordingly issued orders to its officers at Lhasa, and Wang Cusho, betrayed by false promises suffered death while he expected to be honoured with marks of the Emperor's favour. The tumult raised by his dependents, in which a great number of the Chinese were slain, was soon quelled. Their attempt to place his son in the government was defeated by the timidity and flight of the mother, and, according to the severe policy of the Chinese, every branch of the family was extirpated.

In consequence of this resolution the Lamas acquired fresh power and rose to political consequence. The Emperor, either in consideration of the Dalai Lama's pacific character, or as a reward of his fidelity, committed the administration into his hands and his mild and popular government continued to the end of his life. Upon this even, which happened about eighteen years ago. Teshu Lama, the next in dignity, came to be considered as the chief man in the country. His character and abilities had secured him the favour of the Emperor, and his representations had great weight at the Court of Peking. About two years after the Dalai Lama's death he discovered the child into whose body, according to their belief, the soul of the departed Lama had passed, and placed him in the chair of Potala, and his influence with the Emperor procured for Gesub Rimboche, the cupbearer of the former lama, the executive administration during his minority.

Two Chinese viceroys, with a guard of a thousand soldiers, are stationed at Lhasa, and are changed every three years. The Emperor of China is acknowledged as the sovereign of the country; the appointment to the first offices in the state is made by his order, and, in all measures of consequence, reference is first had to the Court of Peking; but the internal government of the country is committed entirely to natives; the Chinese in general are confined to the capital, no tribute is exacted, and the people of Tibet, except at Lhasa, hardly feel the weight of a foreign yoke.

The executive administration is in the hands of Gesub Rimboche and four other ministers, styled Kahlons. The governors of forts and provinces are appointed by them, and the revenue is collected by persons sent annually from Lhasa. But as the Dalai Lama is now nearly of age, it is expected that the Emperor of China will invest him with the supreme authority which his predecessor enjoyed.

The influence of Teshu Lama in the government proceeds chiefly from the veneration that is paid to his character and the weight of his abilities. The Emperors of China being of Tatar extraction, profess the religion of the Lamas, and reverence them as the head of their faith : and the present monarch undertakes no expedition without consulting Teshu Lama, and sending him offerings to engage his prayers for its success. The influence which an able pontiff may derive from this is obvious, and although Gesub Rimboche is jealous of it, yet he is obliged to pay attention to the advice of Teshu Lama.

Any one that would give himself the trouble, might draw a striking parallel between the Lamas and the ancient Roman Pontiffs. The situation of the former, with respect to the monarchs of China, might well be compared to the protection and authority, which the successors of St. Peter derived from the German emperors. Their pretensions to infallibility, the veneration in which they are held by the people, the wide extent of their spiritual dominion reaching over all Tatary and a great part of China, are perfectly similar. But this influence over the minds of the people, possessed by both, has been exercised by the Lamas, perhaps, in a manner more conducive to the happiness of mankind. The oblations of their followers are voluntary : their government is mild and equitable; they enter into no wars, but, on the contrary, often exert their authority in settling the quarrels among contending states. In their private character they are decent and exemplary, and, if I may judge of others by one under whose roof I lived, they are humane, charitable and intelligent.

The religion of the Lamas is either derived from that of the Hindus, or improved by it. They retain, therefore, the greatest veneration for the Ganges and the places held holy in Hindustan. Before that country was invaded by the Mussulmans, the Lamas had monasteries and other religious foundations in Bengal, to which the Tibetan clergy used to resort in order to study the doctrines and learning of the Brahmans. But the conquest of the Moghul put an end to the intercourse. The Lamas' temples were plundered and destroyed, and their people driven out of the country; since which there has been little connection between the inhabitants of Tibet and Bengal.

The trade, however, which used to be carried on between the two countries was formerly very extensive, and the returns being made in gold dust, musk, cowtails, and the valuable articles, it was highly beneficial to Bengal. I formerly took the liberty to represent to you the causes which of late years have occasioned the decline of the trade, and I now beg leave to lay before you an account of the steps that I took to remove them.

Although Teshu Lama is not entrusted with the actual government of the country, yet his authority and influence appear fully equal to accomplish the views which you entertain in regard to the encouragement of trade. His passports to merchants and travellers are obeyed universally throughout Tibet. He is reverenced by his own people, he is respected by his neighbours, and his mild and pacific character seems peculiarly suited to promote commerce. I found in the Lama, therefore, the readiest disposition to co-operate which you in removing the obstacles to a free trade, and in adopting such measures as might increase the intercourse between the country and Tibet.

The tyrannical and faithless character of the Gorkha Rajah, and his invasion of the territories of Demo Jong, a Rajah subject to Lhasa, left, however, no room for any negotiations with him towards reviving the trade through Nepal. But immediately upon the news of his death, which arrived while I was at Teshu Lumbo, the Lama wrote to his successor, Sing Pertab, advising him, in the strongest manner, to allow merchants to trade through his country. His letter on this occasion was short, and I may be excused perhaps in inserting a translation of it :

"To Sing Pertab,—

"[After a number of titles] I have heard of the death of your father, Prithi Narayan. As this is the will of God you will not let your heart be cast down. You have now succeeded to the throne, and it is proper that you attend to the happiness of your people, and allow all merchants, as Hindus, Mussulmans, and the four castes, to go and come, and carry on their trade freely, which will tend to you advantage and to your good name. At present they are afraid of you, and no one will enter your country. Whatever has been the ancient custom let it be observed between you and me. It is improper that there should be more on your part and it is improper that there should be more on mine."

The Lama wrote also to the merchants at Lhasa and Teshu Lumbo, the two principal towns in Tibet. He informed them of the security and protection which merchants enjoy at Bengal, and advised them to send *gumashtas* thither. The Kashmiri and Gosain merchants afterwards assured me, that in consequence of the encouragement and assistance which the Lama had offered them, and the promises which I gave them of freedom and security in Bengal, they proposed, in case they could obtain leave from the Deb Rajah, to pass through his country, to send *gumashtas* to Calcutta to purchase goods, as soon as the rains were over: and a wealthy Gosain merchant, afraid to travel through Nepal, actually embraced the opportunity of accompanying me to Calcutta. The Tibet merchants also came to visit me. But at the same time that they expressed their desire of complying with the Lama's commands, they enlarged upon the heat and unhealthiness of Bengal, and declared their apprehensions of travelling into, what they considered, a distant and unknown country.

Prejudices of this kind are to be cured only by habit, and your compliance with the Teshu Lama's desire of funding a monastery and temple on the banks of the Ganges will probably tend to remove these strong prepossessions against the climate of Bengal and to produce an intercourse with the northern nations. The safe return of the people whom the Lama proposes to send next winter to visit the holy places in Bengal will serve to inspire their countrymen with confidence; the fondness of the Tibetans for everything strange or curious, strengthened by religions, will probably lead many others to undertake so meritorious a journey; and these pilgrimages,, like the Hajj at Mekkah, may in time open a considerable mart for the commodities of Bengal.

Nor is the benefit which Bengal may derive from the resort to Tibetans the only advantage which the Company may obtain by their connection with Teshu Lama. He has written to the Changay Lama, who is the high-priest at the Court of Peking, and in great favour with the Emperor, advising him to send his people to visit the temples in Hindustan. He has also promised to use his best offices with the Emperor of China to procure leave for the Company to send a deputation to Peking. The first, I am convinced, will take place; and although, from the cautious and jealous policy of the Chinese, I am not too sanguine as to the last, yet the advantage of opening even an indirect communication with the Court of Peking is, I humbly apprehend, an object of some importance to the Company.

I could have wished, while I was in Tibet, and within a few days journey of Lhasa, to have proceeded to that city, in order to have formed a connection with Gesub Rimboche, and the rest of the administration there. But their jealousy rendered them averse from it. I could not have seen them, considering the public character I bore, without a considerable expense for presents; and while the Company's views in a communication with Tibet are only to an extension of commerce, I am inclined to think that Teshu Lama's influence is fully sufficient to accomplish them.

After passing five months in Teshu Lama's palace I returned to Bhutan. The Lama at the same time wrote to the Deb Rajah on the subject of merchants, and sent one of his people to assist me in my negotiations at Tassisudon.

But I had now to prosecute my commission under circumstances very different from what I had experienced in Tibet. Teshu Lama's accustomed to an intercourse with strangers, fond of negotiation, and attentive to everything that can raise his character, entered warmly into views which coincided with his own. He had long wished for an opportunity of forming a connection with some of the powers in Hindustan. The authority of the Company was well-known to him, and he had already got great reputation by the peace which his mediation had procured for the Bhutanese. His desire, therefore, of cultivating a friendship which tended to increase his influence, led him zealously to second your application, while his endeavours for the ease and convenience of merchants served to extend his fame. As he speaks the Hindustan language, and possesses a great degree of candour and affability, he conversed with me freely on every subject, and desired me to make my application immediately to him. He communicated to me the opposition which the government at Lhasa had made to my journey; he gave me their correspondence to read; he explained to me the letters which he wrote to them about trade, and told me plainly what could be accomplished and what could not.

The Deb Rajah , on the contrary, secluded from any connection with foreigners, is difficult of access, stiff and ceremonious in his manners, and indecisive in business. He is guided entirely by his officers, who are reserved, suspicious, and evasive; and in every matter of consequence the humour of several hundred priests is to be consulted, and the opinion of Lama Rimboche, who, without experience or abilities, considers himself as supreme in the government, is to be received.

The administration at Tassisudon accordingly made many objections to allowing merchants to pass through Bhutan, insisting that it had never been the custom for strangers to come into their kingdom; that the inhabitants were of a hot and violent temper, and the country woody and mountainous, and, in case of a merchant being robbed, it might occasion disputes and misunderstandings between them and the Company's government. I will not here take up your time with a repetition of the arguments I employed in combating their objections, and in endeavouring to convince them of the benefit which their country would derive from the resort of merchants; for I was sensible, while I used them, that the opposition of the Bhutanese to my proposals proceeded from motives which they industriously concealed. They were apprehensive that the admission of foreign merchants into their country would lessen the profits which they at present derive from their trade with Tibet, and they were still more afraid that by allowing strangers to come into Bhutan they would open a door to the introduction of Europeans.

Neither of these reasons, however, were ever avowed, or even mentioned by the Bhutanese, but they were on this account more difficult to overcome. Without quieting their scruples about Europeans, I foresaw that it was impossible to obtain a communication with Tibet through their country, or to procure the aid and concurrence to the ministry at Lhasa in encouraging and extending the trade with Bengal. I therefore gave up a point which it was impossible to carry, and gave them assurances that no European merchants should enter Bhutan.

Sometime after my arrival at Tassisudon I received your commands of the 9th of May, in which you direct me to endeavour to render the Deb Rajah's capital the centre of communication between Bengal and Tibet. As I found it necessary to deviate in some measure from the letter of these orders, I hope you will believe that it proceeded only from my desire to accomplish more effectually the purpose of my commission, and that the following reasons will serve to justify my conduct.

If the Deb Rajah allowed freedom of trade through his dominions, and permitted the merchants at Tibet to come and purchase goods in this country, I should only have had occasion to have applied for permission for merchants to bring the commodities of Bengal to Rinjipu, which, being the capital of Bhutan, being situated on the road from Pari-jong, and having a communication with Bengal by Lukhi-Duar, Dalim-kotta, and Buxa-Duar, is well-adapted for a central market for the merchandise of Bengal and Tibet. But the whole trade in the more valuable sorts of goods is engrossed by the Deb Rajah and his officers, who are in fact the merchants of Bhutan. The few Tibetans who come to Rinjipu (Paro) are allowed only to exchange the salt and wool of their country for the rice of Bhutan. Had I, therefore, procured permission for merchants to bring their goods only to Rinjipu (Paro) without obtaining leave for those of Tibet to come the trade to that place, the Deb Rajah and his officers—men not wealthy, and who being engaged in the affairs of government carry on their commercial concerns but to a small extent, and without that enterprising spirit which merchants possess—would in fact have been the only purchasers, and the trade would have remained on much the same footing as formerly,only that Rinjipu (Paro) instead of Rangpur would have become the market for the commodities of Bengal. The consumption of Bengal goods, except tobacco, betel nut, and other bulky articles, is very small in the Deb Rajah's dominions, and while the people remain poor, and preserve their present simple manners, will probably continue so. It is no object to Bengal, and their only commodities for exportation are musk, horses, munjit, blankets, and some thin twilled cloths. The first three have always been monopolized by the rulers of Bhutan, and they would reluctantly part with them; the importation of the last ought rather to be discouraged.

In the dread which the administration at Tassisudon was then in of the insurrection in favour of Deb Judhur, supported by the administration at Lhasa, I could not have applied for permission for Tibetans to trade freely to Rinjipu (Paro) without awakening suspicions of treachery, and I therefore judged it best to refer everything in regard to the merchants of Tibet entirely to Teshu Lama.

After many tiresome conferences and fruitless negotiations, in which I was assisted by Teshu Lama's people, I at length obtained the Deb Rajah's consent to allow Hindu and Mussulman merchants to pass through Bhutan under some restrictions and concessions which I have now the honour to submit to you, together with the reasons upon which they are grounded.

I transmitted a copy of those articles to the Lama from Tassisudon, requesting him at the same time to give them all advantages with the government at Lhasa, and to write to the Deb Rajah on the subject. I have since received a letter from him, written in answer to the accounts which his people sent him, of the difficulties that the Deb Rajah started to my proposals, of which I beg leave to jay before you a translation, as it strongly marks the earnestness and zeal with which the Lama interests himself in the success of the different objects of my commission.

In regard to procuring permission for

Europeans to trade into Tibet, it was a point which I have already mentioned impossible of obtaining. In former times, when Europeans were settled in Hindustan merely as merchants, there would have been no difficulty in establishing factories and freedom of trade; but the power and elevation to which the English have now risen render them the objects of jealous to all their neighbours. The opposition which was made to my proceeding into Tibet, as well as the many difficulties I had to encounter in the execution on my commission, arose from this source. The government a Lhasa considered me as sent to explore their country, which the ambition of the English might afterwards prompt them to invade, and their superiority in arms render their attempt successful.

I was at much pains during my stay among the inhabitants of Bhutan and Tibet to remove their prejudices; but I am convinced they can be effectually conquered only by the opportunities which a greater intercourse and more intimate acquaintance with the English may afford them of observing their fidelity to engagements, and the moderation of their views, and by an interchange of those good offices which serve to beget confidence between nations as well as between individuals. The increase of influence which Teshu Lama will derive from the government of Tibet being committed to the Dalai Lama, and other circumstances which your connection with him may enable your to improve, will perhaps open the way to a privilege which at present I could not obtain.

I will now beg leave to submit to you may ideas on the nature of the trade between Bengal and Tibet, and on the measures which appear most likely to revive and extend it.

The most important commodity in this traffic is broadcloth; all the Tibetans of a station elevated above the populace are fond of wearing gowns of it, and it forms also an article of their commerce with the neighbouring tribes of Tatars. The sale of broadcloth, however, from the causes which I have already mentioned, has greatly decreased of late years, and even of what is now consumed a large portion is of French manufacture. I had occasion to buy several pieces in Tibet to give away in presents, and except once, I never could meet with any English cloth.

The article of next importance is coral beads; great quantities of these are used in Tibet, and from thence also sent into Tatary. The want of supplies, and the consequent enhancement of the price, have affected this commodity in the same manner as the former.

I will not her particularize the different kinds of merchandise which have hitherto been exported from this country to Tibet, but beg leave to refer you to the accompanying list, in which I have put down the prices of the principal articled, together with the expense of transporting them. I must observe, however, that most of them were not to be had. The Bhutan caravan, on its return from Rangpur, would no doubt carry a supply of goods from Bengal, but in no degree equal to what the consumption of the country used formerly to take off.

But besides the articles hitherto employed in the trade with Tibet, there appears room to introduce or extend the sale of many new ones. The inhabitants are fond of everything that comes from a strange country, and even the lowest class of people possess a curiosity seldom to be met with. This promises a good opening for the sale of cutlery, glassware, and many other European manufactures.

The most eligible and effectual way in my opinion of extending the sale of British broadcloth in opposition to that of France, of increasing the sale of those goods which have usually been exported to Tibet, and of opening a mart for new articles of commerce, is to encourage the resort of Kashmiris, Gosains

Bhutanese, and Tibetans to Calcutta during the winter time, by making a sale of English broadcloth at that season they will be enabled to procure it at the lowest rate; and by granting them passports and escorts to the northern frontier of Bengal, they will be engaged to purchase the Company's cloth in preference to any other; while the variety of unknown merchandise which they will here find will naturally create a desire of carrying them with them on their return to their own country.

To remove the dread which the natives of Bhutan and Tibet entertain of this climate may, no doubt, require time and use. But when curiosity, religion, and interest conspire to prompt them to visit Bengal, nothing further appears necessary but the encouragement and protection of government.

The Kashmiri and Gosain merchants who propose to come to Calcutta during the next winter will, when furnished with Teshu Lama's passports, find next difficulty in travelling through Tibet; and the Deb Rajah, from the assurances he has given me, will, I am persuaded, readily grant them a passage through his kingdom from Pari-jong to the frontier of Bengal. But as the road has never yet been frequented by merchants, it may be necessary, on their arrival on the borders of Bahar, that that they should received countenance and assistance, and that orders for that purpose should be issued.

The opening of the road through Nepal, and obtaining the abolition of the duties and exactions which have lately been imposed on trade in that country, appears an object of great importance towards establishing a free communication between Bengal and Tibet. The death of Prithi Narayan, the late Rajah of Nepal seems to afford a favourable opportunity of effecting this point. Teshu Lama is ready to second your endeavours for that purpose; and a proper management of the different interests which prevail among the chiefs on the borders of Nepal will, I am convinced, easily accomplish it. The steps which it may be proper to pursue it becometh not me to point out. But I may be excused, perhaps, in suggesting the advantage which you may derive, in all your negotiations with the people who possess the mountains to the northward of Bengal, by taking your measures jointly with Teshu Lama. His acquaintance with the state of those countries renders his opinion of much weight, and the influence which his holy character gives him among the different chiefs, being employed only to settle disputes and promote harmony, may enable you to accomplish by negotiation and peaceful means what that jealousy of the people and the strength of their situation might otherwise render it difficult of obtain.

When a road is opened through Nepal as well as Bhutan nothing further appears to me necessary towards accomplishing the business upon which I have lately been employed. In matters of commerce I humbly apprehend that freedom and security is all that is required. Merchants, left to themselves, naturally discover the most proper manner of conducting their trade, and, prompted by self-interest, carry it on to the greatest extent.

The disadvantages to which the novelty of my journey and the jealousy of the natives subjected my may, perhaps, entitle me to indulgence. I have executed my commission to the best of my abilities, and I now wait in solicitude for the judgment which may be passed upon my conduct.

[From *Narratives of the Mission of George Bogle to Tibet, and of the Journey of Thomas Manning to Lhāsa*, 1879.]

15

My Mission to Lhasa

By

CHARLES BELL

Our journey to Lhasa and our return journey a year later were full of interest, and still more so was our long sojourn of eleven months in the centre of Tibetan Buddhism. For visiting Lhasa, as I did, on the repeated invitations of the Dalai Lama and his Government, I was welcomed everywhere and all facilities were accorded for my seeing the festivals and ceremonies, the manners and customs in palace and cottage; in fine, all that goes to make up the life of this strange and interesting people. I had already of necessity acquired a good knowledge of the Tibetan language, and a considerable acquaintance with Tibetan—life as indeed who but the stupidest of mortals could fail to do after so many years of residence?—and thus was able to understand and appreciate what I saw and heard. But to deal with these things in the present book would be to overweight it with matters which, however interesting in themselves, are foreign to its purport. I will therefore reserve them for a future volume, and in this one touch in the main only upon such events as bear directly upon the political life of the country.

On the 2nd November we covered a long stage of 37 miles from Gau-tsa to Tuna over the Tang La, avoiding as much as possible the intervening town of Phari, for it was the centre of the influenza epidemic. We could not, however avoid changing our transport animals there; and, whether from this or other cause, the infection caught us and took its toll of our party. For in high altitudes, with the consequent difficulty of breathing, the pneumonia that supervenes on an attack is more than ever deadly.

The cold was intense; there was ice everywhere but no snow, for the air was too dry, the winds were strong, but less severe than usual at this season of the year. I went via Gyantse and Nan-kar-tse, crossing the Ka-ro La and Kam-pa La, the former somewhat over, the latter somewhat under 16,000 feet above sea-level. At Gyantse I was met by an emissary deputed by the Dalai Lama to conduct us to the capital. At Chu-shur, on the banks of the great river—which is marked on maps as the Tsanpo or Sanpo, but is known to Tibetans as the Tsang-chu-I was met by one of His Holiness's secretaries, sent to bring me the last forty miles of the journey, to welcome me to Lhasa, and to convey an invitation to lunch or dinner, whichever I might prefer, though, of course, His Holiness could not himself be present at this. This secretary, named Lo-tro, i.e. Wisdom,' was usually known as the Tsen-dron, i.e. the 'Secretary at the Peak,' the term 'Peak' being commonly used for the Dalai Lama's palace of Potala, which is situated on a small hill. He was a man who in any country would be singled out as the fortunate possessor of exceptionally high intelligence. The Tsen-dron and Ne-to Dzong-pon, the office who conducted us from Gyantse, a priest and a layman, were attached to my Mission when I arrived in Lhasa.

I halted for a day at Chu-shur in order to arrive at Lhasa on the 17th, an auspicious date in the Tibetan calendar. I arranged to call on the Grand Lama on the 19th, this being another auspicious date, the 8th of the tenth Tibetan month. When dealing with Tibetans, one should be careful to utilize dates of good omen as far as possible, for its is a matter to which they attach great importance.

Here, at Chu-shur, a rumour reached us that there was a European in Lhasa, a man with grey eyes, who came on one occasion to change gold, mostly in the form of gold medals, with a trader in Lhasa. The report, however, proved to be without foundation, and was probably due to the presence of several Buriats in Lhasa. These people are Mongolians who live in that portion of northern Mongolia which has long been annexed by Russia to her Siberian territory. They trade a good deal in Russian merchandise, and many, living, as they do, in the latitude of southern England and in a Canadian climate, have grey eyes and fair complexions.

The representative of the Ladakh community in Lhasa met me at Chu-shur with a scarf of welcome. These people from Ladakh number several hundred souls, all Mahomedans, who have been settled in Lhasa for many decades and earn their livelihood by trade. It is believed that the settlement had its origin in the prisoners captured by the Tibetans form the Dogra Army, under Zorawar Singh, that attacked western Tibet unsuccessfully in 1841.

Eight miles out of Lhasa, the diplomatic Agent of Bhutan in Lhasa came to greet me, followed by the land agents of my old friends, the heads of the Pa-lha and Do-ring families. Our party growing thus larger and larger, we rode on till two miles from our destination, we were welcomed by representatives of His Holiness the Dalai Lama, as well as by those of the Prime Minister and the Grand Council of Tibet. Here a tent had been erected, picturesque with its blue designs on the roof, after the manner of Tibetan tents, and we were regaled with rice, biscuits, and tea, all after the Tibetan style. In the tea butter, as well as soda, is boiled, so that a scum forms on the surface. This you blow aside before drinking; and each time that you drink, even though but a little, your cup is immediately refilled. You must drink once again after the first refilling, and then, if you like, you can stop. Europeans almost invariably dislike this tea, but it is well-boiled and is not unwholesome. No Tibetan drinks less than fifteen or twenty cups a day, and some drink sixty or seventy.

Outside the tent we were met by the Captain in charge of the small Gurkha detachment which had been sent as a Guard of Honour by the Nepalese Agent in Lhasa. A second Guard of Honour was furnished by a hundred Tibetan infantry, drawn up by the wayside under their officers. Stalwart fellows they were, and, dressed in their modern khaki uniforms, adopted from India a few years ago, they appeared a workmanlike body. The crowd growing larger and larger, we were by now a veritable cavalcade and could sample to the full the restless unending dust to Tibet.

The Grand Council had proposed to accommodate us in the house in which Sir Francis Younghusband and his Staff were lodged in the Expedition of 1904, but the Dalai Lama wished me to be nearer to him, and so we were given the summer residence of a former Regent of Tibet. It lay on the bank of the river, about half a mile from the entrance to the grounds of the Dalai Lama's country Palace, known as 'The Jewel Park' (Nor-pu Ling-Ka). The Regent had never lived in this house during the winter, and it was feared that we might find it cold then; but it was chosen because it was clean.

On the next day the Ministers who constitute the Grand Council made a joint call of ceremony upon me. Among them was my old fiend the Commander -in-Chief, whom I had first met in Darjeeling in 1910, when he was an attendant in the private household of the Dalai Lama. By the favour of His Holiness on the one hand, and by his own energy and devotion on the other, he had risen to his present rank, and furnished an example of that rare phenomenon among the laity of Tibet, a man of humble birth raised to a high position. I say 'laity' adivisedly, for in the celibate ranks of the clergy, separated from their families and having an independent status, such events are of common occurrence.

My reception by the Dalai Lama, in the Jewel Park, was of extreme friendliness. He was not seated in formal fashion on his throne, as is usual, but received me in his private apartments, as he had done in the old days at Darjeeling, when he came to us in trouble and we did our best to make things easy for him. His eyes lighting up with pleasure, he rose from his European chair, and coming to meet me, grasped both my hands in his, as he told me how glad he was that I had come. We sat together alone, as we always had done, and I noticed, when I came out of the room, that there was nobody even within earshot. Thus, we could talk freely. In all my subsequent visits similar privacy was observed. Business had to be held over for my second visit; it would have been contrary to etiquette to have discussed it at this first one.

I then visited my old friend, Lon-chen Sho-kang, who, as the only survivor of the three Chief Ministers, may rightly be termed the Prime Minister. From him too I received an extremely cordial welcome. 'When I heard,' said he, ' that you had come as far as Gyantse and then returned to the Chumbi Valley, I was almost in despair of our ever meeting again. But I used to set your photograph before me and pray that somehow this might be brought about. And thus has my prayer been granted.

An old man now, he spent some two hours daily in prayer, offering supplication for himself, his family, and his native land; and not for these only, but for the whole human race; nor stopping even then, but also for all 'mind-possessors *(sem-chem)* i.e. for birds, beasts, and fishes, the entire animal creation.

He gave me one good piece of advice. 'You will find it best' he said, ' to conduct all your business direct with the Dalai Lama, and not with the Grand Council nor even with me. Otherwise, all kinds of people will come to know secrets which ought to be kept from them, and harm will result.

He paid his return call on me in an hour's time. I had some difficulty in restraining him from paying it at once, but I insisted, for I felt sure that he needed a rest. The sooner a call is returned, the greater is the honour done to the caller.

Visits and entertainments, on the Tibetan side and on ours, now occupied us a good deal, especially for the first two or three months. For the Tibetans are a hospitable people, very fond of entertaining and of being entertained. Ceremonies and etiquette are to them of prime importance, a fact which anybody who has dealings with them does well to recognize.

At this time therefore we were often in the streets of Lhasa. The Tibetan gentry prefer to live in their town houses during the winter, rather than in their villas scattered over the neighbouring country-side, for the town is warmer than the country. Crowds gathered to stare at us for the first week or two, as we rode past, for many of them had never seen a white man before. But we met with no rudeness. The Tibetan from prince to peasant, unless greatly incensed, is essentially courteous and dignified.

An interesting personality in Lhasa at this time was the governor of the Ili Province, in the north-western corner of Chinese Turkestan, on the Siberian border. There were good grounds for believing that this official—a

Mongolian by race, and therefore akin to the Tibetans—had come to Lhasa to negotiate on behalf of China with the Tibetan Government, in order to bring Tibet back to the Chinese fold and to oust British influence from the country. The Tibetan Government were well-aware of the risk of Chinese domination that was likely to result from negotiations unattended by a British Representative. But prevented, as they were, from importing ammunition from or through India, they were of necessity considering how to make the best possible terms with China. My arrival in Lhasa was opportune in that it frustrated the further progress of this Mission.

Three or four months before I came to Lhasa, the Royal Geographical Society and the Alpine Club had requested our government to ask the Government of Tibet for permission to ascend Mount Everest from Tibetan territory. Our ally, Nepal, had refused permission to attempt the ascent from the Nepalese side. I felt sure that, if I wrote, the Tibetan Government would grant the permission, for I do not think that the Dalai Lama has ever refused me anything that I asked for. But I felt bound to oppose the project of writing to the Tibetan Government for this permission; for I knew that the scheme would raise suspicion in the mind of a people circumstanced as are those of Tibet. They would not understand the plea of geographical and scientific aims, and would suspect that some secret and possibly sinister object lay behind the proposal. They would also fear that, whatever our motives, the spirits of the place would be disturbed. The fact that the part of Tibet to be visited lay near the Nepal frontier would further increase their uneasiness, since Tibet and Nepal were not on the best of terms. Difficulties of this kind cannot be smoothed out in letters; personal conversation is essential. The Indian Government and the home Government agreed with my views.

When, however, I came to Lhasa, the India Government asked me to sound the Tibetan Government on the subject, provided that I saw no objection to doing so. The matter being thus left to my discretion, I did ask and obtain permission for the Everest Expedition. Personal conversation, direct between the parties, no interpreters being present enables suspicions to be removed or minimized, when each side trusts the other. In this, as in all talks with the Dalai Lama, I found him full of tolerance. It was certainly a noteworthy fact that Tibet should grant to Britain, her former enemy, a privilege which Britain's own ally, Nepal, had consistently refused.

On the 11th December Rai Bahadur Achuk Tsering died of heart failure, brought on by a combined attack of influenza and gout. His death was a great shock to us all and especially to me. We had worked together, almost continuously, for just twenty years, having been first associated in the census of the Kalimpong sub-division. He was a man of great acumen, whose opinion on questions of Tibetan, Bhutanese, or Sikkimese politics was invaluable. I applied immediately for an old friend, Sardar Bahadur Laden La, a Sikkimese in the Bengal police, who had on my behalf looked after the Dalai Lama and his Ministers during their stay in India from 1910 to 1912. A considerable time, however, elapsed before he was deputed to my Mission, so that he did not join me until the 15th March.

My private conversations with the Dalai Lama, which were frequent, ranged over a wide variety of subjects. Sometimes the power of Tibet to defend itself came under discussion. During one of these conversations—which were entirely informal—being asked by opinion, I expressed my view that the Tibetan army was inadequate. It consisted only of some five thousand men. I thought that it should be increased gradually, as funds and equipment became available, till it reached about fifteen thousand. This seemed the lowest number that would offer a reasonable prospect of defence against foreign foes and internal disturbances;

at the same time there was no hope of finding funds to pay for more.

When I found that the Dalai Lama and the Tibetan Government intended to adopt the opinion, which I had expressed, as a settled line of policy, I expressed it in more detail, suggesting that the increase should be gradual, that recruitment should be spread as evenly as possible over the whole country, that not many should be taken from the district round Lhasa, that in no circumstances should monks be recruited, and that neither the monasteries nor the landed estates should be subjected to direct taxation to meet this expenditure. Whenever mentioning this subject, I also made it clear that my views were entirely my own; that they did not emanate from, and were in no sense inspired by, my Government. The Tibetan Government framed their scheme substantially on the above lines, and commenced acting on it as circumstances permitted.

Many of the monks no doubt were opposed to any increase in the army. Some even urged that, since Tibet was useful to India as a barrier against outside foes, it should be protected by British and Indian troops. But this was not the view of the Tibetan Government, and not even of the responsible heads of the monasteries themselves. The latter control the Assembly, and the Assembly voted for the increase of the army.

The leaders were able to realize that Chinese domination in Tibet, though accompanied by subsidies to the monasteries, would in the end harm the religion and their own influence more than the domination of their own government. They knew that with modern rifles they could keep out large bodies of Chinese troops. Those on the frontier knew it also. For, when volunteers were called for in eastern Tibet, the usual reply was, 'Lend me a good rifle and I will come.' They were well-aware of the uselessness of men without training or equipment; they had not forgotten that a dozen or so Chinese soldiers had kept the whole of Sera monastery at bay.

During January the Indian Government pressed me to come away from Lhasa, but I urged the necessity of remaining, on various grounds, and this view ultimately prevailed. The Tibetan Government were greatly relieved; they were surprised and distressed at the idea of my leaving before our Government replied to a letter which they had written on my arrival in Lhasa. The Dalai Lama, the Prime Minister, and the Councillors all urged me to remain. The Prime Minister, who came twice to see me on the subject, said, 'I was ill for some months, but your coming here has made my illness better. We are old friends. When I looked at your photograph, I used to pray that you would come to Lhasa. The Dalai Lama prophesied that you would come here and settle the Tibetan question. When I heard you were coming, I felt that the prophecy would soon be fulfilled. If you leave now, with nothing accomplished, you will be rubbing my face in the dust.'

The leading priest official said to a friend of mine: 'We will first beg Minister Bell with folded hands to stay. If he does not agree to stay we will throw our arms round his neck to keep him. If he still insists on going, we will hold on to him with our teeth, so that he will have to knock our teeth down our throats before he will be able to get away.'

February is the beginning of the Tibetan New Year. The festival known as 'The Great Prayer,' the chief festival of the whole year, takes place and lasts for three weeks. Lhasa as usual was crowded with monks. Owing to quarrels between the leaders of the monks and certain military officers, there was at this time a grave danger that the monks, of whom there were some forty thousand in the neighbourhood, might break out, loot and kill. The Dalai Lama was aware of the danger and did the most sensible thing by putting

Lhasa out of bounds for the military. The good people of Lhasa were openly terrified, and many of them removed their belongings and hid them in villages far and near. Lhasa has an unenviable reputation for murderous outbreaks in which many people are killed and a great deal of property is destroyed. in the towns of Darjeeling and Kalimpong, on the Indian frontier, rumours were rife to the effect that we of the Mission had been assassinated.

The Tibetans everywhere attributed to me the increase in their army which was destined to curtail the influence of the powerful priesthood. And no doubt they had good reason for thinking so, for His Holiness had apparently taken the suggestion from me and was pushing the matter through with characteristic energy. When, therefore, I announced my desire to attend the Butter Festival, which takes place at night in the heart of Lhasa, those in authority were very nervous. There were a good many monks in Lhasa at the time, the streets were narrow and unlighted, and a stone could easily be dropped or a shot discharged from the darkness of a neighbouring house. The monks, as the Dalai Lama said, act without reflecting, and, being celibate, have neither family nor property to consider.

But I had been present at other ceremonies, and people would have drawn wrong conclusions if I had not been present at this also. As we left his house, the Commander-in-Chief offered Colonel Kennedy a revolver, which the latter fortunately refused. Twelve soldiers accompanied us and six monks armed with long staves. The atmosphere was indeed somewhat electric, but we were well-treated everywhere. And indeed throughout this period of unrest, though we rode and walked unescorted day by day, neither I nor other members of my party received anything but courtesy and kindliness from the people.

Owing to the Dalai Lama's personality and skill, the trouble was eventually averted. Out of the four Councillors on the Grand Council, which constitutes, under the Dalai Lama and Prime Minister, the Government of Tibet, one was dismissed and two were fined. Three colonels were dismissed and two lesser military officers, including the Dalai Lama's nephew, were fined. The leading priests were summoned before His Holiness and warned to keep the monks under strict control. They were reminded that, if fighting broke out, their monasteries would be seriously damaged and they themselves heavily punished.

It was more than sixteen years since a Councillor had been dismissed from his post. He had to remove his official dress then and there at the meeting, in the presence of his fellow councillors, and to go home in ordinary garb.

Shortly afterwards his Holiness fell ill, and this caused renewed anxiety, for none can hold Tibet together as he can. Always a worker, he remained at his tasks when he was in not fit condition to do so. Thus, growing steadily worse and worse, he became dangerously ill. His physician, who had some years previously been promoted to the headship of the priest-officials, was seriously alarmed, and after bowing his head to the ground as usual, addressed him as follows: 'Your Holiness please instruct me what you intend to do. I asked you not to go to the Potala to conduct the ceremony, but you went there. I keep asking you to rest, but you continue working. Do you intend to change your body (i.e. give up this present life), or to remain with us.

The Dalai Lama laughed and replied : 'There is no harm done; give me your medicine. After that he was more careful. He was in fact too ill to work, however much he might wish to continue. The Court officials wisely kept their counsel regarding the gravity of the illness, for, had it been known, there might have resulted a panic in Lhasa and grave uneasiness throughout the whole of Tibet.

Another outbreak occurred five months later in the Dre-pung Monastery, but on a smaller scale, only five thousand monks being involved. It was not directly connected with the former outbreak, having originated in a question of internal discipline. The monks threatened to attack Lhasa. Affairs of this kind are apt to turn against the foreigner of alien religion who has penetrated into the land. The priestly classes, scenting in the foreign influence a menace to their religion and themselves, are especially inclined to be hostile. We had, however, by then been long enough in Lhasa to gain the good will of all classes. So far from our being an object of suspicion, some leading members of the Tibetan Government desired me to intervene with advice; and the monks themselves went so far as to desire my arbitration in the entire dispute. This was undesirable, but I tendered advice on certain aspects of the case in the proper quarter; and this was acted on.

The Tibetan Government summoned three thousand troops to Lhasa and besieged the monastery, which in due course submitted. The affair was settled with a wise admixture of force and leniency. As the Dalai Lama himself informed me during one of our conversations, 'I had to show myself the master. Otherwise, Sera, Ganden, and other large monasteries would be encouraged to break out when they wished to gain any end of their own.' But having shown his power, he used it with the utmost moderation. Even uprisings of this kind help to show how much more orderly is the administration of Tibet than that of China, a fact that is brought home to those Europeans in China who visit portions of Tibet under the Dalai Lama's rule.

[From *Tibet—Past and Present*, 1924.]

16

Lhasa

By

EKAI KAWAGUCHI

I

ON TO LHASA

THE SOLDIER, whose company proved not altogether unwelcome in a travel like mine, happened to be one of the Legation Guards of the Minister of Nepal at Lhasa. His love of his mother had tempted him from the duty, but at Shigatze on his way to Nepal his thought turned to his love of a woman at Lhasa and this was so much greater than his love for his mother that he suddenly changed his mind and determined to go back to Lhasa. Among other things I asked him how many soldiers the Nepal Government kept stationed at Lhasa, and he answered that it was but a few years ago that his Government first sent a guard to the Tibetan capital. He told me that a great calamity befell the capital over ten years ago.

It seems that there were about three hundred merchants of the Palpo tribe of Nepal at Lhasa. They are the most active and alert of the Nepalese tribes, with regard to trading, and follow Indian, not Tibetan Buddhism. They engage in trade at Lhasa in woollen cloth, cotton, silk, coral, jewels dry goods, rice, beans and corn.

Some thirteen years ago, a Palpo merchant at Lhasa searched a Lhasa woman on the charge that she had stolen a piece of coral from his shop. When the coral was not found be became so angry that, in spite of her protesting tears, he took her by force into his house. When she was allowed to go out again, she told the people all that had happened. The 'warrior-priests' of the Sera monastery heard of the affair and became so irritated about the ill-treatment of the woman that some of them came to enquire into the matter, and having ascertained what they wanted went back to Sera and told their chief, who at once called out the warrior-priests.

These warrior-priests are under one chief, at whose summons they gather themselves together. Many of them were not in residence at that time, but about one thousand assembled. These were preparing to march on Lhasa to wreck vengeance on all the Palpo merchants, when the latter got wind of the matter, Sera being only about four miles from the capital. So they had fled from the city before the bellicose priests entered Lhasa, each armed with sword or a large iron hook. These men broke into the deserted houses of the merchants, and carried off what they found. Among the raiders there were, besides the priests, vagabonds of the city, who dispersed with their spoil the next morning at daybreak. Presently, the merchants returned to their houses, and were much distressed to find their merchandise gone—their only property, as they owned no land. Their loss was estimated at something under 230,000 yen.

This affair became a diplomatic question,

and it took over five years to settle it. The Tibetan Government had to compensate the merchants and a party of twenty-five Nepalese soldiers came to be stationed at Lhasa. The chief diplomatist in this affair on the Nepal side was Jibbahadur, whose name has already been mentioned; he was the Clerk of the Nepalese Government, and is the present Nepalese Minister to Tibet.

As we walked on we found ourselves at the foot of a steep hill called Genpala, which has an incline of about two and a half miles to its top, from which I obtained my first view of Lhasa. From the summit I could see, to the north-east, the Brahmaputra running south-east. There is a large tributary called Kichu running from the north-east that flows into this river. It runs through a large plain in the middle of which is a mountain with a high building; and this I saw showing beautifully in the golden sunshine. This was the residence of the Dalai Lama of Lhasa, and is called Tse Potala. Beyond the castle are to be seen roofs towering high in the air, which look like those of a town. These are the streets of Lhasa, which look very small, when seen so far off. I rested for a while, and then gradually went down a great slope for about seven miles till I came to Pache, where I stopped for the night. Having walked all day in the snow and ice I was very foot-sore and fatigued, as well I might be, for I had made twenty-five miles on foot that day.

The following day, the 17th of March, I descended for another two miles and a half and found myself on the banks of the Brahmaputra. I walked some six miles along the southern bank of the river before I came to the ferry of Chaksam, where I had to cross the river. Formerly, there was an iron bridge at this place, the remaining chains of which may still be seen a little lower down the stream. The ferry boats are rectangular in shape like Indian boats. But it is only in the winter that these boats are used, for in the summer large vessels cannot pass across. The Tibetans then use instead the yak-hide canoe. They sew together the hides of three yaks, and the seams are painted over with a sort of lacquer, to make them waterproof. These hide canoes float on the water, and are used as ferry-boats even in the winter when there are not many passengers. In Tibetans the word *Kowa* (meaning 'hide') also signifies a boat. The hide boat naturally absorbs much water and soon gets too soft and heavy for use, and the Tibetan therefore dries his hide boat in the sun after he has used it for half a day in the water. It is so light that a man can easily lift it, and the Tibetan will carry it on his back to the higher part of a stream, and will float it down for a day or two loaded with goods or men. When the boat is unloaded, it is again carried up the stream. But our party being too many for a hide canoe I was ferried over the river in one of the regular wooden boats.

Walking for about three miles on the dry sandy bed of the river. I came to a beautiful place where I saw rocks and high trees casting their shadows on the water. The ground about Lake Yamdo, of which I have spoken elsewhere, is so elevated that it looks as much as 13,500 feet above sea level, but here it is only 11,500 feet high. Here, in sunny places beside the water, the buds of the willows were already out. After seeing only bald mountains and dead leaves for a long time, the green leaves were a delightful sight. Though my coolie carried my baggage, and I was not much troubled on that score, the old wounds on my feet began to smart again, and I could hardly walk. In the midst of my trouble there came along a horseman, to whom I gave a little money to carry me on horseback. About two miles and a half further on we came to a town called Chushur, a rather bustling place, situated in the delta formed by the rivers Kichu and Brahmaputra, the former running from the north-east and the latter from the north-west.

I hardly know any town on the way to Lhasa worse and more wicked than this. The people of the town are indifferent, even unkind, to strangers, and are much skilled in robbing them of their luggage. They will steal both luggage and goods in transport in such a skillful manner that they can hardly be detected. It is widely known in Tibet that no place is richer in thieves that Chu-shur and I had often been warned to be on my guard against them. There being so many skilful thieves and the place being so much frequented by travellers, there is consequently a good circulation of money, and one would suppose that Chu-shur had many rich men; but strange to say, I was told upon enquiry that there were more poor men in that town than in most of the other towns and villages of Tibet. After dining there, I started towards the north-east (on foot, as I could procure no horse) along the stream of the Kichu river and walked on until I felt so much pain in my feet that I could proceed no further. I had laid myself down on the grass to rest when, to my boundless joy, a donkey-driver came along and I was given a lift on the back of his animal for some ten miles, till I arrived at Jang. At Jang something happened that prevented my coolie from following me any further, and he deserted me. My feet were aching worse than ever, for I had travelled about twenty-five miles that day by the help of the donkey; but what to do on the following day I was at a loss to conceive. Happily I was told of some men who were going with tax-meat to the Government at Lhasa, and I asked them to take me on one of their horses. They were going to pay the tax to the Government, yet they did not take their horses from their own village, but hired them elsewhere. They did not travel more than eight or nine miles a day, and I, too, hired a horse for myself, placed my luggage in their charge, and started together with them. We halted at a little village named Nam to take rest, and here stopped for the night. On the following day we went about six miles along a narrow rocky mountain path, which ran north-east along the Kichu river, till we came to Nethang.

II

ARRIVAL IN LHASA

At Nethang there is a temple of the Mothers of Salvation, who are most devoutly worshipped in Tibet, and it is said that it was founded by an Indian hermit, Shri Atisha by name, who organised a new sect in Tibet. I went there to worship the twenty-one Mothers of Salvation (Dolma Nishu tsa chik in Tibetan) whose images I found very well made. On the following day, the 20th, I again went on towards the north-east, along the river, over a plain of about five miles, till I came to a large bridge which I crossed, went on north-east for another four miles, and came to a village called Sing Zonkha, where I stopped for the night. I was to arrive at Lhasa, the capital of the country, on the following day, March 21st.

I hired a horse at the village, and asked my companions to take care of my baggage while I rode on amid the beautiful scenes of the place. After about two miles, I saw on the left a splendid monastery, which at first sight looked more like a large village, though it was in reality the Rebung monastery, the largest of the kind in the vicinity of Lhasa. It is indeed the largest monastery in the ecclesiastical district under the Dalai Lama, and has an army of priests who number some 7,700 as a general rule, though sometimes their number rises as high as nine thousand. During the summer, when the priests go out into the country on pilgrimage, there remain some six thousand only. This is one centre of Tibetan learning, and has a college. I saw in all three colleges in Central Tibet, the other two being the Sera college in Lhasa and that at Ganden.

The former has 5,500 students, and the latter 3,300. But these numbers are only nominal, and the colleges can, like the Rebung monastery, take in either more or fewer students than their fixed number. At the side of the road below this monastery is a place where yaks, sheep, and goats are killed for the table of the Dalai Lama, and the Tibetans have so superstitious a regard for the sheep (seven in number) the meat of which is offered to the Dalai Lama daily, that they ask for such things as the wool and other parts of the animal as keepsakes. Besides sheep, the Dalai Lama eats other kinds of meat, which is also sent from the same place.

It is not very sensible of the Pontiff to get his meat from such a distant place, while he lives in the city of Lhasa; but he takes another view. Lhasa is too near to his palace for the slaughter of animals, and he does not want to have it thought that the animals are killed for him. He desires to get his meat without being responsible for giving the order to kill the animals. This looks very good, but since it is settled that the meat served to him shall be taken from this place, special care is taken in selecting the animals for slaughter, and at bottom, therefore, it makes no difference whether his meat is brought at Lhasa or at that particular place.

I went on for another five miles, and came to the foot of the hill on which stood the place of the Grand Lama, the place which I had seen from Genpala.

The palace is so splendid that even its picture looks beautiful. I am not going to describe it in detail, but there is a quaint little story about it which shows the impression it creates at first sight. A certain countryman once drove to Lhasa some asses heavily loaded with butter. He saw the magnificent palace, and was so struck with its beauty that he stood gazing at it, thinking that it must be a palace of the Gods. When he recovered himself, he was mortified to find that his asses had strayed away. When he had gathered them, he found that there were nine instead of ten, and looked about anxiously to find the lost one. When asked what he was looking for, he answered that some one must have stolen his ass while he was looking at the palace, for he had come thither with ten asses. It was some time before he found that he had not counted the ass on which he was riding. This shows how the magnificence of the palace had affected him. I went half a mile along a wide road, south-east of the palace hill, and came to a bridge called Yuthok Samba, a hundred and twenty feet by fifteen, over which is built a roof in the Chinese style. I crossed the bridge and went on another hundred and twenty yards before I found myself at the western gate of Lhasa, constructed somewhat after the Chinese fashion. I passed through the gate and rode on some two hundred and fifty yards, when I came to a sort of large open court. Here I had to alight, for I was before the large temple of Buddha. I enquired how the image of Buddha came to be placed in the temple. It was before king Srong-tsan Gambo (who later introduced Buddhism into the country) was won to the religion, and when he was engaged to Princess Un-ching, a daughter of the Chinese Emperor Ta-sung of the Thang dynasty. She demanded a promise from his father that Buddhism should be widely preached in Tibet, and required at the same time that she might be permitted to take with her an image of Buddha, which had just been brought from India. The request being granted, the Princess took it to the city of Lhasa, where it has remained ever since. The image was thus brought into the country by the Princess at the same time as Buddhism itself. It was soon found necessary to preach a new form of Buddhism and to invent new characters in which to write its teachings. So learned men, sixteen in number, were sent to India to study Buddhism, and to invent new characters. Consequently, new Tibetan letters were formed, and Buddhist doctrines were translated into Tibetan. Buddhism was thus taught for over thirteen centuries, to the great advantage both of Tibet and of Buddhism. The images of Buddha was not originally carved in China, but was made by a Buddhist sculptor, Vishvakarma by came, in India, whence it was introduced into Tibet through China. When I lifted up my thanks before this image of Buddha for my safe arrival in Tibet, I could not help shedding tears over the goodness of Buddha, which enables me to see His image at this temple as well as at Buddha gaya in India. I need not say, for the whole story shows it, how great is my faith in Buddha. I do not mean that I do not respect other Buddhist deities; still Buddha claims the greatest worship from me, and I have entirely given myself up to Him and His religion.

There are many cheap inns and hotels in Lhasa, but as I had been informed that they were not respectable, I desired to stay with a friend, a son of the premier of Tibet. While at Darjeeling I had become acqainted with this young-noble, and he had offered me a lodging during my stay in Lhasa. I liked him, and did many things for him, and now, though I did not mean to demand a return for what I had done for him, I had no alternative but to go to him. So I called at his house. It was known as Bandesha—a magnificent mansion on a plot of about three hundred and sixty feet square. I entered the house and asked if he was in, but heard that my friend had become a lunatic. They told me that he had gone out of his mind two years before, and that he went mad at regular periods. I learned that he was staying at his brother's villa at Namsaiing, and was obliged to go there for him, but there also I could not find him, and was told the same thing. I waited there for over two hours, as I was told he might come, and then I reflected that it would be of no use for me to see a mad-man, on whom I could not depend, so I made up my mind to direct my steps to the Sera monastery, for I thought it would be better for me to be temporarily admitted in the college, and then to pass the regular entrance examinations. So I at once hired a coolie to carry my baggage, and started for the monastery.

Like the Rebung monastery, it was built on the slope of a hill, and when seen from a distance looked like a village. Guided by the coolie, I arrived at the monastery at four o'clock and at once called at the dormitory of Pituk Khamtsan, giving myself out as a Tibetan, as I came from Jangthang. Hitherto I had passed for a Chinaman, but as such I should have had to go to Pate Khamtsan, where I feared I, might be detected. I had not trimmed my hair nor shaved my face, nor bathed for a long time, and I cannot have been much cleaner than a Tibetan, so I made up my mind to pass for one and to live among them. The examinations for a Tibetan might be too difficult for me; still I could command the Tibetan language almost as well as a native, and I was often treated as one. I thought, therefore, that I could pass without detection, and so for my own safety I entered the monastery in this guise. The dormitory is occupied by several priests, who in turn, by the year, take the charge of the house. The then head of the dormitory was a very kind and simple old man, called La-toe-pa, and when I told him about my desire to obtain temporary admission, he gave me every particular as to what do do.

Before I go any further in my narrative, I must say something briefly about the Sera college. It is divided into three departments—Je-Ta-tsang, Maye Ta-tsang, and Ngakpa Ta-tsang. The first department contains 3,800 priests, the second 2,500 and the third five hundred. The former two departments have eighteen dormitories, named Khamtsan. They differ in size, for the small ones have about fifty priests in them, while there are over a thousand priests in the largest ones. There were two hundred priests in the house at which I stayed. Each Khamtsan has its own property, and all the Khamtsans as a whole are called Sera. These are the largest divisions of the monastery, but I will not enter into the sub-divisions.

[From *Three Years in Tibet*, 1909.]

17

Ta-Chien-Lu (Darchedo)—Its Commerce. Notes on the Government, Commerce, System of Taxation, Population, Foreign Relations, Etc., of Tibet

By
WILLIAM WOODVILLE ROCKHILL

I FOUND myself so comfortably installed in Yang lama's house in Ta-chien-lu, that I made up my mind to wait there the arrival of the two men I had been obliged to leave behind at Jyekundo. But even if the place had been less comfortable I should have stayed there to enjoy the society of the good bishop and the fathers of his mission, to whom I shall ever feel under a debt of deep gratitude for the kindness they showed me and the information they so freely gave to me about the country where they had lived and suffered for so many years. Monseigneur Biet has been in Tibet for twenty-six years, and though still a comparatively young man, is broken down by the many hardships he has had to endure. The history of the work of this mission has been written by the brother of Abbe Desgodins, and to that I must refer those whom the subject interests, only adding a few lines concerning the last persecution to which the faithful priests have been subjected.

The principal station of the mission, since the destruction of Bonga in the Tsarong, was Yerkalo on the Lantsang chiang, to the south of Gartok. Here a fine church, a seminary, a bishop's house, and other costly buildings had been erected, and a considerable stretch of land had been cultivated. The bishop was rejoicing in the completion of his work, when in 1887 a general uprising, instigated by the lamas, took place. Yerkalo was soon a mass of smoldering ruins and from every other station on Tibetan soil the priests were driven away and forced to seek refuge at Ta-chien-lu. At Bat'ang the lamas took from the grave the bones of Father Brieux, killed in 1881, filled their place with ordure, and made a drinking-cup of his skull. The native Christians who remained were not allowed to cultivate their fields by the lamas, and have been reduced to beggary. Since then Mgr. Biet has been obliged to support them from the meager funds at his disposal, but none of the fathers have been able to reenter the country beyond Tung Olo, a little village two days west of Ta-chien-lu. The bishop has appealed in vain to the Chinese authorities of Ssu-ch'uan, and to the French minister at Peking. He can neither obtain indemnification for the losses the mission has sustained, nor promise of reinstatement even in those stations situated on territory under the direct rule of China (as in Yerkalo). The fact is that ever since the miserably managed "state of reprisals" which exists between France and China in 1884-85 foreign prestige in the interior has fallen lower than at any period since the Anglo-French expedition in 1861. Everywhere, in Shen-hsi, Kan-su, Ssu-ch'uan, I heard it said that the officials had changed entirely of late in their manners towards foreigners; nearly all of them showed such marked hostility and arrogance that their conduct could be explained only on the supposition that they were acting under orders from Peking. Every foreigner living in the interior of China is kept under constant surveillance; his daily doings are fully reported to the local officials, his every act pried into, his servants suborned or maltreated, and no occasion is ever lost to snub or humiliate him publicly. In some parts of Ssu-ch'uan the missionaries have been in the last year or two so constantly and maliciously tormented by the officials, that when I was passing through Chia-ting Fu the bishop was about to recall them and put Chinese priests in their places. More than one old white-headed father told me that there had been more real liberty for them in the old days before the "opening" of the country than in the last few years, and I can readily believe it.

Ta-chien-lu is the most westerly sub-prefecture (T'ing) in the province of Ssu-ch'uan, and is also the capital of the Tibetan prince, or king (*jyobo*), of Chala, or Ming-cheng, as it is called in Chinese. The Dar Ch'u passes through the town and is spanned by two bridges. The valley above and below the city is closed by crenelated walls in which are three gates known as the northern, eastern, and southern. The buildings are mostly in the Chinese style of architecture, but many of them retain some of the peculiar features of Tibetan houses, chiefly the two stories and the flat roofs. The population, which I roughly estimated at between 6000 and 8000, is, as might be expected, very mixed, the trade of the place bringing there Chinese from Shen-hsi, Yun-nan, and other remoter provinces, besides large numbers of Tibetans and aborigines from every part of the western border. This floating population, which I have not counted in my estimate, is quite considerable, and is greatly increased by the tea-porters, bringing brick tea from Ya-chou and other localities, of whom at least four hundred come or go daily. There are also eight lamaseries, two of each of the four sects mentioned, in which dwell probably one thousand inmates, besides a certain number of Bonbo priests who do not, however, inhabit convents, and are hence called *ao-gomba*, or "lay lamas." Ten thousand would therefore appear to be a fair figure for the usual population of this town.

An army commissary (*Chun-liang-fu*) administers this sub-prefecture, besides forwarding all the money, supplies, etc., necessary to the Chinese garrisons in Tibet. The post was a highly lucrative one on account of the large sums levied as duties on tea, so that this officer made some $40,000 a year. But of late a deputy (*Wei-yuan*) has been sent here by the governor-general of the province, to superintend the levying of likin dues, and the Ta-chien-lu commissary is no longer able to feather his nest as comfortably as of yore.

The chief military officer of the place is a colonel styled Ch'in-ning Hsieh, Commander of the Fu-ho battalion (ying), from which are taken the various detachments stationed in eastern Tibet. He is supposed to have some two hundred men with him at Ta-chien-lu, but I do not think that, as a matter of fact, he has a hundred.

Prior to 1700, Ta-chien-lu and the country east of it for nearly a hundred miles was not occupied by the Chinese and was under the rule of the King of Chala, but since that date this tract has been annexed to China, though the natives have been allowed to retain their tribal organization. The native prince still resides at Ta-chien-lu, and is one of the most powerful chiefs of eastern Tibet, for among them he alone demands and obtains obedience from the lamas dwelling in his principality. He has the right to levy duties on all goods taken west of the city by Chinese or natives, and exercises exclusive control over all his people, native culprits arrested by the Chinese being turned over to him or his officers for punishment.

To the west, the state of Chala confines on the Manya (*Chan-tui*), and Lit'ang, and the prince has had much difficulty of late years in resisting the encroachments of the Lh'asa people, who have annexed the former country. The alliances he has made by the marriage of his daughters to the powerful chiefs of Derge and Lit'ang have, however, greatly strengthened his power and prestige.

On the western frontier of his state, at a place called Nya ch'u-k'a, or Ma-Nya ch'u-k'a, on the river Nya, is an important station garrisoned by a few Chinese and Tibetan troops. By some this place is considered the frontier post of Tibet, for here all travelers, natives only excepted, must show their passes. The post seems to have been primarily established to arrest deserters from the Chinese forces stationed in Tibet, and this is its principal utility at the present day.

Ta-chien-lu's chief importance is as a trading centre; it is the emporium between China and Tibet. Tea is the most important product exported to the latter country, from ten to thirteen millions of pounds being brought to this town annually for the Tibetan market. This tea is brought from Ya-chou and neighboring localities by porters, who are paid two-tenths of an ounce of silver for each *pao* weighing from eighteen to twenty-three pounds. On arriving at the eastern gate of the city they pass through the likin office, where a duty of Ti. 0. 8 is charged for every five *pao* (or one *t'ao*) of Ya-chou, Yun-chin Hsien, or Tien-chu'an Chou tea, that from Ch'iung Chou paying one mace more. The tea is next taken to the packing houses owned by the great Ya-chou tea firms in the city, and each *pao* is divided into four separate packages or bricks, called in Tibetan *parka*, and made up into cases of nine bricks and securely sewn in rawhide; then it is ready for exportation to Tibet, two cases or *gam* making an ordinary yak-load. On leaving Ta-chien-lu for Tibet a further duty of two tael cents is levied by the native ruler of Chala on every four bricks when exported by Chinese, and of one tael cent when exported by Tibetans.

I cannot do better than to quote here from a pamphlet written by Father Desgodins on the subject of the Tibetan tea trade.

"All the tea bricks prepared for the Tibetan market are not of the same quality; but, according to the maturity of leaves, to the more or less perfect fermentation, to the colour, to the proportion of leaves or of wood to the weight, are divided into five standards. There are besides some dozen loads of fine tea, also packed into bricks, to be sent as presents from the Emperor to the Dalai lama, or to be used by the Chinese officials and some few amongst the native gentry. This fine tea is never an article of trade.

"The first standard is called *Shih chang chin* by the natives, and *Go-mang chu-pa* by the Tibetans. These tea bricks do got contain any tea wood, but only the best fermented leaves of a dark brown (not black) colour. A light sprinkling of fine tea is generally added on both ends of each brick. As it is better flavored, and as less quantity is required, it is the tea preferred as drink by those who can afford to buy it. Each brick weighs generally five and a half English pounds, and is sold at Rs. 14 at Ta-chien-lu, Rs. 2 at Bat'ang, Rs. 3 out of the highroad, Rs. 3.8 in the districts of Tsarong and Zayul, adjoining upper Assam, from Rs. 3 to Rs. 4 at Lh'asa, according to the supply in market.

"The Second standard is called *Guie-tse kioo-pa* by the Tibetans. This brick is nearly of the same size and weight at the first standard, but the quality is much inferior on account of the leaves being of yellow or greenish colour. As the fermentation has been less perfect, the tea is worse flavored, and a larger quantity is required for the same decoction. Unscrupulous merchants sometimes try to sell it as *Go-mang chu-pa* to unwary customers, or to mix some bricks of it with the first quality. The second standard brick is sold at Re. 1 at Ta-chien-lu, Rs. 2 at Bat'ang, Rs. 3 out of the highroad as far as Tsarong and Zayul, Rs. 3.4 at Lh'asa.

"The third standard brick is called *Jya-pa* by the Tibetans, and *Pa chang chin* by the Chinese. Each brick weighs two and a half English pounds, and is sold for ten annas at Ta-chien-lu, Re. 1 at Bat'ang, Rs. 1½ to Rs. 2 out of the highroad at Tsarong and Zayul, Rs. 2 to Rs. 2½ at Lh'asa. Inferior in quality to No. 1, but superior to No. 2, this tea, made of leaves with a few tops of small branches, well fermented and of a dark yellow colour, is by far the most generally used in Tibet, not only as a beverage, but especially as a staple of trade, and as the current money of traders. Men bargain by stipulating so many bricks or packets (of four bricks) of tea. They say, `This sword has cost three bricks' this horse is worth twenty packets,' and so on. The wages of workmen and servants are paid in so many bricks of tea, etc. When bricks or packets of tea are mentioned as money, it is always the third standard, or *Jya-pa*, which is understood; then the bricks are not weighed, but counted. If it is agreed that tea be weighed, and not counted, then the fifth standard is understood to be the medium of exchange.

"The fourth and fifth standards are both called *Jong-ma;* so there are two kinds of *Jong-ma* tea. The first quality or fourth standard, which is made up of half of leaves and half of branches or wood mixed together, is of little use either as a heverage or as an exchange token. It will be enough to say that one brick weighs five English pounds, and is sold for Re. 1 at Ta-chien-lu.

"The fifth standard, or second quality of *Jong-ma*, is made almost exclusively with the wood of the prunings mixed with a few leaves. Sometimes there are no leaves at all. For that reason it is called *Shing ja* (wood tea) by the Tibetans. Each brick weighs nearly five English pounds, is sold at twelve annas six pies at Ta-chien-lu, Re. 1 at Bat'ang, Rs. 1½ to Rs. 2 out of the highroad, Rs. 2 to Rs. 2½ at Lhasa. This tea, after being pounded in a mortar, is drunk; and is used as current money, as above stated, because it is heavier than No. 3, though inferior in quality."

I was told by the likin officials at Ta-chien-lu that the amount annually levied by them on tea brought into the city was between Tls. 110,000 and Tsl. 120,000. Supposing that all tea pays TI. 0.8 a hundredweight (or t'ao), we find that about thirteen and a half millions of pounds are imported yearly.

Besides the tea entering Tibet by this route there is a considerable amount, possibly a million of pounds, taken in *via* Sung-p'an, and probably the same quantity from Li-chiang Fu and Ta-li Fu *via* A-tun-tzu and southeastern Tibet.

Incidentally the amount of tea imported into Tibet may throw some light on the vexed question of the population of that country. Five pounds of *Shing ja* a month is not a large allowance for a Tibetan or Mongol: so, taking thirteen millions of pounds as the average yearly consumption of tea in Tibet, we find that at the above rate it would supply little more than two millions of people, a figure arrived at by slightly more rigorous methods later on. However, notwithstanding the large amount of tea imported, it is no uncommon thing to find people reduced to using roasted barley of peas, chips of wood, willow leaves, etc., anything in fact which will impart a little color and taste to their drink, as a substitute for tea.

Exclusive of tea, the following are among the principal exports from Ta-chien-lu to Tibet: Cottons, silks, satins, gold brocades (*chinkobs*),

K'atag from Ch'eng-tu, tobacco, red leather, chinaware, sugar, furs, gun-barrels, hardware, drugs, and a variety of other articles which we may for convenience class as "notions."

Central and Ulterior Tibet send to Ta-chien-lu pulo, tirma, yak hides, lambskins, lynx, fox, and leopard skins, musk, gold, coral beads, pearls, and other precious stones, saffron (from Kashmir), incense sticks, rugs, dried fruit, tincal, medicines (principally deer horns), dried fruits, soap (from India), a variety of coarse unbleached silken fabric (from Assam?), brown sugar cakes (puram), etc. The total value of these goods is far below that of the tea bought here by Tibetans, who pay in Indian rupees for much the larger part of their purchases. Prior to the recent troubles between India and Tibet the quantity of rupees brought to Ta-chien-lu was so great that eight forges were kept going melting them into ingots, in which shape, and under the designation of *chiu pa*, "nine eight (fine)," this silver is in use all over western Ssu-ch'uan.

After tea, the most valuable trade of this town is in musk. Some conception of its magnitude may be had from the fact that the agent of one foreign firm of Shanghai purchases over $150,000 worth annually. Nearly all the musk before it is brought to Ta-chien-lu is adulterated by the Tibetans with blood, liver, etc., so that of one cod they make four or five. The usual test to ascertain its purity is running a thread rubbed with garlic through the cod; if no odor remains the perfume is held to be sufficiently pure.

Rhubarb is also an important branch of trade at Tachien-lu, but the supply greatly exceeds the demand. At Yerkalo and in the Tsarong hundreds of tons could be brought annually at a nominal price. On the hills around Ta-chien-lu it grows abundantly, but the natives, so as to be able to dispose of it rapidly, dry it by artificial heat and thus injure its quality. The price usually paid for it in town in TIs. 1.5 a picul; the sun-dried sort fetches as high as TIs. 3.

The Tibetan traders of each locality are organized into companies or guilds, and keep agents or vakils stationed at Ta-chien-lu, who make all purchases for them and dispose of their goods. These are called *tson-pon* or *kar-pon,* and, as at Tankar, are the responsible representatives of the merchants who appoint them. The size and importance of their caravans is very great; thus while I was stopping there I saw one leave for Shigatse in which were over 3000 pack-animals, mostly mules, and I was assured that not a day passed without a hundred or two hundred yak-loads of goods leaving the town for Tibet.

A considerable portion of the trade of Ta-chien-lu is in the hands of Shen-hsi men, but the most enterprising traders hereabout and in the Tsarong, Zayul, etc., come from Li-chiang Fu in Yun-nan, and are known as *Yun-nan ko*, or "Yun-nan guests." The Tsarong, a rich and populous country along the Lan-tsang chiang, inhabited principally by the Lissus, is their principal field of operations, and they realize large profits from the unsophisticated natives. Mgr. Biet told me that they had opposed, tooth and nail, the establishment of missionaries in that country on the score that the natives were unaware of the real value of the products of their soil, and unacquainted with weights and measures, but that if the missionaries got a foothold among them they would teach them so much that profitable trade would be destroyed.

While speaking of the tsarong it is proper to note that slavery exists there in a more aggravated form than in any other portion of Tibet. While now and then a poor Tibetan pilgrim, on his way through the Tsarong to the Dokela, or to some other famous sanctuary, may become indebted to some one for the amount of his board or the like, and be obliged to work out by four or five years of labor his little indebtedness, he at least eventually gains freedom; but such is not the case with most of the slaves in the Tsarong, who are taken from among the Lissus and other non-Tibetan tribes inhabiting the country. When one of these is in debt to a Tibetan and unable to meet the demands of his creditor, he becomes his "life servant" (ts'e yo). The master has the right to sell, kill, or otherwise dispose of him: he is given a wife, or a share in a woman, and all the children born to him are slaves. Even if he should be able to get together enough to pay off his debt, the master may refuse it and count his labor as only a set-off for the interest of the sum due. The missionaries have brought and freed a number of these *ts'e'yo,* but usually they have been able to buy only slave children; this class of persons have formed the nucleus of several of their little Christian communities.

While at Ta-chien-lu I learnt some further details concerning the Tibetan customs relating to the disposal of the dead. No funeral services take place before the crops have been gathered, except in the case of very poor people, whose corpses are thrown into the streams at once after death. All those bodies which are to be disposed of by cremation or by being fed to birds or dogs are put in wicker baskets, well salted, and kept until the time of the funeral. In the case of the bodies of rich laymen which have been cremated, the ashes are sometimes collected in a box and a *do-bong* built over it, but generally they are left on the spot where the cremation took place. When the body is to be devoured by dogs and birds of prey the usual method is to lay the naked corpse on the ground, fastening it by a rope tied to a stake so that it cannot be dragged about. But there is another more *recherche* and desirable mode sometimes followed, as was done some years ago with the body of the "living Buddha" at Lit'ang. This was carried out of the lamasery on a stretcher which was followed by the abbot and his 3500 monks. Many of the latter (probably *ri-tru-ba*, or ascetics) had human jaw-bones fastened to their left arms, and skull-bowls hanging from their sides. The procession marched slowly to the top of a hill outside the town; the corpse was laid on the ground, and the abbot took his seat on a stone near-by. Then some lamas stripped the flesh off the body, commencing with the arms, and handed the pieces to the abbot. These he held at arm's length in the air, when vultures, which were sailing around in expectation of the feast, swooped down and snatched them from his hand. In this manner all but the bones were disposed of; then these were pounded into a pulp, and the abbot mixed this with tsamba in his eating-bowl, and fed the balls thus made to the birds, reserving for his own private delectation the last ball of the unsavory mess. With this the ceremony was at an end. This form of obsequies, known as "celestial interment," is the most esteemed.

One of the first questions I asked Mgr. Biet was concerning the mysterious Indian traveler who in 1882 had reached Ta-chien-lu, coming from the Ts'aidam by the same route I had recently followed, and who had made an excellent survey of the country. To the outer world he is known only as Pundit A—K—, or Krishna, and the greater part of the results of his wonderful four years' journey, in which he crossed Tibet from north to south, and from east to west, has been carefully pigeonholed by the Indian government, the method always followed by it where the work of any of the native explorers attached to the Great Trigonometrical Survey is concerned. If any British explorer had done one-third of what Nain Singh, lama Urjyen jyats'o, Sarat Chandra Das, or Kishen Singh (alias A—K—, accomplished, medals and decorations, lucrative offices and professional promotion, freedom of cities, and every form of lionizing would have been his; as for those native explorers a small pecuniary reward and obscurity are all to which they can look forward.

A—K—reached Ta-chien-lu on the 9th of February, 1882, in a penniless condition, after travelling from Sa Chou in the capacity of mule-driver with a Tibetan trader. For days he hung around the door of the bishop's house, afraid to disclose his identity, lest the Tibetans should learn his true character. Finally he gained admission to Mgr. Biet, and told his story. He was most anxious to return to India through China, but the Bishop dissuaded him, advised him to try and reach Assam through the Zayul, and gave him money to help him on. He was a very clever young fellow, a native of Kumaon in British Tibet. During the greater part of his journey he had passed himself off as a peddler, carrying his sextant, aneroid, etc., in a roll of pulo. His survey, as far as I was able to control it, is wonderfully accurate. Unfortunately the names on his map had been so badly transcribed that they were absolutely unrecognizable by any of the people of the country. This is the more to be regretted as probably the fault does not lie with Kishen Singh, whose native language is Tibetan, but with those who transcribed his notes.

In a preceding chapter I have attempted to give an idea of the political and social organization of Kamdo or eastern Tibet. A few notes on the form of government existing in the Kingdom of Lh'asa find place here.

In 1751, the Chinese army having quelled a rebellion in Tibet fomented by the king, Jyur-me nam-jyal, the Emperor abolished the royal dignity and put the government in the hands of a council of ministers (*Ka-lon*), over which presided a lama, popularly known as "King of Tibet." This was made an elective office, the incumbent to be chosen in turn from one of the three great lamaseries of Drebung, Gadan, or Sera. To insure an uninterrupted succession, two lamas were chosen, one to reign as viceroy of the Tale lama, the other to live in a cloister (*rechu gomba*) surrounded with all the pomp of royalty, awaiting the death of the first-mentioned so as to succeed him; until this time came he was cut off absolutely from the outer world. This mode of selecting the *Peu-gi jyabo,* or "King of Tibet", has been retained to the present day, and I was assured that these elections are often the cause of great rioting among the lamas of the convents interested in the question, and have several times ended in serious loss of life. Usually the Chinese Amban intervenes, and puts a stop to the quarrel by giving his *placet* (subject to the final sanction of the Emperor) to the candidate whose party pays him the largest sum of money.

Subordinate to the Peu-gi jyabo, but acting in conjunction with him, are the four ministers or Ka-lon (also called *Shape*), chosen from among the most influential or wealthy laymen. Their appointments are also subject to the approval of the Emperor of China.

Furthermore, as a means of preventing the office of Tale lama and of other incarnations falling into the hands of a powerful family, possibly inimical to China, the Emperor Ch'ien-lung instituted the system of the "golden vase" (*ser-gi bum-ba*), by which lots are drawn by all the candidates for such dignities, the name of the successful one being submitted to the Emperor, who, if it meets his approval, issues a patent of investiture.

It is only since 1793 that the Chinese Amban in Tibet has taken an active part in the administration of the country. The colonial office of Peking (*Li-fan-yuan*) has the general superintendence of Tibetan affairs, but it is the governor-general of Ssu-ch'uan who is the immediate superior of the Amban. To him the Amban reports his actions; of him he asks instructions, even sends him copies of his despatches to Peking. The regulations of the colonial office contain the following rules for the guidance of the Amban in his relations with the native authorities.

"He is to consult with the Tale lama or the Pan-ch'en Rinpoch'e on a footing of perfect equality on all local questions brought before them. All officials from the rank of Ka-lon down, and all ecclesiastics holding offices, must submit to him for his decision all questions of whatever nature they be. He must watch over the condition of the frontier defenses, inspect the different garrisons, control the finances, and direct Tibet's relations with peoples living outside its border. Whenever vacancies occur among the Ka-lon, or Sha-dso-pa (treasury assistants), a report is to be made to Amban, who, in conjunction with the Tale lama, will select suitable persons to fill the offices. These positions cannot be held by relatives of the Tale lama.

"The money in the Tibetan treasury for the pay of native troops is to be used only for that purpose under instructions from the Amban; and, even in relations with foreign nations, the Tale lama must do nothing without his sanction. The relations of the Gorkhas of Nepal with Tibet are under the supervision of the Amban. When this people bring products of their country to the Tale lama and the Panch'en Rinpoch'e, return presents are necessary, and the Amban must decide as to their nature"; and so for all foreign tribes (the British not excepted).

Further on we read that "although the Kalon are the ministers of state of the Tale lama, they may not hold direct intercourse with the tribes outside the frontier. Should these tribes have occasion to write to the Ka-lon, the latter must forward the letters to the Amban, and he, acting in concert with the Tale lama, will prepare answers, but the Ka-lon must not answer them directly. Should letters be exchanged surreptitiously between the Ka-lon and tribes beyond the frontiers, the Amban will remove them from office at once".

The same authoritative work supplies us with some interesting details of the revenues and expenses of the Lh'asa government. "The Tibetan people have to pay annually to their government a certain amount, *per capita*, of grain, cloth, incense sticks, cotton cloth, salt, butter, cheese, dressed mutton, tea, etc. In view, however, of the frequent remoteness of their habitations and the difficulty of transporting goods, they are allowed to pay the equivalent in money. Any family owning cattle or sheep may pay as tax one silver coin (for *tranka*) a year for every two head of cattle, or ten head of sheep. The people can also give, whenever and in such amounts as they choose, money or goods as voluntary gifts to the state.

"Exclusive of the products of the country paid in to the government as taxes, the annual revenue in money amounts to probably 127,000 ounces of silver (about $177,800). All products and money received as taxes are stored away in the treasury in the Jo k'ang (in Lh'asa) and are under the control of three Sha-dso-pa (treasurers). As to the cloth, incense, and money, received as fines, as well as the various donations and the half of the estates, both real and personal, of deceased persons, they are placed in the chief treasury under the care of two other Sha-dso-pa. The Tale lama draws from these two treasuries for governmental and other expenses.

"The annual expenses of the Lh'asa government may be estimated as follows: In the first moon of the year the lamas of Potala, as well as all those from the various temples and lamaseries of Lh'asa, and from all Anterior and Ulterior Tibet, amounting to several myriads, assemble in the Jo K'ang to read the sacred books for twenty days. In the second moon there is another gathering at the Jo K'ang, for the same purpose, which lasts eight days. For these two celebrations some 70,900 ounces of silver (about $100,000) are used in giving the assembled lamas money, k'atag, butter, tea, tsamba, etc. Besides this the daily religious services of the year at Lh'asa absorb some 39,200 ounces of silver (say $55,000) for supplying the officiating lamas with butter, tea, and various presents. Finally, 24,400 ounces of silver ($34,160) are required yearly for providing the lamas of Potala with food and other necessaries, and for the purchase of objects to be given as return presents to persons making offerings to the Tale lama.

"It thus appears that the expenditures are greater than the receipts. Moreover, there are the lamas of the great lamaseries of Sera, Gadan, Drebung, etc., who have to be provided for.

"When the harvest has been abundant, voluntary gifts to government are very numerous, and there is a surplus. Now in the chief treasury there is a minor or special treasury over which is a Sha-dso-pa, and every year, if there is a balance left over in the chief treasury, it is put away in this minor one. The Sha-dso-pa, having general supervision over all expenditures and receipts, make, in conjunction with the Ka-lon, reports to the Amban on the condition of the treasuries.

"Concerning moneys necessary for governmental expenses, to be withdrawn from the chief treasury, the Amban must examine, in conjunction with the Chyidrung Hutuketu (i.e., the King of Tibet), into the nature of the expenses and resources. Any malversation must be at once reported by the Chyidrung Hutuketu to the Amban, whose duty it is to investigate the matter and inflict the prescribed penalty.

"As regards the people of Ulterior Tibet, they pay into the chief treasury (of their province) taxes in grain and money, but the larger portion is paid in kind. Taking into account both the products and money received, the annual receipts are about 66,900 ounces of silver (about $94,000). Formerly, voluntary gifts so increased the sum that there was annually a surplus, but since the Gorkha war (1794) the regular revenues, together with the voluntary gifts, about balance the expenditures. The Amban, acting in conjunction with the Chyidrung Hutuketu, must carefully examine the budget of Ulterior Tibet so that it always balances."

The authority of the Emperor's representative extends even to ecclesiastical appointments, for we learn from the same work that "When there occurs a vacancy among the K'anpo lamas, or abbots of the large lamaseries, the Tale lama informs the Amban of the fact, and they, having consulted with the Hutuketu under whose supervision the lamasery where the vacancy has occurred is placed, choose a new incumbent, to whom a seal of office and a patent of investiture are given, and who thereafter resides in the lamasery.

"When vacancies occur among the K'anpo of minor lamaseries, the Tale' lama fills them as he sees fit."

I cannot enter here into a complete discussion of our sources of information concerning the population of Central and Ulterior Tibet. Recent writers estimate it at from four to six million, but these figures are certainly mere guesses. The latest general census of the country of which I have any knowledge was made by the Chinese in 1737; partial enumerations have been made since then, and wherever I have been able to compare the figures thus obtained with those supplied us by recent travelers I have found the former in excess of the latter. The census of 1737 fixes the population of the kingdom of Lh'asa, or Anterior and Ulterior Tibet, at 852, 162 laity, and 316,200 lamas. It is highly probable that a large portion of the nomads were not counted, but this would not make a difference of 50,000, so it would seem that in the middle of last century the total population of Central Tibet did not exceed a million and a half. What can have been the rate of increase of the population in the past 150 years, is the next question to inquire into. The steady increase in the number of lamas, the Polyandrous marriages and general promiscuity in the relations of the sexes, the fearful and frequent ravages of small-pox, the enslaved state of a large portion of the people in the most fertile parts of the country, and other causes too numerous to mention, tend to prove that the increase has been undoubtly of the smallest, and we positively know that in many localities there has been a notable decrease. I am thus led to believe that even the estimate of 4,000,000 by Father Desgodins is largely in excess of the truth, and that the total population of all Tibet (inclusive of Lahul, Sikkim, etc.), the Kako-nor, and K'amdo (the non-Tibetan tribes living in the southern part of the country, in the Tsarong, Zayul, Poyul, etc., excluded), will not much exceed 3,500,000 souls, of which about 2,000,000 inhabit the kingdom of Lh'asa.

I remained at Ta-chien-lu until the 10th of July awaiting the arrival of the men I had left behind at Jyekundo, but, getting no news of them, I finally made up my mind to leave for Ya-chou Fu. They reached Ta-chien-lu a few days after my departure, yet were unable to catch up with me, and I came home without ever seeing them again; but from a letter received since my return to the United States I have learned of some of their adventures, and they prove how well my Chinese friends at Jyekundo advised me when they said to push on without delay. It will be remembered that shortly after my arrival at Jyekundo the chief of that locality went to Tendo to concert with other chiefs as to the best way to treat me. On his return he found that I had left, so he sent out men with orders to stop me dead or alive, and had my men seized, heavily chained, and locked up. After the lapse of twelve days, my friend Fu T'ung-shih fortunately arrived, and with much trouble had them finally released, given a guide, and started down the road I had followed.

Some two or three days below Jyekundo the lamas of a convent seized them, and, forced them to abandon their horses and luggage, carried them off to the lamasery, where they were again imprisoned. This time they bought their freedom by paying a considerable sum of money, but when they got back to their camp they found that two of their horses had been killed by wolves. They pushed on, however, and after sundry other adventures reached Kanze, where they were most kindly received by Lieutenant Lu, who sent them on, after a few days' rest, to Ta-chien-lu. Considering what those Chinese had to suffer from the lamas, one can imagine how pleasant these would have made it for me if they had laid hands on me. The old K'amba in Mar-jya-kou had said with truth: "Your only chance to get through K'amdo is to travel without losing a minute on the way."

[From *The Land of the Lamas*, 1891.]

18

A Himalayan Romance

By

EKAI KAWAGUCHI

I WAS still in the company of the party of pilgrims I have already referred to. It appeared that some of the party had come to form a rather high opinion of me as a person of reverend qualities. Among them was a young damsel who, it was not difficult to perceive, had conceived a passion for me. The moment the thought dawned on me, I said to myself: "It may be; it is nothing uncommon, rather is it quite usual for women to cherish vain thoughts. She must have heard her elders talking well of me, and have taken a fancy to me." I at once set about raising a barrier between us, which was none other than the teaching of our common Buddhism. When occasion allowed, I explained to her all about the vows with which all true priests bind themselves and why they do so. I depicted to her the horrors of hell that sinners create for themselves even in this world, and which follow them into eternity as the price they pay for momentary pleasures. These things I taught, not only to the girl but to the whole party. For all that, I could not help pitying the little innocent thing. A maiden of nineteen, with few or no restraints on her romantic fancies, she must have thought it a grand thing to be able to go back to her folk with a bridegroom of whom all spoke so well. She was not beautiful, and yet not ugly; a comely little thing was she. But I, though not old, had had my own experience in these matters in my younger days, and I was able to conquer temptations.

Here I may stop to observe that the country through which we were travelling is called Ngari in Tibetan and Ari in Chinese. The region is an extensive one, and includes Ladak and Khunu.

Purang, of which mention has been made more than once, is its central mart and enjoys great prosperity, though located rather to the south. Purang also forms a mid-HImalayan post of great religious importance as a sacred spot for Buddhist pilgrims. The town boasts, or rather boasted, of its possession of three Buddhist images of great renown—those of the Bodhisattva, Mahasattvas, Manjushri, Avalokiteshvara and Vajrapani. According to tradition these were brought thither from Ceylon in olden times. Unfortunately about six months prior to my arrival in Ngari a big fire broke out and destroyed two of these idols, the image of Manjushri alone being saved. Much as I wished to visit Purang, I was apprehensive of many dangers to my impersonation if I went thither, as the Tibetan Government maintains there a challenge gate. My companions went there, however, leaving me behind, and I spent the days of their absence in religious meditation. Joining them again on their return, I continued my travels westwards, coming out in due time to the north of Lake Lakgal. We next took our way along the lake towards the north-west. Facing west and looking over the lake, I saw islands spread out on its surface like the legs of a *gotoku*, or tripod. So I gave them the name of Gotoku jimu, or Tripod islands. Several days afterwards we arrived at a barter port called Gya-nima; it was the 17th of August, 1900.

At Gya-nima barter is carried on only for two months in the year, that is to say from the 15th of July to the 15th of September. The traders chiefly come from the Indian part of the Himalayan mountains and meet their Tibetan customers there. I was just in good time to see brisk transactions going on. I saw no less than one hundred and fifty white tents covering the otherwise barren wilderness, and some five or six hundred people rushing about to sell and buy in their own fashion.

The Tibetan articles offered for sale here were wool, butter, yaks' tails, and the like, while the purchases consisted of about the same category of goods as I gave when speaking of the Mabcha Khanbab mart. I stayed over night and spent the whole of the next day at the fair, making a few small purchases. On the day following we went back to Gya-karko, another barter port. Gya-nima was the most north western point I reached in my Tibetan journey. So far as reaching my destination was concerned, I had hitherto been proceeding in an exactly opposite direction to it, steadily going north-west instead of towards Lhasa, the capital of Tibet. But from the point—Gya-nima—onwards, each step I walked brought me nearer to the main road into Tibet, as also to its capital. In Gya-karko I stayed for three or four days. Here there were about one hundred and fifty tents, trade being carried on even more vigorously than at Gya-nima. Gya-karko is a trading port for people coming from the north-west plains of Tibet on the one hand and the Hindus inhabiting the Indian Himalayas on the other, who are allowed by the Tibetan Government to come as far as this place.

Here I saw many merchants from the towns and villages of the Himalayas. Among them was one from Milum, who spoke English. This man invited me to dinner on the quiet, so to say. I accepted his invitation, but the moment I had entered his tent I at once saw that he took me for an English emissary. When left to ourselves he immediately addressed me thus: "As I live under the government of your country, I shall never make myself inconvenient to you. In return I wish you would do what you can to help my business when you go back to India." I thought that these were very strange words to speak to me. On interrogating him, I found out that he had conjectured that I was engaged in exploring Tibet at the behest of the British Government. When I told him that I was a Chinaman, he said: "If you are Chinese, you can no doubt speak Chinese?" I answered him boldly in the affirmative. Then he brought in a man who claimed to understand Chinese. I was not a little embarrassed at this turn of affairs, but as I had had a similar experience with Gya Lama in Nepal it took me no time to recover sufficient equanimity to answer him, and I felt much re-assured when I found that he could not speak Chinese so well as I had anticipated. Then I wrote a number of Chinese characters and wanted him to say if he knew them. The man looked at me and seemed to say: "There you have me." Finally he broke into laughter and said : "I gave up; let us talk in Tibetan" Then my host was greatly astonished and said : "Then you are indeed a Chinaman! What can be better? China is a vast country. My father, who is now living in my native country, was once in China. If there is any business to be done with China I wish you would kindly put me on the track;" and he gave me his address written in English. His manner showed that he was in earnest, and that he was a man to be trusted. So seeing that this man was going back to India, I thought it would be a good idea to ask him to take with him my letters and deliver them for me in India. It would have been imprudent for me to write things in detail, but I scribbled just a few lines to my friend and teacher, Rai Sarat Chandra Das, informing him that I had penetrated the interior of Tibet as far as Gya-karko, besides asking him to post some letters for Japan which I enclosed, addressed to Mr. Hige Tokujuso and Ito Ichiso of Sakai. A few coins put into the hand of the Milum man secured to ready response to my request. The man proved the honest fellow I took him for; for after my return to Japan I found that my letters had been duly received by both Mr. Hige and Mr. Ito.

To return to my romance. We were still staying at Gya-karko, and I was much embarrassed to find that little Dawa-for that was my little maiden's name—had by no means given up her affection for me. Dawa, I may perhaps mention here, though I shall have occasion to refer to the matter at greater length in another chapter, is a Tibetan name meaning moon, given to persons born on a Monday; those born on a Friday being named Pasang, and those on a Sunday, Nyima.

Well, my little Dawa provided herself to be an adept in the art of love-making. It is wonderful how a little spark of passion, when once kindled, burns up and fashions daring schemes and alluring pictures. The maiden was always at my side, and spoke only of the good things she would make mine, if I would only accompany her to her native country. She said her mother was a lady of an exceedingly kind heart; that her father owned about one hundred and sixty yaks and four hundred sheep; that therefore her family was very rich and their life one perpetual *charchang pemma* or round of pleasures. She added that she was their only daughter, and that she had not yet come across a man to her heart, save one. I may perhaps explain that chachang pemma means drinking tea and intoxicants alternately, and that in Tibet one is considered to have attained the highest pinnacle of happiness when he is able to indulge in a perpetual symposium—drinking, in turns, tea with butter in it and then a spirit brewed from wheat. Only rich persons can enjoy the luxury: but the mass of Tibetans consider this to be the main object of life. Consequently chachang pemma is generally used in the sense of earthly beatitude. By the way, the method of manufacturing the butter-tea is very curious: butter, boiled juice of tea and salt are first thrown together into a nearly cylindrical tub of three feet in height; then a piston, if I may so call it, with a disc large enough to fit the cask exactly, is worked up and down, to obtain a through mixing of the ingredients. This pump-like action of the piston is carried on by sheer force of hands and arms, and as may be imagined, requires a large amount of strength. The motion of the piston transforms the mixtures into a new beverage which the Tibetans call *solcha*. It is said that these people can tell whether the solcha, or butter-tea, will prove good or bad by listening to the sound produced by the piston as it works up and down.

But to return to my story: Dawa never tired of telling me that her family was prosperous; that even Lamas were allowed to marry in her country; that it was really an excellent thing for every Lama to live happily with a wife in this world; that it would be wise for me to do so, and so on. Seeing that all her words were only wasted on me, she seemed to imply that I was an incorrigible fool. Wiles of temptation now came thick and fast upon me: but in such moments I happily remembered the triumph of our Lord Shakyamuni at Buddhagaya. The wise One was about to attain to the state of Absolute Perfection. The king of all that is evil was very much afraid of this, and sent his three daughters to tempt him. The women tried all manner of allurements to secure the fall of the Enlightened One, but in vain. When all had failed the daughters of the King of Devils sang thus:

How like a tender graceful flower am I,
With all the lovely fragrance of my mouth,
And its melodious music soft and sweet!
Am I not mistress of all mirth and joys?
Even Heav'nly bliss is naught to him who lives

In amorous dalliance, dearly loved, with me.
If thou rejectest me, there's none so dull
And stupid in the world compared with thee.

So sang the Sirens, but even they were powerless to conquer the Lord. My Dawa could not of course approach the charms of the arch-devil's daughters, but her plaintive pleadings were there. And I—a common mortal struggling on, but far from the gate of emancipation—I could not but pity the poor little creature, though I strengthened myself by saying: "Let it be so—a fool let me be." I composed an *uta* then:

You call me stupid; that am I, I grant;
But yet in love-affairs being wiser grown,
'Tis safe for me to be more stupid still.

It is true that women never let their mouths be the doors to their mind; but they know a language unspoken, which is far more telling, appealing and enticing, than that which were sound and articulation can convey. And my Dawa had never yet said in so many words what she yearned to say. It happened, however, that Dawa's father and brothers were out shopping one day, and that the girl and I remained alone in the tent. She thought probably that she could not get a better opportunity for her purposes and she tried to make the most of it. Just then I was mending my boots, and she almost frightened me with her boldness. I am neither a block of wood, nor a piece of stone, and I should have been supernatural if I had not felt the power of temptation. But to yield to such a folly would be against my own profession. Moreover I remembered with awe the omnipresence of our Lord Buddha, and was thus enabled to keep my heart under control. I said to the maiden: "I have no doubt that all is excellent at your home; but do you know whether your mother is still living or dead?" The question was unexpected and almost stunned her, put as it was at a moment when she had allowed her mind to wander so far away from her dear mother. She was just able to say: "I do not know whether my mother is living or dead. I have been on a pilgrimage with my father for one year and perhaps more. My mother is a weak woman, and I parted with her in tears, asking her to take the best care of herself, so that she might be preserved. I do not know how she is faring now." Here was my chance—a chance of diverting the girl's attention from me. "H'm! you don't know that?" said I; "only now you were telling me of the bliss of your home, and yet you don't know how your mother is faring now?" Poor little maiden, her mind became disturbed. I almost scolded her, pleaded with her, warned her. She, who claimed to be a good daughter, to be so intent in the pursuit after ephemeral pleasures as to let her thoughts wander away from her dear, good mother; could it be possible? This somewhat highly colored statement of mine seemed to cool down her passion and change it into fear and apprehension. Nor was it extraordinary that she should have become so affected. For in Tibet nothing is supposed to be too great for the Lama; he possesses superhuman powers and can work miracles.

Instead of an object of love, I had now become an awe-inspiring Lama to my little Dawa. As such, I counselled her with a good deal of earnestness, and finally succeeded in subduing her passion and conquering the temptation.

We prolonged our stay at Gya-karko for several days more, and on the 26th of August I started again with the pilgrims. As we travelled on in a north-easterly direction we came to a marshy plain interspersed with pools of water. Farther on the marsh became deeper. I tried to probe its depth with my stick, but the solid bottom was beyond my reach. Knowing then that the marsh could not be forded, we retraced our steps for about three miles and proceeded thence due east. Further on we found that the waters flowing out of the marsh formed themselves into three streams. We waded across them, and about ten miles further on the marsh came to an end and we found ourselves among mountains, and encamped for the night. Here there were many merchants on their way to Gyamina and Gya-karko, and many were the tents they had pitched all round. While there I went on a begging tour amongst the tent occupants—a practice which I put into execution whenever possible, in pursuance of the Buddha's teaching. A day's round, besides, generally earned me enough to carry me through the next day. I may add that the evening, whether after a day of journeying or of begging, I used to spend in preaching among my travelling companions. I had my own reasons for being painstaking in these preachings. I knew that religious talks always softened the hearts of my companions, and this was very necessary, as I might otherwise have been killed by them. I do not mean to say that my life was in any immediate danger then, for there were numbers of people always about, and besides, the region we were going through was a country sacred to Buddhism, and once, within the holy zone, even the most wicked would not dare to commit either robbry or murder. But it was necessary for me to take precautions in anticipation of dangers that might befall me as soon as I should be out of this sacred region. Such were the reasons why I did so much preaching, and fortunately my sermons were well received by my companions.

On th 28th of August we travelled about twenty miles over an undulating country. Throughout that distance we could not get a drop of water, and I had nothing to drink except a cup of tea which I took in the morning just before starting. We were of course all terribly thirsty; yet to me the suffering was not half so great as that I had felt during the former distressing experiences already narrated. Towards the evening we came upon the upper course of the Langehen Khanbab. This is the river called Sutlej in English. It is the head-water of a river which flows westward into India, and, after meeting with the Sita, forms the great Indus that empties itself into the Arabian Sea. My companions volunteered to tell me that this river started from Lake Manasarovara. When I pointed out to them that the Lake Manasarovara was surrounded by mountains on all sides and had no outlet, they replied: "True, but the river has its source in a spring to be found under a great rock, east of the monastery named Chugo Gonpa (the monastery of the source of the river), in a gorge on the north-western side of Mount Kailasa. That spring is fed by the waters of Lake Manasarovara that travel thither underground. Hence it may be said with equal truth that the river flows out of the lake." This was indeed an ingenious way of accounting for the popular belief. But judging from the position of the river, it seemed to me that it must take its origin on a higher level than that of Lake Manasarovara and I was not (nor am I now) ready to admit the correctness of the native contention. On arriving at the bank of the river we pitched our tents as usual and passed the night. On the following day, we visited a sacred place of great fame in that neighborhood, called Reta-puri in Tibetan pronunciation, but originally in Pretapuri. Having left our baggage, tents and other things with two men to take care of them, I went on the journey thither with Dawa, her father and another woman, four of us in all. As we proceeded westwards along the Langchen Khanbab, we saw large boulders of rock making a walled avenue for a distance of about 400 yards. Out of the rock region, we came upon a river flowing down from the north to the Langchen Khanbab. There were two others running parallel and at a short distance from one another. They are called Tokpo Rabsum, which in Tibetan means three friendly streams. We forded one of them and went up a hill for about a hundred and twenty yards, when an extensive plain lay spread before our view. I noticed that the plain was thickly covered with low bush-growths of some thorny family, and the sight reminded me of our tea-plantations of Uji. About a mile and a quarter further on we came to another stream, the name of which is identical with that of the one we had already crossed. Both these rivers were loin-deep and exceedingly cold, with small ice-blocks floating in them. In fording the river I was much benumbed, and on reaching the opposite banks I found that I had almost lost my power of locomotion. So I told my companions to go on while I rested a few minutes, and applied burning moxa to my benumbed limbs in order to recover their use. Off they went, after telling me that nothing could go wrong with me if I would only take the road in the direction they pointed out to me. Tibetans are strong and healthy, and extremely swift-footed into the bargain. I was no match for them in this respect, especially with half-frozen feet and that was why I told them not to wait for me. The smoldering moxa had its effect on my legs. I felt then more alive, and after an hour's rest I proceeded westwards for five miles to a place where the plain came to an end. Thence I walked down stream along a river until the temple for which I was heading rose into view. The sight was a grand one, with its mani-steps of stone which looked, at a distance, like a long train of railway cars. Nor was this the only place where the mani steps could be found. Many of them are to be seen in the Himalayas. I should add that in that mighty range of sky-reaching mountains there lives a species of strange birds, whose note is exactly like the whistle of a railway engine. The mani-steps looking like a train before me made me think of the whistle of those birds, and I felt as if I had arrived once more in a civilised country!

[From *Three Years in Tibet,* 1909.]

19

Under the Northern Rim of Tibet

By

C.P. SKRINE

IN THE spring of 1924 official business along the south-eastern road once more demanded my personal attention. Leaving Kashgar on 1st March and spending a busy fortnight at Yarkand, we reached Keriya on 12th April after short halts at Posgam, Karghalik, Goma and Khotan. On the way home we broke new ground between Keriya and Khotan and again between Khotan and Karghalik; but on the outward journey we used the same direct caravan route which we had already twice traversed, and I will therefore confine myself as far as Keriya to a few passages from diaries and letters.

Yarkand, 7th March, 1924

On the wide grassy plain south of Yangi Hissar this morning we overtook a caravan of camels carrying Tashkend sugar and Baku oil from Kashgar to Khotan. They were fine shaggy brutes and as impressive as camels always are when you see them in long strings filing across the wide spaces of the earth. But what marked this caravan among all I have ever seen—or heard—was its music. Never was there such a carillon of bells as that which rose to heaven from this slow-moving train of unmusical-looking antediluvians. There were loud bells and soft bells, big clanging bells and little bubbling bells, high-pitches bells and low booming bells and cracked bells, double bells one inside the other, copper bells from Kashgar and iron bells from Toqsun far along the road to Mongolia. Some of these latter have as clappers—what do you think? Camels' bones. I bought one the other day as a curiosity. There is something grimly pathetic about the idea of camels padding week after week, month after month, across Asia with the bones of their predecessors tinkling in the bells at their necks.

We had a really brilliant day for our "triumphal entry" into Yarkand with about a hundred British subjects of all kinds and religions mounted on more or less unmanageable ponies behind us. Yarkand as a whole took the utmost interest in our arrival, for it had been rumoured that we had gone back to India and that a former incumbent of the post had returned. I was amused to hear a woman in the bazaar say to a friend as I rode past *Bulturki Consul shu* (This is last year's Consul).

10th March

The new Commandant of the Yarkand garrison is of a type that is new to me, for unlike all the officials I have met hitherto he is a native of Sinkiang, though pure Chinese. His forebears, he tells me have been in the military service of the Urumchi Government for six generations, i.e. ever since the last reconquest but one, in 1758. Incidentally, he is about as un-martial-looking a person as can be imagined but he has had quite a varied and interesting career none the less. He has been to Manchuria and Moscow; he has been on expedition against brigands in wild Kansu; he was once staff officer to a general who was banished to Sinkiang for implication in the Boxer rising But perhaps his most unusual job was when he and two other "weiyuans" (officers on special duty) were detailed to take 500 Kalmuck horses from Urumchi to Peking as a present to the great Yuan Shihkai. I asked him whether the whole number arrived safely after the 2,000-mile journey, mostly across the desert? "Oh, we lost a lot," he replied, "but we had a big margin and delivered the 500 all right." I thought of the Hami melons they used to send to the Emperors, and reflected how the methods of the Chinese resemble natural processes in their disregard of waste.

11th March

Last night the missionaries and ourselves were the guests of ex-Taoyin Chu at a Chinese dinner-and-theatre party at the Tientsin merchants' club. In China you do not go to the theatre after dinner, as we do; the theatre comes to you during it. A large courtyard had been roofed over with cloth for the occasion; on one side was a temporary stage, on the other a dinner-table set for about twenty persons. The place was filled to overflowing with hordes of Chinese attendants, clerks, interpreters, soldiers, policemen and bottle-washers of all kinds, behind whom crowded Turki hangers-on, street-urchins and other sight-seers. Several delicious children of Chinese guests were present; the prettiest was an exquisitely made-up little girl dressed in embroidered red silk with a wonderful ornament in her hair consisting of a butterfly in jewelled enamel and bright green Yunnan jade, with a quivering aigrette of fine gold wire spraying downwards from it. There was also a tiny boy dressed like a miniature mandarin in a fur-lined black satin jacket and black silk skirt, surmounted by an absurd green Homburg hat, who planted himself solidly in the middle of the narrow open space between our table and the stage and stared solemnly at the players for a long time. His back view was that of an exceptionally fat Amban about two feet high, one of the funniest sights I have seen for a long time.

For nearly six hours we sat at the big table while course after course of a full-length Chinese dinner came and went, and a travelling company of Chihli actors performed play after play opposite us. Except for its inordinate length, the entertainment was quite an enjoyable one, and most interesting. On the Chinese stage all the parts are taken by males; the characters speak in a curious and very ugly kind of falsetto sing-song, the voices of the "actresses" differing from those of the actors only in being shriller and more strident. In the classical plays, which from the majority of the repertoire, the chief personages, Emperors, Courtiers, Generals and the like, wear magnificent embroidered cloaks surmounted by vast fantastic head-dresses and masks. A feature of some of the pieces was the acrobatic dancing. The evolutions performed by the acrobats and the speed of their movements on the small and crowded stage, especially in the battle-scenes, astonished us. The most extraordinary dance was that of four very stout Generals in one of the old war-plays. They came on wearing wonderful cloaks, masks and enormous pagoda-like erections on their heads, at the back of which rose a kind of trophy of four small flags. These vast grotesque figures danced like two-years-olds, the flags behind their heads waving wildly in the breeze. Their ordinary walk, too, was inexpressibly comic; it was a kind of goose-step, and every now and again for no apparent reason they would stand for several seconds on one leg with the other held out horizontally in front of them, toes upright, the body perfectly straight and leaning well *forward*. How they could stand up at all in such a position was a mystery; they must have had some sort of Little Tich shoe-attachment, cleverly concealed.

At these "command" performances it is customary for the actor-manager to put on plays from his repertoire (they all seemed to be short, about the length of an average curtain-raiser) according to the wishes of the chief guests, who are expected to reward him liberally for the compliment. A long red paper scroll is brought round inscribed with the names of the plays, from which you choose your fancy. We foreign guests had, of course, to rely on the Consulate interpreter, C., to tell us the titles of the plays; D. and I chose classical war-pieces, Mrs. L., of the Swedish Church Mission, one about brigands which she thought would be exciting. It was, but not quite in the way she expected. It proved to be highly improper—the only improper play we had the whole evening, and also, I am sorry to say, the most popular. The "gallery," of course, thought that the foreign lady had chosen it on purpose. They approved highly of her taste and kept looking round at her with delighted grins to make sure that she did not miss any of the points, especially during what was apparently a most realistic imitation by the leading "lady" of a Chinese nautchdance. What made matters worse was that C., who is immensely proud of his command of the language, in spite of furious winks and head-shakes from me, insisted on explaining in a loud voice exactly what was happening and which of the female characters were no better than they should be. It was most embarrassing and we were all covered with confusion.

Another of the "classical" plays, which was also about brigands but not in the least *risque*, had the following plot. Robbers kidnap the Governor of a province, and a band of public-spirited citizens determine to rescue him by means of a ruse. Dressing up as a troupeators in full rig, with swords and clubs concealed under their costumes, they drive in carriages through the mountains in which the brigands have their fastness. The carriages and horses are represented by an amusing convention; the occupant of the "carriage" holds a pole horizontally in each hand by his side, the fore ends of the poles being held by a boy who prances in front of him representing the horse, the rear ends by a much-padded "coachman" who walks sedately behind. This gives much scope for comic relief; the "horse" jibs and bolts, the driver falls off the "bod" and the carriage upsets. The supposed actors are duly captured and dragged off to the brigands' lair. Here they are made to play and dance for the amusement of the Chief, who is a magnificent sight in the voluminous yellow embroidered robe, huge black and red mask of appalling ferocity and head-dress of immense size and complexity. At the psychological moment the actors throw off their cloaks and draw their weapons; a battle-royal ensues in which the Chief of the Brigands, fighting for his life, lays about him in the most approved style. Eventually the rescue-party defeat the robbers, take their Chief prisoner, and escort the Governor back to his capital in triumph. During the last half hour of this performance the noise made by the orchestra passed all bounds. The musicians were specially reinforced by men with brass trays and large solid cymbals which they clashed and banged until I, for one, felt as if they were performing directly on my nervous system. D. said afterwards that hers, especially in her feet, was so numbed by cold and the absorption of thirty odd courses of shark's fin, sea-slug, etc., that the noise scarcely affected it. We eventually escaped with difficulty at midnight, having been there since a quarter past six; the theatre was still in full swing and the children were still looking on. Wonderful people, the Chinese.

Zanguya, 30th March

Two rather interesting persons were in possession of the rest-house when we arrived and courteously turned out to make room for us. They might be called "Sino-Turkis," for they are Muhammadans of Khotan who for the sake of preferment have adopted Chinese manners, speech and dress. I asked them round to tea and made them tell me all about themselves in their native Turki. One of them said that he had been sent to the Chinese school as a child (doubtless by ambitious parents of the Beg class), and at the age of twenty-five or so had been selected by the Amban of his district (Lop) out of twenty-seven candidates to represent it on the Provincial Council at Urumchi; "Doumalik" he called himself, explaining. The Council or "Douma" of Sinkiang is an advisory body summoned by the Governor, the members of which are theoretically representative of the people, one from each administrative district, but are really nominated by the Ambans; they sit for a fixed term of three years. Our friends had been much impressed by their time at Urumchi and spoke with bated breath of the capital and its ruler; the process of Sinization has evidently been complete. The men impressed me favourably; their manners were perfect and their speech cultivated. One of them in particular, Rajab by name, was most intelligent and looked a thorough gentleman with his neat, short black beard and moustache, black velvet cap trimmed with marten-skin and black satin fur-lined Chinese clothes. He said he was on his way to Karghalik where he had been appointed "Suloya" or chief of police; his friend was going to Goma in a similar capacity.

It seems that Chinese dress is essential for all Turkis who are candidates for Ambanships. But I notice that these men's costume is not purely Chinese; like the designs on Khotan embroidery and carpets, it is a mixture of Mussulman and Chinese. They wear the Turki *tumaq* or cap, as well as the *otek* and *kafsh-massi* or Russian boots and overshoes of Kashgar. Besides Wang Tungling of Uch Turfan, I have heard of two or three other cases of Sinized Turkis holding office. Not long ago I met a Bai man of the same type who was passing through Kashgar on his way to the Pamirs as a *wei-yuan* to inquire on behalf of the Urumchi government into the complaints of the Sariqolis against their Magistrate. Then there was a Mussulman Amban of Kelpin who was relieved of his appointment quite recently after two or three years' tenure; he was not a success, I believe.

Zawa, 1st April

We have been lucky in having perfect weather at this time of year for the crossing of the sandy belt between Zanguya and this place. We might have been caught in one of the sandstorms (Turki *burn*) for which early summer is notorious in these parts. Harding had a most unpleasant time in one last May. Whole caravans have been lost on this section of the road, missing the track in a storm and wandering out into the Takla Makan, where the water is 200 ft. or more below ground-level. For centuries the track has been marked every hundred yards or so on the worst bits by "basket potais" or curious elongated baskets about four feet in length placed on end and filled with sand. It is wonderful how long these last and how the baskets, or remnants of them, remain in position even when upset, as they usually are; stone posts would have sunk into the sand long gap. There are also of course the ordinary "potais" or towers of mud-brick at intervals of ten Chinese li (2 1/4 m.) which are, or ought to be, found along all main roads;these make excellent landmarks.

Khotan, 7th April

The first of Ramazan began a few days ago, and is rather a trial to us as well as to the greedy Turkis. They miss their food in the daytime; we miss our sleep at night. Badruddin's house where we are staying has a fine garden at the back, but the house itself is in the middle of the bazaar and we get the full benefit of the turning of night into day which marks Ramazan in the towns. The walls of the houses are merely lath and plaster and sounds travel through them like paper. The whole town seems to be talking at once until nearly midnight, when the chief meal of the 24 hours is cleared away. Then at 2.30 a.m. the drums begin beating to awaken the Faithful for the preparation of the second meal of the night. These tomtoms are dreadful;

they go on for an hour or more, varied only by the monotonously-chanted refrains of the singing dervishes. From four onwards the whole town is wide awake and busy either cooking, talking or intoning the *sahri* or prayer of dawn. Add to this the normal early-morning noises of Kashgaria, cocks crossing, donkeys braying, birds twittering, pigeons cooing, cows lowing, horses neighing and stumping about in their stalls..... If one's blood is well oxygenated, as it is on the march, one listens to this sort of thing for an hour or so and sleeps the rest of the night soundly enough; in a town this is not so easy.

Lop, 8th April

W——, Amban of this district, is a refreshingly unconventional official. Last year when he was late at the wayside tea-drinking he explained that he had been cooking our lunch; and an excellent lunch it was, with a minimum of sea-slugs and other atrocities and plenty of well-cooked pilaus and roasts. This time owing to an interesting event—the arrival of his ninth daughter—on the very day we came, we were let off both the arrival and departure tea-drinkings, a great concession. Usually as cheerful as could be, W—greeted me later with a long face and his right hand raised with the forefinger bent in the shape of a hook, which I understand is the Chinese finger-language sign for "nine". He appears to have had a most anxious time about his wife this morning, not so much because she was unconscious for two hours, but because of her fury when she came to and found she had given birth to a ninth daughter, having had no sons.

We have a fellow-traveller in Lop to-night whom I would very much like to meet, only I fear he will be starting very early to-morrow. He is a young man of 22, known as the "Gong Amban" or "Gong Beg" He is the great-grandson of Niaz Hakim Beg, last of the indigenous rulers of Khotan, who like Taj Hakim Beg of Kashgar and Durgah Beg of Yarkand was shorn of his power by the Khoquandi upstart Yakub Beg "Bedaulat" in 1864 and finally reduced to the position of a political pensioner by the Chinese when they came back in 1877. The present Gong Beg I am told, receives a pension of 400 taels £46 a month in return for which he is supposed to be always ready to assist the Chinese with a contingent of men in case of need. The interesting thing is that he received orders from Urumchi a short time ago to proceed to Aqsu with five hundred men. The poor boy was horrified, as he has never shot so much as a sparrow in his life and could only find twelve retainers to go to Urumchi with him. As one would expect, he has no influence in Khotan—the Chinese see to that—and all he has been able to do is to raise 5,000 taels from various sources with which to buy himself off at Urumchi. He and his party are not travelling by the usual route along the Khotan River to Shahyar and Kucha, but by the very trying eastern route via Cherchen and Lop Nor. I cannot understand why he is doing this, especially with the hot weather coming on. Something is happening in the north, I can't make out what; ex-Taoyin Chu at Yarkand received sudden orders a fortnight ago to proceed at once to Aqsu, and the Pamirs garrison has also suddenly been sent to the same place.

Besh Toghraq Langar, 9th April

Once more we are in the midst of desert sands. The Khotan oasis never looked so beautiful as it did this morning when we said good-bye to it for a while soon after leaving Lop. The tender mist of spring rested upon fields along the very verge of the dark-grey wastes of gravel desert, pale green where the wheat was sprouting, emerald for the young lucerne. Over the road drooped gracefully the long fronds of the weeping willows, trees which in the Khotan oasis grow to a size undreamed of in England. Tall flame-shaped poplars and the ubiquitous pollarded willow of Kashgaria marked the boundaries of every plot. But we had no eyes for green when on all sides glowed peach-blossom of every shade from rose to delicate shell-pink, set off here and there by the luxuriant foam-white of the quince-orchards. On the trunk of every tree hopped and tapped and peeped at us a pretty kind of woodpecker I have not seen elsewhere; it is larger than the English bird and has a scarlet crest, black and white bands on its wings and scarlet again under its body and tail.

Keriya, 13th April

We had a welcome diversion on the long and rather dreary march between Achma and this place yesterday. In the middle of a belt of sandy steppe 20 miles wide we were suddenly accosted by a weeping peasant woman and her son, a sturdy shepherd boy, who informed us that their hut close by had just been robbed. The father, it appeared, had gone to market, and two thieves had seized the opportunity to come and loot the few pots and pans the poor folk possessed. The lad, who seemed plucky and intelligent, had run after the thieves and thought they had dumped the booty somewhere among the reeds and would come back for it. He pointed out the direction in which they had gone. Without a moment's delay I, my three orderlies, the Beg who accompanied us and his servant charged off helter-skelter across the steppe, spreading fan-wise as we went, while D. and Murad Qari remained on the road comforting the lady. It was bad going and the horses floundered about among dunes and patches of long grass, but before we had gone a mile there was a hurroosh on my right and a view-holloa from Hafiz; two running figures could be seen dodging among the dunes, and off we went after them in full cry. My horse went head overheels in a bad bunker, so that I was not in at the death, but when I came up there were two hulking scoundrels in custody of the Beg. After some prevarication they confessed that they had robbed the poor woman, so we tied their hands and dragged them back to the road where they were duly identified by the delighted boy. At first they refused to say where the booty was, but threats of the Amban's wrath soon prevailed upon them to show us where they had hidden it in the long grass. It was pathetic—a couple of battered copper tea-pots and a small basin, all black with the soot of years, and a dilapidated oil blue quilted coat with brass buttons, evidently the absent bread-winner's only change of clothes. We visited the poor woman's home near by, a couple of tiny huts more than half underground and roughly roofed with reeds and turf. Here I photographed the scene and the entire caste, together with the properties, and then the woman fetched us a jug of water from a neighbouring spring by way of hospitality. Poor thing, she could do nothing but weep and quaver "Ashkalla! Ashkall-la!" (thank you) and try to embrace D., whom she evidently looked upon as her deliverer and sole refuge among all the rough men who surrounded her. We took the robbers off with us, trotting at the stirrups of Hafiz and the Beg, and made a present of them to the Amban of Keriya. They turned out to be real bad characters who had been convicted of robbery a year previously and had been punished with a thousand stripes and banishment to Cherchen; it had not been known that they had already found their way back from that remote spot. The Amban, I am sorry to say, did not seem quite as grateful as he might have been. Perhaps it was tactless of us to catch his robbers for him--the preservation of a Chinaman's "face" is a difficult and delicate matter, not to be lightly meddled with by the Western barbarian.

Boghat Langar, 17th April

How we took the Pelican to the Wilderness

The pride of the Yamen here is, or rather was until yesterday, a full-grown pelican which was caught straying near the town and presented to the Amban two months ago. Yesterday I somewhat rashly showed an interest in the bird (I had no idea they were found in these parts) and tried to take its photograph, whereupon to my dismay the Amban presented it to me on the spot. I refused and refused, I protested that we were going back through the mountains with pony transport and could not possibly carry the huge bird, but without avail. When a Chinaman really wants to unload a present on you, he is adamant and makes it impossible for you to refuse it without hopelessly blackening his face. Accordingly, the same evening the pelican appeared at our house, escorted by two infantrymen carrying the Amban's red visiting "card."

What on earth were we to do? We could not take the poor beast with us on top of a baggage pony, nor could we without cruelty to both parties insist on the Mir Munshi taking it with him in his Chinese cart by the main road. At first we thought we would send it with one of our servants on a cart specially hired; accordingly the local carpenter was set furiously to work constructing a strong and roomy wooden cage for him. Then we found that the pelican had to be forcibly fed; he either would not or could not swallow any food, even fresh fish, unless three strong men rammed it down his throat and kept it there by *force majeure*. The Yamen soldiers told us that they had been doing this the whole of the time they had had the bird. They gave us a demonstration, and the process was so unpleasant and so obviously cruel that we decided then and there that the pelican must be returned somehow or other to its proper place—the wilderness. But how to effect this without the Amban hearing of it? We were starting the very next day for Polu and had a 20-mile march in front of us; time was very short. Far into the night we cogitated and schemed, and finally we made our plan. Next morning I sent word to the Amban that I would not be leaving till about noon, as I had work to do; this was to prevent the Amban going out to his farewell tea-drinking too early. I then borrowed the Mir Munshi's cart, swearing him to secrecy, and arranged that the pelican in its cage should be put on it at the same time as the rest of our baggage was loaded up. The cart, in charge of one of the orderlies, Niaz (also sworn to secrecy), would leave with the caravan so as to put the hosts of inquisitive Keriya sightseers off the scent; at the first opportunity it would cut down a side-lane and double back by devious paths until it struck the Cherchen road to the east of the town, where D. and I would meet it. Having found a secluded spot among the marshes two or three miles along the road, we would liberate the pelican and return quietly to Keriya, whence we would make our official departure in due course.

The plan did not work without some alarming hitches in its initial stages. First of all it was found that the cart could not be brought up to the door of the Aqsaqual's house (which is in the middle of the bazaar) because the lane was too narrow. The cage with the pelican in it had therefore to be carried down to the main street. Then it was found to be too big to go under the hood of the cart. Tableau! There was nothing for it but to leave the cage behind and put the pelican into the cart by itself. This was done under D.'s supervision (I was busy with case-work and farewell interviews in the house) to the delight of the crowd. Our hopes that the pelican would be able to leave Keriya *incognito* were thus frustrated. Off went the caravan along the Polu road, D., pelican and all. Half an hour later, having ascertained that the coast was clear, I slipped out with Hafiz and galloped by a roundabout route to the ford across the Keriya River on the Cherchen road; here I overtook D. and the cart, which was jogging along with Niaz on guard in front and the curtain carefully drawn behind him as if it concealed my harem. He passed many country-people, families coming in to Kariya market from Oi Toghraq or Niya, wood-sellers driving donkeys loaded with faggots and so on; I wondered what they would think if they knew what was in the cart. Beyond the last fields of the oasis a shallow valley among grassy dunes led to the main river-bed half a mile to the north. For once we blessed the dust-haze of the Takla Makan which veiled our movements from a far. Loitering until a favourable moment when no passers-by were in sight, we dived off the road down the little valley, the lumbering vehicle pitching and swaying like a ship in a storm. Turning a corner we appeared to be absolutely in the wilds and were just congratulating ourselves on having shaken off all possible witnesses, when there on the top of a hillock were two boys watching us. Strong measures were necessary. I knew only too well that if even the smallest child saw us depositing the pelican in the wilderness, the bird's fate would be sealed; it would be recaptured and either done to death or taken back to the Yamen, whence the Amban would undoubtedly send it after us as lost property.... I decided to give the boys the fright of their lives, so I galloped straight at them; they ran like hares, I pursuing, until we arrived together at the small farm where they lived. Here I informed an agitated mamma that if she valued the children's lives she would send them to bed and keep them there.

Fate now smiled on us and we found that we could take the cart right down to the edge of the marshes. Here we took the long-suffering pelican out of "purdah." It was worth all our toil and anxiety, and more, to see the beatific expression on his face when he found himself once more on his native health. On the grassy edge of a clear pool he stood proudly with his poor clipped wings outspread, as if offering thanks to the pale sun for his new found liberty. But we could not leave him in too open a place, and so Niaz and I carried him down a secluded channel among the marshes and deposited him where no enemy would find him, safe from the Yamen and its forcible feeding, safe from the spying urchins of Keriya....And there we hope he will find a living among the frogs and minnows until kindly Nature has lengthened his clipped feathers (already half grown), so that he may spread his wings and fly away northwards, far over the Takla Makan to the untrodden solitudes whence he came.

Before returning to Khotan we treated ourselves to a long anticipated holiday trip among the Altun Tagh or "Mountains of Gold" which from the northern rim of the Tibetan plateau. Our first objective was the hill-village of Polu, three short marches south of Keriya; thence we proposed to visit the oases along the foot of the Qaranghu Tagh or Mountains of Darkness, that wildest and most inaccessible central section of the Kunlun which rises in the great massif of K 5 to a height of 23,890 feet. The trip proved somewhat disappointing, for the hateful dust-haze persisted and we saw little along the road beyond our immediate surroundings. Only once, for a short hour or two, did the veil lift. Nevertheless the journey was interesting in the extreme and on the whole enjoyable. Very few explorers had visited this secluded bay beneath the northern ramparts of Tibet, and the region may certainly be classed among the remotest and least-known inhabited corners of High Asia, outside Tibet itself.

The village of Boghaz Langar, at which the last of the above extracts was written, is the southernmost village of the main oasis of Keriya and lies at a height of 5,150 feet above the sea, or 700 feet higher than the town. Close by we visited the famous shrines of Imam Ghazz 'Ali, one of the heroes of local Muhammadan tradition, and of a lady known as Bu Hanifa. The place is remarkable for its plane-trees of immense age and bulk, veritable mountains of ancient wood, gnarled and monstrous like boulders in a torrent-bed. Next day we marched up the left bank of the Keriya River, passing one or two small isolated oases, and camped at a point 6,500 feet above the sea where the stream cuts through the foothills in an almost straight canyon 300 or 400 feet deep. It was a curious camp; though our tents were pitched fifty yards from the edge, the river could be neither seen nor heard and we seemed to be in the middle of a bare rolling moor of sand and scrub. Every drop of water for man and beast had to be brought by hand in buckets and gourds up a terrifying cliff-track known only to the guides we had brought with us. Next morning the haze was thicker than ever and we could see nothing of the massifs of the Altun Tagh, 21,000 feet high, which we knew impended over us at a distance of scarcely 25 miles. For hours we toiled up sandy tracks, new reaches and abysses of the river-gorge coming dimly into view at each corner. I was impressed by the quantities of drift-sand everywhere; even at this height the whole hill-side seemed to be silted up with sand blown from the distant Takla Makan, is marked contrast with the approaches to the Kashgar Range which we knew so well, four hundred miles to the north-west. At midday we were met by the friendly people of Polu who had pitched for us a tiny tent made of sacks on a cliff-top 800 feet above the river-bed. With the indefatigable hospitality of remoter Asia, they had brought all the way from Polu, several miles further up among the mountains, an enormous meal of boiled sheep, bread, tea and hard-boiled eggs dyed bright blue, the favourite colour of Khotan.

Polu is the largest of the hill-villages at the western end of the Altun Tagh or Mountains of Gold, a branch of the Kunlun stretching for a thousand miles to the E.N.E. until it merges with the Nan Shan. The relative importance of Polu is due to the fact that it commands the only possible track leading up over the Kunlun to the northern plateau of Tibet and so to Ladakh and India. The defiles on the north side of the pass are exceedingly narrow and almost, if not quite, impossible for pack transport of any kind; but for a distance of 530 miles, from the Hindu Tash Pass (17,750 ft.) over the Sanju range in the west to the Qarasai gap above Cherchen in the east, there is no other path at all by which men can cross the tremendous barrier of the Kunlun. Polu is picturesquely situated at a height of 8,500 feet on a ridge between two branches of the Keriya River's chief tributary. Its fields are lined with tall poplars and dotted with clumps of fine planes and walnuts. The village consists of closely-packed, flattopped houses of wood and stone with curious raised skylights in the middle of the roof, and has a look of Baltistan or Tibet which differentiates it at once from the settlements of the hill "Sarts" and Kirghiz of the Kashgar Range and the Tien Shan. Stein thinks that there may be Tibetan blood in the people, and certainly they do not regard themselves as belonging to the same race as the people of Khotan and Keriya. Polu and neighbouring villages do not belong to Keriya district, as one would have expected; they are grouped with Imamlar, Chakar, Hasha, Nura and other oases of the great "bay" of the Kunlun into the "Begship of the Three Hundred Hill Families, which is under the jurisdiction of the Amban of Chira. The people of Polu complain of this arrangement, for Chira is twice as far from them as Keriya. They told me however, that whereas they have always been assessed at ten families only, they number about eighty, so that their cultivation is taxed very lightly. They are industrious cultivators, raising crops of barley, millet and lucerne on every available yard; but the dryness of this part of Asia is such that even here, right under snowy mountains 21,000 feet high, crops have to be carefully irrigated. There are two methods of irrigation in use; where the slope is slight, the fields are terraced in the usual manner; where it is steeper, the entire surface is covered with a key-pattern of channels about six inches deep, down which the water trickles over the whole field, a most laborious business. The chief industry, however, is stock-raising; though they look barren enough, the uplands in this neighbourhood grow excellent grass, owing probably to the fertility of the aerially-deposited loess which is found at the very highest elevations and gives a slightly dirty tinge even to the eternal snow. An excellent type of hill-pony, shaggy but better-looking and with finer hair than the Kalmuck ponies, is found here together with a black and very woolly breed of donkey; I bought one of the former for 32 taels (£4 5*s*.) and it turned out one of the best hill-ponies I have ever ridden. "Polu pony" as we always called him, besides being strong and willing, was a remarkably intelligent little animal and took in everything that was going on. On the long bare plateaux of Poma Qir and Chata Qir west of Polu we saw herds of yaks and camels as well as the ubiquitous sheep and goats.

An industry which would be of greater importance locally than it is, if the Chinese did not strictly control it and limit the output, is gold-washing. There is no doubt that gold exists in large quantities throughout the length, not only of the Altun Tagh but of the whole Kunlun system. I heard of gold-washing high up among the almost inaccessible gorges of the Upper Yarkand River; Stein mentions it at Pisha in the Qaranghu Tagh (Central Kunlun), and speaks feelingly of the appalling conditions under which the gold-miners work in the Zailik valley, 13,500 feet up among the peaks to the south-west of Polu; the well-known mines of Surghak and Chizghan, 60-85 miles E.S.E. of Keriya, employ 2,000 labourers even under the Chinese system. Gold is continually being found in new places between Chizghan and Tunhwang in Kansu province, 700 miles eastward. I heard at Keriya of three new mines, all rich, to which there had been miniature "gold-rushes" during the previous two or three years. All the mines between Polu and Cherchen are under the control of the Amban of Keriya, who farms them out to a Beg for a fixed annual weight of gold-dust to be delivered to the Chinese at the fixed rate of 25 taels per tael weight, about five-seventh of the average market price at Khotan. The Beg is not supposed to extract more than that amount from the mines, but of course he does. He finds, pays and feeds his own miners, whose numbers are augmented at Surghak by numerous convicts. The Chinese do not allow the local people to wash for gold except for the Beg, and as his total output is limited by contract he does not often give the inhabitants of a village like Polu leave to wash for him. As a special favour we were given a demonstration of the primitive methods used. Three boys crawled into a hole in the conglomerate bank of the Polu stream and passed out tray after tray of blueish gravelly earth; a fourth washed it in a wooden pan shaped like a very shallow cone with a slit in it. From each trayful the boy got from two to seven tiny grains of gold, some red, some yellow; in a quarter of an hour he had washed out a quantity which he told us was worth a tenga (2*d*) at the Beg's rates. In a day's work, he told us, he would get anything from one-tenth of a tael to 10 taels worth (3*d*.—£1 7*s*).

The men of Polu are exceptionally friendly and hospitable to Europeans, a fact noticed by Deasy, Stein and the few other travellers who have come this way. The villagers still remember Deasy, though his visit took place as long ago as 1897. The stable in which his ponies were kept is pointed out with pride, also the room in which stayed the Chinese ssu-yeh or secretary who was sent by the Amban of Keriya to watch Deasy and prevent him at all costs from finding the secret path over the Kunlun. One of the *bais* or chief men, Tokhta Khalfa, told me with pride that it was his father, Rahim Khalfa, who really helped Deasy to cross the mountains. He gave me a graphic description of how poor Qasim fell off the path on the way up to the pass and was dashed to pieces. He agreed with me that it was a little thoughtless of Qasim, on the edge of the path with a 100-foot drop behind him, to tighten a knot in a home-made rope by hauling at it with one foot pressed against the pony's side.

They offered us the pick of their houses,

but we preferred to camp on a sheltered field under a low bluff of loess above the village. If only the air had cleared for an hour, the glorious snows which we could sometimes just descry far above our heads would have completed an unforgettable picture; but the haze was inexorable. In front of us the Tereklik ("poplar-y") side-glen sloped steeply up; perched on a crag above it was a conspicuous shrine which I visited one day. Besides the usual sacrificial yak's tails and pieces of clothing I found a curious and very old votive sign of wrought copper shaped like a hand-mirror with a fine pierced-work inscription. It reminded me of an object of similar shape and size, only with a chased design and inscription, which I saw at the shrine of Mir Umar at Sangun, under the Kuh-i-Taftan in the Sarhad district of Persian Baluchistan. How I coveted that votive sign! I would have paid quite a large sum for it; but it has never seemed to me quite "playing the game" to tempt unsophisticated people to part with things which they hold sacred.

Four days we waited at Polu for the weather to clear, and then, on 24th April, we gave it up and started for Khotan. Marching three miles up the Tibet trail we struck westward at the village of Hong across the Chirikoldi ("The soldier died") pass and the wide grassy tableland of Chata Qir. The morning had been a little less hazy than usual, but by three o'clock as we descended into the valley of Zinjik Aral a violent storm of wind laden with dust and gravel and a spatter of rain swept down upon us from the Kunlun. Followed two unpleasant hours during which we hurried half-blindly down wild moor-land paths. Only one incident do I remember; under the lee of a steep hillside above us we saw three huge black eagles squatting on the rocks, gorged doubtless after some grim feast. D. put them up; fine birds they were, with dark grey ruffs, light brown heads with black round the eyes and black beaks. In this country as in the Tien Shan they tame these black eagles and hunt gazelle with them. In the evening the wind was still blowing strong when, after ten hours' hard marching, we came to the pleasant orchards of Jai Tuz at the upper end of the Imamlar oasis, scattered over a wide expanse of stony river-bed.

That night the wind dropped and the stars shone out brighter than we had seen them shine for weeks. I was up early, full of hope, and I was not disappointed. Right across the southern sky, above the orchards of the Imamlar valley, above the great rolling downs of Buzang and Chata, above the rocky homes of the mountain people, stretches a wondrous panorama of eternal snow . Our prayers had been granted, not a day too soon; before us stood revealed at last the Kunlun, shyest and most elusive of the great ranges of the earth, the almost impassable barrier behind which lay Tibet. Between eight and half-past I took a telepanorama of five plates which, though far from perfect, is one of the most treasured pictures; not because of its intrinsic beauty, which does not equal that of my Kashgar Range and Tien Shan panoramas, but because of the extreme rarity of the spectacle recorded. An hour later, the haze had reappeared, and by noon not a vestige of the snowy vision remained.

From Imamlar we marched to Khotan in six days without undue haste. Though we did not see the mountains again, even the isolated massif of the Tikenlik Tagh (18,780 feet), across the wide apron of which we trekked for three days, we had some delightful glimpses of Arcadian villages tucked away in folds of the bare moorland. Nura was the loveliest; a green island in a sea of grey and yellow, six miles by two, with old wooden farms and mosques mirrored in clear pools, water-mills shaded by tall planes and orchards ablaze with apple-blossom, white and rose-red. On 27th April we entered the Khotan oasis south of Lop Bazaar and camped near the inn of Kutaz Langar ("At the Sign of the Yak"), where there is a domed tomb among desert poplars called the Shrine of the King's Daughter who Died in the flower of her Youth. Next morning we rode the 18 miles into Khotan in a couple of hours.

Two day's halt was all that we could allow ourselves, for I was as usual behind my programme and the news from Kashgar was somewhat disquieting. Chinese troops were being concentrated at Aqsu in considerable numbers, and the Titai was reported to be arming. Could it be that the civil war which had been so long endemic in the inner provinces of China was now to spread to the Far West? Reluctantly I decided to curtail my homeward tour-programme and abandon a plan which I had long been nursing; this was to climb one or more of the easternmost summits of the Sanju Range and reconnoiter from the north the untrodden gorges of the Qara-qash river, 60 miles long, which had baffled even Stein. But the prospect of a fourth journey along the well-beaten Pialma-Moji-Goma track did not appeal to us, least of all under what we fondly expected would be the grilling sun of May. We therefore decided to take the comparatively little-used upper road to Karghalik via Duwa, Sanju and Kosh Tagh and thus break ground that was new to us.

On 3rd May at Zawa we bade farewell to the Kingdom of Jade and crossed the sand-hills of the Pigeon Shrine to lonely Takhtuban Langar, where the water is drawn from a well 200 feet deep. Thence leaving the main road we struck south-west, reaching Lamus in the Duwa valley late in the evening after a gruelling march of 36 miles. It was here that I visited the charming old Haji who narrated to me the local legend explaining the name of Lamus, recorded by me in another chapter. I shall never forget the scene in the central room of the Haji's farm where Murad Qari and I sat sipping tea and talking to the old man and his well-mannered sons. The family were evidently animal-lovers. A very fat white pigeon sat on the back of a Qur'an-stand and joined in the conversation with such loud cooings that we had to raise our voices to make ourselves heard. An immense tortoiseshell cat purred furiously if anyone even looked as if he intended to stroke it. Best of all, a plump white lamb walked unconcernedly about the room throughout the proceedings, finally jumping up on the dais beside me and helping itself from a plate of raisins on the low Chinese table by my side. When lifted down it repeated the performance, the Haji remarking delightfully that the lamb had become his *mihman* (guest) as well as I!

Resting a day at Lamus we performed another long march across the *sai* by Poski Langar to Chaskam in the beautiful Sanju Valley, where we halted another day for sightseeing. Then the weather changed and we had a most unpleasant march through Sanju Bazaar and along the main Leh-Yarkand caravan-route to Sulaghiz Langar. Icy wind and torrential rain caught us unprepared on the top of a pass, and we had to gallop for it 11 miles, only to find scarcely even the humblest accommodation available at the tiny settlement of Sulaghiz. Next day it was still cold and cloudy, but on 9th May when we marched to Oi Toghraq we were rewarded with the longest panorama of snows we ever saw, even in Chinese Turkistan. From the eastern end of the Sanju range they stretched in an immense arc to the northernmost peaks of the Takhta Kuram west of Karghalik, a glittering panoply of ice 180 miles long.

The rest of our return journey must be passed over quickly. Yarkand was reached on 14th May, and eight days later we were back at Kashgar, having covered a total distance of 936 miles on the last and by no means the least enjoyable of our longer tours in Southern Sinkiang.

[From *Chinese Central Asia—An Account of Travels in Northern Kashmir and Chinese Turkestan*, 1926.]

20

In Northern Tibet

By

SVEN HEDIN

I

OVER THE ASTYN-TAGH

But at last we grew tired of waiting for the storm which never came. I spent most of my time reading Selma Lagerlot's and Heidenstam's books, and studying Buddhist mythology. The gad-flies, however, did not relax their siege, and the wind failed to come and give us an opportunity to break through their investment. At last I lost all patience, and determined to start, let the cost be what it might, on the evening of the 30th June. Sending the caravan by land, by the seven hours' route round the marsh, I directed them to meet me at Yoll-arelish, the point where the road branched, one portion of it going on to Sa-chow, the other bending away to the mountains of Tibet. Meanwhile, I proposed crossing by canoe the same lakes which I had already traversed in April, and at Yoll-arelish, which I had already mapped on a previous expedition, I intended to resume my cartographical work.

The 30th June was a busy day, what with packing up, settling accounts, and getting the two Cossacks off to Kashgar. Besides commissioning the latter to carry my letters to Europe, I gave each of them two yambas (£16), and promised to recommend them warmly to their highest commanding officer, the Czar. They also carried a letter to Jan Daloi, amban of Charkhlik, asking him to send at once 3,000 *jings* (30 ass-loads, or about two tons) of maize to my new headquarters.

We began to load up at five p.m. The moment the camels emerged into the open air, they were surrounded by a swarm of buzzing gad-flies. However, they bore the infliction patiently; and as fast as each animal was loaded up, four men were told off to protect him with big kamish brooms. When all was ready, Turdu Bai mounted his horse, and putting himself at the head of the cavalcade led off at a good round pace.

Then it was the horses' turn; but they made a tremendous pother, kicking and even flinging themselves on the ground, so that we had to lash their loads with extra ropes to keep them on. At last, however, they too set off in the wake of the camels, conducted by Mollah Shah, Kutchuk, and Tokta Ahun, the son of Kunchekkan Beg.

The big and comfortable canoe which was to carry me to the rendezvous was already provisioned and equipped with felts, pipe, matches, etc., and lamps; and it only remained to say good-bye to my faithful Cossacks. I thanked them warmly for their services, and after a hearty shake of the hand saw them mount their black horses and set off along the road to Charkhlik, which town they hoped to reach next morning. They carried with them letters of recommendation to the ambans, begs, and aksakals all along the road, and intended to take the mountain route through Kopa and

Sourghak, and after that travel by night to Kashgar *via* Khotan and Yarkand.

When I started with my boatmen it was pitch dark; but the current helped us, and we went down the river at a smart pace, leaving its dark banks rapidly behind us. At Kum-chappgan I only stayed to change my canoemen. When we started again, the moon had disappeared; but the night was clear and the stars glittered like diamonds above the wandering lakes. A faint, but refreshing, breeze flickered through the reeds, and happily, on that my last night on the waters of the Tarim, the gnats were not troublesome.

At eleven o'clock p.m. we left Tuzun-chappgan, guided by a man in a small canoe. It was perfectly wonderful the way he steered his course in the darkness through that labyrinth of high, dense reeds, across the lagoons and lakes, and through the chappgans and narrow, confined waterways. The other canoemen paddled on without a moment's hesitation and without once stopping, as though their canoes were running on invisible metal tracks, off which it was impossible for them to get astray. They did not talk, they only paddled—paddled unceasingly, and in good time together. But the breezes of the summer night failed to penetrate into those dense reedy wildernesses, and it was oppressively warm, close and stuffy; and the miasmatic vapours rose from the tepid waters of the marsh. At intervals I slumbered, and on towards morning the men began to sing, to keep themselves awake. The lake of Satehkoll was a good deal shallower than it had been in April, so that the men were obliged to get out and draw the canoes after them. Soon after that we were forced to abandon the big canoe altogether, and take to the smaller one. Yet even that soon ceased to float, and we had to wade ashore through the mud.

Then followed two or three hours of waiting in the silence of the dark, dreary waste. At length, however, we heard shouts in the distance; then they came nearer, and lighting our lamps we went to meet them. It was Shagdur and Tokta Ahun, with the horse caravan. They had travelled faster than the camels, so that we had to wait again for them. I thought I could not employ the time to better advantage than by having breakfast; but the Lop-men had to row a long way out into the lake to get a can of fresh water, as well as a few bundles of Kamish to boil it with, before even that simple meal could be prepared, for the shore was absolutely barren.

The camels came up just as day was breaking. They had gone astray in thee darkness, and, misled by an ass-track, had turned off too soon. They continued without stopping, and as soon as breakfast was finished the rest of us got to horse and followed them.

The country was a mere barren waste. On the north side of the marsh the sand-dunes gave at least some relief to the desert, and the dead forest witnessed to the existence of life at a former period. But here there was nothing; the ground was as level as a pavement, and consisted of hard, rough, saliferous clay, which had once been under water. The only break in the monotony was the winding track we followed.

We struck away from the shore at an acute angle; and when the sun rose, and poured a flood of light and warmth across the desert, we could just discern the last lakes of the Tarim system like a dark line hovering above the horizon behind us. The sun rose with unusual splendour. Its beams broke amongst the light and delicate clouds which hung like a veil before its face; so that their edges, lit up from behind, glowed like molten gold, while the middle parts were stained various shades of violet. The air was clear and still, and the sky a pure pearly, spotless blue.

But an even finer spectacle was presented by the panorama of the mountains which, in the oblique, almost horizontal, light, stood out in sharp and distinct relief. Their colouring varied from light blue to violet, shading off through silvery tints. The transitions were not at all harsh, being tempered by the distance, so that they formed a harmonious and enchanting background to the arid desolation at their feet, just as the sunrise is all the more beautiful when it follows a gloomy and stifling night.

But the sun was not without its shadows. No sooner did it show above the eastern edge of the desert than the air became filled with myriads of gad-flies, which, in clustering clouds, followed horse and rider as they moved. Long before noon the heat was oppressive, and we yearned for night to come to free us from our tormentors.

Just on the edge of the desert, where the outer skirts of the mountains began their slow ascent, we halted at the little oasis of Dunglik, or the Hills. Its altitude was 3,415 feet above the sea, and as Abdall lay at 2,750 feet, we had consequently climbed 665 feet whilst crossing the desert. The horses were put inside a shelter which had recently been built, but the camels were turned out to graze on the thin sparse steppe. We were all tired after our night march. As for myself, I dropped asleep under the first tamarisk I came to and lay there until the sun burnt my head; after which I went inside the tent, and sat and worked, scantily attired. There was a well, 10¾ feet deep with brackish water, which, however, did not prevent the animals from drinking it. For our own use we had brought water with us from the lake, and sinking it into the well, which had a temperature of 14.3°C., or 57.7° Fahr., we kept it nice and cool, and every now and then I gave myself a douche from a pail. The temperature of the air rose to 40.1° C., or 104.2° Fahr. in the shade.

I was awakened at three o'clock on the following morning, lamps and candles were lighted, and my breakfast of tea, eggs, and bread was served. We packed up and loaded the animals, and by the time that was done it was dawning in the east. When we started at 4.30 a.m. it was broad daylight, and the gadflies had begun their strenuous day's work. They buzzed about us in myriads, and followed us a mile or so on our road, literally red with frenzy as the rising sun shone through their blood-swollen bodies. I myself killed two or three hundred which had got entangled in the camels' naked skin. Crack! went a whip, and crack! went the suctorian as his inflated body burst. But we soon got too far away from the vegetation, and they durst no longer follow us, so that for the rest of the day we had peace from them.

We were now marching across the open, gravelly *sai*, which slope gently up towards the mountains. It was a perfectly barren and desolate region, without a single blade of grass, without an insect or any other sign of life, nothing but gravel and sand, thinly scattered over a soil as hard as asphalt. On the left was the narrow belt of vegetation which marked the oasis of Dunglik; while on the right were the mountains, gradually unfolding themselves, as their reddish-yellow outlines became shedded out into separate chains and valleys. I took the bearings of every conspicuous peak from several different points, and noted them all down on my map. Behind us on the distant horizon was the faint, dark line of the Tarim lakes, and beyond them a low diffused haze suggested the sandy desert of the Lop country.

At irregular intervals were a number of small stone pyramids intended to mark the road during the continuance of the storms. Asiatics consider it their duty to show a certain amount of gratitude towards their roads and tracks, and they do it by adding one or more stones to these pyramids as they pass them. Without them, they could not find their way to the springs and grazing-grounds; and when a traveller is fortunate enough to escape the storms himself, he is grateful enough to think of those who may travel that same road under less favourable conditions, and so adds his contribution to help make the road plainer.

The heat of the day began to make itself apparent in warm exhalations and warm breezes. I knew it was a long way to the first spring to Tattlik-bulak, for at every point where I had previously crossed it. This gravelly slope at the northern foot of the Kwen-lun was excessively broad. But my hope, that we should soon get amongst the mountains, was doomed to disappointment, for when we reached two huge cairns, one on each side of the trail, Tokta Ahun gave me the very comforting intelligence that we were only half-way, and yet we had been tramping steadily on at the usual caravan pace for fully seven hours.

The little pups, Malenki and Malchik, which were only five months old, had tired very soon after we started, and were then stowed away in a basket on the back of one of the camels. When the sun began to burn, we covered them with a felt, and after that heard nothing more of them until we reached camp, when they jumped out of their hiding place as brisk and lively as possible, though a little stiff. Mahka and Yolldash were more sensitive to the heat, and when we began the second half of our day's march, they appeared thoroughly exhausted. Although we gave them water two or three times, they kept loitering behind and had to be fetched. Finally, we put them on the back of a camel. Yet they did not relish that method of travel, but struggled down as soon as the camel began to walk. Thus they dropped behind again, and Shagdur rode back to fetch them, taking some water with him. After a pretty long absence he came back with. Yolldash, and reported disconsolately that Mashka was dead. When he found the dogs, they were both lying at the bottom of a dry ravine in the shelter of a shady terrace. He gave the whole of the water he had with him to Mashka, who gulped it down greedily. Then he put a cord round Yolldash and led him, while he took Maskha on the saddle in front of him. But before he had gone far, the dog turned very strange, bit the horse in the neck, and let her head fall hopelessly. Thus died the best of our dogs, and had to be left by the wayside. But we had not one drop of water, and I feared the worst for Yolldash. After several unsuccessful attempts, I managed to lash him fast on the top of a camel's load, where he lay rocking and jolting half dead with "sea-sickness."

But the rest of the animals and all the men bore the journey well. It was worth while making an extra push to escape from the killing heat in the lowlands. Getting tired of riding, I walked for several hours. The country was still the same, and the ascent imperceptible, while all day long we had the same peaks constantly on our right. But towards evening the ground became more broken, and we got amongst low hills of gravel-and-shingle, sand, and clay. Further on we could see the bare rock, a light green schist and granite, greatly weathered and brittle. Our path lay up a dry and steeply scarped glen, which was entered by numerous natural watercourses from both sides, and by numerous torrents, which, although now perfectly dry, and cut deeply down through the sides of the glen. The path wound away to the east across an infinite number of ridges, hills and gulleys.

Through the upper part of a narrow gap in the side of the glen we caught a glimpse of the brook, oasis, and refuge of Hunglugu, an especially welcome sight after such a day as we had had. The first thing we did when we reached the spot was to send the dogs off to get water. Their delight knew no bounds; they drank, they coughed, they rolled in the grass, they barked with delight, and then drank and drank again.

There was an abundance of vegetation, chiefly noble tamarisks, which attained the dimensions of trees, though there were also grass and kamish, and a great variety of herbs; while in an expansion of the glen stood a group of rugged old poplars. But we did not stop there. We pushed on farther up, the brook growing bigger and clinging to thee mountain-wall which shut in the glen on the right. We found the horse caravan, which had been a long way ahead all day, encamped at Tattlik-bulak, in a grove of magnificent tamarisks, besides a little caravan of seven asses and seven sheep, which Numet Beg had sent on from Abdall the day before, with a store of provision for our use.

I know nothing more delightful, after a 14½ hours' march through a burning desert, than to encamp in a beautiful oasis like this, and here we had one of the most comfortable camps I have ever had anywhere. My little Mongolian yurt was put up, for the first time, on the outer margin of the tamarisk grove, and it was so neat and cosy and inviting, with its bed, and carpet, and boxes, that I did not really miss the old ferry-boat and its snug cabin. Shagdur, Turdu Bai, and Mollah Shah erected the white tent under the tamarisks, while the other men encamped in the midst of a bower-like thicket. At nine o'clock the temperature of the air was 20.0 C. or 68.0 fahr. and of the water 12.8 C. or 55.0 Fahr, so that my usual wash-down was very refreshing after all the heat of the march. We were now at an altitude of 6,408 feet, or 3,658 feet above Abdall.

When I gave orders that we were to rest the 3rd July at Tattlik-bulak, or the Sweet Spring, the rejoicing was general. We no longer had occasion to complain of the heat; for, although the sun was hot enough at midday, it was tempered by a southwest breeze. This, however, came, not as the steady, continuous blow of the lowlands, but in gusts, which were sometimes so violent that they threatened to bowl over my yurt, yet sometimes again so gentle that they died away into a dead calm. The left side of the glen was bounded by a perpendicular wall of gravel-and-shingle, and it was out of its crannies that the spring gushed; the water was quite fresh, as clear as crystal, and had a temperature of 10.0C., or 50.0 Fahr. The rivulet it gave origin to ran straight into the glen brook, which was somewhat discoloured by dust and mud. The glen itself was from 50 to 200 yards wide, and after hard and long-continued downpours of rain appeared to have been filled from side to side. On the top of the wall above the spring was a cairn of stones, surmounted by two or three staves, on one of which I read "P. Splingaert, 1894," and "C. E. Bonin, 1899;" the former was the Belgian mandarin known as Ling Darin.

The vegetation was luxuriant, although it consisted of but few species. The fauna embraced a few small birds, besides ants, spiders, flies, ticks, and beetles. We also saw two or three gad-flies; but they had no doubt been brought up by our own camels. Had we not lost Mashka, who was a general favourite with everybody, we should have been perfectly in clover. When we started again I had the canvas skiff sewn up in a felt, to protect it against chafing, and the yurt was carried by one of the horses, because they travelled faster than the camels. Thus, from this time onwards, I always found my "house" ready for me when I reached camp in the evening.

The route led up the glen, beside the brook, between cliffs of black slate, which were often connected with the bottom of the valley by seeds of gravel-and-shingle. As we advanced, the vegetation gradually died away. The tamarisks were just in flower, and the pure violet tints of their clusters of blossoms imparted a touch of life to the otherwise monotonous brownish grey of the mountain landscape. We crossed the little stream repeatedly; it was delicious to have it beside us when the day grew warm. In winter the entire glen becomes choked with ice, and travellers then avoid this route for fear their animals should fall and break their legs. In fact, we did observe one camel, which had belonged to a caravan of Mongol pilgrims, lying by the side of the brook.

The sky was cloudy, and we should have had a pleasant march had we not been pursued by swarms of mosquitoes, which showed an unhappy predilection for our ears and nostrils as their chosen field of operations. Their incessant tickling and stinging made the skin sensitive, and irritated it until it itched intolerably.

That evening, when we reached the little pasture ground of Bash-kurgan, or the fortress at the Head of the Glen, my portative hotel stood ready erected and furnished by the side of the track. But there were several things to be done before I could step inside and enjoy a much-needed rest. First, I unpacked my meteorological instruments; then I labelled and put away the geological specimens which I had collected during the day; then I drew my maps, and wrote my notes and observations. By this dinner was ready. Then at nine o'clock came the reading of the meteorological instruments and the boiling-point thermometer, and the winding up and comparison of the chronometers; after which I went out and played with my dogs, and fed them. My day's work was seldom over before eleven o'clock at night. When it was, I usually lay and read for half an hour, and then went to sleep and the fresh, strong, healthy mountain air made me sleep the sleep of the just. At nine p.m. The thermometer stood at 12.1°C. or 53.8° Fahr. What a difference two days' journey made!

During the night the temperature dropped to 0.1°C., or 32.2° Fahr., and next morning we unpacked our warm winter wraps.

I had made up my mind I would not travel up to our new headquarters at too rapid a rate, and so we sacrificed another day to rest at Bash-kurgan. The place was named from the ruins of a small Chinese fort, crowning an isolated hill, and built at the confluence of three other glens with the long ravine of Tattlik-bulak.

As this trench or ravine pierced the lower range of the Astyntagh, or Astun-tagh, we were already on the other side of it when we reached Bash-kurgan. The next day took us up towards the main crest of the same system; but we were unable to get over it in one march, and stopped for the night at Bashyoll, a little grazing ground with a splendid spring (temperature, 5.8°C, or 42.5° Fahr.), beside the ruins of a Chinese fort.

On the 8th of July we had a long and desolate piece of road before us, and consequently carried a supply of water. On both sides our path was overhung by steep, denticulated, irregular masses of rock; but gradually it widened out, and eventually led up to an easy, flat-topped pass, which, strange to say, bore no other name than simply Davan (the Pass). Hitherto the road had run east; now it turned towards the south, although a defile did lead on to the east between cliff-like rocks. There we saw two wild camels, but they were in full flight. This made the third region in the centre of Asia where I had observed these animals; so that, with the information I gathered subsequently, I am now in a position to trace out a map of their distribution.

There was a slight dew on the summit of the pass; but when we descended into the broad, flat latitudinal, or parallel, valley which separates the Astyn-tagh from the Akato-tagh, and were crossing it, it began to rain merrily, and the thunder rumbled amongst the mountains. The valley was a perfect desert, without a single sign of life. After a ride of 13 hours we reached a nameless steppe, where there was neither water nor grazing, though the teresken shrubs did afford a supply of firewood.

II

THE START FOR TIBET

On the morning of the 9th July the sky was perfectly clear; during the previous night the temperature had fallen to 0.7 C. or 33.3 Fahr.

Our order of march was as follows. The asses and the sheep started first. Then followed Mollah Shah and Kutchuk with the horses, which always arrived at the next camping ground a long way in advance of the rest of the caravan. After them came Turdu Bai and Mollah with the camels; while I, Shagdur, and Tokta Ahun brought up the rear. The last-named, who was well acquainted with all that region, acted as my cicerone. Shagdur held my horse when I took the compass bearings of the mountain-peaks, or collected geological specimens, though I left him to pack them up in newspaper. All this generally made us an hour or two behind the others in reaching camp.

To the south-west lay a magnificent mountain mass crowned with perpetual snow, called Illveh-chimen, and on this side of it were two small salt lakes, Uzun-shor and Kalla-koll. At the foot of the Akato-tagh we rested for an hour beside a small spring and pool, called simply Bulak, the water of which was beautifully fresh (12.0 C or 53.6 Fahr.), and our thirsty beasts, which had had no water the day before, were allowed to drink their fill. There was also luxuriant grass around the spring, though its extent was limited. During our short half the weather suddenly changed. The sky clouded over, and it began to rain heavily. It was evident we had already entered the zone of the characteristic Tibetan weather, in which sunshine, rain, and wind alternate incessantly at intervals of only a few short minutes.

Leaving the spring, we followed a dry ravine towards the south-west, and were met by a violent storm from that direction. It was not rain, but wind, which made the dust and sand spin, and drove them with cutting force into our faces, till the skin felt quite sore. The storm advanced upon us like a compact, yellowish-grey wall of spinning whirlwinds, and enveloped us in an impenetrable haze, which completely blotted out every feature of the country. We could see nothing except the path in front of us. It was as much as I could do to sit in my saddle, and when I tried to jot down my notes, it was like tearing the paper to pieces. But after two hours the hurricane stopped quite as suddenly as it began. It was as if we had waded through a river of rushing wind. And no sooner was the storm past than the air cleared at once, and became as pure and transparent as it was before. A very different storm from the storms in the lowlands! But we soon had convincing proof that these violent mountain hurricanes really do carry drift-sand with them; for on the top of the double easy pass of the Akato-tagh we found a number of sand-dunes in miniature, which had been formed there by the south-west wind.

The southern flank of the Akato-tagh, which we crossed to the south-east, was a repetition, in point of orographical relief, of the northern flank of the Astyn-tagh. The *sai*, or hard gravelly slope, descended gradually to a broad valley, which ran from west to east, and on the south was fenced in by another mountain-range, the Chimen-tagh. This gravelly formation was succeeded by *kakir*, or a horizontal deposit of argillaceous mud laid down in water after rain. There we found the skeletons of the two horses belonging to Cherdon and Faisullah's caravan, which had died on the way up. At length we caught sight of the yurt standing on the shore of a small lake, which we had seen in the far-off distance from the *sai* above. It was known simply as *koll*, was about one-third of a mile in diameter, and surrounded by grass.

Strange to say, the gnats and gad-flies again honoured us with their company even at this altitude; the former even kept with us until after we left the main camp in the Chimen-tagh. The moment the wind dropped, out they came in swarms. The horses and dogs suffered the most; the camels' skin was too thick for their delicate proboscis to penetrate. The gnats haunt the mountains for about two and a half months in the summer. You would think it impossible for their larvae to survive the bitter cold which prevails in those altitudes in the winter; but they do.

On the 10th of July we still continued towards the south-east, striking obliquely across the valley, over several deep gullies, which, when in flood, helped to swell the large stream that, farther east, emptied itself into Ghaz-nor (or Gaz-nor) on the frontier of the country of the Tasidam Mongols. We halted beside some springs, surrounded by fresh grass, on the edge of a gully called Temirlik. To take my astronomical observations next day was a veritable baptism of fire, because of the gnats. They used maliciously to wait until I had both hands engaged with the screws of the instrument, and then opened fire.

At a subsequent stage of my travels, Temirlik (9,715 feet above the sea) became a very important centre. Even now several visitors came to our camp. Simultaneously with us there arrived four gold-hunters from the mines of Bokalik, who had been two or three months in the mountains hunting for gold, but had discovered nothing worth speaking about, and were now returning discontented to their homes in Khotan. Here, also, we were overtaken by the maize caravan, which I had ordered from Charkhlik, led by five men, who brought a polite letter from the amban. And, last of all, came a couple of messengers from my principal camp, from which we were still two day's journey distant, who reported that all was well. One of these messengers was Khodai Vardi, whose name means "the God-given," but who, as a matter of fact, was a disagreeable individual from Yanghi-koll, who subsequently tried to play me an unfortunate practical joke. The other was an afghan named Aldat, from Cherchen. He had spent the winter in the mountains shooting yaks, the skins of which he sold in Keriya. He was a fine, handsome young fellow, who lived the life of a real Nimrod amongst these wild mountains. Coming up in the autumn with a good stock of ammunition, his musket, and his furs, he used to spend the whole winter hunting, carrying neither tent nor provisions, but living on the flesh of the yaks he shot, and drinking of the springs which are fed by the everlasting snows.

In the summer his brothers used to come up with a train of asses, collect his stock of yak skins, cut out the serviceable parts, and carry them down to Cherchen. He had been engaged by Islam Bai because of his knowledge of those mountainous regions right away to the foot of the Arka-tagh, though he had never been south of that range. I took a great fancy to Aldat, and proposed he should accompany us on our first expedition into Tibet, and he closed with the proposal without hesitation. His manner of life struck me as being remarkably strange, and yet, at the same time, as very fascinating. I asked him what he did when he had no luck, and failed to kill any game, and so got nothing to eat. "I go hungry till I do find a yak," said he. Where did he sleep? In crevices and ravines, sometimes in caves. Was he not afraid of wolves? No, he carried tinder and flint with him, and always made a fire in the evening to cook his yak steak, and trusted to his musket. Did he never lose his way? Oh, no, he couldn't lose his way! He knew every pass, and had hunted every valley times without number. As for being alone, he thought nothing at all of that. There was nobody he cared anything about, except his old father and his brothers.

What a restless, wandering spirit! I can hardly conceive a more dreary country to be alone in than Northern Tibet. The desert could not be worse. One might get through the days—but the nights! When the cold freezes you to the marrow, and the dark mountain ranges shut you in and menace you will all sorts of imaginable evils! Aldat's life was, of a truth, "dangerous, poor, and great," and even now, when he has long been dead, I cannot understand how he stood it; he remains a mystery to me down to this very hour. I was surrounded by everything I needed-servants, a bodyguard of Cossacks, night-watchmen and watch-dogs—and yet, when the snowstorms raged around my yurt and the wolves howled in the mountains, I often felt a sense of utter loneliness steal over me.

Every one of the men who accompanied me on this expedition of the Chimen-tagh was destined to distinguish himself in some way or other. Turdu Bai was the best Mussulman I ever had in my service; and when the camels were under his care, I was always perfectly comfortable about them. Shagdur was above praise; I do not know how to describe sufficiently the services he rendered me. He learned to do everything; he never forgot anything, and wanted no reminding; life was very pleasant in his company. There was a something about him which was very sympathetic. I especially admired his bold and impetuous courage in moments of danger, and the calmness with which he received commissions of real difficulty. Twice, subsequently, he had occasion to show that he was ready to lay down his life for me. It was elevating to have about one a man who exhibited such a degree of disinterested fidelity; no wonder, then, I became attached to this Buriat Cossack. In his own country he worshipped the idols of Lamaism; but now he turned his back contemptuously upon them. This was not my fault, for I did not consider it my business to shake the faith of any Asiatic; but there was much that went on in my caravan that gave Shagdur, and indeed all the other Asiatics as well, occasion for a good deal of thought—things they had never even dreamt of.

Tokta Ahun of Abdall was a thorough honest good fellow, a man of sound understanding, who proved himself exceedingly useful. I have already said, that he accompanied both the horse and the camel caravan to Temirlik, and he now went with us for the third time when we started for our new head-quarters at Mandarlik, whither they had recently been flitted from Temirlik, because of the gnats. As he will play a conspicuous part in a later expedition, I will say nothing more about him here. With Kutchuk, also, the reader will become better acquainted later on. He, also, was a fine fellow, and uncommonly useful, a sort of Asiatic "Seven Dufva," Mollah Shah was also with us in Northern Tibet. It only remains to mention Mollah, the "Doctor", a comical little fellow of fifty, a thin wrinkled old man, without a trace of beard or moustache; for which reason we sometimes asked him in jest, whether he were not really an old woman, or at all events a Mongol—an appellation which the faithful of the Prophet do not regard as altogether flattering. His voice was shrill and piping, and he was fond to talking to himself, especially of an evening. He was very full of fun, however, and knew what he was about, and everybody liked him. With Mollah, too, we shall become better acquainted, for he accompanied me on my second expedition to Lop-nor. This man must be distinguished from Mollah Shah, previously mentioned, for he also took part in this expedition.

The evening was celebrated by a furious tempest from the west, which threatened to batter in my yurt, until we stayed it down again all round.

On the 12th of July, our course being eastwards, we were not long before we turned our backs upon the zone of vegetation, in that we rode across hard, barren, gravelly ground, though we had all the time on our left the light-coloured belt of grass-land, which stretched away to the debris which muffled the foot of the Akato-tagh, whence two or three troops of *kulans* (or wild asses) watched us with curiosity. Just after we passed the spring of Kumutluk, which filled up the greater part of the valley, we caught a glimpse of the large lake of Gaznor to the north-east. At its west end the lake was broad and rounded, but gradually narrowed towards the north-east, until finally it issued in a little brook. Owing to the treacherous marshes which surrounded it, it was only approachable at a single point. Its shores were in places as white as snow, and its water as salt as brine. In front of it was a little freshwater pool called Ayik-koll, because bears were said to visit it for the sake of the berries which grew on the bushes near it. This pool was overgrown with kamish, and abounded in wild duck, which winter in that district; but Gaz-nor was entirely destitute of vegetation. The *boghana* bushes, kamish, and rushes which grew at Chigghelik (9,768 feet), or the "Place of Rushes"—the Mongols call it Dundu-namuk, or the Middle Spring—south of Gaz-nor, were the cause of the air there being literally thick with gnats and mosquitoes, which tormented us worse than they did anywhere along the Tarim; for their bites produced an eruption of the skin like eczema.

We had now only one day's journey to go to reach our head-quarters camp. It took us up the glen of Mandarlik, deeply trenched between gravel-and-shingle terraces twenty-five feet high. Higher up we met a bubbling brook of bright crystal water. When we entered this transverse breach in the northern face of the Chimen-tagh, we left behind us the northernmost outcrop of the rocks and came amongst the granite, which thrust out its fantastic craggy buttresses nearer and nearer towards each other from both sides. Looking backwards, we saw as through a wide gateway the lake of Gaz-nor, and beyond it in the distance the Akato-tagh. Upon reaching an expansion of the glen, we turned our horses, mules and camels loose to graze. Cherdon, Islam Bai, and Faisullah came to meet us on foot, and an hour later we were snugly housed in our new quarters.

Before starting on our first Tibetan expedition, we granted ourselves a week's rest in the glen of Mandarlik (11,277 feet). It was a splendid place, with plenty of grass. Our camp stood on a terrace on the left bank of the brisk little brook, which sang as it danced down the glen, except after rain in the higher regions, when it swelled to a considerable torrent. The Cossacks and Ali Ahun, the tailor, whose hands were never idle, lived in the big Mongol yurt, behind which Shagdur made a fence of planking, to protect the meteorological instruments from the attention of the camels. Some of the Musulmans lived in two spacious tents, others behind the sheltering barricades made by the maize sacks and the camels' pack-saddles when ranged round in circles. My own quarters were in the smaller Mongolian yurt; and in front of it stood all my big cases, stacked up close together, and covered with a white felt, to protect them against the frequent showers. The view up the glen was magnificent, the background being formed by the main crest of the Chimen-tagh, with its glittering snow-fields. Those of the camels which had already been grazing two months in the mountains were as fat as could be, and in the pink of condition; indeed, all the caravan animals looked well. Only 42 of our 50 sheep were left, and we had acquired three fresh dogs from the nearest Mongol camp at Jurkhak.

Shagdur went over to see the Mongols there, and had a very friendly reception. They promised to sell us any animals we required, and hoped that I should visit them. One day Cherdon rode up the glen and fell in with a herd of 50 yaks, one of which he killed, a fine fat cow. As for me, I took astronomical and other observations, made little trips in the neighbourhood, and got ready for the next big expedition. We told off provisions to last seven men for two and a half months, and then fastened them ready on the pack-saddles. Two cases accommodated the instruments and my own personal belongings.

At the headquarters camp I left behind Islam Bai as caravan-bashi, or head-man; Faisullah, to look after the four camels from Abdall; Khodai Kullu, Kader, and Khodai Vardi, to attend to the horses; Ali Ahun, to do tailor work, and Shagdur as guard and meteorologist, it being his duty to take the observations three times every day. Musa, from Osh, was to go with us as far as the lake of Kum-koll, taking six horses for the purpose of lightening the loads of the other animals; but from Kum-koll he was to return in company with Tokta Ahun. The last named begged that he might spend the summer at Mian, where he was growing wheat; but I asked him to join us again at the end of two and a half months, and at the same time bring with him half-a-dozen fresh camels.

I bestowed great care upon the selection of the caravan I was to take with me in my projected expedition. It was composed as follows: Cherdon, as my right-hand man, body-servant, and cook, as well as tent-man: Turdu Bai, caravan-bashi of the seven camels; Mollah Shah, for eleven horses and one mule; Kutchuk, to act as boatman in my boating trips across the lakes. One Niaz, from Keriya, a gold-seeker, whom we chanced to meet in the mountains, was to act as hodman to the other Mussulmans, and Aldat, the Afghan, was to be our guide as far as his topographical knowledge extended. Yolldash, of course, went with us, and generally slept in my tent. But we only took two of the other dogs, Malchik and a big yellow Mongol dog resembling a wolf. We were also accompanied by sixteen of the sheep, which Niaz, the gold-seeker, drove and guarded in the wake of the caravan.

III
OVER THE CHMEN-TAGH, ARA-TAGH AND KALTA-ALAGAN

Once more we turned our backs upon the abodes of men, and set our faces towards the unknown parts of the world which were still a *terra incognita*. We soon left the principal valley on our right, and struck into a smaller glen without water, but studded with isolated grass-grown hills, backed by high black rocks, with a serrated edge. Thence, after crossing a secondary pass, we followed a path, frequented by hunters and gold-seekers, which led towards the south-east across extensive undulating pasture-grounds. On our right we had magnificent mountain scenery, with almost vertical cliffs. Then over another pass, and we began to descend the glen of Dung-sai, the brook of which never dries up, because it is fed by perennial springs. But although we zigzagged up and down over hills and passes, we were all the time gradually ascending to higher regions. The declivity which led down from the second of the two passes just mentioned, although as easy as possible for the horses, was steep and difficult for the camels, which made a glissade down the gravel.

The mountains began to assume a more Alpine character in the glen of Kar-yakkak (the Glen of the Falling Snow,) which had a altitude of 13,072 feet above sea-level. A clear brook bubbled amongst the waterworn granite blocks which strewed it, while small and pretty flowers grew amongst the moss and grass. We had plenty of fuel in the shape of the droppings of wild yaks and kulans. Two or three yaks' skulls, which we came across, proved that the district had been visited by hunters, and ashes in a cave close by showed where they had spent the night. In several places the ground was burrowed by marmots (*davaghan*) and we often saw these nimble and wide-awake little rodents sitting at the entrances of their runs as we approached. The partridges called busily to each other on the mountain sides, and Cherdon brought in a brace for my supper.

We pitched camp in the upper part of this fascinating glen. It is true, we had not made anything like a full day's march; but fresh animals, carrying big loads, ought not to be over-taxed at the start. As time went on, however, the loads would naturally grow lighter, for the geological specimens which we gathered, although amounting to a goodly collection, did not really add much to the total weight of baggage.

Towards the afternoon a north-easterly

gale sprang up, and a perfect cascade of heavy black clouds came pouring down the glen; farther on, they condensed into a continuous down-pour. When we left Mandarlik the sun was burning hot, and the air thick with dancing gnats; now it was already bleak autumn. And on the following morning, when I stepped out of my yurt, it was quite wintry; the snow fell in thick flakes and the ground was everywhere covered with snow. The depth of winter in the middle of July, and that in the hear to of Asia! If the summer was like this—well, we could not help feeling a certain sense of respect for the winter.

We thought we would wait for better weather; but the snow did not stop, and the day was lost. Sometimes the snow ceased to come down in flakes, and took the form of hail, which rattled noisily against the coverings of the yurt. The temperature, however, kept just above freezing-point, and at midday the snow began to melt, causing the water to trickle in at every seam. The clay soil around the camp became slippery and sticky; you felt as if you were paddling about in the mud of a duck pond.

A slight acquaintance with this, the fourth of the parallel ranges of the Kwen-lun system, was sufficient to show that it differed very greatly from the preceding three ranges. Whereas they were bare, possessed no perpetual snow, and exhibited rounded and weathered forms, this range, the Chimen-tagh, was Alpine in its character, and had a copious precipitation, with a resulting abundance of vegetation. A short distance back we had been obliged to tramp 13 to 14 hours to get from one spring to the next; here we found water at every step.

Although it was still snowing on the 22nd July, we decided to wait no longer. By noon, most of the snow had melted, though the mountain-tops still glittered white. In the depressions the snow fell in the shape of big moist, feathery flakes, which disappeared the moment they touched the ground, leaving it wet and slippery; but on the heights above it was granular, light, and round. This last variety was more pleasant for the equestrian, for the hail readily rolled off; whereas the flakes stuck to us, and wetted us. There was a constant drip, drip, from our caps, our hands got wet and numb with cold, and my mapping sheet wrinkled up and was spoiled. We were unable to see far ahead, and could obtain no general view of the contour and arrangement of the mountain peaks. To the north, however, the weather lifted once or twice, affording us glimpses, as through a tunnel, of the done-shaped, flat-arched ridge of the Akato-tagh.

Our day's march described a wide curve from the south-east to the west, round a massive knot of the Chimen-tagh, crossing over innumerable gulleys on the way. We were all glad to stop when we reached Yappkaklik-sai (13,117 feet), where there were teresken shrubs, but poor grazing. Yet it was not very pleasant sleeping on the ground with nothing but a carpet between one's ribs and the mud. As the temperature during the night fell below freezing-point, the snow did not melt, but lay very much thicker, especially as it came down faster than ever the whole of the evening. Strangely enough, it was sometimes so clear immediately above our heads that we saw the stars glistening, whilst all around us the snow was tossing its huge flake in every direction. It was, however, a good thing it no longer melted, but lay as it fell, thus making a warm blanket for the yurt. The thermometer went down to –4.8 C. or 23.4 Fahr.

Next morning I was awakened at daybreak by a fearful commotion in the camp, and upon hurrying out I learned that the shephert Niaz, and all the sheep except four, were missing, and tracks in the snow plainly showed they had been visited by wolves during the night, which had been pitch dark. I at once sent out all the men after the marauders, Cherdon riding with his rifle in his hand; and about ten o'clock they came back with Niaz and one sheep. They found nine others torn to pieces amongst the hills, and one was missing entirely.

Niaz's story was as follows : He slept as usual under a felt carpet close beside the sheep, which were all loose except four; for if you prevent a few of them from straying, the others will remain beside them. In the middle of the night he was awakened by a trampling in the snow and by the bleatings of the sheep; but owing to the howling of the storm he could not hear very distinctly. However, he at once jumped up, and saw three wolves, which had crept up against the wind, on the very point of attacking the sheep and driving them out of camp. Niaz stupidly never thought of calling up the other men, but rushed off after the sheep, and had kept on after them all the rest of the night, though he only managed to save one. The wolves had planned their, attack so cunningly that the dogs heard nothing of it. Our Mongol had already run away; Yolldash was sleeping in my yurt; and the in experienced Malchik lay curled up like a hedgehog behind the men's tent. The men cursed and swore at every wolf in existence. But what good did that do when we had lost more than one half of our supply of meat?

Soon after we left this till-omened camp, and were striking up into the pass, we were amazed to see the mizzing sheep coming running through the hills, terrified, and beside itself. Upon perceiving us, it stopped, and looked at us narrowly, evidently wondering whether we were friends or enemies; yet seeing its five companions, it no longer hesitated, but hastened to join them. It had no doubt been wandering about all night, having, luckily for itself, got separated from the others that were killed.

The day turned out clear and bright, and the snow melted fast. We were now close to the sumit (14,007 feet) of the principal pass of the Chimen-tagh, and upon surmounting it a magnificent panorama opened out before us. Rightacross our field of vision from east to west stretched another mountain-range, the Ara-tagh, entirely sheathed in snow from top to bottom, although only a few of its peaks, in the south-west, actually bore perpetual snow. Between the Chimen-tagh and the Ara-tagh was a broad, latitudinal or parallel valley, called by the simple name of Kayir (the Clay Mud Valley). It was traversed by a small river, which flowed towards the west; later on we explored where it went to. Beyond the stream to the south were wide grazing-grounds, dotted over with troops of wild asses and herds of antelopes.

With regard to the orographical structure of the Chimentagh, I will only saw now, that it is asymmetrical. The valley of CHimen lies at an altitude of 9,715 feet above the sea, but the valley of Kayir at 13,731 feet; thus we had ascended another of the huge steps which lead up to the plateau of Northern Tibet. Seen from the north, the Chinten-tagh wore the appearance of a gigantic mountain-chain; seen from the south, it had quite an insignificant appearance, owing to the slight difference in the relative attitudes.

At this camp, too, we had a little mishap with the sheep. When I as usual made the round of the camp after taking the meteorological observations, I found that only two out of the six sheep were tethered, but as wolves were probably prowling about in this quarter also, I ordered that they should be all tethered. But when they tried to fasten up the four that were loose, off they went in a mad panic. Although it was now quite dark, off went the men after them, and their shouts soon died away amongst the hills. At length Cherdon returned, bringing two of the sheep, which he had caught with a lasso. But the other man did not come in until two hour later; they had been obliged to drive the poor brutes down the glen and there catch them in traps. After that we always kept them fastened up, until we gradually killed them off.

The next day, favoured by beautiful weather, and a blue sky, without a speck of cloud to mar its serenity, we prepared to storm the next barricade in the border-ranges of Tibet, namely, the Ara-tagh, or Middle Chain. The ascent was by a little ravine, traversed by a rivulet from a natural spring. The top of the pass of Ak-chokka-aytuseh (14,348 feet), or the Pass of the White Cliff, afforded us a repetition of yesterday's panorama, except that the range we now looked upon was a fresh one, namely, the Kalta-alagan, from which the Aratagh was separated by another latitudinal valley, which farther west was connected with the one previously mentioned. There the two rivers which flowed down these valleys merged together, and the united stream then broke through the Chimen-tagh into the Chimen valley.

The transverse valley which led down from the pass was very deeply scarped between its erosion terraces.

My caravan always outstripped me and got a long way ahead, for I was continually delayed, taking observations in the passes and at the entrances of the glens on both sides, collecting geological specimens, photographing, sketching, etc. The road still went up and up, until we reached the top of a rounded pass; then down it dipped again into another glen, deeply trenched in the mountain side. It began to get dusk, and cold, and we were longing for a glimpse of the column of smoke, which generally announced that the caravan leaders had discovered a suitable place for camping in. But on and up went the trail, without our being able to perceive the least sign of a tent. The vegetation came to an end, and we ascended to colder regions. It was evident the caravan had pushed on over the next pass; although the large river which flowed beside us seemed to indicate that the pass over the Kalta-alagan must still be a long way off. We wondered why the men had gone in, and not stopped where fuel and grass were plentiful. Eventually the trail swung round a projecting elbow of the cliffs, and entered a little side-glen, which plainly led up to a nearer pass, where, however, except for two or three pools amongst the stones, there was no water. But it was now dark and I could not see to work any longer. What was to be done? We could of course easily ride on; but I could not leave a gap in my map, and least of all at such an important point, where we were about to cross a pass of the first magnitude. I therefore simply stopped where I was, and bade Tokta Ahun go on until he overtook the caravan, and then return with my yurt and boxes.

In the meantime, Cherdon and I did not have a particularly lively time of it in the cold and darkness, at an altitude of 15,263 feet above the sea. At nine o'clock we took the usual series of meteorological observations, and the reading of the boiling-point thermometer, which, owing to the strength of the wind, occupied us a considerable time, and was only taken at all after we had screened the lap with a cloak. That finished, we had nothing to do but wait. We crept close together to keep one another warm, and mutually related our experiences of similar situations. Cherdon had not much to boast of in that way from the maneuvers in Transbaikalia, but I had spent the night amongst jackals in Persia, had been nearly frozen to death on the shores of the lake of Kara-kul, and many a night had lain awake in the weird desert of Takla-makan.

It was too cold to sleep, and the forest grew keener; as we had no furs, we were forced to keep moving about to prevent ourselves from freezing. But we had been in the saddle II hours besides doing a good deal of work during the time, and nature at last asserted her rights, and we grew heavy and drowsy. Then we again crouched together between two big stones, which afforded us a certain amount of shelter. Before many minutes passed, we were both startled by the long-drawn howl of a distant wolf. We at once sprang up and fastened our horses, which were impatiently scraping the ground close beside us, and Cherdon held his rifle in readiness. If only we could have made a fire, the situation would have been very much less disagreeable, but although he hunted all over the neighbourhood we failed to find either yak-dropping or teresken scrub. Besides, it was so dark that we had to feel where we were going with our hands. The only way to keep the blood in circulation was to stamp our feet and flap our arms together.

After waiting five weary hours, we at length heard a rattling amongst the gravel. It was Kutchuk and Tokta Ahun, with two horses and the yurt. Half-an-hour later they were followed by Turdu Bai, with my cases and the dinner service on camels. The men blamed Mollah Shah for going on with the horses after Aldat told him there was good grazing near a little spring on the other side of the pass. As they also brought fuel with them in a sack, we soon had a fire alight, and I can assure you that when at last I did get my dinner at three o'clock in the morning it went down famously after the seventeen hours' fast. Day was already breaking on the barren mountains when we retired to rest.

Wearied by the exertions of the preceding day and night, we did not get started the following morning until ten o'clock. After traversing the remainder of the distance to Camp no. XIV. We picked up the rest of the caravan, and proceeded up the gentle slope to the pass of Avras (15,703 feet), by which we crossed the Kalta-alagan (Kalta's Hunting-Ground). Here a view of immense smplitude and sublimity unrolled itself in the south. It was no longer a single definite mountain-range, but a whole world of mountains, which it would take months to unravel. Far off in the south-east were gigantic mountain-masses covered with snow, which seemed to belong to one of the usual east-west ranges. More immediately south of us, and forming a continuation of the foregoing, was another stupndous isolated group, or mountain-knot, also mantled with perpetual snow. In the south-south-west we saw the white shimmer of yet another mountain=range, clearly situated to the south of the valley stream which picked up the Kum-Koll. Along the line of the souther horizon were snow-fields and glaciers or fleecy clouds, it was difficult to tell which. I inferred, however, that they were the tops of the Arka-tagh, the culminating range of the Kwen-lun system.

A dry transverse valley led down from the pass to the open flat country, and thee, beside a spring situated amongst low hills, we found the caravan encamped. I gave Musa and Mollah Shah a good wigging for making such a long march the day before.

On the 26th of July we turned due west, and travelled at right angles to the route which we had been pursuing during the past few days; that is, we struck off in the direction of the upper lake of Kum-koll, which was visible in the distance through a field-glass, though it was afterwards hidden from us by lower hills and undulations of the surface. Our route thus lay down the broad and spacious latitudinal valley which ran along the southern foot of the great range of the Kalta-alagan. This range not only thrust our several spurs and ramifications across the valley, but overtopped it in occasional snowy peaks. On the opposite side of the valley was a wide belt of sand, which I at first took for a smaller range of hills running parallel to the bigger ranges; but when we approached nearer to it. I perceived that it consisted of pure sand-dunes, of the same yellow colour as those of the Takla-makan, and very nearly as much developed. Thus the general conditions for the formation of an "ocean of sand," like that which existed down in the desert, obtained here also, at an altitude of 12,000 to 14,000 feet above the level of the sea. The transition from the soft or gravel-strewn valley bottom, with its scattered teresken scrub and other combustible vegetable growths, to the belt of sand was extraordinarily sharp. The crests of the dunes ran from north to south, and appeared to have been built up by predominant westerly winds.

With the sand continuously on our left and the Kalta-alagan on our right, the day's march was extremely monotonous, although vast numbers of kulans were grazing and frisking all over the steppes, which sloped gently westwards towards the lake. Marmots were common, and used to sit up with their fore paws crossed over their breasts until the dogs got near them, then they darted into their holes. Hares, too, abounded, and wildduck flew overhead on their way to the lake. Once more the gnats came and assailed us, but retired shortly after sunset. It was summer weather all day. The temperature rose to 20.0 C, or 68.0 Fahr., and it felt oppressively hot, because of the stillness of the atmosphere. We were only reminded of the great altitude by our shortness of breath and the beating of the heart which ensued upon even very slight exertion.

Aldat and Cherdon rode towards a troop of wild asses (kulans), 34 in number, which, however, fled at their approach, except a she-ass and her foal. But as the men still continued to press on, the mother finally deserted her offspring, which proved to be only four days old. The little creature made no attempt to escape, but stood quite still, until the two hunters picked it up. Aldat placed it on the saddle in front of him, and brought it in. We then packed it in a felt, and hoisted it upon a camel's back—a method of travelling to which it took quite kindly. We also captured another kulan foal at Camp no. XV. inprecisely the same way.

When we encamped, we let them both range at will amongst the tents and stores, and they showed no fear when we patted them. I was anxious to rear them on milk porridge, until they could shift for themselves, which, it was said, they would to able to do three weeks after birth. But when I consulted Tokta Ahun about the matter, he said they would not live longer than five days; he had no less than eight times tried to rear wild asses, but on every occasion had failed. Upon this, I ordered that they should be taken back to the places where they were captured, so that their mothers might find them again, and Cherdon and Aldat were already mounted to carry out my order, when Tokta Ahun said it would be useless. His experience was that once a young kulan had been touched by the hands of man, its mother fled from it as from the pestilence. Nor did she appear to miss her offspring or grieve for it, but kept with the troop she belonged to, and shunned the place where she lost it.

Had we had a brood mare with us, I dare say we could have managed to rear our two little captives. The men told me that a great number of kulan foals perish every year in the Chimen valley, because, during the first few days of their existence, they are unable to accompany their mothers on the approach of danger. When thus deserted, they die of hunger, or are torn to pieces by the wolves. The older kulans are no doubt able to protect their young, so long as the latter are with them, otherwise their numbers would not increase.

In the meantime we took the greatest possible care of our captives, which readily learned to sup up their sloppy porridge. But they were doomed, and as in the evening they showed sings of pining away, and were longing greatly for their mother's milk, I ordered them to be killed. The Mussulamans took possession of their skins, and ate the meat, which they declared to the particularly tender and tasty. But before the little creatures were killed, I photographed them from various positions. One stood 35-½ inches high, the 35-½ inches. The head was disproportionately large, and the legs absurdly long in comparison with their body; but then the latter are in their case the limbs which are first used, as well as those which are the greatest importance to them.

The body was very short and compressed, and gave scarce and indication of the noble and harmonious lines which distinguish the full-grown kulans. The little ones we had in captivity were too young to be afraid of human beings, or of the camels or the tents; but had they been a week older, they would neither have let themselves be captured nor would they have been at liberty without making attempts to escape. When we gave them a finger, they sucked at it greedily, a proof that they were hungry.

During the night of the 26th of July the temperature fell to only 1 1/2 above freezing-point, though the following day was beautifully warm. These latitudinal or parallel east-west valleys, which of course are, relatively speaking, the lowlands of the elevated regions, have, as a rule, a more temperate climate than the higher mountainous parts.

Next day we still continued westwards, riding close to the edge of the belt of sand, and having on our right all day long an unbroken succession of marshes, morasses, and pools, all more or less connected, or, at any rate, linked together, by small channels or watercourses. They were surrounded by luxuriant grass, but the ground was extremely treacherous, and even dangerous; it would not bear so much as a man's weight. Some of these depressions were a couple of hundred yards long. All of them were fed by subterranean springs, which trickled underneath the sand, and lower down they became united into a single stream, which entered the Kum-koll at its eastern end. Six of these rivulets were of considerable size, and one of them carried as much as 70 cubic feet in the second, the water, after filtering through the sand, being as bring as crystal.

We kept a good look out for the lake, and at last saw it gleaming like a silvery ribbon in the west. The day was warm and still, and the mosquitoes troublesome. Moreover, a species of gad-fly called *ila* tormented the horses, and made them nervous and restless by getting into their nostrils. The kulans protect themselves against these insects by keeping their nostrils close to the ground when they graze, the orongo antelopes by spending the hot part of the day deep in the belt o sand, and by coming down to the grazing-grounds in the evening only. The yaks protect themselves in the same way, but go higher up in the sand, so that we did not get a glimse of them all day, although we observed their foot-prints and droppings everywhere. At four o'clock a violent squall of hail and rain came on, and the yaks, which knew this would banish their enemies, made their appearance in little companies on the crests of the dunes. First appeared a clow tih her calf, glissading down the steep slope; but upon catching sight of us, she turned tail about and went back. After that a herd of over 30 arranged themselves in a line on the top of a high sand-dune, and fearlessly stood watching the caravan. I stopped and observed them for some time through my field-glass. The wild yak is in truth a magnificent animal. The herd stood out with remarkable distinctness, black as coal, against the yellow back-ground of the sand. They were on their way down to their grazing-ground beside the lake, when they found themselves thus cut off from it by our caravan. We could almost see them literally rejoicing in the refreshing rain, which patter-pattered on their shoulders. The yaks that live in this region always graze all night, but at sunrise return up amongst the sanddunes, where they remain until it gets dark, or a storm tempts them down again.

The slopes of the sand-dunes were depend in colour by the rain. You would think that a violent downpour such as that was would convert them into soft mud from end to end; but if did not even affect the sharp outlines of their contours, and only formed little shallow pools on the surface. The sand gradually decreased in height as well as swung back from the middle of the valley. We now had the lake on our right; its southern shore extended 60 west of north. Here 14 big yaks were already grazing. Cherdon, who rode with me, could not take his eyes off them, and at last begged that he might try his luck. He crept as stealthily as a cat forwards a powerful bull, which simply stood still and looked hard at him without showing the slightest trace of fear. Cherdon did not like the look of him, and thought discretion the better part of valour. I had warned him to be careful when hunting yaks, and not to go after them alone if he could help it; for when a yak is wounded, he will often turn and attack his hunter.

A little bit further on Cherdon caught sight of a solitary wolf-cub, four months old, and galloping after it, managed to catch it. Upon reaching camp, he tied up his captive; but the dogs showed the greatest possible indifference to it. The men, however, bestowed upon it all the most endearing epithets they could think of; they had not forgotten the nine sheep which the wolves tore to pieces. Tokta Ahun wanted me to keep good watch upon the sheep; for the she-wolf, which no doubt had her lair somewhere close by, would not lose sight of her cub, and if any harm came to it, she would take her revenge upon the sheep. He had twice caught wolf-cubs himself, and on both occasions the older wolves had killed an ass of his. Wolves will not try to meddle with full-grown kulans, because they could never catch them; but they will sometimes chase the young ones into soft marshy ground, and then bite their throats till they kill them. We intended to take our young wolf-cub with us, and try to rear it; but it proved too cunning for its captors. During the night it gnawed the rope through, and ran away with a piece of it round its neck. The Mussulmans hoped that as the beast grew the rope would throttle it; but I thought it more likely that it mother would gnaw the rope away before that.

Camp No. XVI, beside the Upper Kum-koll, which lay 12,737 feet above the level of the sea, was all that could be desired. We had plenty of grass, and plenty of fuel, and the water in the lake was fresh. On the north the imposing range of the Kalta-alagan stretched its rugged sharp-cut spurs down into the valley, and itself extended as far as to the west as we could see. The mountains on the south were, on the contrary, entirely enveloped in clouds. The next morning my little boat lay ready screwed together on the shore; so taking Kutchuk with me I sailed across the lake before a steady breeze. We carried with us the yurt and such instruments as I required for my cartographical work, for taking soundings, and so on. But before we got very far from shore, a sudden squall snapped the sail yard, and we were forced to row back and mend it, by lashing the ends together and strengthening the fracture with pieces of tamarisk wood. Then we steered for a snowry peak which lay 13 east of north. This lake was shallower than I had expected to find it; its greatest depth only measured 12 1/4 feet. We landed, on a little gravelly island about 35 yards in diameter near the northern shore.

The sky in the east now began to assume a threatening aspect, and the valley filled with dense clouds, while columns of rising sand were driven like smoke across the sand-dunes. Accordingly, we thought it best to wait a little; and sure enough, down came the storm. We sheltered ourselves as well as we could against the driving rain by crouching behind the boat. But although the lake was alive with big, foam-crested waves, I could not resist the temptation of dropping the sail and pushing off. We had, however, to exercise the utmost vigilance, for the flat valley acted like a funnel for the wind, which thus swept the lake with umitigated fury. We kept as well as we could to the crests of the waves, so as not to get filled with water. But the gale increased in violence, and the mast threatening to break, I at last called to Kutchuk to furl the sail; but even under bare poles we went along at a spanking pace before the wind. I was only able to get an occasional sounding, we travelled too fast; but I easily managed to obtain the velocity and also took my compass bearings.

In this way we soon reached the western end of the lake, and found that it contracted into a little stream, which carried off its superfluous water, and emptied it into the big salt lake of Ayag-kum-koll, or the Lower Sand Lake, which lay further to the west, and which we shall encounter again on another excursion. Here the Kum-koll was very shallow, its depth seldom exceeding 3 1/4 feet; while the shelving southern shore was continued by mud-banks, over which the water was stained black after being stirred up by our paddles. This part of the lake swarmed with wild-duck and wild-geese. The latter were sitting on their eggs, and unwilling to fly far; but they were all the cleverer at diving, as we soon found out when we tried to row down a flock and attack them with our paddles.

But our return was nothing like so glorious as our departure. We paddled our hardest; but the wind freshened again, and after a while it began to rain, so that we got wet through, a result to which the waters also contributed by occasionally washing over us. At length, however, we perceived the tents, though still a long way off; in fact it took us two or three hours longer to reach them. I was always unlucky in my lake excursions; no matter how fine the weather was when I started, it always came on stormy before I got back.

IV

ACROSS THE ARKA-TAGH

On the 30th of July I sent Tokta Ahun and Musa, with six horses, back to the headquarters camp, although this made the loads somewhat heavier for the animals that remained behind. Besides myself, our strength now consisted of six men-Cherdon, Turdu Bai, Mollah Shah, Kutchuk, Niaz, and Aldat—seven camels, 11 horses, one mule, five sheep, and two dogs. The day's march ran to the south-south-west through open monotonous country for a distance of 23 miles. In the morning the basin of the Kum-Koll was enveloped in a moist, impenetrable mist, and the range of Kalta-alagan had entirely disappeared. The air was warm and still, and full of mosquitoes, which faithfully followed us all day. We longed to reach altitudes where these wretched creatures could not live, and once there we should not return to their native habitat until they were all perished in the winter cold.

The surface of the Kum-koll glittered like plate-glass, but we soon lost it in the mist behind us. In between the dunes, which jutted out like headlands into the valley, we found firm ground, and a series of small basins, each containing a pool of saltish water. When the sand-belt came to an end, we travelled over a gently undulating surface, with patches of grass here and there, until we reached the stream known as Pettelik-daria, which was enclosed between scarped terraces of loose yellow earth. This stream, which flowed due north-west and issued into the lake of Ayag-kum-koll, had a volume of about 353 cubic feet in the second, and a maximum depth of 2 1/2 feet. But Turdu Bai and Mollah Shah, in trying to find a suitable crossing-place, nearly perished in the mud at the bottom, man and horse together. Barely a tenth part of its bed was now under water, but thee moisture still clinging to its sides showed that it had recently been full to the brim. It would then have been quite impossible to ford it.

The next day's march, our fourth at these sublime altitudes, took us to the south-south-east, and was equally as long as the preceding stage. After fording the river once more, we found our road blocked by a minor range, probably a spur of the Arkatagh. The atmosphere was again clear, and in the east-south-east we saw the glittering, snowy mass of Chullak-akkan, which we had first observed from the pass of Avras. The belt of sand still continued on our left hand. These dreary steppes were haunted by innumerable orongo antelopes; but in spite of all their endeavours our hunters failed to bring one down. This country was sometimes visited by gold-seekers and yak-hunters, and this had taught the animals to be on the alert, so that they took very good care not to let us approach too close to them. We were now at the end of Aldat's geographical knowledge. He had never been so far south before, nor any of the other men either; so that for the future I had to take this responsibility of guiding the caravan myself.

We directed our course towards a notch in the mountain-chain, up to which a promising glen appeared to lead. But when we entered it, we found it was destitute of water. However on the right hand, that is to say, the west side of the glen, in an elbow or recess, we discovered a little fresh green grass, and a small spring, which yielded enough water for our wants.

On the 1st of August we did eighteen miles to the south-south-east. On the whole we travelled towards the south, because I was anxious to cross these successive mountain ranges at right angles, and in addition to geographical observations, together also material for a geological profile. My plan was to get as far south as I possibly could, and only turn back when our supplies were half exhausted. In making this calculation I deliberately left one important factor out of account—namely, that on the return journey the animals' strength would become so reduced that they would travel very much slower, and consequently take a longer time. I did not overtook this; but the main thing was to penetrate as far south as I could possibly get. We could somehow or other manage to pilot the caravan home, and if the worst came to the worst we could walk ourselves. I hopes we might have to turn back in a region where there was plenty of grass, so that the animals could obtain a good rest before starting. But I had no conception what a strain the return journey would put upon them, and what trouble it would cost us to get the remnants of our caravan safely home again.

It proved no easy task to force a passage over the granite wall which now towered up across our path. Although it took the whole day, we managed it successfully at last. It was a parallel range of the Arka-tagh. After groping our way up to the watershed.of the new range through winding gorges and glens, over spurs and secondary passes, we beheld, upon reaching the main pass at the top, a stupendous range, black as ink, but capped with snow. This I took to be the Arka-tagh, the same difficult mountain-range which I encountered in 1869; and I feared we should have as tough a job to get over it now as we had them. We pitched camp beside a little brook in the longitudinal valley at the foot of this new mountain-wall, at an altitude of 15,217 feet above the sea.

It had been a splendid day, and we had not been molested by either mosquitos or gad-flies. But at seven o'clock the rain began to patter on the yurt; and when I stepped outside, the whole landscape was steaming with rainy mist, and not a mountain visible. The horses stood tied together in pairs, with their heads hanging down; they were half asleep, and the raindrops ran down their sides and drip-drip-dripped from their pack-saddles and manes. The camels crowded together in a clump-to keep themselves warm, and in spite of their heavy breathing they seemed to enjoy the rest. The camp-fire was smoking in front of the men's tent, and whilst Cherdon prepared my dinner, Mollah Shah got the men's ready. After a while Kutchuk and Niaz turned the horses out to graze. We left them out all night, but told off a watchman to give an eye to them, to see that they did not stray too far. The camels could not see to eat before day-break, and therefore lay where they were all night; but we gave them a few pecks of maize for their supper. Yolldash took very good care not to venture out in such very disagreeable weather, but lay curled up inside my tent. Malchik had a sore foot, and during the last day or two had been packed on a camel's back, where, with the skill of an acrobat and a certain degree of elegance, he adapted himself to the cradling movements of his "steed". With the rain falling like slanting arrows in the darkness outside, I was very glad to creep back into my well-lighted yurt.

We stayed where we were all the next day, for I wanted to take an astronomical observation—a process that is very trying to the patience when you are continually interrupted by passing hailstorms and flitting clouds. The morning did not look very promising. It had snowed ever since midnight, and continued snowing until about nine o'clock, burying what little pasture there was under a white sheet, so that, although our animals were groping about all day, they came home at nightfall only half satisfied. The mountains exhibited a variety of colouring; sometimes the snow-fields glistened intensely white against a background of dark clouds; sometimes the sky was clear in the distance, and the snow-fields assumed a cold, steel-blue tone, while heavy black clouds obscured the sun. Yesterday the perpetual snow, with its rudimentary glaciers, stood out in very sharp relief; to-day it and they were alike hidden under the white mantle of the fresh-fallen snow.

The night of the 2nd of August was the coldest we had had for some time; the thermometer dropped to -5.2 C. or 22.6 Fahr. In the morning every pool and rivulet was covered with a thin sheet of ice, which, however, thawed in the splendidly bright weather that ensued, although in sheltered crevices it did not melt at all. To-day the animals showed the first symptoms of fatigue; one horse was allowed to go without a load, and one of the camels turned sluggish soon after the track began to ascend. We penetrated the next range at a point where it appeared to be lowest, and came eventually into the expansion of a glen in which were hundreds of orongo antelopes—big, beautiful animals, with horns that stuck straight up like bayonets. They sped swiftly and easily up the mountain sides, if apparently costing them no effort at all to exert themselves in the rarefied atmosphere.

From this expansion two glens left off, one to the south, the other to the south-west. We chose the former, for it had a little brook running down it. But it soon narrowed and grew steep, and at the head of it a snow-clad mountain towered up like a wall directly in our path. As our advance in that direction appeared barred, I sent Cherdon on to reconnoiter, and whilst we were waiting for him to return, I took a couple of photographs. He soon came back, however, and said that it would be impossible for the camels to get through that way; so we tried the other glen. Then, whilst the caravan was making a detour round a steep spur, I rode over the top of it with Cherdon, and found it equally steep on the other side. From the top we perceived forty or fifty antelopes grazing on an acclivity not very for away, and made signs to the men with the caravan to drive them into the corner where we were waiting. But they were too knowing for us, and going off up the glen, were speedily out of sight.

The glen soon turned to the south-south-west, and ran up towards a pass which was free from snow. I rode on ahead. The ascent was dangerously steep, and on the top of the pass—the highest point we had hitherto reached, namely, 16,280 feet—I had to wait half-an-hour while the rest of the caravan struggle slowly up the debris-strewn slope towards me. The prospect on the other side was anything but encouraging, a chaos of rocky pinnacles, mountain-spurs, and snow-capped crests extending away to the south. It was plain we were not yet at the summit of the Arka-tagh—we had merely crossed one of its many parallel chains which run from east to west, and consequently still had the worst obstacle to surmount.

At last the others scrambled up to the top of the pass beside me. The poor camels, their legs actually trembled under them! Their nostrils were widely distended, they wanted more air; and their eyes turned with a weary and indifferent look to the south, as if, amid this universe of barren, naked mountains, they had abandoned all hope of ever getting a good feed of grass again. From the summit of the pass we zigzagged down between the craggy headlands into a gorge which led to the south-south-west, and was itself cut through solid rock of black slate, porphyry, and diorite. Moss was only thing that grew beside the brook which traversed it, until we came out upon the broad longitudinal valley into which it issued. There there was some *yappkak* scrub, which the man gathered for their evening fire. This valley was drained by the biggest stream we had encountered since we left the Tarim; it was 213 feet broad, had a maximum depth of 23 1/2 feet, and carried 954 cubic feet in the second. It appeared to have its source in three large rounded mountains, which stood side by side like three-cornered hats in the east-south-east, and flowed towards the west-north-west. Its left bank was twenty-five to thirty-five feet high, and vertical—an obstacle which we should have been unable to surmount had it not been for a little side-ravine which led up to the top of it. After that we struck into a transverse valley, and, entering a glen on its southern side, encamped in open ground beside a little tributary of the big river, at an altitude of 15,693 feet. A little higher up we saw thirteen big black yaks grazing.

They did not at first perceive us, but as soon as we stopped and began to pitch the tent, the leader of the herd caught the alarm and off they all went in a body towards the Arka-tagh, whose main crest did now really loom up before us in all its gloomy majesty. Once safety over that, the country beyond ought to be fairly open.

The next day we decided to rest, so as to give Cherdon and Aldat an opportunity to reconnoiter the nearest glens leading over the Arka-tagh. They reported that the glen in whose mouth we were encamped was impassable; and so, on the 5th of August, we proceeded a good bit down the latitudinal valley, until wee came to a deep-cut watercourse, with a large stream flowing down it. Here, were we turned south again, I stopped for a short time to enter the main geographical features on my map. From that point the latitudinal valley extended as far west as I was able to see. But some distance down I observed a transverse valley or breach, where the river probably cut through the range which we had crossed over the day before. My point of observation was situated a long way above the bottom of the valley, and offered a panorama that was overpowering, both because of its gigantic dimensions and its sublimity. The river, split into several arms, wound through the light grey mountain debris, interrupted occasionally by large sheets of ice. I could just hear the murmur of the water. The spurs of the Arka-tagh lay like sphinxes looking towards the north, with their stony paws just hanging in the stream. But the desolate beauty of the landscape was soon veiled in clouds and steaming rain. Turning our backs upon the scene, we resumed our toilsome march up the glen, the air in which was cold and raw.

The east side of the glen was bounded by a range of snowclad mountains, but the opposite side was more open. However, it soon came on to rain and the wind blew hard. Then while we made haste to run up the tent as fast as we could, Mollah Shah rode on further to ascertain where the glen went to. If there was no practicable pass, we should only tire thc animals to no purpose by proceeding with the whole of the caravan. Even as it was, our animals were beginning to lose flesh. Cherdon's black horse refused to eat, and looked in a bad way, which distressed the poor fellow a good deal, for he was passionately attached to the animal. He had trained him splendidly. When he called him by name, the horse came and put his head over Cherdon's shoulder. The little Buriat Cossack was quite an acrobat. Whilst his horse was moving, he would stand on his hands on the saddle, play at leap-frog over his hind-quarters, and turn somersaults across him without the animal being in the least degree startled by these performances. No wonder, then, Cherdon tended him as the apple of his eye, and was very much distressed to see him ailing. Our four remaining sheep were extraordinary animals. They followed the caravan like dogs, climbed the steepest slopes with ease, and appeared to be perfectly satisfied with the scanty and miserable grass we found for them.

By this we had become accustomed to the extraordinary altitude. So long as I sat still in the saddle or the tent, I did not notice any difference; but the least exertion, such as chipping at a rock with a geological hammer, occasioned shortness of breath and accelerated action of the heart. It was, however, a great advantage to be freed from the attentions of the mosquitos and gad-flies. IN place of them we had a species of gigantic humble-bee, which, when the sun shine, came out and sailed through the air, humming like the bassnotes of an organ. It was specially equipped for the intense wintry cold of these regions, being clad throughout in coat and greaves of thick yellow hair.

As there was not a scrap of pasture at this camp, it was useless to turn the animals out. Although it was scurvy treatment, all we could do for them to give them a shower bath of commingled water and ice, instead of food.

Mollah Shah came back after an absence of six hours, and reported that the pass in which our glen terminated was practicable. But what it was like on the other side he did not know, for the view was obscured by a driving snowstorm. And, indeed, when we left that inhospitable camp next morning, the whole country was once more shrouded in snow. But as the morning wore on, the sun peeped out, and the snow began to melt. The glen led by a slow, gradual ascent up to the pass. Its bottom was strewn with black, slaty debris, which crunched under the horse's hoofs; and down its middle ran a bright, cheerful little brook, picking up a number of smaller tributaries on each side as it proceeded.

The pass formed a rounded, flattened saddle, which even the camels surmounted without any special difficulty. With the help of the camera-stand I made a little temporary shelter for the boiling-point thermometer, and found the altitude was 16,996 feet—thus we were standing on the highest *mountain chain* on the face of the earth. At our feet stretched the latitudinal valley which I traversed in 1896. Immediately on the other side of it was a stupendous mountain group crowned with perpetual snow and *neves*, with short glacier arms radiating in every direction; seen from a distance it might be compared to a starfish. On its northern face were three broad truncated glaciers, with enormous terminal moraines of black debris. Of the naked rock itself there were only a few black and brown pinnacles visible; all the rest was buried under ice and snow. Each glacier-arm gave birth to a little rivulet, which ran down and joined the river that drained the valley from east to west.

After we had thus for several days been struggling up to higher regions, it was quite a treat to go down again. The animals travelled more easily, and we were buoyed up by the hope of finding grass in some hollow or other. Thus we swung at a good pace down the transverse glen which led from the pass to the next valley below. Near its lower extremity

Aldat surprised an orongo antelope, and brought it down with his clumsy, primitive muzzle-loading musket. It proved a welcome addition to our larder, and enabled us to grant our three remaining sheep a few days longer reprieve.

Instead of continuing right down to the river at the bottom of the valley—its banks looked grey and sterile—we turned to the west, and encamped on a gentle declivity where there was a little thin grass. Here Aldat managed to bag a big orongo, which puts us all in better humour, for this supplied us with meat for several days. At these high altitudes rice did not make a very appetising dish; the "pudding" baked into a tasteless dough, and we did not want to kill our sheep until we were really forced to do so. Unfortunately Cherdon had only brought a small supply of cartridges with him, and had used them up too lavishly at first; so that for the future we were compelled to rely upon Aldat's gun. He, fortunately, had a sufficient supply of ammunition.

V

ON THE TIBETAN HIGHLANDS

Thus we had at last climbed the gigantic wall which nature has built up like a bulwark to guard the secrets of Tibet on the north. Wee had long left behind us the paths of the half-civilized yak-hunters and fatuous gold seekers, and plunged into a region which was an absolute *terra incognita*, except that I should cross my own former route, Wellby's, Rockhill's, and Bonvalot's each at a single point. As I had now exhausted the topographical knowledge of my guide, Aldat, my map from this point embraced only a narrow belt on each side of our actual route; but I hoped in the future, that other routes which I proposed to take would enable me to obtain a clear conception of the orographical structure of the region.

I had always plenty to do from morning till evening. Leisure moments were few, and such as I did get I spent in reading Geikie's *Great Ice Age*, Hann's *Klimatologie*, and Kern's *Bhuddismus*. Although we led the lives of dogs in the country, which was as desolate as the moon is supposed to be, yet we reaped more than an equivalent reward in the discoveries and observations which we made from day to day. It was a delicious feeling, to know that we were the first human beings to tread those mountains, where there existed no path, where there never had been a path, and where there was not a footprint visible, except those made by the hoof of yak, antelope, or kulan. It was a no man's land; rivers, lakes, and mountains were all nakeless; their shores, banks, and snow-fields had never been seen by any travellers's eyes but mine; they were mine own kingdom of a day. It was delightful—it was a great thing, to cruise, like a vessel that leaves no track behind her, amongst those upswelling of the world's "high sea", to make our way over those gigantic mountains waves. Only the waves which roll across the Tibetan highlands are petrified; and all distances and dimensions are cast on such a gigantic scale, that you may march for weeks at a time and still find the situation unchanged—still find yourself the centre of a universe of mountains. And it was just as wonderful to live up amongst the eternal storms, those insurgents of the atmosphere, which drive across the howling mountain wastes and set their swift-moving batteries—namely, showers of clattering hail—to play upon the mountain sides.

That night when I stepped out of my tent the sky was mantled with clouds, their edges tipped here and there with the silvery rays of the moon. The wide-spread glaciers, out in the open, were flooded with the pale, frigid moonshine. The men were all asleep, the caravan animals safely tethered, the fire extinguished; and the only sound that disturbed the solemn hush of the night was the little brook murmuring its pensive song amongst the flaky shales. The night was keeping its silent, solitary watch over the mountain wastes, and all around it flitted the ghosts of a multitude of questions and problems craving their answers. Far away in the south I pictured to myself the crests of the snowy Himalayas, and beyond them again India with its stifling jungles. In the west our mountains linked themselves on to the Pamir highlands, and by the time the sun rose here, he was already pouring a flood of brilliant light over the kingdom of the Middle and its mountainous western borders. With the north, where lay the heart of Asia, we were to some extent familiar; but, here in Tibet, we were alone in an unknown land. In vain did we strain our eyes for a glimpse of a fire or the footprint of a human being; we had reached an uninhabited and uninhabitable part of the earth. I felt like an atom of dust in the midst of the illimitable wastes, and fancied I could hear the swish of the planet as it rolled without rest, without cessation, along its everlasting orbit.

On the 7th of August we went on down the latitudinal valley, in the hope of finding one of my lakes of 1896. It was now all over with Cherdon's horse; he kept falling, and had difficulty in getting up again. But, as his appetite remained good, we did all we could to save him. Cherdon treated him in the Mongol fashion; that is, he bled him at the tips of the ears, and cut away a couple of pieces of glandular connective tissue in his eyelids. This seemed to revive him a little, and he managed to go longer stretches at a time. At first I thought it would be best to kill him; but as Turdu Bai was of opinion that he might be saved, I ordered Mollah Shah to lead him slowly after us, whilst the caravan pushed on at the usual pace. As we failed to find a lake, I determined to wheel south again, and cross the mountain-chain which stretched west from the glaciated mountain group already spoken of. The latitudinal valley we were traversing was rather narrow, its steam very nearly dry, and on the south side, immediately underneath the moraines, was a belt of drift-sand, piled up precisely as it was beside the Kum-koll, into big dunes, which were very often detached from one another. They were regularly formed, and crescentic in shape, with their steep concave slopes toward the east. Within the arms of two or three of them were small crescentic pools formed by the melting glacier-arms. We forded several of these little brooks, the water of which was red and muddy. One of them had a volume of as much as 106 cubic feet in the second. The water in the pools, however, was transparent, and of an intense ultramarine blue colour, making a striking contrast to the yellow sand. We encamped beside one of these little brooks, close under the western shoulder of the glaciated mountain group, which we were thus half-way round. The grass, however, was worse than usual.

Mollah Shah came up five hours later. He had left Cherdon's horse a couple of miles from camp, neither better nor worse than in the morning. But when Cherdon went to look after him the animal was dead.

Turdu Bai rode up a transverse valley through the range which we were now about to cross, and returned in the evening with the report that the pass was not dangerous, and there was a big lake over on the other side of it; but he had not seen any grass. The ascent next day was smooth and gradual, and the pass occasioned us no exceptional difficulty, although one of the camels gave up, and had to be relieved of his load. From the top (16,805 feet) we had the same characteristic scene which our eyes had so often rested upon before-namely, immediately below us a latitudinal valley running east and west, backed by a mountain-range covered in part with perpetual snow. This latter was, I concluded, identical with the Koko-shili mountains. The bottom of the new latitudinal valley was in great part filled with a new lake, prolonged both east and west. The caravan had, as usual, a good start of me; but instead of going straight down to the lake, they swung off a good deal to the west of it. This they did, only in the hope of finding grass, but also that they might avoid the soft and treacherous strip of alluvium which encircled the lake. We encamped for the night at its western extremity, our Camp no. XXIV. (alt. 16,497 feet), counting from Abdall, being the very worst we had yet chosen. There was not a blade of grass, nor a scrap of fuel of any description; and we could only obtain a little hot tea at the cost of breaking up a packing-case. All that the beasts got was a handful of maize each. Scarcely was the camp settled down when a furious tempest burst upon us from the west. It began as rain, then turned to hail, and finally came down a regular deluge, until the felting of my yurt was sodden, and the rain dripped through upon me. Then during the night it changed to snow. The camels were just shedding their coats, and shook with cold, so we threw two or three felts over them. It was interesting to note that the new hair grew faster up here in the mountains than it did down in the warmer lowlands. Thus wonderfully does nature adapt herself to her surroundings.

The new mountain-range appeared to be low and easy to cross at a point south-west of our camp. Indeed, in comparison with the many which we had already crossed, we believed it would be a mere trifle. Its northern slopes were not even hard rock, but consisted only of low, rounded hills, which we never anticipated would occasion us the slightest trouble; but in reality this proved to be the most difficult bit of country we had yet encountered. In the first place, it was by no means easy to reach the foot of the hills, for the ground was everywhere marshy, necessitating the utmost caution to keep the horses out of the worst pitfalls, into which they sank up to their withers. But we assumed that, once we did reach the foot of the slope, the ground would be hard, and would bear us as usual. And at first the going was indeed not bad: the surface consisted of yellow clay, littered with stones and flakes of shale, and the ascent was easy. The only difficulty we experienced was with one big camel, which had a rooted antipathy to passes of all kinds, and which simply lay down at the foot of this. We left ridge, we continued along its crest to the south-east, having a deeply-eroded escarpment on each side of us. I led the way in the tracks of a wild yak, which went at first over firm ground, but higher up disappeared into the soft rain-drenched mire, which splashed at every step my horse took. At last he dropped in to such a depth, that I thought it better to get off and lead him. I ought, of course, to have turned back; but the next ridge looked so enticingly near. When, however, one of my boots stuck fast in the mud, I thought it really was time to stop, and wait for others. The men came up panting. The camels, patient and submissive, as they always were, struggled along in their wake, sinking in a foot or more at each step; and yet their broad, flat pads were better than the horses hoofs. One of the former fell, and we had to unload him, get him up, and reload him.

Walking on a veritable quagmire like this, at such a high altitude, completely took our breath, and made us feel quite giddy. Nor did we get on any better when we used as stepping-stones the big pieces of flat slate which lay scattered over the bog. For when we stepped upon them, they too sank into the ground, leaving a little pool of water where they had been. We could hear the water bubbling and trickling under the debris; so that I almost fancied we were walking over a subterranean river, which might suddenly open and engulf the entire caravan. I could not help thinking that the whole bunch of hills would, like a viscous fluid or thick porridge, gradually flatten themselves out to a uniform level. This conformation was caused by the incessant precipitation searching into the ground and making it like s sponge; for only a very small quantity trickled into the superficial brooks and rivulets, and so flowed away. The absence of vegetation with its interlacing roots also contributed to the same result. In two or three places the shales stuck up edgewise and cut the camels' feet. In one place two of the horses would have been literally smothered in the oozy mire, but that we hurriedly freed them from their loads and hauled them up. As the situation became at last absolutely intolerable, I sent Cherdon on to reconnoiter. He came back and said that this ridge was the first of a whole series, which extended a long distance to the south, and that all were flecked with melting snow, which of course would make the going even still more difficult.

This was the signal to return. We had lost more than four hours over this wretched piece of road, besides climbing up to an altitude of 17,219 feet to no purpose whatever; but the worst was that we had taxed the animals' strength severely, and all to no avail. After a little search we found a natural watercourse, or gully, and descended actually in the brook which traversed it—the only direction in which the ground was firm enough to bear us. But upon reaching the latitudinal valley at the bottom, the ground there proved to be not a whit better than it was higher up. Several other brooks poured into the one we were travelling down, until the united stream swelled to the volume of 283 cubic feet in the second. Coming at length to a patch of grass on its right bank, at an altitude of 16,441 feet above sea-level, we encamped, and decided to give the animals—what they sorely needed—a good two days' rest at Camp no. XXV.

A queer sort of rest it was, too! The morning, it is true, was promising enough; but just as I was going to take an observation of the sun, the sky clouded over. A little while after that the men carried out my bed, and felts, and carpets, and had just got them hung on the ropes to dry, when the sky blackened in the west. In we bundled all our belongings again as fast as we could, and had barely finished when down came the hail, rattling and crashing about our ears like bullets. This over, I managed to obtain my solar observation, but had scarcely finished when I saw a new storm advancing, quite as black as the former, but seven times more violent. It was preceded by furious squalls, upon which followed hail and wetting snow. I have seldom seen worse weather in Tibet. It thundered and lightened several times in the minute, and both thunder and lightning were quite close to the surface of the earth, immediately above our heads. The reverberations of the thunder were like mountains being cleft asunder, or mountains crashing flank against flank. The dazzling lightning made us involuntarily flinch, and we actually felt the ground trembling under our feet when the thunder crashed. It was a solemn and aweinspiring sensation to be in the very centre of such a convulsion of nature, exposed to its uncurbed violence. We stopped working, we watched it, we listened to it, we wondered. The dogs howled pitifully. The men's tent was torn open, and it was as much as they could do to get it fastened again. The landscape was sheeted with hail and snow, underneath which the poor hungry horses had to seek their niggardly sustenance.

The second day proved, however, better : sun came out and melted the snow, and the hail-storms kept off until five o'clock in the afternoon. One camel and one horse showed signs of exhaustion; and when, on the 12th of August, we continued, towards the south-east, over the "mud-range," Turdu Bai went on ahead, with the two sick camels carrying no loads; although this of course made the loads of the others all the heavier. In spite of that, however, we soon passed him, for he was travelling terribly slowly, owing to the big pass-hater wanting to lie down and rest so frequently.

On our left we now had a chain of mud-hills; in the far distance on the right a string of reddish eminences, while the ground between the two ascended imperceptibly towards the south-east; but there were no high mountains immediately in front of us. The ground we were travelling over was, however, abominable—one gigantic morass of yellow plastic mud, saturated through and through like a sponge. Although covered in places with a thin sprinkling of gravel, which looked tolerably firm, the animals nevertheless sank in up to their knees at every step, and as each foot had to be drawn in turn out of the tenacious, adhesive mire, it was very exhausting work to get on at all. The surface was, in fact, so soft that no sooner was a deep footprint made in it than the ooze closed round it and filled it in again. It was a piece of exceptional good fortune when the animals did not sink in more than four inches, and we were glad for their sakes when we came to comparative oases like this in the midst of that interminable slough of despond. But our joy was always short-lived: they were soon in again up to the knees, stumbling, falling, so that we had to unload, haul them up, and reload time after time. Truly an accursed land! That grass and fuel should be wanting at an altitude of 16,000 feet above the level of the sea was easy to understand; but why on earth should the ground as big as a three penny-piece; it was everywhere saturated, sodden, through and through. In fact it was like the muddy bottom of a lake just after the water has been drained out of it. To tell the truth, I was astonished that our animals were willing to face it at all. I should have expected they would lie down and absolutely refuse to budge an inch. The big camel, that had such a rooted objection to passes, was quite right in refusing to exert himself. The heart of the Takla-makan Desert was not more destitute of organic life than were these truly abominable mountain wastes. Everyone of the men was obliged to walk. Our hearts beat as if they would burst, and we literally gasped for breath; while to climb into the saddle was like bringing the horse down over his own head. He moved as if he had a stone's weight of sticky soil adhering to each foot, and was unable to complete his pace until he had kicked it off. I rode on in advance to see what the country turned to. But the baggage animals were shy of stepping in the actual foot-prints of the animals which preceded them, and preferred to strike out a fresh track for themselves, though this was really no positive advantage to them.

Thus we plunged on hour after hour. This country threatened to be our doom! Our advance was like that of an invading army, which has burnt its bridges behind it, and is in the midst of the enemy's country, surrounded by dangers on every side. And yet there was a peculiar charm in a rash undertaking such as this. The farther we went the greater obviously grew the difficulties we should have to encounter on our return; but it was just these difficulties which enticed us on. We kept wondering. Shall we overcome them? Yet never for one moment did we think of turning back.

It is a remarkable thing, that in such a relatively short distance as that which intervened between the Akato-tagh and this region there should be such a striking difference in the natural conditions. There we might travel a whole day before we came to a miserable spring; there we had only to stamp on the ground in any spot we chose, and instantly the print of our foot was filled with water.

In the south-west stood a small, conical, detached eminence, and between it and the muddy ridge on our left was a low saddle, the water-parting of this particular district. On the way up we met a solitary wolf, which, however, took to flight the moment it saw us. Here we lost the big camel which hated passes: he failed to reach the top of the saddle, and died before morning. We had just reached the summit (16,769 feet) when the usual storm came on, and the thunder rumbled like the rolling of the ball in a giant's skittle-alley, or like the firing in the bombardment of a distant fortress. Although it was only four o'clock, it was as dark as an autumn evening. The horses walked side-ways to avoid the hail. We ran up our tents hurriedly on the south side of the conical hill, where,although the ground was muddy, there was nevertheless a little grass (16,654 feet); but before we had finished our work, we were all wet to the skin. The storm lasted two hours, then the sun peeped out; but we were in the shade, and the sunshine played on the hills in the east as if in mockery of us. As the earth was relatively warm, the hail soon began to melt, and the men dug a trench round my yurt to draw off the water.

At last, on the 14th of August, the sun shone out. During the night preceding the thermometer fell to –3.2°C. or 26.2° Fahr., so that in the morning the ground was frozen hard, and the holes made by the animals' feet were covered with thin coatings of ice. But our mutual congratulations were short-lived. Before noon the surface turned as soft and spongy as ever. This day, however, we managed to turn our backs upon this abominable range, which had cost us o much trouble. From the easy rounded saddle by which we crossed it, we saw below us another latitudinal valley, shut in on the south by yet another lofty range. In the south-west was a vast glaciated mountain-mass; in the south-east a lake, and behind the latter the contours rose up into snow-clad heights of great altitude. The lake was fed by a stream which came from the west. Higher up the valley, that is towards the south-west, the ground assumed a green tinge, and accordingly we steered our course towards it; for grass was the thing we now needed most.

Upon reaching the place, we at once halted, for the ground was dry, firm sand, and it was quite a pleasure to see how the animals brightened up when they found themselves amongst the grass. Thin and sparse though it was we spread out all our bedding and every felt we had on the sand to dry in the blazing sun; but the tent and the yurt dried best erected in the usual way.

The next day, the 15th of August, it was exactly fifteen years since I started on my first journey to Asia, and I thought that the best way to celebrate the anniversary would be to take a day's holiday in this hospitable spot; and I was glad we did, when I saw how the animals picked up. Although it rained for a couple of hours, the weather was, on the whole, fine, and thee thermometer went up to over 15.0°C., or 59.0° Fahr. This was a veritable oasis in the dreary mountain wastes, and as both animals and men visibly gathered strength, I agreed to give them yet another day. The men really had nothing else to do except bake bread, wash their clothes, and collect fuel, which they obtained from a little plant called *yer-baghri*, which put forth bunches of leaves on the top of a dry stalk.

On the 17th of August we started to climb over the next mountain-range, fording on the way the stream which flowed down the valley from the glacier in the south-west, and which carried from 250 to 280 cubic feet in the second. We began the ascent in a transverse valley, which our animals soon began to feel. After crossing three secondary passes, we reached the main pass, which was flat, and had two pools on the top. On our right, that is in the west, was the mountain-mass sheathed with glaciers and snow-fields; in the east, a flat-topped mountain, the edge of which was as straight as if it had been drawn with a ruler. It was probably capped with the porous tuff which is so common in these regions. From the summit of the pass we descended by an easy watercourse through the red, rounded sandstone hills; but the glen soon contracted into a veritable ravine, which in two or three places was so narrow that we were obliged to scramble up out of it and climb over the hills at the side. Finally, we came out upon a glacier stream with a volume of 350 cubic feet in the second, the water of which was muddy, and reminded me of 'hip' (*nypon*) soup. As there was a little scanty grass beside the stream, and the sandy ground was at least dry, the caravan halted, for the night. Here Aldat, in shooting at an orongo antelope, had the misfortune to break his musket by bursting off a screw, which nearly struck him in the face. But, fortunately, he found it again, and was able to fasten it on with wire and a leather strap, so that, in case of need, the weapon could still be used.

During the greater part of the next day it rained again, and rained-all night until seven o'clock the following morning, when we again started down the valley. The stream flowed almost due south-east, at the rate of nearly 3¾ miles an hour, and we followed it for over 18½ miles. We did not care where it took us, provided we got down to a lower level and found grass Early in the day the men made a very unexpected discovery—namely, a piece of an old shirt, of Mohammedan make, a piece of rope, and a wooden pin with notches in it, such as is used in fastening a pack-animal's load. Whether these things were left by a caravan of Mongol pilgrims, or by Captain Wellby, I could not say. The latter, however, is not unlikely. Wellby and Malcolm crossed Northern Tibet from west to east—that is, from Ladak to Tasidam--at the time I was in Tibet in 1896, their route running along the valley which lay immediately south of, and parallel to, my own route. A few years later Captain Wellby fell in the Boer war; where Lieut. Malcolm also was seriously wounded.

On the 20th of August we did 17 miles in a due south-easterly direction, over slightly undulating country, with a gentle fall, where the going was excellent. In fact, the ground was, on the whole, so level that the water instead of flowing off by any sort of distinct watercourse, collected on the surface in a vast number of little muddy pools. The grass gradually improved, until it was better than any we had hitherto found in Northern Tibet, and mingled with it were patches of luxuriant wild garlic, a herb which the camels ate greedily, and which also made a welcome flavouring in our soup.

The aspect of the region now changed entirely: it was open right away to the horizon. On the horizon there were, it is true, one or two mountain crests; but they appeared quite insignificant. The country assumed in fact a plateau-like character, and consisted of immense table-lands. Three big black yaks, grazing beside a pool, set off in a heavy gallop after us, thinking no doubt that we were somehow old acquaintances. But when they arrived within a couple of hundred yards of us, they perceived their mistake, and swinging round, went off at a clumsy jog-trot. Before us were two smaller lakes; but when we attempted to march between them, we were stopped by the channel which connected them, for it was 6½ feet broad and 5 feet deep. Striking the more southerly of the two lakes, we became aware of a third lake of great area, farther towards the southwest, backed by low, dome-shaped hills. As there was good grazing on its nearer shore, we stopped there and pitched Camp no. XXX.

The 21st of August was devoted to rest and astronomical observations. The weather was splendid, beautifully warm, and the flies were buzzing about in the sunshine. We pitched our tents a little bit back from the lake shore, on some sandy hills, which absorbed the rain without making the ground soft and muddy. The strip of shore itself was low, and strewn with gravelly debris. The water of the lake was salt and bitter; but, fortunately, we discovered a fresh spring close by. And we had no lack of fuel, for yappkak bushes were very plentiful, and grew larger than usual. Two or three of the men, who came in carrying big armfuls of it, were a good deal disturbed in their minds by an uncanny howling they had heard, and asserted it was men shouting. But Aldat, who had been outhunting, explained that the noise was made by wolves. It was getting high time we did have fresh meat, for we were living almost entirely on rice and bread, although I still had a few tins of preserved food left, and every day Cherdon made me a good, nourishing soup of green peas, wild garlic, and Liebig's extract. This last I found of immense service during the journey; it was light of weight, went into small space, and possessed relatively great nourishing value.

VI

ADVENTURES ON A SALT LAKE

On the 22nd of August I made the following arrangements. Kutchuk was to row me across the big lake, in a diagonal direction, towards a dominating peak which lay 50° east of south. Meanwhile the caravan would march west and south round the lake, until they came to the foot of this same peak. As their road might possibly be stopped by the considerable glacier-stream which we had followed a couple of days ago, and which entered the lake at its south-west corner, I sent on Mollah Shah on horseback to find out. He came back in the evening, and assured us there was no hindrance; but at the same time he reported another lake farther to the west, and equally large, which no doubt received the melting waters of the glacier. I assumed, therefore, that the caravan would have no difficulty in reaching the rendezvous before us, for we should spend a good deal of time in taking soundings and other observations. I ordered Cherdon on arrival to light a big fire, to serve as a beacon for our guidance.

It was a warm, bright day, the lake was like glass, and the turquoise-blue of the sky was only flecked by a few light, fleecy clouds. Whilst the caravan was loading up we got the skiff ready, putting into her the sail, the oars, and the life-belts, as well as the necessary instruments. We got started some time before the caravan, which we subsequently saw skirting the lake in a long string.

The bottom of the lake was covered throughout with a layer of salt, from ¾ to 1½ inches thick quite close to the shore. The salt rested upon red mud, and broke under our naked feet; for we had to drag the boat a good mile before it would float. Even at that distance from the shore the lake was barely 20 inches deep. First we directed our course towards a little islands in the east-south-east, Kutchuk punting, not rowing; and every time the oar touched the bottom, it produced a sound as though it struck against a stone. This extensive lake was nothing more than a gigantic salt-pan, utterly destitute of life-not an aquatic bird, not a lacustrine animal, not an alga. The very shore itself was barren as far as the water washed up it. The grass only began on the sandy hills several feet above the water. On its west side were some peculiar islands of rocky debris, semicircular in form.

The little island we were making for was shaped like a pear, with its stalk pointing towards the north, and its maximum height above the lake did not exceed 16 feet. It was a peaceful fragment of virgin soil, carpeted with excellent grass; but the only indication of organic existence it bore was the skeleton of a bird. Nevertheless, it afforded me a splendid view all round. Both east and west the country was perfectly open right away to the horizon. To the north-west was the massive mountain-knot, covered with glaciers, beside which we had encamped two or three days before. On the south the principal features were low, softly rounded ridges; in the north, the range we had last crossed, overtopped here and there by snowy peaks. The island was encircled by a narrow belt of blue clay; but beyond that was the layer of salt, all the irregularities of its surface being visible through the transparent water. After a while Kutchuk was unable to punt, and had to take to rowing, which of course made our advance somewhat slower.

The soundings of this lake gave a result I did not at all expect. Its floor was almost perfectly level; the maximum depth only slightly exceeded 7½ feet, or one-half the depth of the marsh of Kara-koshun. The difference of depth given by the various soundings did not exceed one inch. Thus, the water formed a thin layer upon the top of the salt deposit. I had brought with me a sounding line several hundred fathoms long, but we found our seven-foot oar, which was accurately graduated to scale, quite sufficient for our purpose. Towards the east the lake appeared to extend to an immense distance, but this was only an optical illusion caused by mirage; for the eastern shore came into sight, though not very clearly, late in the afternoon.

It was altogether a remarkable day that I spent on this salt lake. The weather was splendid, the air perfectly still and the few white clouds which hung about the crests of the adjacent mountains where every one reflected on the surface of the lake. The sun, that rare visitant in these unfavourable regions, was very warm; we were delighted to get a glimpse of summer, and dream of its fleeting pleasures. It was delightful, too, to bathe our faces in its hot beams, and feel that we were dry after the many wettings we had had in the Arka-tagh, and at the same time delightful also to escape from the poisonous insects which, in lower regions, were such devoted associates of the summer sun. All around us was, the silence of the grave, not a fly buzzing in the air, not a fish leaping in the water, the lake as lifeless as a chemical solution. The restless spirits of the air were taking a holiday, though doubtless only to prepare themselves for fresh outburst. It was, in fact, as tranquil and peaceful as a Sabbath-day.

Viewed through the pure and rarefied atmosphere, there was something light and evanescent about the landscape. I can only liken it to a bride in an "Empire" robe of white and sky-blue silk; it was the airiest *aquarell* in diluted colours; everything was ethereal, transparent, like a *fata morgana* or a half-remembered dream. The water, except in the immediate vicinity of the skiff, where it was green, reflected the light blue colouring of the sky.

After the slow, dragging pace of the caravan, it was delicious to travel in this way. My place in the fore was as comfortable as an easy chair, and there I made my observations and sketched, precisely as I had done some months before on the big ferry-boat on the Tarim. I had no need to trouble about steering; a glance at the mountain we were making for was sufficient to control our course. Kutchuk sang and hummed as he rowed; or rather he did not row, he paddled. The mast and sail were lashed across the boat amidships, so as to be out of the way. I had brought no overcoat or furs with me; if I turned cold, I could of course take a turn at the other oar. But I was perfectly warm; the temperature of the air was 14.°0 C., or 57°.2 Fahr., while the temperature of the water was 17°.1 C., or 62°.8 Fahr. I revelled in the enjoyment of existence, and forgot all about the showers of hail.

The water was so heavily charged with salt that the drops which fell into the boat stiffened like stearine; after the water evaporated, there was left a thin, chalky-white hollow ball, which generally collapsed. The oar with which we took the sounding looked as if it had been painted white, our hands got white and rough, our clothes were spotted white from top to toe, from the sprinklings of the spray, and the velocity-instrument glittered all over with crystals. The bulwarks and bottom of the boat looked as if she had been recently employed in transporting flour. For the first few hours we saw the caravan duly marching along the western shore, and after that I saw it from time to time through my glass, plodding along in its usual orderly fashion. It was making a detour, whilst we were going in a straight line towards the rendezvous. Thus at first our routes diverged, until the caravan disappeared behind the hills, and after that I lost sight of it.

Mile after mile the depth remained constantly six feet. Hour after hour Kutchuk paddled steadily on, and yet we seemed to get no nearer to the southern shore. Towards the afternoon light clouds began to gather in the sky, and the bright surface of the lake became as it were marbled over. The lap—lapping of the water against Kutchuk's oar was the only sound that broke the brooding silence of this Tibetan Dead Sea, which lay at an attitude of 15,634 feet above the level of the sea.

At four o'clock the sun peeped out again, and now the lake appeared to extend farthest to the west, this effect being, of course, due the low angle of the sun's rays as he was setting. I failed to see the caravan; but then the distance was great, and they might be hidden behind the hills. Further on in the afternoon the surface of the lake clouded over along the southern shore, and we heard a rushing noise, which gradually approached nearer. Kutchuk thought it was a stream entering the lake somewhere close at hand; but it soon became evident that it was a tempest rising. The wind blew from the east, and made it hard work to paddle; but it soon grew stronger, and we hoisted the sail and turned to the south-west. Then away we bowled at a glorious pace across the high waves, which, with a hollow roar, lashed themselves into white foam against the gravelly beach. We were afraid the sharp gravel would cut the canvas hull of the boat. but we managed to get the sail down in time. Kutchuk jumped out into the water, and helped her up, whilst I pushed with the oar, and in that way we got her beached without damage.

It was now dusk, and we hurried to the top of the nearest hill to look for the caravan; but not a trace of either man or animal! The whole region was silent, uninhabited, almost weird in its loneliness. It was like entering the ruins of a monastery in which no man has put foot for a thousand years. Whilst Kutchuk gathered an armful of yappkak fuel—the shrub grew plentifully just there—I penetrated farther up amongst the hills, but was stopped by two or three creeks and lagoons, in which the salt lay like ice, merely covered by a thin film of water. On a hill-side was the bleached skull of a kulan, and not very far away we noticed the foot-prints of a bear. I shouted, I listened, I shouted again, but no answer. The caravan was nowhere within hailing distance.

When I got back to our landing-place it was already dark. Kutchuk had gathered together a big pile of fuel, and as I had nothing else to do, I set to work and helped him to make it bigger. It was abundantly clear that some unexpected hindrance had arisen to prevent the carvan from reaching the rendezvous. Otherwise they would at least have sent a mounted messenger or two to tell us where they were, and—what was to us more important still—bring us food and water and warm clothing. Our first idea was to make use of the favourable breeze, and sail on to the west; but second thoughts showed that would be very risky in the darkness, especially as the wind was still increasing in violence. And, after all, the circuit round the lake might be a good deal longer than we anticipated, so that there really had not been time for the caravan to get round.

The best thing, therefore, was to make ourselves as comfortable as we could for the night. Choosing a level space, we stacked up our fuel, lifted all the things out of the boat, and took the boat to pieces; then, raising the two halves on end, we made, as it were, two sentry-boxes, which sheltered us capitally against the wind. Scarcely had we finished our preparations when it began to rain. Then we tilted each half of the boat at an angle of 45, propping it on an oar, and in this way procured a roof over our heads as well. Converting the life-belts into pillows, we each managed to get a short nap. At nine o'clock I wound up the chronometer, and took a meteorological observation, whilst Kutchuk lighted the fire. Then we sat and chatted for a couple of hours; but it would have been much more enjoyable if we could have had a cup of warm tea and a slice of bread, or even a cup of water. From this I learned never to embark again without taking food and extra clothing with me.

When we had used up all our fuel, it was time to think of going to bed, and here the two halves of the skiff again came in very handy. We spread the sail on the gravel, though that did not make it very much softer. Then half burying the life-belt in the ground, and doubling myself up, I lay down, while Kutchuk tilted the half-boat over me. After that he stopped up every crevice with gravel and sand, using the oar blade as a spade. The bottom of the boat was only an inch or two above my head, and I was packed into it like a corpse into a coffin—an idea which was a good deal strengthened by Kutchuk's digging and scraping outside. Inside it was as dark as the grave, and the space was so confined, that I had the greatest difficulty in turning myself round.

After spending a whole day on the water, and getting no supper, I naturally felt cold; but in my cold "tent" I very soon grew warm. Kutchuk made himself comfortable in a similar way. Capital thing that boat! First she carried us all day across the lake, then she sheltered us all night on shore, and when, a little afterwards, it began to pour with rain, and the heavy rain-drops rattled like drum-sticks against the taut canvas, we only felt all the more comfortable. We chatted for a little while, Kutchuk's voice sounding through the double canvas walls like a voice from the grave, and my own hollow and sepulchral. But Nature soon asserted her right, and we slept as sound as the dead, oblivious alike of wolves and bears and our own faithless caravan.

I was awakened two or three times by the insidious cold, but at length daylight blinked in under the bulwarks, and I was astonished to find it was already seven o'clock. I called Kutchuk, who came and helped me to open my coffin lid, and, sure enough, there was the sun high above the horizon. We were both stiff with cold, and made haste to gather a fresh supply of fuel, which we lighted with our last two or three matches. The fire put fresh life into us. As there was a fresh and steady east wind, and we neither saw nor heard anything of the caravan, I decided we would go and look for them. We put the boat together again, rigged her up, launched her, manned her, and shook out the sail, using one of the oars as the boom and the other as the rudder, and away we skimmed like a swallow, hugging the southern shore. The wind blew hard, and the lake rose high, so that the skiff rolled a good deal, and Kutchuk, who sat in the bow, was seasick. I was busy taking soundings, measuring the velocity, and mapping the route. At the end of an hour or a little more, I saw through the glass two white objects at the western end of the lake, surrounded by a number of small black dots. The former I took to be the yurt and the tent, the latter the men and animals of our caravan.

At the end of another three hours we reached our destination. Cherdon and Aldat waded out and hauled us carefully ashore. It was as I supposed : the caravan had been stopped by a broad river, which was too deep for them to ford, and which flowed out of the large lake farther west. Turdu Bai had tried it in several places, but always found the water so deep, that his horse lost his feet and began to swim. After that they turned back and encamped beside the spring where we found them. They had kept a fire burning all night on a hill, to serve as a beacon to us, in case we should be driving about on the lake. As they were in urgent need of fresh meat, Aldat had managed to shoot a kulan or wild ass. During my absence our young wolf-cub was so generously fed that he died from over-eating himself.

Directly we landed, Cherdon brought me coffee and break-fast. The rest of the day I spent in making up arrears of work. The next question was, which way were we to go? If we turned to the west, it would take us three days to get round the new lake; and to the east lay the big salt lake which we had just crossed. On the south we were stopped by the river, which ran from the evidently fresh-water lake into the salt-water one. To turn back was not to be thought of I would not go back until the miry high ground had frozen sufficiently to bear us. Finally I resolved to convoy the entire caravan across the river with the aid of the skiff.

Whilst I and Kutchuk rowed round to the mouth of the river, which was about 325 yards across, the caravan went down to the spot where it was narrowest. Just outside the mouth we found a ridge of bank, with only about 20 inches of water on it; this would have made a first-rate ford, except that there was a gap in the middle of it 8½ feet deep. At the spot where the animals were being unloaded the water, notwithstanding there was a strong current flowing out of the fresh-water lake, was intensely salt. We saw the two waters blending together—turning thick, and giving rise to eddies, as when a spoonful of sugar is put into water.

Both banks consisted of hard gravel. The place where the crossing was to be made was 190 feet wide. The principal difficulty was getting a rope stretched from one side to the other. Having tied together the greater part of the ropes with which we lashed on the loads, we made one end fast on the left bank and dragged the other end up stream; then, whilst I rowed across as hard as I could pull, Kutchuk stood up in the bow with the end of the rope in his hand ready to jump ashore. But we failed to hit the little headland on the other side; the rope was too short. Back we hauled ourselves, joined on another piece of rope, and repeated the manoeuvre again-this time with a better result. Thereupon we made the rope fast on the right bank and tightened it until it hung clear of the water.

We tried to drive the horses across, but they refused to enter the river until we had towed one of them over. But the worst business was with the camels. As it was impossible to get them to swim across themselves, there was nothing for it but to tow them over with the boat one by one. Having forced a camel into the river, we slipped a rope round is neck, with which Turdu Bai, crouching in the stern, supported the animal's head above the surface. Meanwhile I hauled the boat across the river by pulling on the rope. But as the camel did not condescend to exert himself in any way, but simply lay and floated like a log, I had his entire weight to bear as well as the full force of the stream, and was obliged to exert myself to the uttermost; if I had let go, the whole bag of tricks would have drifted out into the lake and the camel been lost. However, I managed to get him far enough to feel firm ground under his feet, and he then condescended to help himself.

After we had in this way ferried across the third camel, the rope grew so slack that it dipped into the water. Whilst we were doubling it, and tightening it up again, the first rope broke, and so we had to do the whole thing over again. As my hands were by this time badly blistered, Cherdon hauled across the remaining three camels. Our last surviving sheep, which was accustomed to keep beside the camels, swam over of its own accord.

We carried the baggage across in 14 journeys, and encamped on the spot where we landed. This river was the largest I had hitherto seen in Middle on Northern Tibet. It carried a volume in 1,678 cubic feet in the second. In all probability it had its sources a long way to the west, and gathered into its basin all the glacial streams of the region. Several small aquatic animals were carried by the current from the fresh water lake towards the salt-water lake; but they would of course perish as soon as the infusion of salt grew too strong for them.

As two or three of the horses and one of the camels had chafed backs, we allowed them to travel for the next few days without loads.

My favourite grey also needed rest, so I rode another horse. It was my custom to train my saddle-horse to stand when I wanted to take a compass-bearing; and the moment I put my hands into my pocket to get my compass, my good grey used to stand perfectly still until I had finished.

We now climbed the hills, consisting of soft material, without a trace of hard rock, which bordered both lakes on the south At intervals we found excellent grass on the hill-side, which, added to the springs and the abundance of fuel, tempted us to stay; but the animals were still tolerably fresh, and so we kept on. After crossing a low ridge, we came upon another lake, which, although without visible outlet, was nevertheless fresh.

Amongst the hills south-west of the lake, we observed 18 yaks grazing, and higher up a herd of above a hundred, young and old together—in fact, the ground was black with them. Whilst we were watching them, the sky darkened in the east and west simultaneously, and the rumbling of the thunder—a warning, like the lion's roar, for us to be on the alert—announced that a storm was approaching. Down burst a hail-shower with overpowering violence. The yaks disappeared in the thick downpour, as also did Aldat, with his gun on his shoulder, as he hurried up the slopes on the other side of the valley. Leaving him to look after himself, we continued along the lakes side, and encamped beside a little pool a mile or so from its southern shore. About nine o'clock we heard shouts in the darkness, and two or three of the men, whom I sent out to see what it was, met Aldat utterly wearied out, staggering under the load of a big hump of yak-flesh and a yak's tail. Aldat's victim was a well-grown calf, which had dropped at the first shot.

The next day, being Sunday, was devoted to rest. Aldat and Kutchuk rode back to the place where the former had killed the yak, and fetched in a whole load of meat—an invaluable addition to our scanty larder. Cherdon cut me some cutlets, which were not at all bad; but then it was a young animal, whose flesh was tender.

On the 27th of August we steered due south, and soon crossed a little brook, the water of which had a temperature of no less than 20°.3 C., or 68°.5 Fahr., and contained an extra-ordinary number of small crustaceans. That evening, too, we encamped on the shore of a large lake, where the grass was too good to be passed; in fact, the hills on its western side were overgrown with that I may describe as luxuriant grass. The water of the lake had a specific gravity of 1.021; but there were springs of fresh water not far away. The next day we skirted the south-west corner of the lake, crossed over a ridge of flattened hills, and were again stopped by a labyrinth of creeks, pools, and other sheets of water. One of these was of considerable size, and had a strong muddy red current. Mollah Shah tried in two or three places to wade across it, but it was too deep, and he was forced to turn back. So, here we were again stopped by an impassable river, and were just on the point of turning up along its northern bank in search of a fordable crossing, when we perceived our old, all too familiar enemy threatening us. Although there was an east wind blowing, the western horizon was darkening rapidly. Masses of cloud, heavy as lead, came rolling across the country, with the sweep of an immense seine-net. Or rather it was like an army advancing both wings at once to the attack with irresistible *clan*. The clouds of the left wing had blood-red edges, but those of the right wing were black as ink. The advanced skirmishers were packed together in the most extraordinary formations, as they raced before the tempest. All this time the country in the east was basking in bright sunshine; but the terrible net of the west was drawing in closer and closer around us. We hastily decided to encamp where we were, though not too close to the stream, for the violent downpour might perhaps cause it to overflow its banks. Every man gave a hand with the framework of the yurt, and we had just got two or three felts stretched across the top spars when the storm burst. The hail-shower literally swept along the ground. Every pellet stung, for they came as if discharged from a pea-shooter. There was quite a race for shelter.

The next morning the weather was not very promising, and it was noon before we got the boat ready for measuring the stream and exploring the intricate network of water-ways which stopped us. To the north lay the big salt lake, which I and Kutchuk had sailed across, while to the south was another lake of very respectable dimensions, which, like the fresh-water lake I have mentioned before, discharged itself into our special friend, the salt-water lake. In its lower course the new river expanded into two or three broad basins. Not knowing in which direction the stream flowed, we entered one of these side arms, but were of course soon turned back. At its inner ends was a flock of about 50 wild-geese, presumably resting on their way to India for the winter. But at our approach they all flew off, except one, which took to the water. We made for him and pursued him for nearly an hour, his divings growing shorter and shorter, until at last we got within about 12 yards of him, when I began to harpoon him with the oar, the only weapon I had at hand. He was several times embarrased by the blade, and at length succumbed to a well-directed shot. He made a welcome change in our bill of fare.

We eventually discovered, that the new stream joined the broad river which flowed from the fresh-water lake to the salt-water lake. Landing on the other side of it, we climbed a hill, and perceived we were almost entirely surrounded by large sheets of water. We were standing at the very extremity of a neck of land which ran due east, and had to the north of us the big salt lake so often spoken of, and on the south the fresh-water lake we had just discovered. About half-way down the neck of land was a low range of hills, with apparently plenty of good grazing and abundance of game at its southern foot. On our way back to camp, I made up my mind to have a sail on these new lakes.

VII

A TIBETAN LAKE-LAND

Camp No. XXXVI. was now the base for further operations, Leaving Turdu Bai, Aldat, and Niaz there with the camels and four tired horses, I, with Cherdon, Mollah Shah, and Kutchuk, besides seven horses, our one mule, and the dogs, went off on the new excursion. We were provisioned for a week, and took with us only such thins as we absolutely needed, in addition to felts and furs. The boat, of course, was indispensable in this land of lakes. I packed my instruments in the big camera case. Of the yurt we only took one half—that is to say, the lower part of the framework, and a couple of felt rugs to cover it. The men made a shelter in bad weather out of a few of the roof-spars and two or three felts. After the horses had waded across the river, getting only the lower half of their pack-saddles wet, we easily carried our loose luggage across in the boat.

Before we advanced very far we were stopped by the sound that connected the two lakes, and had to unload, swim the horses across, and ferry over the baggage in the boat. As soon as we were once more loaded up, we got started in real earnest, skirting the northern shore of the fresh-water lake. Very soon, however, we came to a place where the hills plunged steeply down into the water—nay, actually hung over it—so that we were forced to climb right over the top of them. Extensive sheets of water stretched both right and left of us.

We put up our temporary yurt beside a little brook that issued from the side glen, about 300 paces up which a herd of big black yaks were peacefully grazing. As they made not the slightest attempt to flee, I was inclined to think they were tame yaks, and must belong to a band of nomads somewhere in the neighbourhood. But when we turned our horses loose to graze, and they slowly made their way up to the richer grass where the yaks were, the latter sniffed and turned and steadily examined us, and then went off at a gentle trot over of the hills towards the salt lake.

My quarters were so confined that Cherdon had to make the bed first, and then fix the lattice framework round it. It was like creeping into a dog-kennel; but once inside, I was very comfortable and warm, especially after I let Yolldash come in beside me.

Although during the night the thermometer fell to –5°.2 C., or 22°.6 Fahr., the next day, the last of August, turned out a splendid summer's day, without a speck of cloud or a breath of wind. The lake was as smooth as a duck-pond. A kulan came and had a look at the horses with as little concern as if he knew perfectly well that Cherdon's cartridges were all exhausted long ago. On the southern side of the lake were two peaks, crowned with glittering white snow, which, with the flawless sky above them, were reflected with photographic distinctness in the lake. A few hours' further march took us to the end of this lake, but a new neck of land, only a few hundred yards broad, separated it from yet another lake, which extended still farther to the east. This also we followed along the northern shore.

For a short distance we travelled on the top of the cliffs, which hung some 230 feet above the surface of the lake, following a kulan path, which ran so near the edge as not to be altogether pleasant. Away below in the water we could see a shoal of very large black-backed fish, which greatly excited Kutchuk's interest. So we stopped, to see if we could not catch some. We made hooks out of the metal in Yolldash's colar by heating it in the fire and hammering it out. At the same time we contrived a bow out of the ribs of our tent; if we came across wildduck we might perhaps hit them with arrows. You see, we were living like Robinson Crusoe, and had to do the best we could with such scanty materials as we possessed.

The evening was raw and windy, and the prospects for the morrow not very promising. My yurt stood as firm as a rock, but the interior was so confined that to dress and undress was attended with a certain amount of difficulty. Early the next morning I walked to the top of the nearest hill, and thence obtained a splendid view of the entire vicinity, in which water was decidedly more abundant than land. The lake, which sent off a wedge-shaped arm towards the north-east, lay spread out below my feet like a map. It was situated at an altitude of 15,906 feet above the sea. We had thus come down to a relatively lower level, but were still higher than—the top of Mont Blanc! In the meantime Kutchuk had launched the boat and got her ready, and as soon as I returned we rowed in under the perpendicular cliffs of red sandstone where we had seen the fish.

Meanwhile the caravan continued its way round the lake, having instructions to stop on the south side, immediately underneath a peak, which I have indicated on my map by the sign O1. We anchored the boat quite close to the shore, with big segments of the mountain wall hanging over our heads, as it were, by a hair, and threatening every instant to topple down and crush us. Although we felt nothing of the north-west wind, because we were in shelter, we nevertheless heard it swishing along the crest of the precipice.

For a fishing-rod we used one of the spase of the boat, our bait consisting of small pieces of yak flesh, while an empty match-box served capitally as a float. The *asmans*—the fish—bit splendidly, yet we only caught four medium-sized fellows. We were not fishing for amusement, but because we wanted food, and our catch was barely sufficient for one meal. However, skimpy though that meal was, it was a great change and the fish was tasty.

But whilst I sat in the boat thinking and enjoying the sunshine and the rest, the hours flew all too fast, and it became time to start for the rendezvous. But it was darkening in the west; the sky was rapidly clouding—a storm was brewing. We had to choose between staying where we were until it was over—which would hardly have been worth while, for it was now two o'clock, and the caravan no doubt by this already arrived at its destination—or we might take the risk of crossing the lake. I preferred the latter course. Before Kutchuk had rowed very far we began to feel the north-west wind, which helped us along first-rate. Right ahead the leaden, grey clouds were trailing long fringes of hail across the mountains, gradually blotting them out. Behind us the sky was thickening in the same way. The storm approached nearer, the lake went higher, its waves hissing white-crested around us. Down came the hail-burst, peppering the water with its big round pellets. In a moment or two the inside of the boat was as white as chalk. Water and hail, water and hail—everywhere! Shores and mountains alike vanished! We had to keep a sharp watch upon the water, for, as the wind went on increasing in violence, the waves broke higher and higher. Still, as they were several times longer than the boat, we had only to keep her head straight before the wind, and we rode on beautifully, up and down, up and down, with the spray dashing from our bow. Immediately south of the red sandstone chiffs the sounding-line had given a depth of 159¾ feet, the greatest depth I ever sounded in Tibet, but this rapidly decreased as we approached the southern side, until I began to fear the lake would shallow to such an extent that our light craft would be dashed like a nutshell against the beach.

The hail ceased, but not so the wind. It, on the contrary raged still more fiercely, for the further we proceeded from the cliffs the more we became exposed to its fury. Still there was one thing in our favour; we were now at any rate able to see where we were going to, and found we were not yet half-way across. We now steered for a headland, behind which we hoped to obtain some shelter. The waves meanwhile rose so high that they hid the shore from us when we went down into the trough of the "sea", and when the sun peeped out through the clouds, as he soon did, they were almost weird-looking: they glittered like the backs of dolphins, changed from blue to green and from green to blue, and were capped with hissing foam, which sparkled like jewels where the sun's rays tipped them. The canvas covering of the skiff was indented every time she pitched, and was strained so tight that a single powerful side-blow would have been sufficient to burst it; hence we had to manoeuvre her with both oars so as to shield her against the onset of the waves. To be brief, this voyage again ended happily. The storm passed over, the wind subsided, the features of the shore came out distinctly, and we altered our course, making straight for the camp. The sun himself was hidden behind a dense black cloud, but his reflected rays glittered like quick-silver as they streamed across the ruffled surface of the lake.

We were now a long way from our base-camp under Turdu Bai's charge, and it was time to think of returning to it. According to my reckoning we could not be very far from the sources of the Yang-tse-kiang, and I had not given up all idea of trying to discover them. But one thing was clear: the three large lakes which we had discovered in this region had plainly nothing whatever to do with the Yang-tse-kiang, but formed a self-contained basin, possessing no outlet; but as I was not yet absolutely sure of this, I resolved to sacrifice the 2nd of September to a ride farther south. This led us over undulating tablelands, with scanty grass and dangerous, yielding ground. After going 16¾ miles, we stopped on the bank of a stream, which entered the next lake—a small salt pool lying south east of the preceding. Beyond this we were unable to proceed, because of our fast diminishing supplies and our exhausted horses. Next day we turned back, but struck off to the west. We again very nearly got stuck fast in the treacherous quagmires, the horses sinking in nearly two feet. A large stream, which issued from the mountain on our left, flowed due north, and emptied itself into the lake in which we had fished. We travelled along its bed, for it was there we got the firmest ground to ride upon.

Game was extraordinarily plentiful thereabouts. We saw fully half-a-dozen herds of orongo antelopes (*Pantholops Hodgsoni*), each consisting of a score of individuals, though the yaks and kulans occurred either singly or in small troops. Rats, marmots, and hares were very common, while wild geese and gulls made the lake shores noisy with their screeching. We rode in two divisions, with a gap of about 50 paces between us. Yolldash was very busy amongst the game. Once he drove three kulans at full gallop through the gap between us, but before I could get my small camera ready to snap them, they were gone. About an hour later he went off after a herd of orongo antelopes, and when he came back was covered with blood; he had evidently had a royal time of it. Wolves and foxes frequented the uplands to the south. During the latter half of the day's march heavy snow drove straight in our faces, so that I could barely see the horse which marched immediately in front of me. We were all sheathed in white armour of soppy melting snow, which kept peeling off in big strips. Mollah Shah led the way, following a yak-track, which, fortunately, in spite of the snow, was pretty easy to see.

I had intended next day to row across the lake from south to north, so as to take a second series of soundings, but when we woke the weather was, to say the least, peculiar. The sky was perfectly clear, the sun shone in all its splendour, but a strong half-gale was blowing from the north, and the waves broke noisily on the flat shelving beach. Of course, crossing it by boat was out of the question. We rode west along the shore, which was nothing but a mud bath, a very slough of despond! What a wonderful—what an utterly God-forsaken region this was! The ground seemed to be as thin as the air; the very mountains themselves as soft as pumice-stone. Everything was in a state of disintegration. The weather the most unreliable it is possible to conceive. To embark on the lake was to put your life in direct jeopardy. In some places, although the ground did bear, it nevertheless quarked under the horses' feet, and undulated before them as though it were an indiarubber sheet.

At length we reached the end of the lake, and found that it, too, emptied itself through a broad, and considerable stream, into the lower fresh-water lake. The latter was black with wild geese, trying their wings after moulting, flying round in short, quick circles, in preparation for their long journey to warmer climes. They were being closely watched by a solitary golden eagle. We pitched camp (no. XLII). besides the embouchure of the river into the lower lake. From this spot it could not be more than a day's journey to the place where we had left Turdu Bai. Whilst Mollah Shah and Cherdon led the horses along the southern shore of this the lower fresh-water lake, I and my trusty boatman, Kutchuk, started to cross it diagonally. When we started it was glorious weather, with a favourable wind, but we had not got very far when the wind freshened, and drove us out into the open, where, however, the depth nowhere exceeded 10 feet. After about an hour the wind changed, and the usual forerunner of a tempest, the black clouds, loomed up in the west. They divided themselves into two sections, one of which went off over the mountains to the south, leaving a trail of white snow behind it, while the other hastened across the lake to meet us, once more churning up the never-resting waves. The most prudent course would have been to run before the storm, except that we should then have been carried away from our men, who were cut off by the broad channel which connected the second fresh-water lake with the first salt-water lake. We therefore resolved to try and row against both wind and waves. In the distance, to the west-north-west, stood the little hill from which I first saw this lake. Our boat was already pitching in such an uncomfortable manner that I, who was sitting in the fore part, was drenched by every billow that broke. A pelting rain came on and helped to make the situation more disagreeable still. Although we each strained at our oars we made no headway. Very often one-half of the boat would hang over on the top of a wave; then down she would plump, threatening a rent in her fragile covering. Soon another ill-omened change took place in the wind, for it swung round to the south, and blew with unparalleled violence, setting up a second system of waves, which ran at right angles to the first. This caused them at the points of intersection to rise to double their former height. All our efforts were now required to avoid these watery pyramids, and to keep to the relatively level spaces between them; but before we were aware of it, the skiff was hovering on the summit of a wave, and had we failed to balance her there, over she would have gone. Of course, I had now abandoned all idea of taking soundings. We might esteem ourselves lucky if we escaped with out lives, and we kept wondering whether it was to be the next wave or the one after it which was to bowl us over. In this way we toiled for an hour and a half before the storm subsided. But even them the sky wore a threatening aspect, being streaked in every direction by storm centres resembling waterspouts, with hanging draperies of black cloud. Most of them went past us on one side or the other; but some of them drifted right across our lake. We were not a bit nearer land when the second storm came and shook out its heavy load of snow and hail over our heads. Although it drove straight in our faces, we could do nothing to ward it off, for one moment's unwariness and over we should have gone. Throughout the whole of that day we toiled like galley-slaves.

During the respite which followed the second squall we made haste to win headway, for the sky was already darkening for the third time; and down charged the third storm upon us with its pouring torrents of rain. The second had painted the inside of the boat white with snow and hail; this half filled her with water, which lapped backwards and forwards as we rode up and down the heaving waves. But the squall, too, passed, and pursued its solitary way across the inhospitable mountains and impressionable lakes which stretched to the east.

After eight hours' hard work we at length came to land, and I was never more delighted to put foot on *terra firma*. Climbing a little hill, I perceived Mollah Shah waiting for us on a headland with the four horses. We paddled round to where he was, and then stopped to take the volume of the stream which we had crossed a week before. We also measured its breadth and sounded its depth, and took three measurements of its velocity, when down came the fourth squall. Although the sun was still above the horizon, it was as dark as midnight, except when the dazzling flashes of lightning lit up the weird chaos of lake and barren mountain. The hail came down from the sky and swept along close to the surface of the earth; the spray rose from the lake and mingled with it. We happened to be just then on the east side of the channel, and it was only by the most desperate efforts that we were able to push our boat over to the other side, although it was not more than 200 feet across. This, however, was the farewell greeting of that day of storms, and I need not say we had had enough of it. We unscrewed the boat, packed sail, mast, oars, and life-belts into the one half, loaded up, distributed the instruments amongst us, mounted, and set off at a smart trot for home.

It was a pleasant change to ride after the long stretch of strenuous rowing. The moon shone through the breaking clouds, mingling her light in a fantastic manner with the incessant flashes of lightning, which seemed to turn her white crescent yellow every time they flamed out upon it. At length we reached camp, and found all well. Aldat had shot four orongo antelopes, so that we were well provisioned for two or three weeks to come. The camels and ailing horses had gathered flesh during their rest. Even after we lay down to sleep, utterly tired out, the storms still continued to chase one another unweariedly over the earth. We rested all the next day, the 6th of September. The afternoon was like a winter's day, without a single glint of sunshine, while one hailstorm followed another without intermission. Whilst Cherdon and Kutchuk went fishing, the other men prepared the skeleton of an orongo antelope, and I was kept busy recording the results of our recent excursion.

Possibly I often dwell upon events, and describe incidents, which may seen to the reader trivial and insignificant, but I do it for the purpose of conveying some idea of the life which the solitary traveller leads in those desolate, uninhabited wastes. Taken as a whole, they will give a consistent picture of how the days passed month after month in our little community. We were not a large company, and we lived under monotonous conditions, the same occupations recurring with uniform regularity, and our lives strictly governed by the clock. It was only the country we travelled through which, with its never-ending variety and change, kept our interest awake.

With regard to my choice of servants, I had every reason to be satisfied. With stoic serenity Turdu Bai tended the camels as if they were his own children. Cherdon was attentive, alert, and punctual, and yet at the same time a comical little man, with his own peculiar philosophy of life. Mollah Shah watched over the horses with irreproachable care, but was somewhat taciturn, abrupt, and reserved. When on the march, one half of the horse-caravan was led by Kutchuk, a young giant of two or three and twenty, always happy and contented, but especially so when he was afloat, for most of his days since he was a child had been spent on the water. Without Aldat our situation would have been very critical indeed; he kept us supplied with fresh meat, and was always after the game. But both in camp and whilst on the march he preferred to be left to himself, and spoke but little. Niaz did all the heavier work, carried water, gathered fuel, drove in the animals of a morning, and gave a hand with loading them up. The dogs had the best time of it, for they had plenty of meat to eat, nothing whatever to do, except to keep watch, and that was a sinecure. And they had a playmate in our last surviving sheep, which nobody had the heart to kill. The creature consorted faithfully with the camels, grazed with them during the day, and at night found warm and cosy lair beside them.

VIII

THE LAST DAYS OF ALDAT THE AFGHAN

Camp No. XLIII, was the turning-point of the expedition. Our supplies would not allow us to proceed farther south. We were only provisioned for two and a half months, and we had already spent six weeks on the tramp. Although we still had a plentiful supply of rice, we were obliged to husband our flour with the utmost care, having used too much of it in attempting to save the camel that died. Winter would soon be here, and we ought to return, making a wide detour, first west, then north, then east, back to our headquarters camp in the Chimen valley.

But before leaving this part of Tibet, I wished to cross a particular east-west range, which culminated in the south-west in a vast mountain-mass, capped-with perpetual snow, After a rather short day' march to Camp No. XLIV. (16,038 feet), I decided to divide our party, sending on the larger portion of the caravan, under command of Turdu Bai, down a latitudinal valley which opened out to the west-south-west. I ordered him to wait for us somewhere in the open country to the north-west of the culminating mountain-mass, while I myself skirted its left flank. This excursion would, I estimated, take only four days, and I selected Cherdon and Aldat to accompany me. We had only six horses, and carried the small temporary yurt, provisions for a week, and fuel enough to last two days. There was a certain element of adventure in the plan, for the Mussulmans might lose their way. But in case our trail should be obliterated by hail or snow, I instructed Turdu Bai to wait for us one week, and if at the end of that time he failed to hear anything of us, he was to abandon all further search, and make his way back as best he could to our head-quarters camp in the Chimen valley. Their provisions could be made to hold out at a pinch; and as for ourselves, we relied upon Aldat to keep us supplied with meat.

Both sections started simultaneously on the 8th of September, and after leaving the upper course of the river, which some days before had stopped our southward march, our routes diverged, and we were soon hidden from one another by a cluster of low hills. Our own course was towards the south-south-west, through fairly open country, except that it was a little diversified on both the right and the left. The contours rose slowly as we advanced, and the ground became barren, except for a few patches of moss. After riding smartly for several hours we reached a chain of flat hills, with small basins of crystal spring-water between them. Each of these last was surrounded by a belt of short, thick, vivid-green grass, soft as an Oriental carpet. Here, as there did not appear to be any grazing towards the south, while there was good spring water, as well as plenty of fuel, for the district was much frequented by yaks and kulans, we halted for the night, our camp being 16,316 feet above sea-level. Apart from a couple of big wolves, the only traces of animal life were two or three ravens. The weather was, of course, unfavourable; this made the eighteenth day that we had hail-storms and snowstorms from the west. But the night was as usual bright and still, with a clear moon, and as early as nine o'clock in the evening the thermometer dropped to –2°.0 C. or 28°.4 Fahr.

On the 9th we continued in very nearly the same direction, the surface being a good deal more broken; we were now approaching higher regions. Before we turned due west we were forced out of our way by a watercourse, which issued out of the flank of the big snowy mass in front of us, and which was filled with soft ooze. We were all drowsy and stiff with cold when we stopped at a patch of grass. As soon as the camp was pitched Aldat came and begged permission to stalk a big yak which he had seen grazing not very far away. I went out and watched him, creeping like a cat along the hollows towards his unsuspecting prey. Thanks to the strong wind that was blowing against him, he was enabled to get within thirty paces of the yak. He fixed his gun on its fork, and fired. The yak jumped, making the earth fly all around him. Then he ran a few yards, stopped, staggered, tried to keep his balance, but finally fell. Then he rose again, and went through the same series of movements. This is repeated several times; but at last tumbled down all of a heap and lay without moving. All this time Aldat lay behind his gun, motionless as a statue, lest he should draw the attention of the dying animal to himself. Cherdon and I now joined him. It was difficult walking; we could only take two or three steps at a time, and then had to stop, for the least effort in this extraordinarily rarefied air brought on quickened action of the heart. The yak was a bull of fifteen years. Out came the knives, his head was cut off, his entrails taken out, and then we left him till the following morning. His fat was the part about him which we desired most. It cost Aldat a real pang to leave behind the magnificent skin, which would have brought him in a good sum at Cherchen; but we could not carry it with us, as we had only three baggage horses. However, I promised to give him full value for his masterly shot.

The 10th of September was a hard day. Before the sun rose, Aldat drove in the horses, which had wandered a long way down the valley, and then went to fetch the head and fat of the yak. That morning our bitterest enemy, the west wind, overslept himself, and did not get up until nine o'clock; but afterwards he took his full revenge for the delay. Our camp was in a bad situation at an altitude of 16,874 feet, and fully exposed to the wind, which blew as it had seldom blown before. We now perceived immediately in front of us the pass on the south flank of the snowy mass which we had to cross over. We trembled as we thought of it; it was so high, and yet it looked innocent enough!

As Aldat did not turn up, I sent Cherdon to look for him; but it was eleven o'clock before they came back. Cherdon found the young hunter lying beside his victim, ill and unable to continue his work. The Cossack helped his comrade down to camp, and also brought some of the yak fat. And, in truth, poor Aldat looked in a very bad way: he was bleeding at the nose and had a violent headache; so I made him sit still, while Cherdon and I took down the tent and loaded up the animals.

The ground was hard; there had been nearly eleven degrees of frost, although at one period of the night the thermometer dropped as low as –10°.7C or 12°.7 Fahr. This was clearly an indication that winter was at hand. Aldat was so unwell that he was unable to get into his saddle without help. On our way up towards the detestable pass which we were about to cross we had on our right, one after the other in succession, the snowy peaks which we had seen at a distance, though now of course they were close beside us; while on our left was a black mountain-ridge, overtopped farther south by yet another snowy mass. As soon as the sun gathered power, the ground thawed, and then began our struggle with the mire. Hour after hour we plodded on up the acclivities, flattering ourselves time after time that we were now quite close to the pass, but time after time we were deceived. We crossed one saddle after another, but always found there looked yet another ridge in front of us, hitherto unseen.

The horses sank in up to the fetlocks, and the fragments of slate which were embedded in the soft ground caused the poor animals to slip and cut their legs against the sharp edges. There were blocks of stone fully a cubic yard in dimensions, and two or three were as large as cottages. Under the shelter of one of these last we stopped for a quarter of an hour or so to thaw our stiffened limbs. About fifty yards or so north of our track hung two small transverse arms of the glacier, and along them two yaks were travelling at about the same pace we did. Yolldash went after them, and barked himself hoarse, but they paid not the slightest attention to him, though they stopped and regarded us. But, finally making up their minds that we were harmless, they turned and climbed a precipitous moraine, with an enviable ease and ability, which, considering their size and weight, the yielding nature of the foothold, and the intensely rarefied air, impressed me greatly. On the top of the pass the aneroids showed an altitude of 17,803 feet, or precisely half the thickness of the atmospheric envelope which surrounds the earth.

During the day the thermometer never rose half a degree above freezing-point; but the wind searched us to the very marrow-skin vests and furs were no use at all against it. Had we been able to walk, we could easily have kept ourselves warm; but we could not walk—we could only stick to our staggering horses and long for a tolerable spot to camp in. The sole consolation we had was that, having now at length reached the summit of the pass, we should next go *down*. The glen by which we descended led to the south-west, and was filled with debris, through which trickled a little rivulet. A short distance beyond its exit from the mountain we encamped at 17,268 feet above sea-level, or nearly 1,500 feet higher than the top of Mont Blanc! We had only a handful of fuel left, while the animals were forced to be content with the few blades of miserable grass which grew there. Aldat was now unable to stand. We left him lying where he reeled off his horse, after wrapping him up well with felt rugs. We could not persuade him to take anything; he refused to drink even a cup of warm tea, but lay moaning all night. As early as nine o'clock the temperature was at –3°.6 C., or 25°.5 Fahr., and during the night it dropped to –11°.9C. or 10°.6 Fahr.

Next morning we crossed the hills towards the north-west. A long way off in the south west there was yet another snowy mass, the south-eastern continuation of which took the form of a line of snowy pinnacles; beyond a shadow of doubt, it was the range of Tang-la. However, we soon came to a main valley extending east and west, which gathered into itself all the streams, brooks, and rivulets of the region. In order to avoid the necessity of crossing all these watercourses, we decided to travel along the bottom of the valley. But on a small detached hill at the foot of the mountain Cherdon's sharp eyes discovered some small black objects, which he took to be either human beings or yaks. We stopped and regarded them through the glass. They were alive that was certain, for they moved. But one of the objects seemed disproportionately big; perhaps after all it was only a yak cow with a couple of calves.

Encouraged by this, we made direct for the hill where we perceived the mysterious objects. Poor Aldat was now so bad that we had to lash him on his horse to prevent him from falling off. He talked incoherently; his mind was beginning to wander, and he kept begging us unceasingly to leave him behind. After advancing some way down the mountain-side, we made out that the mysterious objects on the hill were two men collecting stones and piling them up into a pyramid, or cairn. An hour later our doubts were cleared up. They were our friends, Turdu Bai and Kutchuk, who had climbed to the top of the hill to look for us. Finding no traces of us they were on the point of returning to camp, but before they did so resolved to build up a conspicuous landmark. The cairn, which was over six and a half feet high, and occupies a conspicuous position, will easily be recognised by any future exploring party.

After giving ourselves a much-needed day's rest at Camp no. XLVIII. (16,645 feet), we resumed our westward journey on the 13th of September. It was repugnant to me to travel when one of our number was sick; but our scanty supplies would not allow us to linger. Aldat's mind had wandered all night; and he moaned, shouted, and sang songs in Persian. The treatment I adopted had produced no effect; he had no longer any command over either body or mind, and sat as limp as a rag, his eyes fixed in a distorted stare. We carried him on an improvised litter fixed between two sacks on the back of a camel, giving him a cushion for his head, and covering him well with felt rugs, and lashing him on to prevent him from falling off.

After crossing over a low saddle of threshold (16,756 feet) of the valley, we travelled along the sandy bed of the stream, a welcome change to the animals after miry ooze. Cherdon caught sight of a herd of twenty *arkharis'* or wild sheep; but when he tried to stalk them with

Aldat's musket, they disappeared like a puff of smoke. The valley we were following led out upon a tableland of soft red sand, overgrown with grass, and open towards the north-west. Here we encamped beside the first fresh-water pool we came to, at an altitude of 16,087 feet. From this time onwards I had my yurt heated both morning and evening; that is to say, one of the men brought in some glowing embers on a bed of ashes, carrying them on the lid of our cooking-pot, or when that was in use, in my hand-basin. Artificial heat of some kind was certainly needed in the incessant winds which cut across those ugly highlands.

Thanks to a favourable country, almost level and with firm ground, we were able on the 14th of September to travel eighteen and a half miles. The characteristic feature of the landscape was a countless number of small pools, each the centre of a self contained drainage basin, with no outlet, and very often without any visible contributaries. After a long search for fresh water, we stopped beside a small spring, surrounded by sparse thin grass. In the early part of the day the weather was splendid; but in the afternoon we were visited by the usual storms of hail and lightning, though now, by way of a change, they came, not from the west, but from the east. Just as we were pitching our tents (altitude, 16,044 feet) it began to snow, and come down it did with a vengeance, much heavier than we had ever seen it before, so that the grass was very quickly hidden. Then the wind veered round to the north-east, and quickened to a velocity of twenty miles an hour. The snow was wreathed up to a great height on the windward side of my yurt. At nine o'clock it was no easy task to take the usual meteorological observations, for not only was it pitch dark, but the snow whirled and blustered so tempestuously that it was quite impossible to see an inch before our faces. Unfortunately my lantern was *hors de combat*: three of its panes were broken and the glass replaced by paste-board, while the fourth was cracked in a dozen directions, and only held together by strips of paper and gum. The snow crunched under our feet, and after being but a few minutes in the open air, we might easily have been mistaken for snow men, such as children make. The men's tent was only two or three yards from mine, but I literally could not see it, because of the driving snow, and I only knew where it stood by hearing the wind whipping the lashing its cords. Truly a strange experience to be snowed up in a region where there existed nothing but water. Nor were the prospects for the future any brighter; for the melting of all this snow would make the ground like a quagmire. At nine o'clock the thermometer went down to –2°.1 C. or 28°.2 Fahr., though at one p.m. it had stood at 11°C., or 51°.8 Fahr. But we were now so deeply buried in snow that the inside of both the tent and the yurt were kept warm all night. Outside, the storm howled dismally, and the fine snow pattered, pattered against the frozen felts as if it never meant to stop.

Our spirits were still further depressed by poor Aldat's condition. He was attacked by a serious illness which I confess I did not understand. He complained of pains in the heart and head, and his feet turned black, and were as cold and hard as ice. I rubbed them for some time, hoping to restore the circulation, but it was without effect. They were as if dead, and he had quite lost all feeling in them, even when I pricked them with a pin. This moribund condition gradually crept up his legs; although late that evening I gave him a hot foot-bath, which seemed to do him good. But what surprised us most was the way his mind wandered. Whilst on the march he chattered incessantly, and kept shouting to his camel to lie down, and for a good hour after he was comfortably tucked up in bed inside the tent he kept on beseeching the other men in the most moving tones to let his camel stop. Mollah Shah, who had known him in Cherchen, told us that he had once been out of his mind, but had been cured by a certain Abdurrahman Khoja, an *ishan,* or "holy man," who went to his father's house and repeated certain prayers over him, making him at the same time swallow slips of paper written all over with texts from the Koran. It was heart-rending to hear this young fellow of four-and-twenty, who had so recently been in the full strength of manhood, rambling in the delirium of fever, and talking of his old father and his brothers in Cherchen. We kept watch beside his bed all night, and did all we could to help him: but the prospects were anything but favourable for a dying man, to be thus carried on the back of a camel through icy snowstorms, and over mountains which almost scraped the sky.

The horses, impelled by hunger, wandered astray during the night in search of grass; and it was late in the morning before we managed to find them again. The snow lay nearly a foot thick, and owing to its dazzling whiteness was painful to the eyes. Although the sun was warm, the day remained cold and raw, for a cutting westerly wind swept across the snow-fields. Once, when it stopped for a breathing space, the sun actually burnt, but within a few minutes we were once more being buffeted by the blinding snow. This soon passed over, and the sun once more peeped out; but the wind still continued chilly. It was winter and summer in fraternal alliance—in a word, thoroughly typical Tibetan weather!

We were now travelling consistently north-west, over a tolerably open country, and consequently had no big mountain chains to cross. The temperature never rose above freezing-point all day, and the ground remained hard; but the snow hid the marmots' holes, which literally honeycombed the ground, and caused the horses very often to stumble and fall. The order of our itinerary was now three days' marching, the fourth rest. On the 16th of September our camp lay 16,395 feet above sea-level. Cherdon had carefully kept a few cartridges, but now expended them upon a young yak, which furnished us with a good load of excellent meat. Yak beef is not good; but when you have nothing else, you cannot afford to be over nice. He also shot a wolf, which was evidently meditating designs upon our last surviving sheep. When we stopped, Aldat begged to be left all night between two camels in the open air; for the Mussulmans believe that the bodily warmth of these animals will restore health and strength to a sick man whose own vitality is slackening. So we made him comfortable amongst the camels, and left Mollah Shah and Niaz to keep him company.

Early on the morning of the 17th of September I was awakened by a terrible din in the camp: men were shouting and dogs barking frantically. I looked out, and there was a big bear slinking off, not fifty paces from the tent. His tracks in the snow showed that he had minutely examined the camp, and made a complete circuit of my yurt; but when the dogs attacked him, he thought it best to sheer off.

The weather was now fine, but the going abominable: the surface undulated and was littered all over with nasty sharp-edged pieces of tuff of all sizes and shapes. There was not a square foot of bare ground between them, and every tiny patch that happened to be free from stones was burrowed into by rats or marmots. Our animals stumbled incessantly on the sharp-pointed stones, or in the treacherous holes, and two of the camels cut the pads of their feet until they bled. After this followed a stretch of soft ground, which at first was frozen on the surface sufficiently to bear the weight of a camel, but later on it gradually thawed. At one place the last camel went through with both fore legs, and in spite of all our efforts to help him sank deeper and deeper into the mire. At last I hit upon the device of slipping felts underneath his feet as we got them up one by one, and by this means we lifted him into his usual attitude when he lay down. Then, after he had rested abit, we induced him to make a desperate effort, by which he succeeded in scrambling on to firm ground, where he stood with the ooze dripping in clots down his legs and sides. He was literally shelthed in mud—we scraped it off with knives—and stood trembling in every limb, breathless and bewildered.

We now approached a peculiar glen, which stretched east-north-east towards a lake about six miles distant. Beyond the latter was a huge mountain-knot, draped with snow, which we had had on our right all day long, and which was clearly the same gigantic peak which I called King Oscar's Peak when I skirted its northern flank in 1896.

The bottom of the valley consisted of low-terraced table-lands, covered with layers of tuff fifty to seventy feet thick, while blocks of tuff were scattered around in every direction. About an hour later we reached the steep edge of a second similar glen, and so precipitous was the descent that it occasioned us a long hunt before we were able to find a suitable place by which to get down. Kulans and orongo antelopes were here numerous, and we counted a herd of forty-two yaks. The next day the sun asserted his supremacy, and we were not harassed by storms. The patches of snow that were left from the last downfall now melted and evaporated. At one o'clock the temperature rose to 12°.0 C, or 53°.6 Fahr.

In this way we plodded on day by day across the barren, inhospitable uplands of Tibet. It was two months since we had set eyes upon a human being except ourselves, and we were growing anxious to get back to our headquarters camp. But every day's march that I plotted on my map only showed how slowly we advanced, and how great was the distance we yet had to go: we were still over 240 miles from Temirilik.

Our spirits always rose with our third day's march, for every-body knew that "to-morrow we shall rest". Thus the 20th of September we spent in Camp no. LIV., at an altitude of 16,133 feet. Cherdon, using Aldat's gun, shot a fifteen-year-old yak, which I photographed in various positions before he was flayed and cut up. In the evening Cherdon came in with an orongo antelope, and we tried another Mussulman cure with Aldat. Undressing the invalid, we wrapped him in the antelope's still moist warm skin, pressing it close to his body all round. I confess I had not much faith in the remedy, and felt sick at heart at being so powerless to do anything for the man. The last evening or two I gave him a few grains of morphia; except for that he never slept a wink.

At our next stopping-place westwards down the valley, the ground was literally honeycombed with marmots' holes. One old fellow, who was basking on a hill-side in a comically killing attitude, being stretched out like a man, or at least like a monkey, was pounced upon by Yolldash. The men kept him two months and tried to tame him, but he was just as wild at the end of the time as he was at the beginning: whenever anybody went near him, he used to sit up on his hind legs ready to lay hold with his sharp fore-teeth, which were endowed with a very respectable amount of power. The marmot's bite was said to be dangerous, and the wound very hard to heal.

Where *davaghan* or marmots occur, you are almost certain to find bears; for the Tibetan bear lives almost entirely on these rodents, which devours bones and skin and all. He doesn't stalk them down, as Yolldash did, but visits one hole after another, until he finds a victim at home; then with his powerful claws he scratches away the soil until he is able to seize his prey. He gets, at all events, plenty of exercise before his meal, for you can always see where a bear has been by the big heap of soil he makes. Several small troops of kulans were galloping about the bottom of this broad valley. There was great natural beauty in the elegant forms and perfect shape of these animals. They would gallop in a half circle, lying over at an angle of forty-five degrees to the ground, then suddenly wheel and halt in a straight line a little distance away. Their evolutions were as regular and as well executed as if they had been ridden by invisible Cossacks.

To-day Aldat was able to sit on horseback, although he had to be tied on fast and well looked after. We all hoped that he was improving, but in the evening he grew worse again. Every breath was accompanied by a groan, and he breathed at the rate of fifty-eight gasps a minute, which even at the height of 15,873 feet above sea-level was abnormal. On the other hand, his temperature was remarkably low, and the most strained attention failed to detect the least sign of his heart beating, and his pulse was correspondingly weak. His intellect still continued clouded: he kept talking about wanting to go out and shoot yaks. Although it was a violation of the order of our itinerary, we halted for a day for his sake, notwithstanding that we had only bread to last two or three days longer, and a dozen more shots would completely exhaust our ammunition.

Although on the morning of the 23rd the invalid's condition was scarcely changed at all, except that he now took his breath twenty-four times in a minute, we resolved to continue. It was evident he could not last very much longer, but we were unable to wait. We packed him in between two bags of fuel, putting soft felts underneath him, and wrapped his feet in carpets, and rolled up a fur and put it under his head for a pillow, then lashed the whole fast with ropes on the back of a camel.

Just as the camel was getting on to his feet to start, Aldat ceased to breathe. His broken eyes—beautiful grey Afghan eyes they were—were fixed a far off upon a country which our glances were unable to reach. He who formerly had ranged over these stupendous uplands with light and hurrying footstep on the trail of the wild yak had succumbed to the hardships of his calling, and closed a life which had been exceptionally lacking in pleasure. "Ghetti!"—i.e., "He is gone!"—whispered the Mussulmans, as they stood in silence round his strange death-bed. But Turdu Bai, looking at the matter from the practical side, asked me what we were to do with the body. I was reluctant to bury him in unseemly haste, and all the men were quite satisfied when I gave the order to start. The camel had carried him several days, and he was not a heavy load. I had promised the men that they should be at Temirlik in eighteen days, which would allow us six rest days, if we travelled at the rate of fifteen miles a day. Consequently, they counted them with growing interest, and were anxious not to lose a single hour.

IX

STRUGGLING BACK OVER THE TIBETAN BORDER RANGES

When we started again, making for a large lake lower down the valley, our caravan was converted into a funeral procession. The men no longer talked, but were silent and grave. Kulans and yaks grazed unmolested near our line of march. The ravens of death hovered around us in wide circles. The lake shore was hard and afforded excellent going. The water was salt and bitter, and had a temperature of 16°.6C., or 61°.8 Fahr., which was abnormally high when compared with the mean temperature of the air at that season of the year. It was, I dare say, partly a consequence of the high temperature of the lake, combined with the absence of wind, that this day, at one p.m., the temperature rose to 17°.5 C., or 63°.5 Fahr.

After passing the lake, we continued, still towards the north-west, over a gently-rising, undulating tableland, furrowed by numerous watercourses, with treacherous mud at the bottom. Beside one of these we came across a small piece of wood belonging to a Mongolian pack-saddle. It was as soft as cork, and must have been dropped either by a pilgrim caravan which had strayed this way from the north, or by Captain Wellby and Lieut. Malcolm's caravan, the route of which we crossed somewhere this same day. When we stopped Mollah Shah and Niaz dug a grave for Aldat, whilst the other men were about their usual duties. After putting in one skin underneath and another on the top of the corpse, they shovelled in the soil, and made an oblong mound above it; and so we left the dead man to his last long rest in the moist and treacherous earth. It was the simplest burial I have ever been present at—no ceremonies, no tears, no prayers, except those I silently breathed for the peace of the dead man's soul. Beside the grave we set up one of the tent spars, and fastened on the top of it, by way of *tugh*, one of Aldat's own hunting trophies, namely, a yak's tail; for this is the usual headstone to a Mussulman tomb. But I scratched on a small piece of wood, in Arabic and Latin lettering, the dead man's name, as well as the date, and my own name, in case destiny should lead any traveller to the spot before Aldat's burial mound becomes finally levelled down.

Later on I was able with my own hands to give to Aldat's brother, who met us in the Chimen valley, the dead man's gun, the wages which were due to him, and his clothes and furs. His old father, Eisa Ahun, son of Dill Mohammed Khan, visited me a year later at Charkhlik, and it was a relief to me to know that Aldat's mother was dead, and so spared the grief of losing such a handsome and splendid son.

On the 24th of September the men were ready to start at an unusually early hour, being anxious to get away as soon as possible from so sorrowful a spot. After the Mussulmans had repeated a *dua* or prayer over his grave, poor Aldat was left alone with the mighty silence of the hills; no pilgrims, except the wild beasts of the wilderness, would hereafter visit his grave. The last we saw of it was the black yak's tail fluttering in the breeze as we dripped below the hills in the west.

We now set ourselves resolutely towards a yawning ravine or gateway in the mountain-range in front of us. But it was no easy matter to reach it. The ground consisted of loose red sand, furrowed by a great number of deep trenches, 100 to 150 feet deep, with precipitous sides and a treacherous morass at the bottom of each, in which we should of course have perished, man and mouse, had we once dropped into them. The glen, which we finally reached after very great difficulty, led gently up to a double pass, beyond which we halted for the night.

The following day we threaded a series of small passes or gaps in a number of minor parallel chains; but when at length we were gratified by the sight of open country, namely, a broad attitudinal valley, stretching as usual east and west, all vegetation had come to an end. Although we had done a good day's work already, we nevertheless pushed on diagonally across the valley, riding for several hours on its hard floor before we reached a fresh-water pool, with a few blades of grass beside it. That day we did 19¼ miles.

As we approached the Arka-tagh the country grew more and more desolate. On the 27th of September we did not see a blade of grass anywhere, nor a single trace of any other kind of vegetation, or the least indication of organic life. Up and down we went, over the mountains and across the valleys, traversing them all at right angles. No sooner did we get down to a stream than we had to begin to work our way up on the other side of it, and although the difference of elevation did not exceed 350 feet, the climb proved a tremendous strain when it was repeated time after time without variation. After many tiresome detours and halts we at length reached the summit of the new range, situated 17,071 feet above the level of the sea. Immediately north of it was a solitary ridge, which we were forced to double either east or west. I preferred the latter, and rode on a long way in advance of the caravan, until it grew dark, when I stopped and waited for them at an altitude of 16,769 feet. They came in in small parties, all dead beat, and reported that they had left behind, in a hopeless condition, a white horse which we had brought from Yanghi-koll. Besides this, two camels and one horse were suffering from some affection of the eyes; they noddle their heads when they walked, as if they were suffering from want of sleep.

The next morning we were again in the midst of winter; but the clouds soon disappeared, the wind dropped and the sun came out and proved scorching hot. At such moments the black bulb thermometer used to register up to 70°.0 C., or 158°.0 Fahr. When we stood and watched the patches of snow attentively we could actually see them dwindling before our eyes. Kutchuk went back to fetch the white horse; but although he was still alive, he fell down and died on the way to camp.

We descended into the next latitudinal valley through a narrow gorge shut in by red cliffs, consisting of sandstones and shales. The brook which flowed along the bottom of it had frozen during the night. As long as we were in the deep cutting, we were in shelter; but as soon as we emerged into the open the caravan was caught by the full force of the gale, which was just beginning, but rapidly increased to a westerly hurricane of the worst description. We had to sit tight to prevent ourselves from being actually blown out of the saddle. Horses, men, and camels—all bent over and literally lay *upon* the wind. The entire caravan was blown sideways. Horses' tails and loose ends of clothing flapped and fluttered like streamers down the wind. It was hard work to get our breath: we were nearly choked. The camels were blown from side to side as they lurched along. The valley in front of us was shrouded in mist,so that we were unable to see which way to go. But the first bite of grass we came to should, I resolved, be the signed to stop; for it was impossible to travel far in such a gale. Those who have never been in one can form no conception of what it is like. It was as though the entire volume of the atmosphere were concentrated into this great trench of the earth's surface and forced through it like a roaring tide. The clouds drove overhead at racing speed; drift-sand-nay, actually small stones were caught up from the ground, and hurled point-blank into our faces. In the more exposed situations the wind had a velocity of over 55¾ miles an hour; but after we got in the shelter of some low hills, beside a little brook at the bottom of the valley where we encamped, it dropped to 31½ miles an hour.

Owing to this fickle weather, and these abrupt and violent changes of temperature, our skin grew very sensitive. The nose and ears suffered most, the skin peeling off time after time. Our nails turned as brittle as glass, and split and cracked; and there was constant pain in the finger-tips.

Several of our horses were now in a bad way, and as we had only maize enough to last two days more, I directed one of the men to see if we could not spare some of the rice for them. Our smallest mule very nearly gave up at this camp, No. LXI. (16,100 feet) but was saved by Cherdon, who treated her according to a practice of the Buriats. She was swollen up to an enormous size, and lay writhing on the ground. The Cossack took an awl and with a powerful push thrust in into her side up to the hilt. The gas streamed out, but not a drop of blood. Then we forced her to stand up, flung a rope round her hind quarters, and whilst one man pulled at her head, another whacked her with a staff. Every time she kicked out behind, two other men pulled away at the rope, so that in this way she was forced to move forwards, swinging from right to left. People may say what they like about this method, but it certainly proved a sure cure in her case. She recovered, was with me when I rode towards Lassa, took part in my journey westwards across Tibet to Ladak, went over the Karakorum Pass, and when I last saw her in Kashgar, at the end of May, 1902, she was in first-rate condition.

After a day's rest, we set to work in earnest, on the last day of September, to scale the entrenchments of the Arka-tagh. Following the eastern shore of the lake of Camp no. LXI., we made for what appeared to be a suitable pass, but were compelled to circle round a creek or bay, which the lake sent out towards the east, and which was entered by a stream at its extremity. This bay was almost a separate lagoon, and contained fresh water sheeted with ice, whereas the ice itself was strongly saline, and when melted yielded water with a specific gravity of 1.0225. The west was shut in by vast snowcapped mountain-masses belonging to the Arka-tagh. We found a good road up to the top of the range in a deeply scarped watercourse, the bottom of which was littered with hard debris, while numerous small lateral glens entered it from both sides. I led the way with Cherdon and Mollah Shah. At three o'clock it clouded over, and became almost dark. The pass was easy to ascent from the south, and we had no difficulty in reaching to summit; but the north side, where the strata cropped out along the strike, was fearfully precipitous.

This range, which overtops almost all others on the globe, resembles a colossal springboard, from which you might take a leap into the void spaces of the universe. Just as we reached the summit, the snow-storm was raging its worst. I thought we were lost. The altitude was 17,071 feet, and I had scarce strength to make the necessary observations; my hands were stiff and entirely destitute of feeling. As the caravan lingered I sent the two men back to see what had become of it, and sat down with my back to the storm to wait for them. The snow whirled about me in huge plumes or tassels, while the abyss at my feet was a seething caldron of tossing snow-flakes. The wind howled and whined and whistled, as it swept over the sharp-cut summit of the pass. At last I heard the camels' bells close beside me—the animals flitted past like spectres—I did not hear a footstep. Turdu Bai marched leaning far forward, with one arm raised as if to protect his face: he walked as a man does when he forces his way through a dense thicket. But how to get down on the other side of the pass? It was like plunging headlong into a black abyss, the bottom of which we were unable to see.

All the men went on foot, so as to be ready to help and support the camels. Kutchuk went first, feeling the way. He took the descent zigzag and at hap-hazard. At every ten or a dozen yards we were forced to stop and rub our faces with snow to prevent them from freezing. We slipped, we slided, carrying the snow with us. One of the camels stumbled, fell turned half a somersault, but, luckily, lay in such a position that he was able to get up again without being unloaded. The snow whirled madly around us; we gasped for breath; everything danced before our eyes. By this the day was well advanced and it grew dark; nevertheless we persevered until the slope began to grow easier. It was pitch dark when we stopped on the flank of the mountain, at an altitude of 16,330 feet. Here there was not a blade of grass, nor a handful of fuel, though of water we had plenty in the shape of snow and ice. Indeed, we had more than enough, for the ground was as white as could be, and the skies were emptying out showers unceasingly upon our devoted heads.

When the sun rose on the 1st of October, we were enabled to see what sort of a place it was where we had stopped in the darkness of the night before. It was still snowing, and the landscape wore a decidedly wintry aspect. The animals were stiff with cold, and hungry, when we started down the chilly valley. As soon, therefore, as we reached a patch of scurvy grass we stopped, at an altitude of 16,074 feet, although we had only gone a very few miles. I gave the order to slaughter our last sheep; but it was like a stab into my own heart. I felt as if I were committing murder.

On the 2nd of October we travelled 18½ miles north, our track at first going downhill, until we reached the hard gravel at the bottom of the valley. We were still unable to see much of our surroundings, because of the blinding snow. The valley, with the gentle fall, gave us friendly help for yet another day. When the air cleared, we perceived the Chimen-tagh a good 60 miles away. But before we started on the second morning, the usual westerly storm was once more on its way to freeze us as we sat astride our wretched beasts. We saw the forerunners of the storm racing each other a long way off across the open spaces behind the projecting cliffs and in the throats of the glens.

We were following a little brook, and ought to have stopped as soon as it came to an end; but, perceiving a lake, the Achikkoll, further north, we hoped to reach it and find fresh springs there. The poor animals were thoroughly exhausted. The horse I had ridden to Andereh lagged behind with Niaz, and another horse, a white one, was left on the road in charge of Kutchuk. It grew dusk, and then dark; but the moon soon came out, and shed her pale spectral light over the frigid waste. As we failed to discover water, we passed the lake, leaving it a good bit on our right. Turdu Bai was leading the way on foot, and we were all overjoyed when he at length stopped and shouted that he had reached a stream which flowed into the lake. We had marched 23¼ miles, the utmost that our animals were now capable of doing in a day. The sick horses did manage to reach Camp no. lXV. (13,948 feet), but it was well on the next day, for the men had been obliged to leave them some way back all night. We tended them the best we could, feeding them with rice.

The basin on the Achik-koll was of very considerable extent, especially to the east and the west. From the latter direction it received a large stream, on which, when we forded it on the 5th of the October, a good deal of drift-ice was floating. The basin lay ensconced between the Arka-tagh on the south and a smaller range on the north, the latter of which did not appear particularly difficult to cross. On the morning of the 6th, the whole basin was shrouded in a peculiar cold, moist, clammy mist, and through it the picturesque outlines of the range on the north were but faintly and dimly seen painted, as it were, with evanescent colours on the canvas of the sky, with the snow etched in more strongly higher up. Owing to these subdued tones the range appeared to be at least a day's march distant.

The caravan was dying, and we breasted the new slopes at a funeral pace. The district was dotted over with hundreds of kulans, and more particularly with orongo antelopes. Yolldash managed to catch one of the latter, and held it fast by the nose until Cherdon came up and killed it. Its meat was very welcome as a change in our monotonous diet. The ascent grew steeper. We crossed an endless number of ravines and passes, where we had to make frequent halts to let the animals recover breath. A man came to tell me that one of the horses was unable to go any farther. No sooner was it slaughtered than down went another, never to get up again. This miserable pass would have been a mere trifle for animals in good condition; but before we surmounted it we lost two more horses, one of them being the faithful grey which had carried me to Cherchen, and then to Altimish-bulak. And when we did at last surmount it, the prospect was not a whit more encouraging. To right and to left were glacier-arms, in front of us a chaos of mountains. Just over the top we halted in a recess of the rocks, although there was not a scrap of firing or food for the animals. Next morning one of the horses was lying dead, his neck stretched out, his eyes fixed, his body stiffened with frost. It was evident we could not go on long in this fashion. Our marches were growing shorter and shorter, and the animals were getting utterly exhausted and worn-out.

Curiously enough, all the camels struggled over this fateful pass without any damage. In the morning we found them lying motionless, and with marvellous resignation, in the same attitudes in which we left them the night before. They were powdered with rime-frost, for the thermometer had not risen above –3°.8 C., or 25°.2 Fahr., and there was an icy, cutting wind. We followed the valley towards the north-east, the country remaining absolutely barren and totally destitute of game. The only sign, I will not say of life, but simply of movement, was the stream breaking against the water-worn block of granite, some of them as much as a cubic yard in dimensions, which littered the watercourse at the bottom of the valley.

The night of the 8th of October was still and cold and bright, and the thermometer went down to –18°.3 C., or –0°.9 Fahr. An icy current of air, the usual night breeze, swept down the valley. From this sharply-defined valley a fresh caravan would have made Temirilik in four days; but it would clearly take us a good deal longer than that. We had only six small pieces of bread left, though our rice would last for three or four days longer. It looked as if we should have to do the last stage or two on famine rations. A little fuel, too, would have been extremely welcome; but, unfortunately, this region was never visited by yaks.

We resumed our way down the valley in a howling snowstorm. Very soon the valley contracted to a gorge, the bottom of which was impeded by cumbering masses of rock, in part water-worn, which had toppled from the heights above. In fact, we were threading a deep transverse glen cut through the granite, and the scenery presented all the characteristics usual in a granite region-rugged, pinnacled forms, at once capricious and picturesque. The stream was for the most part frozen over, although at the cascades we could see it rippling along underneath the transparent bridges of ice. We crossed it a great number of times, our object being to keep as far as possible as long the same level on the erosion terraces between which it flowed. Very often the ice was strong enough to bear even the camels; but where it would not bear them, we broke it up with poles and stones. The veterans amongst the camels traversed this difficult piece of road in a wonderful way, especially as they now carried bigger loads, in consequence of the horses having died.

The name of the glen was Togri-sai, or the Straight Glen; and it was very well known to the gold-seekers of Cherchen and Keriya, for it contained a gold-field, which we passed in the course of that day's march. The miners seemed to have been there only about a month before; but there were no indications of the valley having been visited since. About half-way up the glen we came to the first three huts, built of granite.

Close beside them were a great number of pits in the gravel beds, surrounded by mounds of sand and gravel, which the miners had dug out. There were several hundreds of these pits, very few of them, however, more than eight feet deep. Most of them were abandoned long ago, but others appeared to have been worked that very summer. The huts were merely temporary affairs, four square, the sides 6 to 10 feet long, the walls composed of unhewn blocks of granite, without any sort of binding material. The roof consisted at the best of a piece of linen or felt flung across as spar. Lanes and alleys wound in and out amongst the gravel heaps of this Asiatic Klondyke; and beside some of the mines there hung an antelope's skull or a kulan's skin, fastened to a stake, in sign of ownership. In some places the owner of a claim had surrounded his property with a low wall of unhewn granite.

Some of the huts contained primitive ovens

for baking bread, for the miners bring flour with them; but for the rest of their food they depend upon the hunters who accompany them, and who for a trifle sell them the flesh of the yaks, kulans, and antelopes they shoot. The miners convey their paraphernalia on the backs of asses, which they then send down into the valleys to graze during the two months that their work lasts. We found household utensils in only two of the huts—namely, a few rough rakes, used in separating the gravel from the goldbearing rock, a wheelbarrow, two or three ridge-spars, and a trough for baking or washing gold. We had no scruples about appropriating this excellent material; it would keep us warm for two or three days.

One of the camels here gave up and was left behind, until we should find an opportunity the next morning to fetch him in. We advanced terribly slowly in the bitterly cold weather, with snow falling and 3°C. (= 5½ Fahr) or frost. At a steep place one of the camels stumbled and rolled down the face of the slope, turning over several times, but happily he took no further harm. This misadventure cost us an hour, for we had to make a road up the cliff to get him back again. It was 11 o'clock at night when we encamped (14,814 feet) after this long and tiring, though interesting, day and the moon was already shining out of the snow-clouds.

X

BACK TO HEADQUARTERS AT TEMIRLIK

The camel which we had left behind died during the night. Of our original caravan there were now left only six camels, three horses, and one mule; and even they were all in a pitiable condition.

The valley widened out again, and ascended by three broad, step-like terraces, twenty-three, forty, and fifty feet high respectively. It was no use pushing on in the hope of finding grass, the animals were dead beat. We were forced to let them rest where they were, feeding them upon the stuffing of the last of our pack-saddles. The next day, the 10th of October, we continued our slow and weary tramp north-north-east along the same valley. I also went on foot now, so as to spare the one horse that was fit for duty. The river was frozen, for the temperature had fallen to −18°.8 C., or −1°.8 Fahr. At starting the sky was clear, but it was not very long before the everlasting westerly wind began to make itself felt. Happening to cross over to the right-hand side of the valley for the purpose of examining the lay of the strata, I lighted, by pure chance, upon some exceedingly interesting rock-drawings. They were made on the surface of what had once been a light-green slate, though it was now stained dark brown, and polished bright by wind and weather, and as the outlines had been cut through the outer laminae of the rock with a sharp instrument they were very conspicuous, owing to the light incised lines showing against the dark background. They must have been of considerable antiquity, because portions of the pictures were obliterated.

They represented scenes from a hunter's life, and he must have been an enterprising fellow. He would seem to have hunted yaks, kulans, orongo antelopes, and wolves in the mountains, and wild duck, wild geese, and tigers beside the lake of Lop-nor. One especially noticeable fact in connection with them was that the hunter represented carried in every case, not the Central Asiatic musket, with its forked rest, but bows and arrows, and the long arrows had their barbs pointing forwards, like the trident of Neptune.

Although consisting of a few strokes of bare outline, the animals were drawn in a characteristic and easily recognisable manner. The hunters were represented in different positions standing, creeping, kneeling, and the one who was aiming at a tiger considered it safest to keep to his saddle. The rock faces on which this work of art was engraved were three and a quarter feet and five feet high, and the pictures very nearly a foot in length. There can be little doubt that they date from a period when Mongols still dwelt around Lop-nor, and probably spent a portion of the summer in the mountains. And at our next camp (13,344 feet), on the left bank of the stream, where the grass was tolerably good, I found strong confirmation of this assumption in a Mongol *obo*, or cairn, built of flat slates and inscribed all over in Tibetan lettering with the fundamental dogma of Lamaism: "On maneh padmeh hum"—which means, "O jewel of the lotus flower!"

These traces of human occupancy invested the place with a certain degree of interest, and we spent the next day beside the *obo*. But before that day came to an end, our position under-went a great and joyful change. Cherdon, with Aldat's last charge of powder, had just brought down a young kulan quite close to camp, when Mollah Shah came running to me to tell me breathlessly that he had seen, a long way down the valley two hunters on horseback. I at once ordered him to go off after them, and bring them back with him at all costs. At first the me were rather shy, but soon recovered confidence, and told me that they had spent three months in the mountains, supplying the miners with kulan meat. But they had not been to Temirlik, so that we were still ignorant as to how our headquarters had fared during our absence.

This unexpected meeting with human beings, after being isolated from our kind for eighty-four days, put fresh life into us all. The first thing I did was to buy their two horses,, which were as English thoroughbeds in comparison with ours. A small parcel of wheat flour also proved an exceptionally welcome acquisition. But what interested us most was the palaver which was held that evening round the camp-fire. Mollah Shah had already offered to tramp all the way on foot to Temirlik, and send a relief caravan to our assistance. But there was now no need for him to do so. Togdasin, one of the hunters, knew the mountain paths better than he did; so I gave him his own horse, which I had just brought from him, and sent him to Islam Bai with a message. He promised to be there in two days, and was instructed to tell Islam Bai to meet us with fifteen horses and a goodly supply of provisions at the springs of Supalik, two days west of Termirlik, in the Chimen valley. Togdasin set off at eleven o'clock at night, taking with him two empty preserved fruit tins by way of credentials, to show that he was an express courier from me; they would also serve as a hint to Islam Bai to bring with him a fresh supply of the same kind. Togdasin took nothing with him to eat, except a small piece of kulan flesh. I did not envy him his night ride, seeing that the night before the temperature had fallen to –20°.2 C., or –4°.4 Fahr.; but I promised him a handsome reward if he executed his commission well.

The next two days took us to the end of the Togri-sai, and a good bit along the Chimen valley. Into this latter the Piazlik, the imposing mountain-chain which overhung the valley on the south, and thus formed the continuation of the Chimen-tagh, thrust out across our path a long series of rectangular spurs *en ichelon*, consisting of sharp-pointed irregular rocks of a brown, grey, or black colour. Our spirits rose high when we started on the 14th of October, nor were they in any degree damped by the fact that we all had to walk, for according to our calculation we should meet the relief expedition at nightfall.

The stream which descended the valley carried about 177 cubic feet in the second, and we kept to its left bank. On our left rose the Illveh-chimen, with its snow-capped peaks. Its flanks were scored by an endless number of dry ravines, each of which we had to cross over, and this occasioned us an infinite amount of trouble. But after we crossed the last of them, the ground became perfectly level and the going first-rate. Mollah Shah assured me, that about twilight, and before it was dark, we should reach the springs of Supa-alik, the appointed rendezvous; but it was evident he did not know the country, and the second hunter who had only accompanied us for two days had now left us. It grew dark—it grew pitch dark—and yet we failed to find any springs. On the contrary, the path we had hitherto followed gradually came to an end, and although there were yappkak bushes at intervals, there was not a blade of grass. But, thanks to the splendid hard surface, the animals held out well through this long tramp.

However, at the end of about another hour and a half, Mollah Shah and Niaz, who were leading, stopped and shouted that they saw a fire in the distance. This news electrified us, and we quickened our pace. It was as though all our toil and privation were suddenly come to an end, and we had no further need to exert ourselves. We pushed on through the darkness straight towards the fire, which dropped, then flared up again. I walked beside the camel that carried the skiff, and held on to it, until my hand got numbed with cold; then I went round to the other side of the beast and held on with the other hand, whilst the first thawed and got warm. Then for a long time we failed to see the fire, and our hopes dropped, and we became doubly sensible of our weariness. Perhaps, after all, the fire belonged to some gold miners. We stopped and shouted. We gathered a bundle of yappkak and made a big blaze, but there was no answer to our signal. We fired two or three shots from a revolver, but the sound died away into space, without awakening so much as an echo. We held our breath and listened. The night was as silent as the grave, and the fire went out.

When we started again away from our own fire, around which we had warmed ourselves for half-an-hour, the darkness seemed ever intenser than before. In fact, I involuntarily glanced up at the stars to convince myself that I had not been suddenly smitten with blindness. Hour after hour we plodded on, dragging our weary animals after us, which as they did not refuse to follow, probably scented grass.

Again the fire flared up. The men who had been plodding along in dogged silence, once more became lively and talkative. Soon after this we came to some *malgun* bushes, a sure indication of the vicinity of water. Then the deceitful fire faded once more, and finally it disappeared for good. Every five minutes or so the men shouted all together as loudly as they could, but their voices died away in the night unanswered. I was beginning to believe we were being deceived by a will-o'-the wisp, which flitted on in front of us and disappeared just before we reached it. Our patience had been too severely tried; as the fire died out, so did our interest, and then fatigue finally got the upper hand. As soon as we reached the next belt of bushes. I commanded halt, to the intense satisfaction of everybody concerned. But although we had been on foot for over twelve hours, we had not accomplished more than 26¾ miles.

We were all completely done up, men and animals alike, and were in a truly pitiable plight; too far gone, in fact, to arrange camp. The men just sat down on the ground, on the very spot where each happened to stop. We had one can of water left, which we had brought from the last river, and with this each of us got one cup of tea; that, and a bit of kulan meat roasted over the fire, was all we had left. On the off chance that relief might be in the neighbourhood, we kept up a big signal fire for about an hour and half. Then we dropped off to sleep, in a kind of swoon, with the frosty stars glittering above our heads. We had by this got down to 11,388 feet above the sea.

Next morning, the 15th of October, the men found a fresh-water stream not more than two hundred paces away, and as the situation was all that could be desired for a camp, there being an abundant supply of rich tall grass and plenty of fuel, we decided to stay there over the day and see what would happen. Mollah Shah, who had been out to reconnoitre, came back and said that the deceptive fire of the night before had been made by a party of hunters, who were on their way back to Cherchen with a load of skins, and had deliberately kept out of our way, not knowing who or what we were. Here we were, then once more thrown back upon ourselves. What were we to think about the relief caravan? and how far dare we trust to our messenger, Togdasin? Cherdon, who had got from him a handful of powder and a little lead, spent the whole morning looking for an antelope, but returned at two o'clock empty handed. This region was frequently visited by hunters, and then animals were shy and difficult to get near, but he said he had seen a dark coloured something moving a long way off in the west, which he had at first taken for a troop of kulans; but he now believed that they were horsemen, and that they were approaching our camp.

I hurried out with my field-glass, and sure enough there was a troop of mounted men galloping towards us in a cloud of dust. Running to the top of a little hill we watched them with bated breath. They were still a long, long way off; but we could see them distinctly over the tops of the thicket. Owing to the mirage, they seemed to be travelling a little distance above the earth, but their bobbing movements showed that they were riding at a gallop. They disappeared amongst the thickets, but the cloud of dust which they sent up showed which way they were coming. It must be our friends, who, having failed to observe our signal fire, had started at daybreak, and pushed on until they came across our trail, and had then turned back and followed after us.

Our excitement reached a climax when we saw two mounted men emerging from the bushes. Then appeared two others, driving a troop of horses in front of them—all coming at full gallop. But I soon recognised Islam Bai by the skin hood of his cloak. He was leading on a white horse. He quickened his pace, and soon outdistanced the others, and, dismounting a little way off, saluted. He looked well and pleased, and announced that all was well at headquarters. The other three men were Musa from Osh, Khodai Vardi, and Tokta Ahun from Abdall. It was, after all, their fire which we had seen; and they, as we supposed they would do, had pushed on westwards during the night, until they came to our trail, when they at once understood that we had gone past each other in the darkness.

Islam Bai brought with him fifteen fresh horses, all in splendid condition, and a good stock of provisions, and at three o'clock we had a thorough Lucullan feast. He brought nothing but good news. The post-jighit Yakub had arrived from Kashgar, and in an instant I was tearing open letters and newspapers from my home in far-off Sweden. Shortly after we left Man-darlik, Islam Bai had shifted camp to Temirlik, pitching his quarters beside some Mongol caves or grottoes. The *amban* of Charkhlik had been to visit me in state, and so had the Mongol chieftain of Pshui in Tsaidam; but both had, of course, returned without seeing me. The former brought with him thirty ass-loads of maize. For the last two weeks Islam Bai and the others had been in a state of the greatest anxiety about us, for we had promised to be back in two and a half months at the outside, and they knew our supplies must be exhausted. Thus question and answer flew backwards and forwards for hours, and it was late when I got to bed that night. But the men sat and talked long after that around a rousing big fire, which there were now plenty of hands to feed. Kader Ahun, Aldat's brother, had come to Chimen to meet him. He surprised me by saying that he was fully prepared for the sorrowful tidings; for some little time before he had dreamt he was riding across a broad tableland and met my caravan. But when he looked for his brother amongst the men, he could not find him, and when he awoke he knew that some misfortune had overtaken him. We made out that he had the dream precisely at the time of Aldat's death, and Shagdur was in a position to prove that the man's story was not invented. For Kader Ahun told his dream to the Cossack long before they had any intelligence of our return, and Kader Ahun added at the time, that he believed Aldat was dead. This was the only instance of telepathy which has come under my observation throughout my journeys in Asia.

After two day's rest, during which I took an astronomical observation, we rode, on the 18th of October, thirty miles to the east, across barren deserts and sand-belts, leaving the camels and surviving horses of our caravan to follow slowly on in our wake, but without loads. It was delightful to have a good fresh horse to ride on; and I was also glad that our surviving animals would now have a good six months in which to rest and graze at leisure. And well they deserved it!

On the 19th we rode along the right bank of a stream which bathed the southern foot of a small detached mountain group, and then shortly afterwards disappeared amongst the sterile gravel at the bottom of the valley, without reaching any of the lakes which lay further east. Upon reaching a wretched little oasis in the midst of this desolate region, called Bagh-tokai, or the Orchard Wood, we met eight men returning from Bokalik to Cherchen, carrying with them the skins of eleven yaks, four Kulans and two orongo antelopes, which they had shot. We gave them what rice we could spare, for they had lived all summer on yak and kulan meat, and we knew how pleasant a thing it is to have a change in a monotonous bill of fare.

Our caravan had once more increased to an imposing cavalcade, when, on the 20th of October, we at last turned our faces north-north eastwards towards Temirilik. But we were not to reach headquarters without a final salute from our all too pertinacious friend, the west wind.

Shagdur met us half-way, and pulled up and saluted in military fashion, as if he and his horse had just been cast in bronze. We were both glad to meet again, and he had a good deal to tell us. He had kept the meteorological records with exemplary care, and the self-registering instruments had never once failed. It was getting dusk when we at length reached the spring of Temirlik. There I was met by Faisullah and Kader, both of whom had been with me on the ferry-boat, and they pointed out to me the six camels which had been out at grass all summer. On the right bank of the little brook which issued from the springs several fires were scattering their sparks into the air; it was the tented village of our new headquarters camp, besides the big Mongolian yurt there were two tents, a hut made of reeds and branches, long rows of maize sacks, and all the heavier baggage. Here I was greeted by Ali Ahun, the tailor, and Yakub, the post-jighit, as well as by a crowd of old men, chance visitors, whom I had never seen before.

Over on the other side of the brook was a two-storied loess terrace. On the lower platform my little yurt was already put up, with the stove lighted inside it. In the vertical face of the upper platform the Mongols had, in time past, hollowed out a number of caves or grottoes. One of these Shagdur had converted into a very convenient dark room for photography, and got everything ready for developing the plates which he knew I should bring back with me.

Thus ended this toilsome journey, and we could now with a good conscience indulge ourselves in two or three weeks rest. The expedition had resulted in geographical discoveries of very great importance, but it had entailed a considerable amount of hardship and suffering and loss of life. Of the twelve horses we started with only two were now left, and of the seven camels only four; and of these four, one stood like a bronze statue for two days amongst the long grass, and on the third day lay down and died, without having attempted to bite a single mouthful. And last, though by no means least, it had cost the life of one man.

[From *Central Asia and Tibet—Towards the Holy City of Lhasa,* Vol. I, 1903.]